Regulatory Autonomy and International Trade in Services

Regulatory Autonomy and International Trade in Services

The EU Under GATS and RTAs

Bregt Natens

Associate, Sidley Austin LLP, Brussels

EE Edward Elgar PUBLISHING

Cheltenham, UK • Northampton, MA, USA

Published by
Edward Elgar Publishing Limited
The Lypiatts
15 Lansdown Road
Cheltenham
Glos GL50 2JA
UK

Edward Elgar Publishing, Inc.
William Pratt House
9 Dewey Court
Northampton
Massachusetts 01060
USA

A catalogue record for this book
is available from the British Library

Library of Congress Control Number: 2016931519

This book is available electronically in the **Elgar**online
Law subject collection
DOI 10.4337/9781785364310

FSC www.fsc.org MIX Paper from responsible sources FSC® C013056

ISBN 978 1 78536 430 3 (cased)
ISBN 978 1 78536 431 0 (eBook)

Typeset by Columns Design XML Ltd, Reading

Printed and bound in Great Britain by
TJ International Ltd, Padstow, Cornwall

Contents

About the author

Dr Bregt Natens is an associate in the International Trade group of Sidley Austin LLP. He advises clients on international trade and investment, including EU and WTO trade remedies, customs rules, market access and regulatory barriers, and trade policy negotiations.

Acknowledgements

This book is based on my doctoral dissertation, which I wrote during my time as a PhD researcher at Leuven University. I am indebted to my doctoral supervisors, Professors Jan Wouters and Geert van Calster, and the other members of my doctoral jury, Professors Geert De Baere, James Mathis and Petros Mavroidis for their helpful comments and remarks on the dissertation. My research was generously funded by the Government of Flanders in the context of its Policy Research Centres. I want to thank Axel Marx and my colleagues at the Leuven Centre for Global Governance Studies for their support. This especially goes for Dylan Geraets, for thoroughly influencing my thinking – the Van den Bossche in hand – and Marieke Koekkoek, for bringing plus to counter minus. Thank you, too, to Eleanor-Jane Martin for editing the dissertation.

Upon leaving Leuven University, I was lucky enough to intern in the Legal Affairs Division of the WTO. I want to thank doctors Graham Cook and Rodd Izadnia for the influential and inspiring legal discussions. I then joined Sidley Austin LLP's International Trade team, where I get to do great work in an exceptionally collegial environment. I particularly want to thank Arnoud Willems and Sven De Knop for getting me on board. Needless to say, the views expressed in this book do not represent the views of Sidley Austin LLP or its clients.

I also want to thank my publishers, Ben Booth and Iram Satti at Edward Elgar.

Tot slot, mama & Johan, papa & Bea, dank je voor alle steun en liefde. Mama, zonder jou was de doctoraatsthesis noch dit boek er ooit gekomen. Ik schrijf hoe ik schrijf dankzij jou, elke dag weer. Anne, dank je voor het houvast doorheen het eeuwige zoeken, en voor alle invloed en inspiratie. Stijn, ruim de helft van dit boek is geschreven in jouw, toen onze, Bronstraat, merci. En tot slot, Sid, dank je om me een gelukkigere, rustigere mens te maken; dat heb ik hard nodig. Dank je voor al je liefde, begrip en geduld, en je onvoorwaardelijke steun. *Todo está bien (futur).*

Brussels (where else!), autumn 2015
Bregt Natens

Introduction

1. TRADE AND REGULATORY AUTONOMY

Globalisation is a fact and one can see its effects particularly well in trade. For almost seventy years, trade liberalisation, which can be defined for present purposes as 'a process introducing greater market openness and a competitive market environment' through legally binding obligations,[1] has been a key element of foreign trade policy for almost all of the world's nations. Although some question the net gains from trade (and especially the redistributive effects), it is undisputable that political leaders have taken the trade liberalisation route. Since the 1940s, international cooperation has led to the global reduction of tariff barriers through subsequent negotiating rounds in the context of the General Agreement on Tariffs and Trade or GATT 1947. In 1994, the Uruguay Round of negotiations culminated in the establishment of the World Trade Organization (WTO). Moreover, in parallel with multilateralism, a wave of bi- and plurilateral trade agreements highlight the perceived importance of trade liberalisation at a time in which the WTO is facing one of the most difficult periods in its existence, exemplified by the gridlocked negotiations in the Doha Round. Although in an altered form, i.e. from multilateral to preferential, it is clear that trade liberalisation is

[1] Markus Krajewski, *National Regulation and Trade Liberalization in Services* (Kluwer Law International 2003) 5. Liberalisation does not equal deregulation, which indicates the removing or reducing of regulation. Complying with liberalisation obligations and commitments does not necessarily require deregulation. See Aaditya Mattoo and Pierre Sauvé, 'Domestic Regulation and Trade in Services: Key Issues' in Aaditya Mattoo and Pierre Sauvé (eds), *Domestic Regulation and Service Trade Liberalization* (World Bank & Oxford University Press 2003) 1–2. Liberalisation does however often need *re*regulation. See Federico Ortino, 'Services' in Simon Lester and Bryan Mercurio (eds), *Bilateral and Regional Trade Agreements: Commentary and Analysis* (Cambridge University Press 2009) 214; Aik Hoe Lim and Bart De Meester, 'Addressing the Domestic Regulation and Services Trade Interface: Reflections on the Way Ahead' in Aik Hoe Lim and Bart De Meester (eds), *WTO Domestic Regulation and Services Trade* (Cambridge University Press 2014) 333.

still at the forefront of international trade policy. However, even fierce supporters of trade liberalisation must recognise that the impact of liberalisation goes beyond what are traditionally seen as trade concerns. Economic concerns, such as the protection of intellectual property rights or competition law, have emerged in trade contexts. The impact of trade liberalisation has also extended to other types of societal choices. This is the result of obligations ascertained under international trade law, which typically limit domestic regulators in the exercise of their regulatory autonomy.[2]

Regulatory autonomy[3] concerns regulatory measures or regulation, i.e. 'measures that a government characterizes as an exercise of its authority to regulate its domestic affairs'.[4] Market failures in a wide sense are at the core of why regulators regulate.[5] In that way, governments provide public goods, redistribute income, and shield and support preferred activities, whether economic or not.[6] More practically, regulatory autonomy is equally valuable because states opt for differing regulatory

---

[2] Sungjoon Cho, *Free Markets and Social Regulation: A Reform Agenda of the Global Trading System* (Kluwer Law International 2003) 1.

[3] The concept 'regulatory autonomy' goes by many monikers, including domestic regulatory autonomy, national regulatory autonomy, policy autonomy, unconstrained policy choice, juridical space, trade policy space, policy space, political space, regulatory room for manoeuvre, regulatory jurisdictional allocation, manoeuvring space, regulatory space, domestic sovereignty, domestic political sovereignty and policy autonomy, and sovereignty. In the context of international trade – and with the exception of sovereignty, of which regulatory autonomy is only a part – these terms have been used in similar ways and to indicate parts of the same concept.

[4] Robert E Hudec, 'GATT/WTO Constraints on National Regulation: Requiem for an "Aim and Effects" Test' (1998) 32 The International Lawyer 619.

[5] Aaditya Mattoo and Pierre Sauvé, 'Domestic Regulation and Trade in Services: Looking Ahead' in Mattoo and Sauvé (eds), *Domestic Regulation and Service Trade Liberalization* 223. See, extensively, Krajewski, *National Regulation and Trade Liberalization in Services* 11–40; Panagiotis Delimatsis, *International Trade in Services and Domestic Regulations: Necessity, Transparency and Regulatory Diversity* (Oxford University Press 2008) 37–83; and Tinne Heremans, 'Why Regulate? An Overview of the Rationale and Purpose Behind Regulation' in Aik Hoe Lim and Bart De Meester (eds), *WTO Domestic Regulation and Services Trade* (Cambridge University Press 2014) 25–44.

[6] Bernard M Hoekman and Patrick A Messerlin, 'Liberalising Trade in Services: Reciprocal Negotiations and Regulatory Reform' in Pierre Sauvé and Robert M Stern (eds), *GATS 2000: New Directions in Services Trade Liberalization* (Brookings Institution 2000) 489.

goals and methods, and their population has different needs and habits.[7] Regulatory autonomy also is the *autonomy* to regulate. The regulator should be competent to enact regulation and this competence should not be restricted. For present purposes, the relevant restrictions are those imposed on regulators by international trade law. Thus, regulatory autonomy is linked to the balance between on the one hand domestic preferences reflecting domestic needs fulfilling domestic regulatory purposes, and on the other hand the adverse trade effects of such regulations. Regulatory autonomy can be defined as: 'how much margin of appreciation is left to [...] domestic governments in crafting their own regulations while at the same time fulfilling their [international trade law] obligations'.[8]

Scholarship has highlighted many aspects of the trading system which constrain regulatory autonomy. I discern five dimensions of the concept of constraints on regulatory autonomy in international trade law:

a. Regulatory autonomy is constrained by exogenous and endogenous factors. Exogenous factors include, for example, international law obligations and interpretations thereof or political decisions in trading partners. Endogenous factors include, for example, domestic political pressure or business decisions by domestic companies. Both types of factors determine the actual amount of regulatory autonomy, which is therefore in a constant state of flux. I focus solely on the constraints on regulatory autonomy from international trade law obligations.
b. Regulatory autonomy may be constrained in so far as a regulator aims to advance an economic interest, or a non-economic interest. This distinction, which lies at the core of much of the debate on regulatory autonomy, has important consequences for the shaping of the tension between regulatory autonomy and trade liberalisation. My wide approach covers both.
c. Exogenous constraints on regulatory autonomy may stem from three inextricable macro-level aspects of international trade law:

[7] Kalypso Nicolaïdis and Joel P Trachtman, 'From Policed Regulation to Managed Recognition in GATS' in Pierre Sauvé and Robert M Stern (eds), *GATS 2000: New Directions in Services Trade Liberalization* (Brookings Institution 2000) 248.

[8] Michael Ming Du, 'Domestic Regulatory Autonomy under the TBT Agreement: From Non-discrimination to Harmonization' (2007) 6 Chinese Journal of International Law 269, 274. Du also notes that the domestic government should be democratic.

trade negotiations, trade rules, and the interpretation of trade rules by the relevant dispute settlement bodies. Considering the practical legal approach taken in this book (see below), I focus on existing trade rules and their interpretation.

d. Considering the trade rules and their interpretation in more detail, constraints on regulatory autonomy are to be analysed according to the way in which a trade law violation is usually established: (i) the measure under scrutiny must fall within the scope of the agreement; (ii) it must violate an obligation contained in the agreement; and (iii) it cannot be justified by an exception.

e. Finally, the extent of constraints on regulatory autonomy may be linked to the nature of a trade law obligation, for example whether the obligation is a non-discrimination obligation, a market access obligation, a transparency obligation or a recognition-based regime.

In the case of trade governance, the liberalisation of trade has led to a binding set of rules and obligations, undersigned by all WTO Members, or, in the case of preferential liberalisation, the signatory parties. As with all international obligations, this necessarily implies a loss of regulatory autonomy: by agreeing to be bound by certain obligations, a domestic regulator may no longer adopt regulations which violate these international obligations. A regulator will normally only agree to restrict its regulatory autonomy if this leads to acceptable *quid pro quos*,[9] because trade liberalisation obligations lead to domestic adjustment problems that can only be solved by enacting measures which may incidentally restrict trade.[10] A similar balance must be struck for all types of international cooperation. However, in the case of the WTO, an international organisation famous for its well-functioning and binding dispute settlement system, it must be stressed that other states may force compliance with these obligations by bringing disputes in an effective manner.[11] Moreover, as noted, economic governance is characterised by the inherent conflictive nature of the interests at play – i.e. offensive trade interests

---

[9] Michael J Trebilcock and Robert Howse, 'Trade Liberalization and Regulatory Diversity: Reconciling Competitive Markets with Competitive Politics' (1998) 6 European Journal of Law and Economics 5, 30.

[10] Dani Rodrik, 'How to Save Globalization from its Cheerleaders' (2007) 1 Journal of International Trade and Diplomacy 1, 21.

[11] Pascal Lamy, 'The Emergence of Collective Preferences in International Trade: Implications for Regulating Globalisation' (Collective Preferences and Global Governance: What Future for the Multilateral Trading System, Brussels, 15 September 2004) 6.

versus defensive non-trade interests, whether economic or non-economic, which may coincide with protectionism.[12] Hence, the balancing of competing rights, principles, values and interests becomes one of the most important challenges for WTO law.[13] In other words, the need for a balance is inherent because trade rules by nature impinge on other policy areas, and because trade restriction is an 'inevitable corollary' of policies with non-trade objectives.[14] Already in 1969, a prominent scholar described the tension between regulatory autonomy and trade as fundamental:

> One of the most fundamental issues facing GATT and international trade is whether or not there is a desirable limit to 'free trade' beyond which the policies of free trade would impose too much uniformity on particular national social or political systems and too greatly restrict the individual freedom of particular nations to pursue goals of their own societies.[15]

The tension between regulatory autonomy and trade liberalisation has become increasingly complex in recent times. Globalisation and other powers have led to increased economic integration. Considering that more economic integration inevitably leads to a reduction in regulatory autonomy,[16] the altered approach of the international trading system, moving from non-discrimination to forms of market integration, and the ever wider scope of what is considered 'trade-related' substantially complicate the puzzle regarding the tension between regulatory autonomy and trade liberalisation.[17] When focusing merely on non-discrimination and not market integration, the balance conundrum is focused on exposing protectionist intent in regulation. Protectionist

---

[12] Ibid. Also see Mattoo and Sauvé, 'Domestic Regulation and Trade in Services: Key Issues' 1.

[13] Mads Andenas and Stefan Zleptnig, 'Proportionality and Balancing in WTO Law: A Comparative Perspective' (2007) 20 Cambridge Review of International Affairs 71, 88–89.

[14] Panagiotis Delimatsis, 'The Fragmentation of International Trade Law' (2011) 45 Journal of World Trade 87, 96.

[15] John H Jackson, *World Trade and the Law of GATT* (Bobbs-Merrill 1969) 28–29.

[16] Robert M Hamwey, *Expanding National Policy Space for Development: Why the Multilateral Trading System Must Change* (South Centre Trade-Related Agenda, Development and Equity (TRADE) Working Paper 25, 2005) 10, figure 4.

[17] Henning Grosse Ruse-Khan, *A Comparative Analysis of Policy Space in WTO Law* (Max Planck Institute for Intellectual Property, Competition & Tax Law Research Paper 08-02, 2008) 10–11.

regulation can be said to frequently favour domestic economic actors from the perspective of competition. This is sometimes intended but may sometimes be a sincerely unwanted consequence.[18] However, from a market integration approach, regulatory heterogeneity itself could be considered a serious barrier to trade.[19] This leads to a delicate balance between international trade objectives, bound by legal obligations, and legitimate domestic regulatory claims.[20]

A legal approach to drawing this line has its limits:

> in some ultimate sense the problem is unsolvable. Taken to their logical conclusion, either free trade or local autonomy could virtually eliminate the other, and negotiating a working border between the two depends as much on history, politics, and local terrain as on any overarching vision. No matter how a legal test is articulated, it cannot satisfactorily resolve the tensions between local autonomy and free trade in all conceivable cases. In the end, the law must have a certain irreducible messiness in dealing with such fundamental tensions. Messiness is not, however, the same as chaos.[21]

Being aware of these limitations, this book can only strive to unravel some chaos – of which there is plenty in the subject of this book: the regulation of trade in services.

2. TRADE IN SERVICES AND REGULATORY AUTONOMY

The issue of constrained regulatory autonomy is especially challenging in the case of trade in services. Whereas services are usually described as being intangible, invisible, perishable and not storable, in practice they are usually defined by a list of activities which are considered to be services. The WTO Secretariat identifies 12 main categories of services:

---

[18] Daniel A Farber and Robert E Hudec, 'Free Trade and the Regulatory State: A GATT's-Eye View of the Dormant Commerce Clause' (1994) 47 Vanderbilt Law Review 1401, 1402–1403; Hudec, 'GATT/WTO Constraints on National Regulation: Requiem for an "Aim and Effects" Test' 619–620; Delimatsis, *International Trade in Services and Domestic Regulations: Necessity, Transparency and Regulatory Diversity* 70.

[19] Cho, *Free Markets and Social Regulation: A Reform Agenda of the Global Trading System* 1.

[20] Hudec, 'GATT/WTO Constraints on National Regulation: Requiem for an "Aim and Effects" Test' 619–620.

[21] Farber and Hudec, 'Free Trade and the Regulatory State: A GATT's-Eye View of the Dormant Commerce Clause' 1438.

business services; communication services; construction and related engineering services; distribution services; educational services; environmental services; financial services; health related and social services; tourism and travel related services; recreational, cultural and sporting services; transport services; and other services not elsewhere included.[22] From this, it is clear that a wide and heterogeneous range of activities in very different areas of economic activity falls under the notion of 'services'.[23] Considering this wide range of activities, the importance of services to the economy is clear. In 2010, services accounted for 70 per cent of the value added to the world GDP. In comparison, agriculture accounted for just over 3 per cent and industry for the remaining 27 per cent.[24] In the case of the EU, services were estimated to compose 73 per cent of EU GDP in 2014.[25] Among other things, services account for an important share of total foreign direct investment and provide a significant proportion of employment opportunities.[26] Importantly, services are inputs into production, for instance by facilitating transactions through space or time (e.g. transport or telecommunications services), or by producing human capital (e.g. education or research and development services).[27] The 'facilitating' role of services leads to productivity gains across all sectors. In turn, this has a positive impact upon growth in the whole economy.[28] Growth in services sectors, whether through size or diversification, is said to be a reflection of and a precondition for economic growth.[29]

---

[22] General Agreement on Tariffs and Trade, *MTN.GNS/W/120, Services Sectoral Classification List* (1991).

[23] Joseph Francois and Bernard M Hoekman, 'Services Trade and Policy' (2010) 48 Journal of Economic Literature 642, 645.

[24] World Bank, 'Services, etc., Value Added (% of GDP)' (2015) <http://data.worldbank.org/indicator/NV.SRV.TETC.ZS/countries/1W?display=graph> accessed 2 August 2015.

[25] Central Intelligence Agency, 'The World Factbook: European Union' (2015) <https://www.cia.gov/library/publications/the-world-factbook/geos/ee.html> accessed 6 August 2015.

[26] Francois and Hoekman, 'Services Trade and Policy' 644.

[27] Ibid 645 and the references there.

[28] Bernard M Hoekman, *Liberalizing Trade in Services: A Survey* (World Bank Policy Research Working Paper 4030, 2006) 21–22 and the references there.

[29] Bernard M Hoekman and Aaditya Mattoo, 'Services Trade and Growth' in Juan A Marchetti and Martin Roy (eds), *Opening Markets for Trade in Services: Countries and Sectors in Bilateral and WTO Negotiations* (Cambridge University Press 2008) 53.

Regardless of its importance in the economy, services underperform when it comes to trade. Indeed, although trade made up 59.5 per cent of world GDP in 2013,[30] trade in services accounted for 12.4 per cent of world GDP in 2013 – or roughly 20 per cent of total trade.[31] However, the emergence of global value chains – producing goods from raw materials to final products not in one place, but wherever the necessary skills are available at a competitive price and quality – highlighted the key role of efficient services sectors in contributing to goods exports.[32] Transport, logistics, finance, communication, other business, and professional services are necessary prerequisites for global value chains. Consequently, services play a more important role in trade than previously suggested.[33] Services content in exports is just over 50 per cent of gross exports in the EU, and 42 per cent on average for G20 countries.[34] In other words, the direct and indirect value added to all exports by services accounts for 50 per cent of the total value of global trade in goods and services.[35] According to forward-looking studies based on computable general equilibrium (CGE) models, further liberalisation of trade in services is likely to generate greater gains than those from goods liberalisation.[36]

A reason for the remaining discrepancy between the share of services in GDP and in trade, aside from the un-tradability of some services sectors and practical reasons such as proximity between the service supplier and the consumer, is that services liberalisation is highly

---

[30] World Bank, 'Trade (% of GDP)' (2015) <http://data.worldbank.org/indicator/NE.TRD.GNFS.ZS/countries?display=graph> accessed 6 August 2015.

[31] World Bank, 'Trade in Services (% of GDP)' (2015) <http://data.worldbank.org/indicator/BG.GSR.NFSV.GD.ZS/countries?display=graph> accessed 6 August 2015.

[32] OECD, World Trade Organization and UNCTAD, *Implications of Global Value Chains for Trade, Investment, Development and Jobs* (Report prepared for the G-20 Leaders Summit Saint Petersburg (Russian Federation), 2013) 2, 6 and 11.

[33] Ibid 16.

[34] Ibid 11.

[35] Francois and Hoekman, 'Services Trade and Policy' 643. 'Value added' is the value that 'is added by the processing of imported components into final products for export as opposed to measuring trade flows on the basis of the gross value of goods crossing the border'.

[36] Hoekman and Mattoo, 'Services Trade and Growth' 21–22 and the references there.

complex due to the breadth of the concept of services[37] and the importance of indirectly trade-related regulation.[38] Services are characterised by extensive regulation, to such an extent where it can be said that '[e]ach regulatory act of a national government increases, at least potentially, the fragmentation of the world economy and, in this manner, might negatively encroach on the efficient delivery of services'.[39] Indeed, services disciplines are 'primarily concerned with how an economy is regulated'.[40] In order to achieve the economic potential of liberalising trade in services, regulators need to be sure that their regulatory autonomy will be preserved. This is linked to two issues for regulators. The first issue is the intrusiveness of obligations. For example, in some cases, the incremental benefit of going beyond non-discrimination is unlikely to justify the political cost of strictly disciplining non-discriminatory measures.[41] The second issue is the inherent incomprehensibility and uncertain implications of constraints on regulatory autonomy.[42] In conclusion, the tension between regulatory autonomy and trade liberalisation is more complicated in the area of trade in services, as the chances of stepping on the ground of trade obligations are substantial and potential conflicts between trade rules and domestic regulatory measures may loom large.

Being aware of these difficulties, negotiators at the WTO and at the preferential level have created a complex legal framework to liberalise trade in services. First, there are multilateral and preferential rules, which

---

[37] Rudolf Adlung and Martin Roy, *Turning Hills into Mountains? Current Commitments under the GATS and Prospects for Change* (World Trade Organization Economic Research and Statistics Division Staff Working Paper ERSD-2005-01, 2005) 6.

[38] Hoekman and Mattoo, 'Services Trade and Growth' 53.

[39] Delimatsis, *International Trade in Services and Domestic Regulations: Necessity, Transparency and Regulatory Diversity* 70–71; Adlung and Roy, *Turning Hills into Mountains? Current Commitments under the GATS and Prospects for Change* 6.

[40] Lim and De Meester, 'Addressing the Domestic Regulation and Services Trade Interface: Reflections on the Way Ahead' 347.

[41] Aaditya Mattoo, 'Services in a Development Round: Three Goals and Three Proposals' (2005) 39 Journal of World Trade 1223, 1224 and 1229–1232.

[42] Hoekman, *Liberalizing Trade in Services: A Survey* 40. Even the EU and the US, with traditionally large resources of trade law capacity and the most experience in WTO litigation, 'claimed to have been surprised by the full implications' of the regulation of trade in services at WTO level as interpreted in the case law, even if the amount of case law remains very small. Mattoo, 'Services in a Development Round: Three Goals and Three Proposals' 1224 and 1229–1232. To some extent, more case law may reduce such surprises.

overlap. On 15 April 1994, the Uruguay Round of negotiations was completed and international trade in services became part of the regulatory framework of the multilateral trading system. Annex 1B to the Marrakesh Agreement contained the innovative General Agreement on Trade in Services (GATS) and its Annexes. Building on principles developed in the context of trade in goods, GATS faced the challenge of creating new disciplines for a complex, heterogeneous and increasingly important aspect of most economies: trade in services. Its rules and disciplines had a large impact on the regulatory landscape, even twenty years after its inception. This is a remarkable feat considering the boom of trade in services as a result of the information technology revolution. These technological advancements and the growing economic importance of trade in services have nonetheless put GATS' rules and disciplines under strain, especially since the agreement has not been updated since its entry into force. The multilateral services regulatory framework is not limited to the GATS and its Annexes. It also includes the plurilateral Agreement on Government Procurement, GATS Protocols, a Reference Paper on telecommunications, an Understanding on financial services, a waiver allowing preferential treatment to services of least-developed countries, and several Ministerial Declarations and Decisions. Additionally, the scope of some key aspects of GATS is dependent on each Member's unique Schedule of specific commitments (Schedule), and Members have submitted their list of exemptions to the Most-Favoured-Nation (MFN) obligation.

Aside from multilateral disciplines, the regulatory framework of trade in services also consists of rules and obligations in various types of regional trade agreements (RTAs) and preferential trade agreements (PTAs).[43] According to the WTO, RTAs are agreements (i) to liberalise or facilitate trade on a regional basis (though parties are not required to belong to the same geographical region); (ii) between two or more partners in a reciprocal way; (iii) leading to preferential treatment. In the multilateral trading system, every formal relation between two or more states can accordingly be considered 'regional'.[44] Hence, in the context of the EU foreign trade policy, all trade agreements which fulfil these conditions are RTAs, although they may have different official qualifications. Consequently, in WTO parlance, all non-multilateral reciprocal

[43] Bilateral investment treaties (BITs) also regulate certain trade in services. For delineation purposes, this book does not address the regulation of trade in services in BITs.

[44] Ousseni Illy, *L'OMC et le Régionalisme – Le Régionalisme Africain* (Larcier 2012) 35 and 68–69.

trade agreements are RTAs, whilst PTAs grant unilateral trade preferences. Both types of agreement can be either bilateral or plurilateral.

Since 1992, there has been a surge in the conclusion of RTAs. The WTO counted more than 350 RTAs in force in 2012. More recently, negotiations for so-called mega-RTAs have dominated trade news, as groupings of states look to conclude plurilateral trade agreements. More recent RTAs contain services chapters. Although architecturally there are two families of services chapters – and some hybrid or sui generis forms – both the GATS-style and NAFTA-style families are built on fundamental GATS principles. These disciplines can build on and extend GATS rules (so-called GATS+ or GATS-Plus obligations),[45] build on and reduce GATS rules (referred to as GATS– or GATS-Minus),[46] or contain obligations not in the current GATS mandate (denoted as GATS-X).[47] As concerns specific commitments on market access *sensu lato*[48] and national treatment, it seems that, generally speaking, RTAs go (significantly) further.[49]

Moreover, the rules themselves are complex. GATS is structurally complex, and its language 'is often awkward and it should come as no surprise that many of the disputes evolve around misunderstandings

---

[45] See for use of these terms, for example, Martin Roy, Juan A Marchetti and Hoe Lim, 'Services Liberalization in the New Generation of Preferential Trade Agreements (PTAs): How Much Further than the GATS?' (2007) 6 World Trade Review 155.

[46] Rudolf Adlung and Peter Morrison, 'Less than the GATS: "Negative Preferences" in Regional Services Agreements' (2010) 13 Journal of International Economic Law 1103, 1136–1138; Rudolf Adlung and Sébastien Miroudot, 'Poison in the Wine? Tracing GATS-Minus Commitments in Regional Trade Agreements' (2012) 46 Journal of World Trade 1045.

[47] The term 'GATS-X' is adapted from Horn, Mavroidis and Sapir's term 'WTO-X'. Henrik Horn, Petros C Mavroidis and André Sapir, 'Beyond the WTO? An Anatomy of EU and US Preferential Trade Agreements' [2010] The World Economy 1565.

[48] It should be noted that the term 'market access' has a more specific meaning in the context of trade in services: Article XVI GATS limits the meaning of the term to a closed list of six types of restrictions to market access, which is market access *sensu stricto*. In this book, the term 'market access' will be used *sensu stricto*, as in Article XVI GATS, unless explicitly noted.

[49] See Juan A Marchetti and Martin Roy, 'Services Liberalization in the WTO and in PTAs' in Juan A Marchetti and Martin Roy (eds), *Opening Markets for Trade in Services: Countries and Sectors in Bilateral and WTO Negotiations* (Cambridge University Press 2008).

regarding the ambit of specific provisions'.[50] The same goes for many equally intricate RTAs with GATS+, GATS– and GATS-X obligations. From a practical perspective, the distinction between goods and services is not always clear (an issue not discussed in this book),[51] and neither are the modal differences of services commitments (analysed further below).

Thus, the law on trade in services is a patchwork of applicable obligations (which do not always apply to all covered services) and commitments (by which any country unilaterally decides which services it subjects to which obligations) found in several regulatory regimes, which attempt to mitigate concerns regarding regulatory autonomy. Therefore, a general approach to assessing regulatory autonomy inevitably distorts the truth as the full *potential* impact on regulatory autonomy will never materialise. No WTO Member (Member) has made full commitments in all services sectors, and preferential liberalisation of trade in services is equally limited. The existence of different regulatory regimes and the zealous use of the available flexibilities in each regime indicate the need for a delineated approach to assess the balance between regulatory autonomy and services liberalisation.

3. A CASE STUDY APPROACH: THE EUROPEAN UNION AND THREE EU RTAs

The complexity of the regulatory framework regarding trade in services and the use of flexibilities therein make it an overly ambitious, even impossible, task to assess its constraints on regulatory autonomy. For the purpose of an in-depth analysis of the impact of multilateral and preferential liberalisation of trade in services on regulatory autonomy, the multilateral and preferential levels must be integrated. This necessarily requires taking a case study approach. In the case of multilateral obligations, all flexibilities will be addressed from the point of view of a

[50] Juan A Marchetti and Petros C Mavroidis, 'From Reluctant Participant to Key Player: EU and the Negotiation of the GATS' in Inge Govaere, Reinhard Quick and Marco Bronckers (eds), *Trade and Competition Law in the EU and Beyond* (Edward Elgar Publishing 2011) 95.

[51] What matters is whether the measure *affects* trade in services. *Canada – Certain Measures Concerning Periodicals* WT/DS31/AB/R, AB report adopted 30 July 1997 17–20. On the differentiation between goods and services, see e.g. Joost Pauwelyn, 'Squaring Free Trade in Culture with Chinese Censorship: The WTO Appellate Body Report on *China–Audiovisuals*' (2010) 11 Melbourne Journal of International Law 119; Tania Voon, 'China and Cultural Products at the WTO' (2010) 37 Legal Issues of Economic Integration 254.

selected WTO Member, and, as concerns bi- or plurilateral agreements, some of that country's RTAs can be analysed. This approach has the benefit of allowing a comparative and cross-cutting analysis.

The selected case study is the European Union (EU). On the one hand, the EU is often considered to be overregulated and overprotective domestically. On the other hand, services make up almost three-quarters of the EU's GDP. Being one of the world's largest economic entities, the EU's services market is of undoubted importance.[52] In 2012, the EU was by far the largest exporter and importer of trade in services.[53] The liberalisation of trade in services is also considered a European offensive interest, exemplified by the fact that the EU is party to a substantial number of RTAs that regulate trade in services. Hence, it is more of a *rule maker* rather than a *rule taker*. Consequently, it may have been and may still be in the best position to foresee the impact of the liberalisation of trade in services on regulatory autonomy, and hence build in necessary safety valves, or to make the most of the available flexibilities. Moreover, the EU played a key role in the drafting stage of GATS: it has been said that '[t]he EU's hand can be traced in all key provisions of the GATS'.[54] Such deep involvement indicates that the EU's use of the flexibilities in GATS (and its RTAs) are likely to have been thoroughly deliberated and to have taken prior experiences into account. Therefore, it would seem that regulators in the EU stand to be substantially affected by constraints on their regulatory autonomy. Europeans are also used to dealing with multilevel governance and balancing of interests,[55] and their implications for regulatory autonomy. Therefore, this book addresses the extent to which the EU's multilateral (through GATS) and preferential (through selected RTAs) liberalisation of international trade in services constrains regulatory autonomy through imposing legally binding obligations.

To conduct the proposed analysis, and for the same reasons that the case study of the EU is necessary, a selection of EU RTAs must be made. Of course, only RTAs for which the text was available when the research commenced (July 2014) could be selected. After mapping the services

---

[52] Daniel Drezner, *All Politics is Global: Explaining International Regulatory Regimes* (Princeton University Press 2007) 32–33.

[53] World Trade Organization, *International Trade Statistics 2013* (2013) 27.

[54] Juan A Marchetti and Petros C Mavroidis, 'The Genesis of the GATS (General Agreement on Trade in Services)' (2011) 22 European Journal of International Law 689, 716. Also see Marchetti and Mavroidis, 'From Reluctant Participant to Key Player: EU and the Negotiation of the GATS' 48–95.

[55] Chad Damro, 'Market Power Europe' (2012) 19 Journal of European Public Policy 682, 688.

commitments in all EU RTAs containing services chapters,[56] the most promising case studies are recently concluded EU RTAs which are primarily designed to open up global markets to European businesses, and the 'new generation' Deep and Comprehensive Free Trade Agreements (DCFTAs) concluded with countries targeted by the eastern part of the European Neighbourhood Policy. Considering the crucial importance of treaty interpretation for the purposes of assessing constraints on regulatory autonomy from legal provisions on trade in services, the selection of EU RTA case studies should also take into account the various approaches to treaty interpretation enshrined in the agreements. There are three such approaches. First, some EU RTAs are to be interpreted based on customary rules of interpretation only. Second, some EU RTAs are to be interpreted based on customary rules of interpretation in so far as the interpreted provision is not identical to a WTO provision. If the interpreted provision is identical, its interpretation 'shall be consistent with relevant WTO [Dispute Settlement Body] interpretations'. Third, the interpretation of some EU RTAs 'shall take relevant WTO [Dispute Settlement Body] interpretation into account'. (The relevance of this distinction may nonetheless be limited, as below, in Chapter 1, it is argued that a rebuttable presumption of WTO-consistent interpretation applies to EU RTAs.) Based on these criteria, and following the order of the three available approaches to interpretation, the following agreements are selected as case studies for the analysis of constraints on regulatory autonomy from the preferential liberalisation of trade in services: (i) the EU-Colombia & Peru RTA;[57] (ii) the EU-Singapore RTA;[58] and (iii) the EU-Georgia DCFTA.[59] Interestingly, both Georgia and Singapore are examples of 'the few countries in the world that [have] chosen a radical

---

56 Bregt Natens and Jan Wouters, *Mapping Services Liberalisation Commitments in European Union Regional Trade Agreements* (Leuven Centre for Global Governance Studies Working Paper 116, 2013).

57 Trade Agreement between the European Union and its Member States, of the one part, and Colombia and Peru, of the other part (OJ L 354, 21.12.2012, p. 3). At the time of writing, the EU and Ecuador concluded negotiations on Ecuador joining the RTA.

58 The latest update on the EU-Singapore RTA states that 'The draft agreement needs now to be formally approved by the European Commission and then agreed upon by the Council of Ministers, and ratified by the European Parliament'. European Commission, *Overview of FTA and Other Trade Negotiations* (Updated 16 September 2015).

59 Association Agreement between the European Union and the European Atomic Energy Community and their Member States, of the one part, and Georgia, of the other part (OJ L 261, 30.08.2014, p. 4).

unilateral free trade opening of [their] economy to the whole of the world'.[60] Consequently, both Georgia and Singapore can be expected to have had a 'constraining' impact on the negotiations, as they would have been looking for relatively unfettered liberalisation.[61]

As a matter of delineation, two important limitations of this book must be set forth. The first limitation is one *ratione materiae*. Aside from limiting the research to a case study of the EU and the three selected EU RTAs, the regulation of trade in services in the selected RTAs cannot be addressed in its totality. First, the investment or procurement chapters of the EU RTAs, which have an impact on trade in services as they also cover a certain form of supply of services, are not addressed. Second, EU RTAs often include sector-specific regulation of services, which do not have corresponding GATS obligations and would lead us too far afield. Third, several general obligations in the EU RTAs also apply to services. Whilst these are addressed where related to GATS obligations (e.g. in the case of current and capital transactions), they are not discussed when unrelated to GATS obligations.

The second limitation is that the methodology adopted to address the research problem is a comparative legal analysis of the constraints on regulatory autonomy from the multilateral liberalisation of trade in services, as compared with the preferential liberalisation. However, in the words of a prominent scholar of regulatory autonomy:

> Sixty years of GATT/WTO dispute settlement history told us that the balancing line between trade liberalization and domestic regulatory autonomy has been drawn, erased and redrawn in the light of the specific facts of the case at hand and the prevailing sensitivities of the time.[62]

Therefore, the comparative legal analysis should be practical and based on the law as it stands. Where guidance from dispute settlement is available, case law serves as the basis of the present analysis. This is because two objectives of dispute settlement, as enshrined in Article 3.2

---

[60] Michael Emerson, *Countdown to the Vilnius Summit: The EU's Trade Relations with Moldova and the South Caucasus* (The EU's Trade Relations with Moldova and the South Caucasus EXPO/B/FWC/2009-01/Lot 7/39, 2014) 13.

[61] See as concerns Georgia, Patrick A Messerlin et al., *An Appraisal of the EU's Trade Policy Towards its Eastern Neighbours: The Case of Georgia* (SciencesPo and Center for European Policy Studies, 2011) 17.

[62] Michael Ming Du, 'Has the WTO Appellate Body Pushed the Limits of Global Governance in the *China–Publications* Case? A Reply to Julia Ya Qin' (2012) 11 Chinese Journal of International Law 227, 231.

of the Dispute Settlement Understanding (DSU) are securing predictability and security, and the filling of gaps and resolution of ambiguities in treaty text.[63] Moreover, it is a goal of dispute settlement to provide a 'reasoned analysis of important policy implications of the rule application, so as to shed light on complex issues and dilemmas requiring a balancing approach'.[64] Undeniably, this applies to the balancing of regulatory autonomy and trade liberalisation. If no guidance from dispute settlement is available, an interpretation of the law must be based on treaty interpretation to devise the Members' common intention, rather than aiming for a perfect legal system.[65] This requires some pragmatism, but that is a necessary corollary of the constructive ambiguity that led to the adoption of any treaty.[66]

4. SUMMARY AND OUTLINE OF THE BOOK

Trade in services is economically crucial, and will be more so when the share of trade in services in global trade rises to live up partially to its weight in GDP. Because the broad scope of activities considered as services includes heavily regulated economic activities that are not usually considered as related to trade, balancing trade liberalisation in services with regulatory autonomy is even more difficult than is the case for trade in goods. The complex regulatory framework created by the multilateral and preferential liberalisation of trade in services creates a further layer of intricacy. It is the purpose of this book to assess the constraints on EU regulatory autonomy resulting from the multilateral and preferential liberalisation of trade in services. The analytical approach taken is an in-depth case study that analyses the EU's obligations regarding trade in services under GATS and under three EU RTAs (EU-Colombia & Peru, EU-Singapore and EU-Georgia). Before assessing the structure of these agreements (Chapter 2), their scope (Chapter 3),

---

[63] John H Jackson, *Sovereignty, the WTO and Changing Fundamentals of International Law* (Cambridge University Press 2006) 148.

[64] Ibid 150.

[65] Lode Van Den Hende, 'GATS Article XVI and National Regulatory Sovereignty: What Lessons to Draw from *US–Gambling*?' (2007) 20 Cambridge Review of International Affairs 93, 105. See *United States – Measures Affecting the Cross-Border Supply of Gambling and Betting Services* WT/DS285/AB/R, AB report adopted 20 April 2005 paras 159–160.

[66] For GATS, see *Mexico – Measures Affecting Telecommunications Services* WT/DS204/R, Panel report adopted 2 April 2004 para. 7.3.

the obligations therein (Chapters 4–7) and the exceptions to these obligations (Chapter 8), it is necessary to explicate the interpretational framework (Chapter 1) for this book's practical comparative legal analysis.

1. Interpretation of GATS and the selected EU RTAs

Before one can commence the analysis of constraints on regulatory autonomy resulting from obligations applicable to the EU in GATS and the services chapters of EU RTAs, it is imperative to explain how these treaties are to be interpreted. In the case of GATS, case law has developed its take on the rules of treaty interpretation extensively. In the case of EU RTAs, despite the dispute settlement mechanisms provided, no disputes have been brought to this day.[1] Although there is some guidance in the text of each of the selected agreements, it is submitted that a presumption of WTO consistent interpretation applies to all agreements. Because the objectives of an agreement shed light on the interpretation of its provisions, these are addressed in this chapter as well.

1. THE MULTILATERAL LEVEL

1.1 Treaty Interpretation in the WTO

To understand many unresolved questions of GATS law, one needs an understanding of how panels and the Appellate Body (AB) have so far interpreted GATS. As treaty interpretation in the WTO has been addressed expertly elsewhere,[2] it suffices here to briefly introduce the applicable rules. Article 3.2 of the Dispute Settlement Understanding (DSU) contains the mandate for the dispute settlement system to clarify the existing provisions of the WTO agreements in accordance with customary rules of public international law. In practice, WTO dispute

[1] See Claude Chase et al., *Mapping of Dispute Settlement Mechanisms in Regional Trade Agreements – Innovative or Variations on a Theme?* (World Trade Organization Economic Research and Statistics Division Staff Working Paper ERSD-2013-07, 2013) 10–11 and 54–55.

[2] Isabelle Van Damme, *Treaty Interpretation by the WTO Appellate Body* (Oxford University Press 2009).

settlement bodies apply Articles 31 and 32 of the Vienna Convention on the Law of Treaties[3] (VCLT).[4] By applying Article 31.1 VCLT, the panels and AB interpret treaty provisions 'in accordance with the ordinary meaning to be given to the terms of the treaty in their context and in the light of its object and purpose'. The ordinary meaning of a term should determine the common intentions of the parties,[5] and all the terms of a treaty must be given meaning.[6] The treaty interpretation techniques of Article 31 VCLT are 'ultimately a holistic exercise that should not be mechanically subdivided into rigid components'.[7] To confirm the interpretation resulting from an application of Article 31 VCLT, or if the cited approach leaves the meaning of a provision ambiguous or obscure, or leads to a result which is manifestly absurd or unreasonable, Article 32 VCLT allows recourse to supplementary means of interpretation, including the preparatory works – i.e. the negotiating history, to which little importance has been given[8] – of the treaty and the circumstances of its conclusion.

In addition to treaty interpretation rules, it is important to note that the AB has 'opted for a strong de facto rule of precedent'.[9] As the AB stated itself:

> the legal interpretation embodied in adopted panel and Appellate Body reports becomes part and parcel of the acquis of the WTO dispute settlement system. Ensuring 'security and predictability' […] implies that, absent cogent reasons,

---

[3] Vienna Convention on the Law of Treaties, 23 May 1969, 1155 U.N.T.S. 331, 8 I.L.M. 679 (1969).

[4] Their customary nature is confirmed in respectively *United States – Standards for Reformulated and Conventional Gasoline* WT/DS2/AB/R, AB report adopted 20 May 1996 15–16 and *Japan – Taxes on Alcoholic Beverages* WT/DS8/AB/R, AB report adopted 1 November 1996 122–123.

[5] *India – Patent Protection for Pharmaceutical and Agricultural Chemical Products* WT/DS50/AB/R, AB report adopted 16 January 1998 para. 45.

[6] *US – Gasoline (AB)* 21.

[7] *China – Measures Affecting Trading Rights and Distribution Services for Certain Publications and Audiovisual Products* WT/DS363/AB/R, AB report adopted 19 January 2010 para. 176; *Japan – Alcoholic Beverages II (AB)* 104.

[8] Peter Van den Bossche and Werner Zdouc, *The Law and Policy of the World Trade Organization* (3rd edn, Cambridge University Press 2013) 192–193.

[9] Joost Pauwelyn, 'Minority Rules: Precedent and Participation Before the WTO Appellate Body' in Joanna Jemielniak, Laura Nielsen and Henrik Palmer Olsen (eds), *Judicial Authority in International Economic Law* (forthcoming) 3; Anne Scully-Hill and Hans Mahncke, 'The Emergence of the Doctrine of Stare Decisis in the World Trade Organization Dispute Settlement System' (2009) 36 Legal Issues of Economic Integration 133.

an adjudicatory body will resolve the same legal question in the same way in a subsequent case.[10]

On a vertical level, 'following the Appellate Body's conclusions in earlier disputes is not only appropriate, but is what would be expected from panels, especially where the issues are the same'.[11]

1.2 The Objectives of GATS

The preamble of an agreement reflects the intentions of the negotiators, and therefore provides context to the obligations in an agreement and sheds light on its object and purpose.[12] The AB stated that the preamble adds 'colour, texture and shading' to the interpretation of an agreement.[13] Moreover, the preamble contains the objectives of an agreement, which constitute its *telos* and 'serve as a lighthouse for our appreciation of its provisions and case law'.[14] The objectives of GATS are reflected in the key elements of its preamble and shape the tension between regulatory autonomy and trade liberalisation.[15] The second recital of the GATS preamble states that the overarching objectives of the agreement are the expansion of trade in services under conditions of transparency, and progressive liberalisation to promote economic growth among all WTO Members. The objective of progressive liberalisation is complemented in the third recital by the words 'while giving due respect to national policy objectives'. The latter is supported by the fourth recital, in which regulatory autonomy is emphasised. It talks of '[r]ecognizing the right of

---

[10] *United States – Final Anti-Dumping Measures on Stainless Steel from Mexico* WT/DS344/AB/R, AB report adopted 20 May 2008 para. 160.

[11] *United States – Sunset Reviews of Anti-Dumping Measures on Oil Country Tubular Goods from Argentina* WT/DS268/AB/R, AB report adopted 17 December 2004 para. 188.

[12] Article 31.2 VCLT and *United States – Import Prohibition of Certain Shrimp and Shrimp Products* WT/DS58/AB/R, AB report adopted 6 November 1998 para. 155.

[13] Ibid. As concerns GATS, see *US – Gambling (AB)* paras 188–189.

[14] Michael Ming Du, 'Domestic Regulatory Autonomy under the TBT Agreement: From Non-discrimination to Harmonization' (2007) 6 Chinese Journal of International Law 269, 273.

[15] Andrew Lang, 'The GATS and Regulatory Autonomy: A Case Study of Social Regulation of the Water Industry' (2004) 7 Journal of International Economic Law 801, 804.

Members to regulate, and to introduce new regulations, on the supply of services within their territories in order to meet national policy objectives'.

The AB has pointed out that there are several objectives listed in the preamble of GATS, but did not express a view on their relationship.[16] In its reading of the preamble of the Agreement on Technical Barriers to Trade (TBT Agreement), the objective of trade liberalisation and a right to regulate were however compared to the balance set out by the national treatment obligation and the general exceptions provision in the General Agreement on Tariffs and Trade (GATT) 1994.[17] This comparison does reflect a relational understanding. This is confirmed by the finding of the Panel in *China – Publications and Audiovisual Products* that the second recital of GATS contains the 'general object and purpose', while the aspect of securing a balance between rights and obligations must be interpreted 'in light of this general object and purpose'.[18] Similarly, the Panel in *US – Gambling* noted that 'Members' regulatory sovereignty is an essential pillar of the progressive liberalization of trade in services'.[19] This indicates that progressive liberalisation and transparency, as conditions for the expansion of trade in services, are considered the foremost objectives of GATS. Of course, liberalisation must nonetheless 'secure an overall balance of rights and obligations'[20] and the right to regulate should not be underrated. The Panel in *US – Gambling* noted that 'it is clear that *WTO Members do have the right to regulate*' and '[w]e have not decided that WTO Members do not have a right to regulate'.[21] In *China – Publications and Audiovisual Products*, the Panel noted that 'China has the undoubted right to regulate trade in services under the GATS'.[22] The Panel in *Argentina – Financial Services* stressed the

---

[16] *US – Gambling (AB)* footnote 271; *China – Publications and Audiovisual Products (AB)* para. 392.

[17] *United States – Measures Affecting the Production and Sale of Clove Cigarettes* WT/DS406/AB/R, AB report adopted 24 April 2012 paras 94–96.

[18] *China – Measures Affecting Trading Rights and Distribution Services for Certain Publications and Audiovisual Products* WT/DS363/R, Panel report adopted 19 January 2010 paras 7.1219 and 7.1348.

[19] *United States – Measures Affecting the Cross-Border Supply of Gambling and Betting Services* WT/DS285/R, Panel report adopted 20 April 2005 para. 6.316, and recalled by the AB in *US – Gambling (AB)* footnote 271.

[20] *US – Gambling (Panel)* para. 6.317.

[21] Ibid paras 5.17 and 7.4 (emphasis original).

[22] *China – Publications and Audiovisual Products (Panel)* para. 7.1139. Also see *China – Measures Affecting Electronic Payment Services* WT/DS413/R, Panel report adopted 31 August 2012 para. 7.569; *United States – Measures*

preamble's right to regulate in conjunction with Article XIX GATS, which refers to respect for national policy objectives.[23] However, panels and the AB have stressed that the limit of regulatory autonomy lies where it impairs the rights of other Members under GATS.[24]

The discussion above highlights that the objectives of GATS can be interpreted as giving substantial regard to national regulatory autonomy on the one hand, or that they can be interpreted under a wholly opposite market liberalisation approach on the other hand.[25] It should be recognised that GATS, as part of a regulatory framework on international trade, is based on the point of view that trade liberalisation is beneficial. The structure of the agreement indeed reflects this approach. However, from its preamble onwards, the tension between regulatory autonomy and trade liberalisation is recognised,[26] and the (limited) use of the preamble in GATS case law indicates that panels and the AB recognise this tension, too. This, in its turn, points towards the nature of GATS as an elaborate political compromise that is 'no monument of clarity'.[27]

2. THE PREFERENTIAL LEVEL

2.1 Treaty Interpretation in RTAs

2.1.1 Rules and guidance for the interpretation of RTAs

The interpretation of RTA provisions is crucial to understand how RTAs limit regulatory autonomy. Being aware of the lack of interpretational

---

Affecting the Cross-Border Supply of Gambling and Betting Services WT/DS285/ARB, Decision by the Arbitrator circulated 21 December 2007 para. 3.45.

23 See e.g. *Argentina – Measures Relating to Trade in Goods and Services* WT/DS453/R, Panel report not yet adopted paras 7.422–7.423.

24 *US – Gambling (Panel)* para. 6.316, recalled by the AB in *US – Gambling (AB)* footnote 271; *China – Electronic Payment Services (Panel)* para. 7.1139.

25 M Krajewski, *National Regulation and Trade Liberalization in Services* (Kluwer Law International 2003) 57.

26 This reflects the fear of developing countries during the negotiation of GATS that the agreement would grant effective control over their services markets to foreign powers. Marchetti and Mavroidis, 'The Genesis of the GATS (General Agreement on Trade in Services)' (2011) 22 European Journal of International Law 689, 698.

27 Juan A Marchetti and Petros C Mavroidis, 'From Reluctant Participant to Key Player: EU and the Negotiation of the GATS' in Inge Govaere, Reinhard Quick and Marco Bronckers (eds), *Trade and Competition Law in the EU and Beyond* (Edward Elgar Publishing 2011) 95.

guidance from case law, concerning both the interpretational rules of RTAs and the substantive content of their provisions, one must resort to an interpretation based on the text of the agreement and the available interpretational tools. As noted in the Introduction, the EU's RTAs contain three types of interpretational provisions, and one of each type is selected as a case study in this book. The three types of interpretational provisions prescribe interpretations: (i) based on customary rules of interpretation only; (ii) based on customary rules of interpretation for provisions not identical to a WTO provision but consistent with relevant WTO interpretations for identical provisions; and (iii) taking into account relevant WTO interpretations. These rules create four scenarios:

a. An identical obligation is interpreted 'in consistency with' WTO case law.
b. An obligation, whether identical or non-identical, is interpreted by 'taking into account' WTO case law.
c. A non-identical obligation is interpreted in accordance with customary rules of interpretation.
d. An identical obligation is interpreted in accordance with customary rules of interpretation.

At first sight, from a. to d., the risk of interpretational variance seems to augment. However, WTO treaty interpretation is based on customary rules of interpretation, and while there is leeway within these rules for adopting a different approach to the one taken in WTO dispute settlement practice, how far could an RTA arbitration panel that is called upon to interpret an RTA deviate from WTO treaty interpretations in situations b., c. or d.? A director at the Directorate General for Trade of the European Commission noted, in his personal capacity, that 'the substantive law of free trade agreements is very largely influenced – and, indeed, dependent upon – WTO law'.[28] Indeed, it is my view that, absent a good reason not to, the provisions in the EU RTAs' services chapters should be interpreted in conformity with WTO case law regardless of which of the three abovementioned types of interpretational provision applies.

---

[28] Ignacio Garcia Bercero, 'Dispute Settlement in European Union Free Trade Agreements: Lessons Learned?' in Lorand Bartels and Federico Ortino (eds), *Regional Trade Agreements and the WTO Legal System* (Oxford University Press 2006) 399.

2.1.2 The presumption of WTO consistent interpretation

Because of the combination of the three main reasons set out below, it is argued that there is a rebuttable presumption that RTA provisions must be interpreted in consistency with WTO case law interpretations.[29] This presumption improves the predictability and coherence of international trade law, and is therefore 'highly desirable'.[30] RTA arbitration panels should apply '*de facto stare decisis*', i.e. precedents are followed for 'extra- and quasi-legal reasons, including custom and habit' and their high persuasiveness, but not because RTA arbitration panels are legally required to do so.[31] Such a 'de facto precedent, like a de jure one, creates a presumption that it is to be followed unless a very good reason for a departure exists'.[32] Hence, it is my view that although RTA arbitration panels are not always allowed to and do not always have to expressly draw upon WTO case law, a *de facto* identical interpretation should be achieved in most cases, i.e. except when the presumption is rebutted. The main proponent of *de facto stare decisis* summarises this approach as follows:

> in a de facto stare decisis regime, a prior holding is like a cane that the adjudicator is only in theory – specifically, legal theory – free to use or toss,

---

[29] The presumption of WTO consistent interpretation also applies to RTAs between the EU and non-WTO Members, as the reasons below do not cease to apply in such a case.

[30] Garcia Bercero, 'Dispute Settlement in European Union Free Trade Agreements: Lessons Learned?' 400, who makes this claim regarding bilateral provisions that are largely independent from WTO obligations. Concerning areas of overlap between WTO and RTA obligations or where an RTA obligation reproduces the WTO obligation without referring to it, he notes 'it is difficult to see how a bilateral panel could properly apply the provisions of the FTA without also referring to WTO law'.

[31] See Marc L Busch, 'Overlapping Institutions, Forum Shopping, and Dispute Settlement in International Trade' (2007) 61 International Organization 735, 740; David M Palmeter and Petros C Mavroidis, *Dispute Settlement in the World Trade Organization: Practice and Procedure* (2nd edn, Cambridge University Press 2004) 56; Locknie Hsu, 'Applicability of WTO Law in Regional Trade Agreements: Identifying the Links' in Lorand Bartels and Federico Ortino (eds), *Regional Trade Agreements and the WTO Legal System* (Oxford University Press 2006) 526–527 and 551–552.

[32] Raj Bhala, 'The Precedent Setters: De Facto Stare Decisis in WTO Adjudication (Part Two of a Trilogy)' (1999) 9 Journal of Transnational Law & Policy 1, 3.

but in fact always uses whenever the opportunity arises, or in the rare cases when it chooses to toss the cane, it takes great care in explaining why.[33]

The first and second main reasons are supporting affirmations vis-à-vis the third, perhaps most convincing, reason for a WTO consistent interpretation.

2.1.2.1 'Supremacy' of the WTO agreements The first reason to interpret RTA provisions in consistency with WTO case law is based on the alleged 'supremacy' of the WTO agreements vis-à-vis RTAs. The argument is based on Article 41 VCLT, which at least 'reflects customary law',[34] and relates to the relationship between the WTO Agreements on RTAs from the perspective of public international law. Article 41.1 VCLT addresses the situation in which two or more of the parties to a multilateral treaty may conclude an agreement to modify the treaty between them as individual parties. Such modification is prohibited if: (i) the multilateral treaty prohibits modification; (ii) if the modifying treaty affects the rights and obligations of third parties; and (iii) if the modifying treaty derogates from a provision, where such derogation is incompatible with the effective execution of the object and purpose of the multilateral treaty in its entirety.

Article 41.1 (a) VCLT reflects the situation where a multilateral treaty provides for the possibility of a modification of the multilateral treaty between two parties alone. According to several authors, the WTO rules on the formation of RTAs, contained in Articles XXIV GATT 1994 and V GATS are thus to be considered superior to RTA rules on the basis of Article 41.1 (a) VCLT, as the formation of the RTA is only in accordance with Article 41.1 (a) VCLT if it respects the rules set out in these provisions.[35] This creates a 'constitutional and hierarchical relationship

[33] Raj Bhala, 'The Myth About Stare Decisis and International Trade Law (Part One of a Trilogy)' (1999) 14 American University International Law Review 845, 939–940.

[34] Kerstin Odendahl, 'Article 41' in Oliver Dörr and Kirsten Schmalenbach (eds), *Vienna Convention on the Law of Treaties* (Springer 2012) 723. Pauwelyn considers Article 41.1 VCLT to be customary international law: Joost Pauwelyn, *Conflict of Norms in Public International Law: How WTO Law Relates to Other Rules of International Law* (Cambridge University Press 2003) 305.

[35] James Mathis, *Regional Trade Agreements in the GATT/WTO: Article XXIV and the Internal Trade Requirement* (TMC Asser Press 2002) 271–285; Thomas Cottier and Marina Foltea, 'Constitutional Functions of the WTO and RTAs' in Lorand Bartels and Federico Ortino (eds), *Regional Trade Agreements and the WTO Legal System* (Oxford University Press 2006) 56–57.

between WTO rules and RTAs'.[36] This may have been visible in *Turkey – Textiles*, as the AB may have hinted at the fact that RTAs are a mere exception to multilateralism, rather than an alternative.[37] Even if 'supremacy' is too strong a term, the link between Article V GATS and the RTA does create a hierarchy between both agreements.

Similarly, it may be argued that Article V GATS does not provide for the *possibility* of modification,[38] but merely does *not prohibit* such modification. Consequently subparagraph (b) of Article 41.1 VCLT is applicable. This reflects the situation where a modification is neither expressly prohibited (in which case a modification cannot be allowed under the rules of the VCLT), nor expressly allowed (in which case Article 41.1 (a) VCLT would apply). In support of such argument, it can be put forth that Article V GATS is an exception,[39] and therefore not a provision explicitly allowing the modification of GATS between RTA parties (even if in effect this is what an RTA does). In order for a modification to be in accordance with Article 41.1 (b) VCLT, the modifying agreement, *in casu* the RTA, should fulfil the two conditions contained in that provision.[40] Failure to fulfil these obligations would imply a violation of Article 41.1 VCLT. Either condition thus is a 'ground of illegality',[41] as modifications that do not fulfil a condition are illegal modifications of the multilateral agreement. The first condition requires that the rights of the other Members are not prejudiced by the RTA. That could appear to be the case as, in principle, the RTA remains *res inter alios* for those Members.[42] Nonetheless, the rights of third parties may in certain situations be affected by interpretations of provisions in an RTA.[43]

---

36 Cottier and Foltea, 'Constitutional Functions of the WTO and RTAs' 57.

37 Peter Hilpold, 'Regional Integration According to Article XXIV GATT – Between Law and Politics' (2003) 7 Max Planck Yearbook of United Nations Law Online 219, 246.

38 The examples given of such clauses in Odendahl, 'Article 41' 723–724 differ from Article V GATS: e.g. '[n]othing in the present Convention shall preclude States from concluding international agreements *confirming or supplementing or extending or amplifying* the provisions thereof' (emphasis added).

39 Van den Bossche and Zdouc, *The Law and Policy of the World Trade Organization* 664.

40 The notification requirement of Article 41.2 VCLT would be fulfilled by the notification of the RTA to the WTO.

41 Pauwelyn, *Conflict of Norms in Public International Law: How WTO Law Relates to Other Rules of International Law* 305.

42 Odendahl, 'Article 41' 725.

43 Compare to Pauwelyn, *Conflict of Norms in Public International Law: How WTO Law Relates to Other Rules of International Law* 308–310, giving

The second condition of Article 41.1 (b) VCLT is more interesting: it requires that the derogation from a certain multilateral provision in the modifying agreement is not incompatible with the effective execution of the object and purpose of GATS as a whole. The Panel in *China – Publications and Audiovisual Products* referred to the expansion of trade in services under conditions of transparency and progressive liberalisation and as a means of promoting the economic growth of all trading partners and the development of developing countries as the 'general object and purpose' of GATS.[44] A case can be made that RTAs may generally be incompatible with this object and purpose.[45] For example, RTAs (and especially GATS– provisions) do not promote the interests of all WTO Members nor do they contribute to progressive rounds of multilateral services liberalisation. However, this is not the question at hand, which is whether *interpretations* that are not consistent with GATS case law, and thus derogate from a GATS provision, are incompatible with the effective execution of the object and purpose of GATS. Article 41.1 (b) (ii) VCLT requires that the modification does not relate to a provision from which derogation is incompatible with the effective execution of the object and purpose of the multilateral treaty as a whole. Where an RTA provision is drafted using WTO law concepts, the RTA itself could well be consistent with Article 41.1 VCLT. It seems, even if not required by Article 41.1 VCLT, that the *interpretation* of such a modifying agreement should adhere to the same guidelines as its creation. Indeed, it may be argued that the establishment of a multilateral framework for trade in services with a view to the expansion of such trade under conditions of transparency and progressive liberalisation could be hampered by inconsistent interpretations between RTAs and GATS, if not frustrated entirely. First, RTAs do not increase transparency of the regulation of trade in services, as this book will demonstrate. Second, there are clear GATS– provisions in the services chapters of

inter alia the example of a multilateral environmental agreement that is modified by a subsequent bilateral agreement in which, between the parties to the latter, an emission reduction target is lowered vis-à-vis the multilateral agreement.

44 *China – Publications and Audiovisual Products (Panel)* paras 7.1219 and 7.1348.

45 Pauwelyn, *Conflict of Norms in Public International Law: How WTO Law Relates to Other Rules of International Law* 317–318, who envisages situations outside of adherence to the conditions in Articles XXIV GATT 1994 and V GATS that may violate Article 41 VCLT.

RTAs,[46] which indicates that RTAs do not necessarily lead to progressive liberalisation. Third, trade diversion effects may indicate that there is no expansion of trade in services resulting from RTAs. The link with 'a provision, derogation from which is incompatible with the effective execution of the object and purpose of the treaty as a whole' can be made because any specific provision from which the RTA deviates has such potential, possibly through linking back to the preamble. Indeed, in many cases, derogation from *any* GATS provision could be said to frustrate the abovementioned object and purpose of the agreement.[47] To avoid such problems (and although it is acknowledged that this reasoning is not sufficient to support the presumption by itself), it is submitted that the interpretation of an RTA should be in conformity with that of the hierarchically supreme agreement,[48] i.e. the multilateral WTO covered agreements.

2.1.2.2 Systemic integration The second reason for interpreting provisions of RTAs in consistency with WTO case law relates to the principle of systemic integration. Article 31.3 (c) VCLT requires RTA arbitration panels to take into account, together with the context of the terms of the treaty and the treaty's object and purpose, 'any relevant rules of international law applicable in the relations between the parties'. According to the International Law Commission (ILC)'s report on the fragmentation of international law, this rule expresses the principle of 'systemic integration'.[49] The ILC notes that 'all that article 31 (3) (c) requires [is] the integration into the process of legal reasoning – including reasoning by courts and tribunals – of a sense of coherence and meaningfulness'.[50] The AB endorsed this interpretation in the context of

---

[46] See e.g. Rudolf Adlung and Sébastien Miroudot, 'Poison in the Wine? Tracing GATS-Minus Commitments in Regional Trade Agreements' (2012) 46 Journal of World Trade 1045.

[47] See, for similar thinking, Rudolf Adlung, 'The Trade in Services Agreement (TISA) and its Compatibility with GATS: An Assessment Based on Current Evidence' 14 World Trade Review 617, 623.

[48] It is supreme for the same reasons expressed vis-à-vis Article 41.1 (a) VCLT.

[49] International Law Commission, *Fragmentation of International Law: Difficulties Arising from the Diversification and Expansion of International Law* (A/CN4/L682, Report of the Study Group of the International Law Commission, 2006) para. 413.

[50] Ibid para. 419.

applying non-WTO law to interpret WTO law.[51] The limit to this approach is that interpretation by way of Article 31.3 (c) VCLT must reflect the common intention of the parties to the treaty that is being interpreted.[52] If the WTO agreements are applicable in the relations between the parties, i.e. all parties are WTO Members, and the rule concerns the same subject matter,[53] RTA arbitration panels should take into account these WTO rules and, hence, their interpretation by WTO dispute settlement bodies. The arbitration panels are only obliged to do so in specific situations according to some of the treaty interpretation provisions in the selected EU RTAs, but should take into account the normative environment of international trade law. It has even been argued that RTA tribunals are 'essentially always required to interpret [R]TA obligations in the light of the relevant WTO law'.[54] I agree with this view. Ignoring WTO case law would run counter to the principle of systemic integration. Similarly, it may be said that WTO case law provides context in the sense of Article 31 VCLT.[55] According to Article 38.1 (d) *juncto* 59 of the Statute of the International Court of Justice, judicial decisions are not binding precedents, but may nonetheless constitute 'subsidiary means for the determination of rules of law'.

2.1.2.3 Pragmatic reasons Finally, and most convincingly, the third reason for a presumption of WTO consistent interpretation is a pragmatic preference for multilateral dispute settlement organs in the context of the fragmentation of international trade law. The presumption could be considered 'a hub-and-spoke model' that 'would be particularly effective in countering fragmentation in the international trade regime'.[56] In comparison to the body of case law from any other international tribunal, the WTO's body of case law is very substantial and well developed. The

---

[51] *European Communities – Measures Affecting Trade in Large Civil Aircraft* WT/DS316/AB/R, AB report adopted 1 June 2011 para. 845.

[52] *Peru – Additional Duty on Imports of Certain Agricultural Products* WT/DS457/AB/R, AB report adopted 31 July 2015 para. 5.95.

[53] The subject matter of the rules must be the same: see ibid and the case law cited there.

[54] Adrian M Johnston and Michael J Trebilcock, 'Fragmentation in International Trade Law: Insights from the Global Investment Regime' (2013) 12 World Trade Review 621, 638. The authors correctly note that this does not work the other way, nor between RTAs dispute settlement organs.

[55] Hsu, 'Applicability of WTO Law in Regional Trade Agreements: Identifying the Links' 527; also see 523–540.

[56] Johnston and Trebilcock, 'Fragmentation in International Trade Law: Insights from the Global Investment Regime' 641.

consequence of this is the *de facto* hierarchy of the WTO dispute settlement over RTA dispute settlement.[57] It therefore has 'procedural superiority' over RTA dispute settlement.[58] It may be that multilateral dispute settlement is 'intrinsically superior to RTA dispute settlement' and is perceived to be more legitimate because of, among other factors, the neutrality of panellists and its rules-based approach.[59] When interpreting provisions which are related to – not just identical to – WTO law, or find their foundation therein, there would be little sense for an *ad hoc* EU RTA arbitration panel to go against a WTO case law interpretation, unless there is a clear indication that the parties intended to diverge from the meaning of the WTO provision. For example, in most RTAs there are references to national treatment or MFN obligations, which induce the scope of cross-treaty interpretation.[60] If an RTA has a *telos* similar to that of the WTO, the RTA's dispute settlement mechanism 'will be inspired by the GATT/WTO case law when interpreting' the RTA.[61] Similarly, an analysis of the ordinary meaning of the words in the RTA could lead to the taking into account of WTO case law.[62] Of course, the RTA panel should not apply WTO law, but it should use relevant WTO (case) law to interpret an RTA provision if the conditions of Article 31.3 (c) VCLT are fulfilled.[63] These conditions are that relevant rules of international law applicable in the relations between the parties shall be taken into account when interpreting a provision. In practice, due to the quasi-universal

---

[57] Erik Voeten, 'Borrowing and Nonborrowing among International Courts' (2010) 39 Journal of Legal Studies 547, 566; Johnston and Trebilcock, 'Fragmentation in International Trade Law: Insights from the Global Investment Regime' 639.

[58] Delimatsis, 'The Fragmentation of International Trade Law' 115.

[59] William J Davey, 'Dispute Settlement in the WTO and RTAs: A Comment' in Lorand Bartels and Federico Ortino (eds), *Regional Trade Agreements and the WTO Legal System* (Oxford University Press 2006) 354–357; William J Davey and André Sapir, 'The *Soft Drinks* Case: The WTO and Regional Agreements' (2009) 8 World Trade Review 5, 22.

[60] Johnston and Trebilcock, 'Fragmentation in International Trade Law: Insights from the Global Investment Regime' 639.

[61] Panagiotis Delimatsis, 'The Fragmentation of International Trade Law' (2011) 45 Journal of World Trade 87, 109.

[62] Johnston and Trebilcock, 'Fragmentation in International Trade Law: Insights from the Global Investment Regime' 637, argue that this may also apply to other RTAs.

[63] In WTO case law, the panels and AB cannot 'determine rights and obligations outside the covered Agreements'. *Mexico – Tax Measures on Soft Drinks and Other Beverages* WT/DS308/AB/R, AB report adopted 24 March 2006 para. 56.

membership to the WTO, the rule will only need to be 'relevant', as it will very often be applicable in the relations between the RTA parties. Consequentially, the relevant rules of WTO law and their interpretation should reflect on the interpretation of the RTA provision, leading to a WTO consistent interpretation.[64]

Moreover, only in very specific cases can a WTO panel decline to exercise their procedurally validly established jurisdiction.[65] Otherwise, according to Article 23 DSU, the jurisdiction of the WTO dispute settlement system is exclusive and compulsory as concerns the covered agreements. Hence, in 'twin' cases concerning the same parties and subject matter, a Member may bring a case before the WTO if it is dissatisfied by the outcome at the level of RTA dispute settlement; for example, if there is an overlap between WTO and North American Free Trade Agreement (NAFTA) provisions and the latter's dispute settlement mechanism adjudicated on issues that could have been brought before a WTO panel. The problem is aggravated in the context of 'double' RTAs, where the relationship between parties is not only governed by WTO rules and an RTA, but potentially also a mega-regional or a plurilateral agreement such as the Trade in Services Agreement (TiSA).[66] The risk of fragmentation and turf wars resulting from such a situation provides no benefit to any of the parties involved.[67] Only in cases where the dispute is based on a WTO+ or WTO-X provision, or in cases where a panel could decline to exercise its jurisdiction, would this risk be avoided.

---

[64] This is very much in line with the case law from the Court of Justice of the European Union on the principle of consistent interpretation of secondary EU law with rules of international law. See e.g. Case C-61/94 *Commission v Germany* [1996] ECR I-3989, para. 52.

[65] *European Communities – Export Subsidies on Sugar* WT/DS265/AB/R, WT/DS266/AB/R, WT/DS283/AB/R, AB report adopted 19 May 2005 para. 312. See, extensively, Bregt Natens and Sidonie Descheemaeker, 'Say it Loud, Say it Clear – Article 3.10 DSU's Clear Statement Test as a Legal Impediment to Validly Established Jurisdiction' 49 Journal of World Trade 871.

[66] Joost Pauwelyn and Wolfgang Alschner, 'Forget About the WTO: The Network of Relations between Preferential Trade Agreements (PTAs) and "Double PTAs"' in Andreas Dür and Manfred Elsig (eds), *Trade Cooperation: The Purpose, Design and Effects of Preferential Trade Agreements* (Cambridge University Press 2015).

[67] See e.g. the EU-Chile 'Swordfish' and EU-Faroe Islands 'Herring' disputes where claims were filed both at the WTO and the International Tribunal for the Law of the Sea. The case was settled.

2.1.2.4 Evidence supporting the presumption There is evidence of the presumption of a WTO consistent interpretation in RTA dispute settlement practice. First, such evidence is found in NAFTA Chapter 20 dispute settlement, one of the few examples of active bilateral dispute settlement (outside of investment). The interpretation of NAFTA Chapter 20 by the Arbitral panel makes substantial reference to WTO case law. To date, three reports have been issued, each relying on GATT 1947 and WTO case law. The NAFTA Arbitral Panel in the *Certain U.S.-Origin Agricultural Products* case does so only in passing, noting that exceptions to trade liberalisation obligations should be 'viewed with caution', as is 'well accepted in the interpretation of the GATT [1947]'.[68] The Panel also hinted at the importance of AB case law, by referring to the AB's acceptance of and reliance on Articles 31 and 32 VCLT as customary rules of interpretation.[69] Consequently, when the Panel was asked to interpret a NAFTA provision 'substantively identical' to a WTO obligation in *Broom Corn Brooms*, WTO case law was referred to.[70] In establishing likeness of products, GATT 1947 and WTO case law was used extensively.[71] Additionally, in its *Cross-Border Trucking Services* report, the NAFTA Arbitral Panel's analysis started by explaining that its approach 'is fully consistent with the practice of the WTO Appellate Body'.[72] In its interpretation of the national treatment obligation under NAFTA, the Arbitral Panel explicitly relied on a GATT Panel Report.[73] WTO case law on Article XX GATT 1994 was also heavily relied upon by the Panel.[74] Hence, in all three cases of Chapter 20 dispute settlement, WTO/GATT 1947 case law was cited.[75] Nonetheless, it should be noted that the point of view taken here is not shared unanimously in legal scholarship. For example, one author notes that '[i]n short, one can speak meaningfully about separate bodies of de facto stare decisis at the WTO

---

[68] CDA-95-2008-01 NAFTA Chapter 20 Arbitral Panel, Final Report 2 December 1996 in the matter of Tariffs Applied by Canada to Certain US-Origin Agricultural Products para. 122 and footnote 109.

[69] Ibid footnote 107.

[70] USA-97-2008-01 NAFTA Chapter 20 Arbitral Panel, Final Report 30 January 1998 in the matter of US Safeguard Action Taken on Broom Corn Brooms from Mexico paras 50 and 53.

[71] Ibid paras 66–68.

[72] USA-MEX-98-2008-01 NAFTA Chapter 20 Arbitral Panel, Final Report 6 February 2001 in the matter of Cross-Border Trucking Services para. 214.

[73] Ibid para. 251.

[74] Ibid paras 262–270.

[75] Johnston and Trebilcock, 'Fragmentation in International Trade Law: Insights from the Global Investment Regime' 636–637.

and NAFTA' and notes that the references to WTO law are merely of 'suggestive' value, *ad hoc* and controversial.[76] Other authors, and I concur with their reading of the case law, have specifically criticised this reading, describing that it is an 'unfair' analysis.[77] In my opinion, the explicit referral to WTO case law is to be understood as giving *de facto* precedential value to the interpretations of WTO panels and the AB.

Outside of NAFTA, a recent dispute between Costa Rica and El Salvador was settled through the dispute settlement mechanism of the United States-Dominican Republic-Central America Free Trade Agreement (CAFTA).[78] The dispute settlement organ, called 'Grupo Arbitral' made explicit reference to WTO law in several instances. Regarding the request for establishment of a Grupo Arbitral, it takes into account the relevant law of the WTO, with explicit reference to a recent AB Report.[79] Costa Rica advanced an argument on the basis of AB case law as well, although it was not considered by the Grupo Arbitral.[80] In a preliminary procedural ruling in, at the time of writing, the only other CAFTA case, addressing Guatemala's obligation to enforce its domestic labour laws, the Arbitral Panel noted that it was 'mindful of the practice of panels in WTO dispute settlement', also because both parties referred to WTO case law – and went on to consider WTO case law.[81] These instances constitute further evidence that RTA parties may also be inclined to apply interpretations of WTO law to RTAs.

Second, when interpreting provisions in bilateral investment treaties (BITs) which are similar to WTO disciplines, panels in investment dispute settlement have also drawn upon WTO case law.[82] For example, the NAFTA Chapter 11 Arbitral Panel in *S.D. Myers Inc. v Canada* held

---

[76] Busch, 'Overlapping Institutions, Forum Shopping, and Dispute Settlement in International Trade' 742.

[77] Johnston and Trebilcock, 'Fragmentation in International Trade Law: Insights from the Global Investment Regime' 636.

[78] CAFTA/ARB/2014/CR-ES, Tratamiento Arancelario a Bienes Originarios de Costa Rica (Informe Final del Grupo Arbitral), 18 November 2014.

[79] Ibid para. 4.41 at footnote 37.

[80] Ibid at footnote 60.

[81] CAFTA/ARB/2014/CR-ES, Guatemala – Issues Relating to the Obligations Under Article 1621(a), Ruling on the Procedure for Addressing Guatemala's Request for a Preliminary Ruling, 20 November 2014 para. 54; Guatemala, *Guatemala – Issues relating to the obligations under Article 16.2.1(a) of CAFTA-DR – Initial written submission of Guatemala (2 February)* (2015) paras 63–64 and 66.

[82] Hsu, 'Applicability of WTO Law in Regional Trade Agreements: Identifying the Links' 549.

that a State must choose the least trade restrictive alternative reasonably available, which respects the State's chosen level of protection. The Panel stated that this approach is 'consistent with the language and the case law arising out of the WTO family of agreements',[83] as found in the necessity analysis of Article XIV GATS. Subsequently, it referred to GATT 1994 case law on 'likeness' in interpreting the term 'like circumstances'.[84] The Arbitral Panel also relied on WTO case law in affirming that NAFTA obligations are to be considered cumulative and complementary.[85] In *Pope & Talbot Inc. v Canada*, the Arbitral Panel referred to the AB's text-based interpretational approach.[86] Outside of NAFTA investment arbitration, a similar reference to interpretative practice in WTO case law can be found in the *ADF Group Inc. v United States of America* arbitral award.[87] The Arbitral Panel in *Continental Casualty Company v Argentine Republic* relied on WTO case law regarding the necessity test found in Article XX GATT 1994.[88]

These examples illustrate the NAFTA Chapter 11 Arbitral Panel's statement in *Methanex Corporation v United States of America* that:

> the Tribunal may derive guidance from the way in which a similar phrase in the GATT has been interpreted in the past. Whilst such interpretations cannot be treated by this Tribunal as binding precedents, the Tribunal may remain open to persuasion based on legal reasoning developed in GATT and WTO jurisprudence, if relevant.[89]

Similarly, in *AES Corporation v The Argentine Republic*, without reference to WTO law, the NAFTA Chapter 11 Arbitral Panel noted that while there is no formal rule of precedent, and 'a different solution for resolving the same problem' may be adopted by each tribunal, once an arbitral tribunal has set a point of law, such 'precedents may also be rightly considered, at least as a matter of comparison and, if so

[83] *S.D. Myers Inc. v Canada* NAFTA Chapter 11 Arbitration Partial Award, 13 November 2000 para. 221.

[84] Ibid paras 244–246.

[85] Ibid paras 291–294.

[86] *Pope & Talbot Inc. v Canada* NAFTA Chapter 11 Arbitration Award on the Merits of Phase 2, 10 April 2001 footnote 68.

[87] *ADF Group Inc v United States of America* ICSID Case No ARB(AF)/00/1, Award, 9 January 2003 footnote 152.

[88] *Continental Casualty Company v Argentine Republic* ICSID Case No ARB/03/09, Award, 5 September 2008 paras 192–195.

[89] *Methanex Corporation v United States of America* NAFTA Chapter 11 Final Award of the Tribunal on Jurisdiction and Merits, 3 August 2005 para. 6.

considered by the Tribunal, of inspiration'.[90] Finally, the Arbitral Panel in *Pope & Talbot Inc. v Canada* expressed the similar view that there are 'very strong reasons for interpreting the language of Article 1105 [NAFTA] consistently with the language in BITs', referring particularly to the aim, context, object and purpose of NAFTA.[91] This cross-treaty interpretational practice is not a legal requirement, but it appears to be practice in the interpretation of BITs, and could be expected in RTA case law, if such case law were to emerge.[92] Hence, the presumption of WTO consistent interpretation thus appears to be a practical reality.

2.1.2.5 Rebutting the presumption As noted, the 'presumption' of interpreting EU RTA provisions consistently with WTO case law is rebuttable. Of course, the RTA interpreter is not stringently bound by WTO interpretations. The RTA is a separate treaty; its interpretation should not blindly or slavishly follow WTO case law.[93] Following the application of relevant rules of interpretation, if the outcome is that RTA provisions should be interpreted contrary to WTO case law, the interpreter should follow this course. Immediately, two situations come to mind. First, the context, object and purpose of the agreements may differ, which may lead to a difference in interpretation – as is the case for the national treatment obligations of Article 2.1 TBT Agreement and III:4 GATT 1994.[94] Second, there may be an indication that the use of a different term indicates a different interpretation from a WTO term. However, if there is no such indication, or it is insufficient, preference should be given to an interpretation which conforms to WTO (case) law. This analysis needs to be made on a case-by-case basis, taking into account all relevant factors. Such an analysis could be based on Article 31.4 VCLT type exceptions to the general principle of interpretation in accordance with the ordinary meaning of the text of a treaty.[95] This provision states that a special (as opposed to ordinary) meaning shall be

---

90 *AES Corporation v The Argentine Republic* ICSID Case No ARB/02/17, Decision on Jurisdiction, 26 April 2005 paras 30–31.

91 *Pope & Talbot Inc. v Canada* paras 115–116.

92 Johnston and Trebilcock, 'Fragmentation in International Trade Law: Insights from the Global Investment Regime' 629.

93 Hsu, 'Applicability of WTO Law in Regional Trade Agreements: Identifying the Links' 541.

94 See e.g. *US – Clove Cigarettes (AB)* para. 181.

95 Oliver Dörr, 'Article 31' in Oliver Dörr and Kirsten Schmalenbach (eds), *Vienna Convention on the Law of Treaties* (Springer 2012) 568.

given to a term if such a meaning can be established as the parties' intention. Here, a 'special meaning' would be a meaning contrary to WTO law.

If the presumption is rebutted, the question arises as to whether there should be coherence between the non-WTO consistent interpretation given to provisions in different RTAs. It is submitted that this is not the case if the treaty interpretation mechanisms do not support such a finding. For example, as addressed below, one of the objectives of the EU-Georgia DCFTA is the integration of the Georgian economy into the EU internal market. By contrast, the EU-Colombia & Peru RTA appears to be concerned with achieving a GATS-type balance between trade liberalisation and other concerns. Thus, it would seem defensible that treaty provisions in these agreements should be interpreted differently.

2.2 The Objectives of the Selected EU RTAs

Considering the broader political scope of the RTAs, it is no surprise that the objectives of the EU-Colombia & Peru (EU-C&P) and the EU-Georgia DCFTA are much wider than those of GATS. The objectives of the EU-Singapore agreement are however limited to trade. The following overview is limited to trade-related objectives.

The objectives of the EU-C&P and EU-Singapore RTAs, listed in their preambles, are the promotion of comprehensive economic development with the objective of reducing poverty and creating new employment opportunities and improved working conditions, as well as raising living standards in the parties' territories by liberalising and expanding trade and investment between their territories. The parties desire to establish clear rules governing their trade and to provide a predictable legal framework for their trade and investment relations. Moreover, the EU, Colombia and Peru, and Singapore stress that they build on their respective rights and obligations under the WTO Agreement. The EU-Singapore RTA lists trade and investment liberalisation and facilitation as its sole objective under Article 1.2, 'Objectives'. This differs from the more detailed EU-Colombia & Peru RTA list of objectives, which lists 11 oriented objectives, all of an economic nature, in Article 4. Concerning services specifically, Article 4 (c) EU-C&P notes that the progressive liberalisation of trade in services, in conformity with Article V GATS, is an objective of the agreement. Articles 107.1 EU-C&P and 8.1 (1) EU-Singapore RTA, again, reaffirm WTO commitments and note that the objective of the chapter on trade in services is the progressive liberalisation of such trade. The objectives of the EU-Georgia DCFTA, listed in Article 1, in so far as they are relevant here, note that Georgia's economic potential should be developed through approximation with EU law. Georgia's sustained and comprehensive regulatory approximation, in compliance with the rights and obligations arising from WTO membership, will gradually integrate the Georgian economy into the EU internal market. As concerns services, and according to Article 76.1, the objective of the agreement is again the progressive reciprocal liberalisation of trade in services. Article 220 EU-Georgia, part of the chapter on transparency, recognises the impact that the regulatory environment may have on trade and investment and therefore obliges the parties to provide a predictable regulatory environment for economic operators.

As under GATS, regulatory autonomy is confirmed in the preamble of the EU-Colombia & Peru RTA by an affirmation of the 'rights to use, to the greatest extent, the flexibilities provided for in the multilateral framework for the protection of public interest'. Note the reference to the multilateral framework, not the RTA. Article 107.5 of the RTA adds that each party retains the right to exercise its powers and to regulate and introduce new regulations in order to meet legitimate public policy objectives. In the EU-Singapore RTA and EU-Georgia DCFTA, it is merely noted in Articles 8.1 (3) and 76.4 respectively that each party 'retains the right to regulate and to introduce new regulations to meet legitimate policy objectives in a manner consistent' with the provisions in the chapter.

Three aspects of these objectives stand out. First, all three RTAs (although it is less prominent in the EU-Georgia DCFTA) mention the desire to create a predictable legal framework. When interpreting an RTA in accordance with this objective, preference may be given to the presumption of WTO consistent interpretation. Moreover, the constraints on regulatory autonomy resulting from these RTAs should be in accordance with the principle of predictability. Second, the EU-Colombia & Peru and EU-Singapore RTAs confirm that these agreements build on the parties' rights and obligations under the WTO. This statement could also be seen as supportive of a WTO consistent interpretation of the agreement, as differing interpretations of key provisions could have the effect of modifying or eroding WTO rights and obligations. Third, in comparison to the objectives of GATS, the balance between trade liberalisation and regulatory autonomy differs between the agreements. The EU-Colombia & Peru RTA can be said to echo the GATS balance. In the case of the EU-Singapore RTA, strengthened by this agreement's sole listed objective of trade liberalisation and facilitation, the balance appears to tip towards trade liberalisation. In cases where the presumption of WTO consistent interpretation would be rebutted, this difference should be taken into account. Similarly, the EU-Georgia DCFTA features less explicit reference to regulatory autonomy, which can be explained by the agreement's focus on integration of the Georgian economy into the EU internal market, rather than 'simply' facilitating and liberalising trade. The need for regulatory autonomy would necessarily be diminished by this objective of approximation: as Georgia is supposed to comply with EU rules, EU regulators are unlikely to face substantial regulatory autonomy constraints. The differences in these objectives, and the existence of broader objectives in two RTAs, are only to play a limited role. In most cases, they do not appear to be a sufficient reason to alter an interpretation based on the presumption of WTO consistent interpretation.

2. Structure of GATS and the selected EU RTAs

1. THE STRUCTURAL FLEXIBILITY OF GATS AND THE EU'S USE THEREOF

To understand GATS, and specifically its impact on regulatory autonomy, one must understand its flexible structure. The flexibility is likely due to the novelty of regulating trade in services at the time of GATS' conclusion and to the difficulties with predicting its implications. The flexibility allowed the drafters to construct a potentially very powerful agreement, which also contained room for moulding obligations which were acceptable to all parties. In other words, GATS has the inherent potential to be encompassing and stringent, but it does not need to be so in practice. The structural flexibility of GATS is evident in two ways: first, in the structure of its obligations, and second, in the approach to scheduling specific commitments. This section further addresses how the EU made use of the flexibilities of GATS.

1.1 Flexibility in the Structure of Obligations

GATS contains non-discrimination obligations, market access *sensu lato* obligations, obligations based on recognition-based regimes and transparency obligations. Concerning their applicability, the obligations can be divided into the following categories:[1]

a. Unconditional general obligations apply to any measure affecting trade in any service covered by GATS. The most important of these obligations is the Most-Favoured-Nation (MFN) obligation. In line with the flexible nature of GATS, the MFN obligation is limited by

[1] For a very clear schematic overview of the structure of GATS obligations, see Rudolf Adlung, 'Public Services and the GATS' (2006) 9 Journal of International Economic Law 455, 459.

a list of individual exemptions, drawn up by each Member at the conclusion of GATS.

b. Conditional obligations apply only to measures affecting trade in services in sectors for which specific commitments have been scheduled by the Member. This category consists of two subcategories:
   1. The specific commitments of Part III of GATS only apply to measures affecting trade in services in sectors for which commitments have been undertaken in the schedules of commitments, and in so far as no limitations to the specific commitments have been scheduled.[2]
   2. The conditional general obligations of Part II of GATS only apply to measures affecting trade in services in sectors in which specific commitments have been scheduled, but these cannot be limited by scheduling limitations.[3] Consequently, these obligations apply in full to a sector if it is scheduled.

1.2 Flexibility in Scheduling Specific Commitments

1.2.1 Scheduling specific commitments

To determine which services sectors the conditional obligations apply to, one must look at the Member's Schedule of specific commitments. The flexibility of the Schedules is crucial to the balance between regulatory autonomy and trade liberalisation, and allows both to be reconciled if the commitments are scheduled 'wisely and cautiously'.[4] The Scheduling Guidelines provide Members with information and guidance in drafting their Schedules.[5] GATS uses a positive listing approach: the specific commitments and conditional general obligations only apply to sectors

---

[2] *Mexico – Measures Affecting Telecommunications Services* WT/DS204/R, Panel report adopted 2 April 2004 paras 7.359–7.362.

[3] Benedict F Christ and Marion Panizzon, 'Article XI GATS' in Rüdiger Wolfrum, Peter-Tobias Stoll and Clemens Feinäugle (eds), *Max Planck Commentaries on World Trade Law: WTO – Trade in Services*, vol 6 (Martinus Nijhoff 2008) 252–253.

[4] Markus Krajewski and Maika Engelke, 'Article XVII GATS' in Rüdiger Wolfrum, Peter-Tobias Stoll and Clemens Feinäugle (eds), *Max Planck Commentaries on World Trade Law: WTO – Trade in Services*, vol 6 (Martinus Nijhoff 2008) 400.

[5] General Agreement on Tariffs and Trade, *MTN.GNS/W/164, Scheduling of Initial Commitments in Trade in Services: Explanatory Note (3 September)* (1993); S/L/92, Guidelines for the Scheduling of Specific Commitments under the General Agreement on Trade in Services (GATS) (Adopted by the Council for Trade in Services 23 March).

which have been listed.[6] Aside from horizontal, i.e. cross-sectoral commitments, the Schedules are comprised of four columns, in which (i) the relevant services sector, (ii) the market access, (iii) national treatment and (iv) additional commitments and limitations thereto are listed per mode of supply. In over 90 per cent of commitments, limitations have been scheduled.[7] The limitations should be seen as minimum guarantees, as a Member may grant more market access or national treatment.[8] Services are usually divided in sectors on the basis of the Services Sectoral Classification List, or W/120,[9] which is related to the Central Product Classification (CPC) of the United Nations (UN). However, the use of these instruments is not mandatory.[10] Moreover, a Member may further specify services sectors listed in these instruments until the required degree of specificity is achieved.[11]

Considering the complexity of the Schedules, it is clear that there is substantial flexibility for a Member to modulate its specific commitments and therefore limit the applicability of GATS obligations.[12] The positive listing approach, in combination with the possibility of diverging from the W/120 and CPC classification where required allows Members to carve out services of specific importance from their Schedules, as does the possibility of scheduling commitments per mode of supply and per

[6] General Agreement on Tariffs and Trade, *MTN.GNS/W/164, Scheduling of Initial Commitments in Trade in Services: Explanatory Note (3 September)* para. 17.

[7] Laura Altinger and Alice Enders, 'The Scope and Depth of GATS Commitments' (1996) 19 The World Economy 307, 316–322, contains overview tables of these limitations, both at sectoral and horizontal levels.

[8] Aaditya Mattoo, 'National Treatment in the GATS: Corner-Stone or Pandora's Box?' (1997) 31 Journal of World Trade 107, 110.

[9] General Agreement on Tariffs and Trade, *MTN.GNS/W/120, Services Sectoral Classification List.*

[10] General Agreement on Tariffs and Trade, *MTN.GNS/W/164, Scheduling of Initial Commitments in Trade in Services: Explanatory Note (3 September)* para. 16.

[11] Martín Molinuevo, 'Article XX GATS' in Rüdiger Wolfrum, Peter-Tobias Stoll and Clemens Feinäugle (eds), *Max Planck Commentaries on World Trade Law: WTO – Trade in Services*, vol 6 (Martinus Nijhoff 2008) 451.

[12] See *China – Measures Affecting Trading Rights and Distribution Services for Certain Publications and Audiovisual Products* WT/DS363/AB/R, AB report adopted 19 January 2010 para. 376.

commitment. In practice, the possibility of including additional commitments in a Member's Schedule has led to a wide variety of commitments.[13] Lastly, cross-sectoral services can be extracted from conditional obligations through limitations based on horizontal commitments.

1.2.2 The interpretation of Schedules

Considering the importance of the Schedules for the scope of a Member's obligations under GATS,[14] their interpretation is of the utmost relevance to regulatory autonomy. The case law on the interpretation of Schedules has clarified four issues. First, as noted in Article XX:3 GATS, the Schedules are an integral part of the agreement. Their interpretation thus 'raises the same interpretative questions as any other kind of treaty language'.[15] They must be interpreted like any other treaty provision, by identifying the *common* intention of the Members – not just the Member whose Schedule is being interpreted – according to the interpretational rules of Articles 31 and 32 VCLT.[16] (It should be reiterated that 'interpretation pursuant to the customary rule codified in Article 31 of the *Vienna Convention* is ultimately a holistic exercise that should not be mechanically subdivided into rigid components'.[17]) This means that terms used in a Schedule that have a specific meaning in the domestic context of the scheduling Member may well not have this meaning in the interpretation of the actual Schedule: it will be interpreted 'as if it was in fact the result of a multilateral negotiating exercise'.[18] Nonetheless, the unilateral origin of the Schedule cannot be ignored, as Members had 'a

---

[13] Markus Krajewski, 'Article XVIII GATS' in Rüdiger Wolfrum, Peter-Tobias Stoll and Clemens Feinäugle (eds), *Max Planck Commentaries on World Trade Law: WTO – Trade in Services*, vol 6 (Martinus Nijhoff 2008) 424. The most important use of the additional commitments is the Reference Paper on Basic Telecommunications.

[14] For example, the Panel in *China – Measures Affecting Electronic Payment Services* WT/DS413/R, Panel report adopted 31 August 2012, spends over thirty pages considering the interpretation of a subsector in China's Schedule of specific commitments.

[15] Isabelle Van Damme, 'The Interpretation of Schedules of Commitments' (2007) 4 Journal of World Trade 1, 22.

[16] *United States – Measures Affecting the Cross-Border Supply of Gambling and Betting Services* WT/DS285/AB/R, AB report adopted 20 April 2005, para. 160; *China – Publications and Audiovisual Products (AB)* para. 405.

[17] *China – Publications and Audiovisual Products (AB)* para. 348.

[18] Markus Krajewski, 'Playing by the Rules of the Game? Specific Commitments after *US – Gambling and Betting* and the Current GATS Negotiations' (2005) 32 Legal Issues of Economic Integration 417, 423.

broader scope of manoeuvring' in determining their commitments.[19] This exemplifies the tension between the Schedules as, on the one hand, an integral part of the WTO agreements (and therefore, they constitute treaty language), and on the other hand, the way in which they are drafted and negotiated.[20]

Second, a service cannot be scheduled in more than one sector and consequentially, the sectors and subsectors in a Schedule are mutually exclusive – deciding otherwise would make the scope of commitments unclear.[21] For a so-called integrated service, i.e. a service made up of several distinct component services, this means that:

> the classification under a single subsector of a service made up of a combination of different services is not incompatible with the principle of mutual exclusivity if these services, when combined together, result in a distinct service that is supplied and consumed as such. [...] In our view, what is relevant [is] whether the component services, when combined together, result in a new and distinct service, the integrated service.[22]

Therefore, there is only an integrated service, with subsequent separate scheduling, if these conditions are fulfilled. If this is not the case, the separate services need to be scheduled individually. Moreover, any service that falls within the scope of the definition of the sector referred to in the Schedule, is included in that sector – it need not be specifically named.[23]

Third, the use of WTO documents supporting the scheduling process has been contested. The AB has explained that the W/120 and the 1993 Scheduling Guidelines are not 'context' in the sense of Articles 31.1 and 31.2 (a) or (b) VCLT.[24] The following elements can be considered relevant context:

---

[19] Federico Ortino, 'Treaty Interpretation and the WTO Appellate Body Report in *US – Gambling*: A Critique' (2006) 9 Journal of International Economic Law 117, 130.

[20] Van Damme, 'The Interpretation of Schedules of Commitments' 24.

[21] *US – Gambling (AB)* paras 180 and 185. The CPC, on which the W/120 is based, which is in turn followed by many Members, is also mutually exclusive.

[22] *China – Electronic Payment Services (Panel)* para. 7.188.

[23] *China – Publications and Audiovisual Products (Panel)* para. 7.1014; *China – Electronic Payment Services (Panel)* paras 7.178–7.179.

[24] *US – Gambling (AB)* para. 178; General Agreement on Tariffs and Trade, *MTN.GNS/W/164, Scheduling of Initial Commitments in Trade in Services: Explanatory Note (3 September).*

a. The remainder of the Member's Schedule of specific commitments. This was further developed in the case law to include, for the determination of the scope of a listing in a Member's Schedule:
   1. The relevant sectoral heading.
   2. The market access, national treatment and additional commitments under the relevant (sub)sector.
   3. Subsectors adjacent to the relevant services.
   4. Commitments scheduled under another related sector.[25]

   The scope of a relevant sector defines the scope of the commitment, and it is hence unsurprising that the determination of the scope of a sector in a Schedule has been a key subject in dispute settlement.[26]
b. The substantive provisions of the GATS.
c. The provisions of other covered agreements.
d. The GATS Schedules of other Members.[27] As concerns this element, it must be stressed that each Schedule has its own intrinsic logic, which tempers the relevance of other Schedules as context:[28] they may be 'of limited utility in elucidating the meaning of the entry to be interpreted'.[29] Nonetheless, the structure of the Schedule is relevant.[30]

The 2001 Scheduling Guidelines are not evidence of Members' interpretation of commitments which were existing at the time of the adoption of the 2001 Scheduling Guidelines, as they were aimed at assisting future

---

[25] *China – Publications and Audiovisual Products (AB)* paras 361–372, summarised and subsequently applied in *China – Electronic Payment Services (Panel)* para. 7.103 for elements (a)(1)–(4).

[26] In *US – Gambling*, the US attempted to demonstrate that the relevant gambling and betting services were included in one particular subsector over another. The Panel and the AB did not agree. In *China – Publications and Audiovisual Products*, China claimed that the non-physical distribution of sound recordings was not covered by the relevant subsector. The Panel and AB found that these services were included in the relevant subsector. In *China – Electronic Payment Services*, China argued that the relevant electronic payment services did not fall within the scope of a given subsector. Again, the Panel did not agree. The emphasis put on this by the responding Members demonstrates the importance of interpreting Schedules.

[27] *US – Gambling (AB)* para. 178 for elements (a)–(d).

[28] Ibid para. 182.

[29] *China – Publications and Audiovisual Products (AB)* para. 383.

[30] As explicitly stated in *China – Electronic Payment Services (Panel)* para. 7.103, referring to the AB's approach in *US – Gambling*.

commitments.[31] In that sense, they are not 'subsequent practice' in the sense of Article 31.3 (b) VCLT.

In the case of GATS, the AB ruled that the 1993 Scheduling Guidelines and the 1991 Services Sectoral Classification List W/120, both provided by the WTO Secretariat, are supplementary means of interpretation as covered by Article 32 VCLT.[32] These Guidelines demonstrate a clear preference for using the W/120 as a basis for Members' Schedules, and indicate that, in case the W/120 is not followed, the alternative classification should be sufficiently detailed as to avoid any ambiguity regarding the scope of the commitment.[33] In other words, 'unless otherwise indicated in the Schedule, Members were assumed to have relied on W/120 and the corresponding CPC references'.[34]

Fourth, the object and purpose of GATS are relevant to the interpretation of the Schedules in accordance with Article 31.1 VCLT. Two key objectives have been raised in this context: transparency and progressive liberalisation.[35] The AB noted that 'the security and predictability of Members' specific commitments [...] is equally an object and purpose of the GATS'.[36] The Schedules must obtain 'the requisite clarity as to the scope of the commitment'.[37] This also goes for an interpretation given to a Schedule by a panel.[38] As concerns progressive liberalisation, the AB stated that this principle does not support an interpretation of the Schedules that 'constrains the scope and coverage of specific commitments that have already been undertaken by Members and by which they are bound'.[39] It has been remarked that this interpretation, taken to its extreme, implies a clear preference for trade liberalisation over regulatory autonomy.[40] However, the interpretative importance of the object and

---

31 *US – Gambling (AB)* para. 193.

32 Ibid paras 196–197 and 206–207. A cover note added by a Member to its Schedule, as the EU has done, or to draft versions of its Schedule is also a supplementary means of interpretation.

33 General Agreement on Tariffs and Trade, *MTN.GNS/W/164, Scheduling of Initial Commitments in Trade in Services: Explanatory Note (3 September)* para. 16.

34 *US – Gambling (Panel)* para. 6.106, confirmed in *US – Gambling (AB)* para. 204.

35 *China – Electronic Payment Services (Panel)* para. 7.196.

36 *US – Gambling (Panel)* para. 6.108, confirmed in *US – Gambling (AB)* para. 189.

37 *US – Gambling (AB)* para. 204.

38 *China – Electronic Payment Services (Panel)* para. 7.198.

39 *China – Publications and Audiovisual Products (AB)* para. 394.

40 Nellie Munin, *Legal Guide to GATS* (Wolters Kluwer 2010) 41.

purpose of GATS should not be overestimated: although an interpretation given by a panel should not contradict the object and purpose of GATS, its objectives do not necessarily provide specific guidance.[41]

Overall, the panels and AB require a more explicit, albeit potentially circumstantial, deviation from what can be expected by other Members in a Schedule for it to reach the conclusion that a service sector would (not) be covered by a commitment.[42] Although acceptable from the perspective of settlement of disputes, this may lead to unexpected consequences taking into account the complexity of services classification:[43] Members may find that they are committed to more than they expected.[44] Indeed, it may be argued that the U.S. was faced with such a situation in *US – Gambling*, and as one author notes: '[i]f even the US can make a scheduling mistake, how much more likely are such mistakes or unintended commitments for countries with much less expertise and negotiating capacity?'[45] This is especially so for (unexpected) changes in the 'real world'. If the terms used in a commitment in a Member's Schedule are sufficiently generic, according to the AB, 'what they apply to may change over time'.[46] Deciding otherwise would, in many cases, render GATS commitments meaningless through time. Nonetheless, this forward-looking interpretation may have serious implications in the digital era, where the supply of services has been facilitated tremendously.[47] The result of the AB's interpretation is that GATS is 'technologically neutral' as concerns the Schedules, as commitments apply regardless of the technological manner in which services are supplied.[48]

More generally, it has been noted that, in the context of the interpretation of schedules (including of specific commitments,) the AB 'has

---

[41] *China – Publications and Audiovisual Products (AB)* para. 393.

[42] See e.g. ibid, disagreeing with the Panel (at paras 7.1237 and 7.1247).

[43] See Rolf H Weber and Mira Burri-Nenova, *Classification of Services in the Digital Economy* (Springer 2013).

[44] See *US – Gambling (Panel)* para. 7.3.

[45] Krajewski, 'Playing by the Rules of the Game? Specific Commitments after *US – Gambling and Betting* and the Current GATS Negotiations' 446.

[46] *China – Publications and Audiovisual Products (AB)* paras 396–397.

[47] Sacha Wunsch-Vincent, 'The Internet, Cross-Border Trade in Services, and the GATS: Lessons from *US – Gambling*' (2006) 5 World Trade Review 319, 328; Aaditya Mattoo and Sacha Wunsch-Vincent, 'Pre-empting Protectionism in Services: The GATS and Outsourcing' (2004) 7 Journal of International Economic Law 765, 774–780.

[48] *US – Gambling (Panel)* para. 6.285; Wunsch-Vincent, 'The Internet, Cross-Border Trade in Services, and the GATS: Lessons from *US – Gambling*' 329–334.

adopted a contextual, effective, and systemic interpretation of the WTO covered agreements, not necessarily also of the VCLT'.[49] In that systemic interpretation, the AB appears to be giving more deference to the common intention than to the treaty language of a specific Schedule. This means less deference is given to regulatory autonomy as the text of a Member's Schedule, or the intention behind it, is to be considered in light of the common intention of all WTO Members.[50] This reflects the ambiguous nature of a Schedule: it is neither a unilateral document, nor a truly multilateral one. Considering the importance of Schedule interpretation to the bargaining process when (re)negotiating Schedules (also at a preferential level), this approach must be approved.

1.2.3 Withdrawal and modification of Schedules

As explained, the Schedules of specific commitments are of crucial importance to understanding the implications of GATS on a Member's regulatory autonomy. The Schedules contain the commitments vis-à-vis the most important GATS obligations: the market access and national treatment obligations. However, as noted, the interpretation of Schedules in the context of a dispute, or technological changes, or a change in policy preferences may lead to a situation where some commitments are unexpected or unwanted.[51] Article XXI GATS therefore foresees the possibility of modification or withdrawal of Schedules of specific commitments. The modifying Member must negotiate compensatory adjustments, made on an MFN basis, at the request of any Member that considers itself to be affected by the modification or withdrawal.[52] The compensation consists of more far-reaching specific commitments in

---

[49] Van Damme, 'The Interpretation of Schedules of Commitments' 32.

[50] Ortino, 'Treaty Interpretation and the WTO Appellate Body Report in *US – Gambling*: A Critique' 131 approves of this approach, Van Damme, 'The Interpretation of Schedules of Commitments' 33 does not.

[51] After *US – Gambling*, the US has invoked procedures under Article XXI GATS to modify its Schedule and exclude gambling services from its specific commitments. See Henning Grosse Ruse-Khan, '"Gambling" with Sovereignty: Complying with International Obligations or Upholding National Autonomy' in Meredith Kolsky Lewis and Susy Frankel (eds), *International Economic Law and National Autonomy* (Cambridge University Press 2010) 155–159, noting that the price to pay for regulatory autonomy is that of compensatory adjustments.

[52] S/L/80, Procedures for the Implementation of Article XXI of the General Agreement on Trade (Modification of Schedules) (Adopted by the Council for Trade in Services 29 October 1999) para. 3.

another sector.[53] If the procedure in Article XXI GATS is followed, the modified Schedule becomes, as all Schedules, an integral part of GATS and no recourse to dispute settlement is possible. As explained below, the EU has modified its Schedule following the several enlargement rounds of the EU. If no agreement is found, the matter may be referred to binding arbitration.

1.3 The EU's Extensive Use of the Structural Flexibility

The EU made extensive use of GATS' inherent flexibility. The EU listed 28 MFN exemptions in 1994,[54] the highest number of all Members and the EU's 1994 Schedule, the longest of all Members, contained 96 pages.[55] The EU's consolidated 2006 Schedule contained 234 pages.[56] Of course, the complexity of the EU as an actor with now 28 Member States and their diverging interests also partly explains this extensive use of GATS' flexibilities. Nonetheless, the EU's experience with and knowledge of WTO law undoubtedly influenced the attention given to a precise and extensive use of these options.

1.3.1 The EU List of MFN exemptions

The EU List of MFN exemptions contains 19 sector-specific exemptions, of which eight are related to audio-visual services and three to publishing.[57] The other sectors for which an exemption was listed are road transport and internal waterways transport (two listings each); computerised reservation systems and air transport sales and marketing services; rental and leasing of ships; and direct non-life insurance and financial services. Not all exemptions apply to all EU Member States, as some

---

[53] Olga Nartova, 'Article XXI GATS' in Rüdiger Wolfrum, Peter-Tobias Stoll and Clemens Feinäugle (eds), *Max Planck Commentaries on World Trade Law: WTO – Trade in Services*, vol 6 (Martinus Nijhoff 2008) 469. Also see S/L/80, Procedures for the Implementation of Article XXI of the General Agreement on Trade (Modification of Schedules) (Adopted by the Council for Trade in Services 29 October 1999).

[54] GATS/EL/31, European Communities and Their Member States: Final List of Article II (MFN) Exemptions (15 April 1994).

[55] GATS/SC/31, European Communities and their Member States: Schedule of Specific Commitments (15 April 1994).

[56] S/C/W/273, Communication from the European Communities and its Member States: Certification: Draft Consolidated GATS Schedule (9 October 2006).

[57] GATS/EL/31, European Communities and Their Member States: Final List of Article II (MFN) Exemptions (15 April 1994).

Member States, such as France and Italy, have negotiated specific exemptions. For example, it appears that France's persistence in protecting cultural diversity required EU negotiators to list a specific exemption. Likewise, not all exemptions address all third countries. In some cases, the beneficiary third countries for which the exemption applies are listed. For instance, an indefinite MFN exemption is listed for the production and distribution of cinematographic works and television programmes in Nordic countries. This exempts Denmark from an obligation to extend the treatment accorded to Finland, Norway, Sweden and Iceland – hence both EU and non-EU Member States – regarding benefits provided in conformity with support programmes that enhance the production and distribution of audio-visual works produced in Nordic countries to third countries. Furthermore, the EU list of MFN exemptions contains nine horizontal exemptions. Three of these exemptions apply to all EU Member States. They address (i) the progressive liberalisation between the EU and Switzerland, San Marino, Monaco, Andorra, and Vatican City State; and (ii) work permits for seasonal workers from states in Central Eastern and South-Eastern Europe and in the Mediterranean Basin.

1.3.2 EU enlargement rounds and the applicable Schedule of specific commitments

The legal situation of the EU Schedule of specific commitments is complex.[58] In 1994, a Schedule was submitted to the WTO Secretariat on behalf of the Member States of the former European Communities, the EC-12 (i.e. Belgium, Denmark, France, Germany, Greece, Ireland, Italy, Luxemburg, The Netherlands, Portugal, Spain and the United Kingdom).[59] Interestingly, the supplements to the 1994 Schedule include commitments for Austria, Finland and Sweden, replacing their national Schedules for those sectors covered in the supplements.[60] In 2006, and thus after the 2004 enlargement, a draft consolidated Schedule was

[58] The remarks that follow apply equally to Lists of MFN exemptions. Considering the relative complexity of Schedules, the comments focus on the latter and not on the Lists.

[59] EU 1994 Schedule. Also see WT/REG39/1, Establishment of the European Union, Services (Communication from the European Communities and their Member States) (24 April 1998).

[60] GATS/SC/31/Suppl.1/Rev.1, European Communities and their Member States: Schedule of Specific Commitments: Supplement 1 Revision (4 October 1995); GATS/SC/31/Suppl.2, European Communities and their Member States: Schedule of Specific Commitments: Supplement 2 (28 July 1995); GATS/SC/31/Suppl.3, European Communities and their Member States: Schedule of Specific

submitted to the WTO Secretariat.[61] Although certified by the WTO Secretariat in accordance with the relevant procedures and originally foreseen to replace existing schedules from 1 September 2005,[62] this consolidated Schedule is still not ratified by five EU Member States.[63] Therefore, it has not yet entered into force. The 2006 consolidated Schedule is said to merely merge the 1994 Schedule with those of the 13 new Member States and insert 'therein the modifications or withdrawals of commitments notified by the EC and the compensatory adjustments agreed', in accordance with Article XXI GATS.[64] The enlargement of the EU with Bulgaria, Romania and later Croatia means the consolidated Schedule is no longer up to date. For the 2007 enlargement round in which Bulgaria and Romania acceded to the EU, the procedure on the modification of Schedules has been conducted and the European Commission has requested the Council to authorise the signature of these agreements.[65] The 2013 accession of Croatia has not yet led to a modification of its Schedule.[66]

Hence, it would seem that the legally binding Schedule is still the original 1994 Schedule and the Supplements in conjunction with the national Schedules of all Member States which joined the EU since, and

---

Commitments: Supplement 3 (11 April 1997); GATS/SC/31/Suppl.4/Rev.1, European Communities and their Member States: Schedule of Specific Commitments: Supplement 4 Revision (18 November 1999).

[61] EU 2006 consolidated Schedule.

[62] S/L/286, Certification: Schedule of Commitments of the European Communities and its Member States.

[63] European Commission, *COM(2013) 0689 final, Proposal for a Council Decision on the signing, on behalf of the European Union, of the Agreements in the form of an Exchange of Letters between the European Union and the Commonwealth of Australia, the Federative Republic of Brazil, Canada, the Hong Kong Special Administrative Region of the People's Republic of China, the Republic of India and Japan pursuant to Article XXI of the General Agreement on Trade in Services (GATS) 1994, relating to the modifications of the commitments in the schedules of the Republic of Bulgaria and Romania in the course of their accession to the European Union* (2013) para. 1.

[64] EU 2006 consolidated Schedule para. 3. For a systematic overview of these modifications or withdrawals, see WT/REG170/8/Rev.1, Factual Presentation: Enlargement of the European Union to 25 Member States (Services) Report by the Secretariat 61-105.

[65] European Commission, *COM(2013) 0689 final.*

[66] Although its goods schedule of concessions has been withdrawn as of 1 July 2013: WT/REG337/1, Factual Presentation: Enlargement of the European Union to 28 Member States – Accession of Croatia (Goods and Services) Report by the Secretariat para. 2.4.

not the 2006 consolidated Schedule which covers the EU-25 in conjunction with the three most recent EU Member States.[67] The delay in EU Member States' domestic ratification of the consolidated Schedule thus leads to legal uncertainty, as noted for example by the US, Colombian,[68] Australian and Japanese[69] representatives in the WTO's Committee for Regional Trade Agreements. Additionally, the new commitments have not yet entered into force vis-à-vis other Members. Considering the negotiated compensatory adjustments for the EU-25 Member States and the certification of the draft consolidated Schedule, there could be a legitimate expectation that other WTO Members will not bring a case on the basis of the 1994 Schedule against any of the EU-25 Member States. This is less clear for Bulgaria and Romania, although the process for such adjustments vis-à-vis the enlargement to 27 Member States is ongoing. As concerns Croatia, the national Schedule would still apply. (The request for consultations from the Russian Federation against, among other things, the EU's Third Energy Package does not indicate which Schedules are considered relevant.)[70] In any case, the 2006 consolidated Schedule is used for the purposes of this book.

1.3.3 Overview of commitments in the EU Schedule of specific commitments

From the perspective of regulatory autonomy, the commitments and limitations in the EU Schedule are crucial. As noted, a Schedule of specific commitments may contain horizontal limitations that apply across the board to all scheduled services sectors. In the case of the EU Schedule, a crucial horizontal market access limitation in Mode 3 is the 'public utilities' limitation, which states that 'services considered as public utilities at a national or local level may be subject to public

[67] Hence covering the EC-12 and the new Member States that acceded in the 1995 and 2004 enlargement rounds: Austria, Cyprus, Czech Republic, Estonia, Finland, Hungary, Latvia, Lithuania, Malta, Poland, Slovak Republic, Slovenia and Sweden.

[68] WT/REG170/M/4, Consideration of the Enlargement of the European Union to 25 Member States, Goods and Services, Note on the Meeting of the Committee on Regional Trade Agreements (1 May 2009) para. 8.

[69] WT/REG170/9, Enlargement of the European Union to 25 Member States (Services) (24 March 2009) 1–2.

[70] *European Union and its Member States – Certain Measures Relating to the Energy Sector* WT/DS476/1, Request for Consultations by the Russian Federation, 8 May 2014.

monopolies or to exclusive rights granted to private operators'.[71] This limitation is further discussed below.

Several important horizontal limitations to national treatment address subsidies – which are considered measures affecting trade in services under GATS. The Schedule contains a horizontal Mode 3 limitation for national treatment that applies to all Member States. This limitation states that eligibility for subsidies may be limited to juridical persons established within (a part of) the territory of a Member State. The same limitation notes that all Member States are unbound for subsidies related to research and development. Moreover, it is explicitly noted that the subsidisation and supply of a service within the public sector is not in breach of the EU's commitments. As concerns subsidies, Poland and Hungary are fully unbound.[72] Sixteen Member States are unbound for branches established in a Member State by a non-EU company.[73] For national treatment in Mode 4, all Member States have reserved, to the extent that any subsidies are made available to natural persons, the right to limit the availability to nationals of an EU Member State. Austria and Poland are fully unbound.[74] Finally, some Member States have explicitly retained the right to grant subsidies for entertainment services that do not adhere to the national treatment obligation.[75]

Three other horizontal national treatment limitations should be mentioned. First, in principle, national treatment accorded to subsidiaries of foreign companies established in an EU Member State and formed in accordance with their law is not extended to branches or agencies of foreign companies. Less favourable treatment may be granted to subsidiaries if they only have their registered office in EU territory. This is the case unless the subsidiary shows that it has an effective and continuous link with the economy of the Member States. Second, about ten EU Member States have added national treatment limitations concerning real estate purchases by foreigners or non-residents. Third, EU Directives on mutual recognition of diplomas do not apply to nationals of third countries and recognition of diplomas to practice regulated professions remains within the competence of the Member States unless EU law applies.

For both market access and national treatment, Mode 4 is substantially narrowed by an elaborate limitation, indicating that all EU Member

71 EU 2006 consolidated Schedule 306.
72 Ibid 310.
73 Ibid.
74 Ibid 310.
75 Ibid 502.

States are unbound except for measures concerning the entry into and temporary stay within a Member State which apply to listed categories of natural persons providing services. This list consists of intra-corporate transfers, business visitors and contractual service suppliers. In order to fall within these categories, a natural person must fulfil conditions set out in the Schedule. These may vary from one Member State to another. It appears that, generally, highly educated natural persons are targeted by the Mode 4 commitments.

The Schedule goes on with sector-specific commitments. The EU Schedule contains at least some commitments for almost all services sectors listed in the W/120. Of course, these commitments do not necessarily apply to all EU Member States and are narrowed by the listed limitations. Lastly, the Schedule also contains some additional commitments and commitments in Annexes.

2. THE STRUCTURAL FLEXIBILITY OF EU RTAs

The structure of the services chapters of the EU-Colombia & Peru RTA, the EU-Singapore RTA and the EU-Georgia DCFTA differs from that of GATS. As with the analysis of GATS' flexibilities, the following two elements are relevant: the structure of obligations and the scheduling approach.

2.1 Flexibility in the Structure of Obligations

A notable difference between the three selected EU RTAs and GATS is the division of obligations in relation to the mode of supply. Whilst GATS obligations are the same for each mode, the RTAs contain separate obligations for establishment, cross-border supply of services and temporary presence of natural persons for business purposes. These categories correspond roughly to GATS Modes 3, 1 and 2, and 4 respectively.

Additionally, the EU-Colombia & Peru and EU-Singapore RTAs do not contain an unconditional MFN obligation, and consequently no MFN exemptions. The EU-Georgia DCFTA does contain an MFN obligation. Moreover, the subsection on domestic regulation is limited to sectors in which specific commitments have been undertaken. Further, in the EU-Singapore RTA, the provision on domestic regulation applies only to the extent that the specific commitments apply. This appears to incorporate the reservations on specific commitments and consequentially render the domestic regulation provision a specific commitment rather than a conditional general obligation.

2.2 Schedules of Specific Commitments

2.2.1 Flexibility in scheduling specific commitments

As with GATS, in the case of the EU-Colombia & Peru and EU-Singapore RTAs, the market access and national treatment obligations only apply to committed sectors in the Schedule, and in so far as they are not limited by reservations in that Schedule. In contrast to the integrated GATS Schedules, the EU's Schedules of specific commitments in the EU-C&P, EU-Singapore and EU-Georgia agreements are divided in several Annexes.

a. For the EU-C&P RTA, they are: (i) Annex VII Section B for establishment; (ii) Annex VIII Section B for cross-border trade in services; and (iii) Annex IX Appendix 1 Section B and Appendix 2 Section B for temporary presence of natural persons for business purposes.
b. In the case of the EU-Singapore RTA, the commitments are listed under Annex 8 in: (i) Appendix 8-A-1 for cross-border supply of services; (ii) Appendix 8-A-2 for establishment; and (iii) Appendix 8-A-3 for key personnel, graduate trainees and business services sellers.
c. The specific commitments in the EU-Georgia DCFTA are listed in: (i) Annex XIV-A for establishment; (ii) Annex XIV-B for cross-border supply of services; (iii) Annex XIV-C for key personnel, graduate trainees and business sellers; and (iv) Annex XIV-D for contractual services suppliers and independent professionals.

Furthermore, the Schedules in the selected RTAs also differ structurally from GATS. Aside from the column setting out the relevant sector, they contain one[76] rather than three columns (market access, national treatment and additional commitments) as is the case for GATS. This approach may simplify the Schedule, and mitigate some uncertainty related to the application of Article XX:2 GATS.[77] From the perspective of regulatory autonomy, this approach seems to preserve more policy

[76] In the case of the EU-Georgia DCFTA, the Schedules take the form of a list.

[77] See below and James Mathis and Eugenia Laurenza, 'Services and Investment in the EU – South Korea Free-Trade Area: Implications of a New

space, as there would seem to be a presumption that the listed reservation applies to both market access and national treatment obligations in case of uncertainty regarding the nature of the reservation. It would seem more difficult in this case, compared to the Article XX:2 GATS situation, for a complainant to argue that the limitation only applies to market access issues (and not to national treatment).

The situation differs in the case of the EU-Georgia DCFTA. The national treatment and MFN obligations for establishment apply to all services sectors within the scope of the chapter except for those situations covered by reservations in Annex XIV-A. In other words, for the first time in an EU RTA and in contrast to the EU's practice of positive listing, a negative list approach was followed.[78] This is also evident from the annex, as it differs from other Schedules by not being formatted in a column-type document. It merely contains a list of horizontal and sectoral limitations. These limitations do not distinguish between national treatment and MFN *per se*. For regulatory autonomy, the negative listing approach means that any unlisted and new services are subject to the non-discrimination provisions. The degree of liberalisation is therefore higher, although it may also be said that legal certainty is increased. Interestingly, the DCFTA contains no market access obligation for this mode of supply. In the absence of such a market access obligation, for which a violation does not require the demonstration of discrimination, this approach may be more deferent to regulatory autonomy. A government is allowed to regulate as it pleases, in so far as that it does not discriminate between different foreign, or between foreign and domestic, services or services suppliers. For cross-border supply of services such an obligation has been added, but no MFN obligation applies. The national treatment and market access obligations only apply to scheduled sectors, consequently following a positive listing approach, and are limited by the reservations in Annex XIV-B. This annex does follow the traditional EU Schedule form with two columns. The domestic regulation provisions in Articles 93–95 mirror the division between the modes of supply. For cross-border supply of services, the obligation applies only to scheduled sectors and to the extent that these

Approach for GATS V Agreements and for Bilateral Investment Treaties' (2012) 13 The Journal of World Investment & Trade 157, 166 at footnote 33.

78 The negative listing approach has been called the most important innovation in services chapters of RTAs because it 'forces states to take an inventory of their restrictions and make them transparent'. J Anthony VanDuzer, 'A Critical Look at the Prospects for Robust Rules for Services in Preferential Trading Agreements' (2012) 39 Legal Issues of Economic Integration 29, 35.

specific commitments apply in accordance with Annex XIV-B. In the case of establishment and temporary stay of natural persons, the disciplines on domestic regulation shall not apply to sectors to the extent that a reservation is listed in accordance with Annexes XIV-A, C and D.

2.2.2 Withdrawal and modification of Schedules

Article 13.2 *juncto* Articles 12 and 14 EU-C&P state that the Trade Committee, consisting of representatives of the parties, may, by consensus, agree to modify the Schedules, in order to 'advance in the achievement of the objectives' of the RTA. No other modification procedure for the Schedule is available, and no withdrawal of a Schedule is possible. Considering the abovementioned objectives of the EU-C&P RTA, it would seem that the modification of a Schedule would, normally, need to lead to *more* liberalisation. Nonetheless, there should be room to correct scheduling mistakes, and there is nothing in the agreement that precludes a modification that leads to the withdrawal of a specific commitment if consensus is reached.

In the EU-Singapore RTA, Article 8.63 states that the parties must review, aside from the integral services chapter, the Schedules within three years of the agreement's entry into force. The Committee on Trade in Services, Investment and Government Procurement may, in the context of such review, decide to amend the Schedules. Although in principle, the review occurs 'With a view to further deepening liberalisation and eliminating remaining restrictions', it must also ensure 'an overall balance of rights and obligations'. Therefore, as with the EU-C&P RTA, there appears to be room for correcting mistakes and, potentially, withdrawal of a specific commitment. Very similar provisions can be found in Articles 80 and 87 EU-Georgia, although here, review is supposed to occur 'regularly'.

2.3 A Complex Structure that is Not More Flexible

In conclusion, the scope of application of the most relevant obligations in the services chapters of the EU-Colombia & Peru and EU-Singapore RTAs is limited to services listed in the Schedule. In comparison to GATS, there are no core unconditional obligations (aside from, for example, the transparency obligation in Articles 130 EU-C&P and 8.17 EU-Singapore RTA). The lack of an MFN obligation and list of exemptions thereto, make the structure of the chapter more comprehensible. The structure of the services chapter in the EU-Georgia DCFTA thus differs substantially from that of GATS and the other EU RTAs. It is a hybrid positive-negative listing chapter, with several flexibilities typical of trade in services. This hybrid approach in combination with the mode-specific obligations creates a complex structure that nonetheless does not seem to be more flexible than GATS in terms of undertaking commitments.

3. The scope of GATS and the selected EU RTAs

Determining whether a measure falls within the scope of an agreement is the first step in establishing whether the measure could be inconsistent with that agreement. Thus, a wide scope constrains regulatory autonomy more than a narrow one. The GATS negotiators' approach to delineating the scope of the agreement was pragmatic: there is no positive definition of the concept of services in GATS. In principle, it applies to almost every service in any sector. The same goes for the EU RTAs. To remedy this very wide scope, the scope of the agreements is limited by exemptions. In GATS, these are limited to what the Contracting Parties agreed to, whereas exemption in the services chapters of the selected EU RTAs are more conducive of EU sensitivities. Because GATS is a *trade* agreement, there must be trade in services, which is defined as the supply of a service through one of four modes of supply. The selected EU RTAs have largely mirrored this approach.

1. THE SCOPE OF GATS

1.1 A Wide Scope

Article I:1 GATS states that the agreement applies to measures by Members affecting trade in services. In paragraph 3 (b) of the same provision, services are defined negatively as any service in any sector except services supplied in the exercise of governmental authority. Articles I:3 *juncto* XXVIII (a)–(c) GATS highlight that three elements need to be considered: (i) what is 'trade in services'; (ii) what are 'measures by Members'; and (iii) when does a measure by a Member 'affect' trade in services.

1.1.1 'Trade in services'

'Trade in services' is the supply of any service in any sector through one of the four modes of supply defined in Article I:2 GATS.[1] Each mode of supply requires an international dimension because borders between Members must be crossed.[2] The four modes of service supply are:

a. Mode 1: cross-border supply of services, whereby the service crosses the border from the territory of one Member *into* the territory of any other Member (both consumer and service supplier remain in their respective home country); for example, a consumer receives market research report services from abroad through the telecommunications or postal network. From the perspective of the 'receiving' Member, i.e. the Member that schedules a commitment to open a service sector in its territory for cross-border supply of services, Mode 1 only covers services that are 'imported' into its territory.[3]

b. Mode 2: consumption abroad, whereby the consumer of one Member goes abroad to consume the service in the territory of any other Member; for example, a consumer has moved abroad as a patient to consume medical services. From the perspective of the 'receiving' Member, Mode 2 only covers services that its consumers consume abroad.[4]

c. Mode 3: commercial presence, i.e. whereby the service is supplied by a foreign affiliate of the service supplier of a Member, in the territory of any other Member; for example, the service is provided by a locally established subsidiary of a foreign-owned and -controlled hotel group. This Mode is often considered less threatening by competing domestic service suppliers as the foreign established suppliers are subject to the same rules and regulations

---

[1] *Canada – Certain Measures Affecting the Automotive Industry* WT/DS139/AB/R, WT/DS142/AB/R, AB report adopted 19 June 2000 para. 170.

[2] Diana Zacharias, 'Article I GATS' in Rüdiger Wolfrum, Peter-Tobias Stoll and Clemens Feinäugle (eds), *Max Planck Commentaries on World Trade Law: WTO – Trade in Services*, vol 6 (Martinus Nijhoff 2008) 44.

[3] S/L/92 2001 Scheduling Guidelines para. 28; Rudolf Adlung, 'Export Policies and the General Agreement on Trade in Services' 18 Journal of International Economic Law, 497.

[4] S/L/92 2001 Scheduling Guidelines para. 31; Adlung, 'Export Policies and the General Agreement on Trade in Services' 497.

as their domestic counterparts.[5] According to the Panel in *Mexico – Telecoms*, Mode 3 includes services originating in the territory of establishment but delivered in the territory of another Member,[6] i.e. to exports of services by establishments of foreign enterprises. Therefore, the scope of Mode 3 is wider than services supplied solely in the territory of the country of establishment.[7] Consequently, a domestically established foreign service supplier may 'supply a committed service to a foreign recipient wherever located, and of whatever nationality or origin'.[8]

d. Mode 4: temporary movement of natural persons, whereby the service is supplied by a natural person of a Member, in the territory of any other Member; for example, a foreign national provides services as an independent consultant or employee of a foreign consultancy firm.[9]

Contrary to the case for goods, GATS may not appear to apply to export measures such as export quotas, restrictions, or incentives because it does not contain any *specific* obligations disciplining such measures.[10] However, such measures are to be assessed as any other measure.[11]

It is not always easy to foresee the implications of the mode of supply approach.[12] Consequently, many inconspicuous measures may come within the scope of GATS. Consider for example a medical tourist, going

---

[5] Daniela Persin, 'Market Access for Small Versus Large Service Enterprises: The Preferential and Multilateral Trade Liberalization Tracks Compared' (2010) 45 Journal of World Trade 785, 795 and the references at footnotes 45–47.

[6] *Mexico – Measures Affecting Telecommunications Services* WT/DS204/R, Panel report adopted 2 April 2004 para. 7.375.

[7] *China – Certain Measures Affecting Electronic Payment Services* WT/DS413, Panel report adopted 31 August 2012 para. 7.618.

[8] Ibid.

[9] These examples for all four modes of supply are taken from World Trade Organization Trade in Services Division, *The General Agreement on Trade in Services: An Introduction* (2013) 3.

[10] Rudolf Adlung, 'The GATS Negotiations: Implications for Health and Social Services' (2003) 38 Intereconomics 147, 151–152.

[11] This is especially relevant for Mode 3; see Adlung, 'Export Policies and the General Agreement on Trade in Services' 507–508. Also note that reverse discrimination is not prohibited by GATS.

[12] See for example Damien J Neven and Petros C Mavroidis, 'El Mess in TELMEX: A Comment on *Mexico – Measures Affecting Telecommunications Services*' (2006) 5 World Trade Review 271, 279–282, who argue that the Panel in *Mexico – Telecoms* wrongly asserted that US service suppliers provided a

abroad to receive medical treatment (Mode 2). The *sending* (or home) state government's refusal to reimburse the costs of the foreign treatment may discriminate against foreign services and could theoretically violate the national treatment obligation.[13] (Of course, establishing the scope of GATS is only the first step of the compatibility analysis.) On the other hand, measures which reserve hospital beds for residents restrict the 'export' of hospital bed capacity and are not disciplined by GATS. Measures that tax 'exported' health services or oblige *domestic* health providers to provide certain mandatory services for domestic consumers before allowing them to move abroad are consistent with GATS. This analysis does not change in the case of specific commitments in hospital services.[14] Domestically established foreign health providers can be subjected to such an obligation if no commitment is scheduled, even if these export restrictions do not apply to domestic service suppliers. If a Mode 3 commitment is scheduled, a non-discriminatory export subsidy or tax is still acceptable (but an export restriction is not).[15] The main source of potential confusion is the fact that, from the point of view of the *receiving* (or host) state, there is no obligation to treat foreign *patients* like domestic *patients*. Rather, Mode 2 applies to domestic patients moving abroad to receive a service, and therefore the relevant comparison is domestic versus foreign medical *service suppliers*.

In some cases, it is equally difficult to predict which Mode is applicable. For example, the distinction between Modes 1 and 2 may depend on the perspective:

> If the transaction is deemed to have originated with a supplier in one jurisdiction selling a service to a consumer in another, then from the point of view of the jurisdiction in which the consumer is located, this would be classified as crossborder delivery, or a mode 1 transaction. If, on the other hand, the consumer initiates the transaction or solicits the service, it could be classified as consumption abroad. This potential confusion between mode 1

Mode 1 service, as the true international supply of services was a Mode 1 supply by *Mexican* service suppliers.

[13] Markus Krajewski, 'Patient Mobility Beyond Calais: Health Services Under WTO Law' in Johan van de Gronden et al. (eds), *Health Care and EU Law* (T.M.C. Asser Press 2011) 9–18 examines this issue.

[14] Adlung, 'The GATS Negotiations: Implications for Health and Social Services' 151.

[15] Adlung, 'Export Policies and the General Agreement on Trade in Services' 507–508. Also see A Mattoo, 'National Treatment in the GATS: Corner-Stone or Pandora's Box?' (1997) 31 Journal of World Trade 107, 121 at footnote 26.

> and mode 2 transactions obviously becomes important if the commitments scheduled by a Member are not identical in both modes.[16]

This has led to the suggestion that both modes should be read as one, or that Mode 2 should be redefined so as to require physical movement by the consumer.[17]

Two important clarifications must be noted. First, as concerns Mode 3, commercial presence also covers investment.[18] The definition of commercial presence in Article XXVIII (d) GATS is said to comprise both pre- and post-establishment,[19] and both existing and new investments.[20] However, it is narrower than definitions in investment law because it defines commercial presence from a physical enterprise point of view and does not comprise assets such as portfolio investments, real estate and all forms of tangible or intangible property.[21] Moreover, there is the requirement that the investment is 'made in order to supply a service in the host Member'.[22]

Second, regarding Mode 4, the Annex on Movement of Natural Persons Supplying Services under the Agreement holds that Members are not prevented from regulating entry into or temporary stay in its territory.

---

[16] Patrick Low and Aaditya Mattoo, 'Is There a Better Way? Alternative Approaches to Liberalization Under the GATS' in Pierre Sauvé and Robert M Stern (eds), *GATS 2000: New Directions in Services Trade Liberalization* (Brookings Institution 2000) 452.

[17] Zacharias, 'Article I GATS' 51.

[18] All modes of supply influence investment, but that this is especially true for Mode 3. Moreover, investment is linked to Articles XI, XII and footnote 8 to Article XVI:1 GATS. Federico Ortino and Audley Sheppard, 'International Agreements Covering Foreign Investment in Services: Patterns and Linkages' in Lorand Bartels and Federico Ortino (eds), *Regional Trade Agreements and the WTO Legal System* (Oxford University Press 2006) 201; Bart De Meester and Dominic Coppens, 'Mode 3 of the GATS: A Model for Disciplining Measures Affecting Investment Flows?' in Zdenek Drabek and Petros C Mavroidis (eds), *Regulation of Foreign Investment: Challenges to International Harmonization* (World Scientific 2013) 100–110.

[19] *China – Measures Affecting Trading Rights and Distribution Services for Certain Publications and Audiovisual Products* WT/DS363/R, Panel report adopted 19 January 2010 para. 7.974; S/C/W/314, Mode 3 – Commercial Presence (Background Note by the Secretariat 7 April 2010) para. 9.

[20] Pierre Sauvé and Christopher Wilkie, 'Investment Liberalization in GATS' in Pierre Sauvé and Robert M Stern (eds), *GATS 2000: New Directions in Services Trade Liberalization* (Brookings Institution 2000) 348.

[21] Ibid.

[22] De Meester and Coppens, 'Mode 3 of the GATS: A Model for Disciplining Measures Affecting Investment Flows?' 105 (emphasis omitted).

This includes measures necessary to protect the integrity of, and ensure the orderly movement of, natural persons across the Member's borders. However, such measures may not nullify or impair the benefits of another Member flowing from the Member's schedule of commitments. Nonetheless, disciplines on Mode 4 supply of services address highly sensitive domestic regulatory issues. Concerns regarding such issues are reinforced by the dynamic nature of labour markets versus the static nature of GATS.[23] This is reflected in the Mode 4 commitments in the EU Schedule. A horizontal limitation sets out the categories of natural persons covered by the EU's Mode 4 commitments, noting that the EU is unbound except for measures concerning the entry into and temporary stay within an EU Member State of specific categories of natural persons providing services. As such, natural persons not falling within these categories do not benefit from the Mode 4 commitments. The covered categories are intra-corporate transfers (ICTs), strictly defined in the EU's Schedule. They are:

a. Intra-corporate transfers (ICTs) of senior personnel or personnel possessing uncommon knowledge essential to the host establishment's service, research equipment, techniques or management.[24]
b. Business visitors (BVs),[25] which are negotiating the sale of services or entering into agreements to sell services for a service provider. BVs cannot supply services themselves. Alternatively, BVs are senior personnel responsible for the setting up of a commercial presence of a service provider of a WTO Member in an EU Member State.[26] Some Member States limit the BVs visit to approximately ninety days.
c. Contractual service suppliers (CSSs).[27] To qualify as a CSS, a natural person engaged by a foreign juridical person can supply services if the latter obtained a service contract for a period not exceeding three months from a final consumer in the Member State concerned. The number of the persons covered by the service

---

[23] Allison M Young, 'Where Next for Labour Mobility under GATS?' in Pierre Sauvé and Robert M Stern (eds), *GATS 2000: New Directions in Services Trade Liberalization* (Brookings Institution 2000) 207.
[24] EU 2006 consolidated Schedule 321–324.
[25] Ibid 324–327.
[26] Finland, Hungary and Poland are unbound for this sub-category.
[27] EU 2006 consolidated Schedule 327–330.

contract shall not be larger than necessary to fulfil the contract.[28] The service contract has to be obtained in one of 16 listed activities, subject to a specific sectoral commitment being undertaken by the EU Member State concerned (including any limitations). The listing includes, for example, legal services and higher education services.

The duration of the stay within an EU Member State is limited to three months in any twelve-month period.[29]

These limitations substantially limit the scope of Mode 4 for the EU vis-à-vis the specific commitments, i.e. market access and national treatment.

1.1.2 'Measures by Members'

'Measures by Members' includes measures taken by central, regional and local authorities. They include laws, regulations, rules, procedures, decisions, administrative actions or any other form of measure. Therefore, measures which are factual, rather than legal or administrative, are also included.[30] The measure can be any act or omission, as long as it is attributable to a Member.[31] Accordingly, the measure may be unwritten.[32] However, the Appellate Body (AB) has not yet explained whether a practice, 'a repeated pattern of similar responses to a set of circumstances',[33] may be challenged as a 'measure' in the context of GATS.[34] In

---

[28] A commitment in the EU's Schedule does not confer the right to exercise a professional title in the EU Member State concerned.

[29] Cyprus, Czech Republic, Hungary, Lithuania, Malta, Poland, Slovakia and Slovenia are unbound for this category.

[30] This includes the implementation of international agreements, standards and decisions of international organisations and their administrative bodies. Zacharias, 'Article I GATS' 54.

[31] *United States – Sunset Review of Anti-Dumping Duties on Corrosion-Resistant Carbon Steel Flat Products from Japan* WT/DS244/AB/R, AB report adopted 9 January 2004 para. 81.

[32] *European Communities – Measures Affecting Trade in Large Civil Aircraft* WT/DS316/AB/R, AB report adopted 1 June 2011 para. 792.

[33] *United States – Anti-Dumping and Countervailing Measures on Steel Plate from India* WT/DS206/R, Panel report adopted 29 July 2002 para. 7.22.

[34] See *United States – Measures Affecting the Cross-Border Supply of Gambling and Betting Services* WT/DS285/AB/R, AB report adopted 20 April 2005 para. 132; *United States – Measures Affecting the Cross-Border Supply of Gambling and Betting Services* WT/DS285/R, Panel report adopted 20 April 2005 para. 6.197.

the context of other agreements,[35] the AB set out three conditions which must be fulfilled before a practice may be challenged as a 'measure'. First, the practice must be attributable to the responding Member. Second, the applicant must provide sufficient evidence as to the precise content of the practice. Third, the practice must have general and prospective application.[36] Hence, the combined effect of measures cannot be challenged as such; it is the *measure* and not its *effect* that must be challenged.[37]

The exact scope of 'authorities' may be derived from GATT 1994 case law. The AB held that the 'essence of "government" is that it enjoys the effective power to "regulate", "control" or "supervise" individuals, or otherwise "restrain" their conduct, through the exercise of lawful authority'.[38] Accordingly, one can argue that measures by non-governmental bodies exercising delegated powers are to be considered as measures by Members.[39] For example, this could include self-regulating private associations that license certain liberal professions.[40] It appears from the GATS text that an explicit delegation of powers is necessary; this means self-regulating bodies which do not exercise formally delegated powers are probably exempted from the scope of the agreement. However, this reasoning is unlikely to hold in the case of bodies that are only formally non-governmental.[41] Additionally, Article I:3 (a) GATS requires Members to take reasonable measures to ensure that their commitments are observed by all bodies taking measures that fall within the scope of GATS. Measures by private actors are, in principle, exempted from the agreement unless they are encouraged and supported rather than just

---

[35] *United States – Laws, Regulations and Methodology for Calculating Dumping Margins (Zeroing)* WT/DS294/AB/R, AB report adopted 9 May 2006 paras 193 and 198; *United States – Continued Existence and Application of Zeroing Methodology* WT/DS350/AB/R, AB report adopted 19 February 2009 paras 183–185.

[36] *US – Continued Zeroing (AB)* paras 193.

[37] *US – Gambling (AB)* paras 115–128.

[38] *Canada – Measures Affecting the Importation of Milk and the Exportation of Dairy Products* WT/DS103/AB/R, WT/DS113/AB/R, AB report adopted 13 October 1999 para. 97.

[39] Krajewski, 'Patient Mobility Beyond Calais: Health Services Under WTO Law' 462–463.

[40] Zacharias, 'Article I GATS' 55–56.

[41] Markus Krajewski, *National Regulation and Trade Liberalization in Services* (Kluwer Law International 2003) 63.

tolerated by the government.[42] This may be difficult to establish. The actions of a monopoly or of exclusive service suppliers that have been, formally or in effect, established or authorised by a Member, may lead to a violation of the Member's MFN, market access and national treatment obligations, or its obligations undertaken as additional commitments.[43] Hence, the scope of 'measures by Members' can, in certain situations, be considered to have been stretched to include actions by these actors.

1.1.3 'Affecting'

The final element of the scope of GATS is determining whether the measure is 'affecting' trade in services. The AB decided that assessing whether a measure is prohibited by GATS first requires an examination of this element.[44] A panel must establish that the measure affects relevant actors in their capacity as service suppliers.[45] According to the case law, 'affecting' implies that all measures having an effect on trade in services are covered, giving GATS a broad reach.[46] Actual trade flows or specific service suppliers seeking to supply a service are not a prerequisite for the application of GATS.[47] This wide approach is comparable to the Court of Justice of the European Union's *Dassonville*-formula, which encompasses all measures that are 'capable of hindering [trade], directly or indirectly, actually or potentially'.[48] For example, a measure does not need to be aimed primarily at regulating a particular service.[49] In practice, this interpretation could mean that non-final or indirect measures are also subject to GATS regulation.[50] Similarly, measures that incentivise or dis-incentivise behaviour may affect trading activities.[51]

---

[42] Zacharias, 'Article I GATS' 56. Private trade barriers are addressed in Articles VIII and IX GATS.

[43] See Article VIII GATS.

[44] *Canada – Autos (AB)* paras 151–152.

[45] Ibid paras 167 and 181.

[46] *European Communities – Regime for the Importation, Sale and Distribution of Bananas* WT/DS27/AB/R, AB report adopted 25 September 1997 para. 220; *Canada – Autos (AB)* para. 158.

[47] *Argentina – Measures Relating to Trade in Goods and Services*, WT/DS453, Panel Report not yet adopted, paras 7.88–7.94.

[48] Court of Justice of the European Union, Case 8/74 *Procureur du Roi v Dassonville*, ECLI:EU:C:1974:82, para. 5.

[49] By analogy to the finding on goods in *India – Measures Affecting the Automotive Sector* WT/DS146/R, WT/DS175/R, Panel report adopted 5 April 2002 para. 7.305.

[50] Zacharias, 'Article I GATS' 45.

[51] *China – Publications and Audiovisual Products (Panel)* para. 7.1450.

And, as further explained below, many provisions in a bilateral investment treaty (BIT) would appear to affect trade in services.

The term 'affecting' also delineates the scope of GATS. As the AB noted in the context of Article III:4 GATT 1994, it is 'not any "laws, regulations and requirements" which are covered by Article III:4, but only those which "affect" the specific transactions, activities and uses mentioned in that provision'.[52] It continued by stating that 'affecting' 'serves a similar function in Article I:1 [GATS], where it also defines the types of measure that are subject to the disciplines set forth elsewhere in the GATS'.[53] Additionally, measures that do not affect trade in services (i.e. not affecting trade or exclusively affecting trade in goods) are not covered by GATS.[54]

1.1.4 Subsidies

Subsidies receive special attention in the selected EU RTAs. Therefore, it is appropriate to briefly address subsidies in the context of the scope of GATS.[55] Unlike in the Agreement on Subsidies and Countervailing Measures (SCM Agreement), a subsidy is not defined under GATS. Generally, it can be said that the term 'subsidy' encompasses direct grants and tax incentives, among other things. These measures are a powerful policy tool used frequently by domestic regulators, especially in sectors such as tourism, transport and audio-visual and financial services.[56] Article XV GATS may give the impression that subsidies are not (yet) covered by GATS, as it merely recognises that subsidies may have distortive effects on trade in services and does not contain disciplines for subsidies. However, subsidies are not excluded from the scope of GATS.

---

[52] *United States – Tax Treatment for 'Foreign Sales Corporations' (Recourse to Article 21.5 of the DSU by the EC)* WT/DS108/AB/RW, AB report adopted 20 March 2000 para. 208.

[53] Ibid para. 209.

[54] *EC – Bananas III (AB)* para. 222.

[55] See Pietro Poretti, *The Regulation of Subsidies Within the General Agreement on Trade in Services of the WTO: Problems and Prospects* (Kluwer 2009) 136–152 for an analysis of existing GATS disciplines on subsidies.

[56] Pietro Poretti, 'Article XV GATS' in Rüdiger Wolfrum, Peter-Tobias Stoll and Clemens Feinäugle (eds), *Max Planck Commentaries on World Trade Law: WTO – Trade in Services*, vol 6 (Martinus Nijhoff 2008) 353.

Rather, they are assessed like any other measure, with all GATS obligations applying equally to subsidies.[57]

Considering the importance of subsidies as a policy tool and the applicability of GATS disciplines to these measures, many members have scheduled subsidies limitations vis-à-vis their national treatment obligation.[58] Importantly, paragraph 10 of a WTO explanatory note on scheduling states that GATS does not contain obligations outside a Member's territorial jurisdiction, implying that the national treatment obligation does not extend to a service supplier located in the territory of another Member.[59] Therefore, in the case of committed sectors without scheduled limitations concerning subsidies, national treatment must still only be accorded to foreign service suppliers located within the Member's territory.[60] Export subsidies would not need to be scheduled as long they are not discriminatory.[61] Nonetheless, the ability to discriminate between domestic service suppliers and Modes 3 and 4 foreign service suppliers remains of the utmost importance with regards to regulatory autonomy, as this allows for a targeted and more affordable set of policies.

The EU has not listed MFN Exemptions for subsidies and no relevant entries were scheduled with regard to market access. As concerns national treatment, two horizontal limitations regarding subsidies are included in the EU Schedule. First, for most EU Member States, the eligibility for subsidies (from the EU or its Member States) may be limited to juridical persons established in the territory (or a sub-division) of a Member in Mode 3. Some Member States are not bound by the underlying commitment for branches established in a Member State by a non-EU company. Furthermore, research and development subsidies are exempted from the underlying commitment. This limitation also states that the supply of a service or its subsidisation within the public sector is not in breach of Mode 3 national treatment commitments. Second, in the case of Mode 4, subsidies to natural persons may be limited to nationals

---

[57] Not all authors agree that subsidies are covered by GATS. For a convincing rebuttal of such claims, see De Meester and Coppens, 'Mode 3 of the GATS: A Model for Disciplining Measures Affecting Investment Flows?' 133–135.

[58] Pierre Sauvé, 'Completing the GATS Framework: Addressing Uruguay Round Leftovers' (2002) 57 Aussenwirtschaft 301, 326.

[59] General Agreement on Tariffs and Trade, *MTN.GNS/W/164, Scheduling of Initial Commitments in Trade in Services: Explanatory Note (3 September).*

[60] Poretti, 'Article XV GATS' 361–362.

[61] Adlung, 'Export Policies and the General Agreement on Trade in Services' 507–508.

of a Member State. This limitation is again applicable to most EU Member States. In addition to the two horizontal commitments, there are some sectoral commitments in entertainment services. For instance, France and Italy are unbound for Mode 3 national treatment as concerns subsidies and any other forms of direct and indirect investment, thereby explicitly reserving the right to grant subsidies in such cases.[62]

1.2 Exemptions from the Scope

As set out above, the scope of GATS does not contain an *a priori* exclusion of measures by a Member affecting trade in any service in any service sector. This broad scope is limited by some exemptions. The first exemption covers most services directly linked to air traffic rights. These services have been explicitly excluded from the scope of GATS.[63] The second explicit exemption, the so-called governmental authority exception, deserves further attention.

1.2.1 The governmental authority exception[64]

The governmental authority exception constitutes the most important exemption from the scope of GATS. Inscribed in Article I:3 (b)–(c) GATS, it is an important aspect of the balance between regulatory autonomy and trade liberalisation. This is the case because the governmental authority exception touches directly upon a government's ability to regulate sensitive areas of a society in which government intervention often plays an important role. Such sectors include medical, education and health services. If the exception applies, the service is considered a service supplied in the exercise of governmental authority and thus not a 'service' in the sense of GATS. For the governmental authority exception to apply, two cumulative conditions listed in Article I:3 (c) GATS must be fulfilled: (i) the service must not be supplied 'on a commercial basis'; and (ii) the service must not be supplied 'in competition with' one or

[62] This does not necessarily mean that any downstream benefits from such subsidies would not be prohibited by other WTO rules. For example, if a government scheme subsidizes a service provider on the condition that it provides cheaper services to domestic goods producers, there may be a potentially prohibited indirect benefit to the latter compared to a foreign goods producer.

[63] Art. I:3 (b) GATS; para. 2 Annex on Air Transport Services. Para. 3 of the Annex lists some specific services that are covered by GATS.

[64] This section has benefited tremendously from discussions with Dylan Geraets, Sidonie Descheemaeker, Laura Verhoeven and Ines Willemyns.

more service suppliers. It is clear that the scope of the governmental authority exception is to be defined for each service, not for a service supplier.[65] The moment in time at which governmental authority must be assessed is less clear. This issue will be addressed first, as it informs the interpretation of the two conditions set out. Next, a potential third condition for the presence of governmental authority is examined. Finally, the relevance of the exception for public services, monopolies and universal service obligations will be discussed.

1.2.1.1 When to assess the governmental authority exception Before assessing the two conditions for the governmental authority exception, it should be established *when* these conditions must be assessed. Three moments in time may qualify as the comparator: (i) the situation at, or just before, the moment the measure was enacted; (ii) the situation in the present time, 'but for' the measure;[66] or (iii) the situation in the present time, created by the measure. This choice has severe repercussions on regulatory autonomy. Usage of the first moment in time has little textual support: Article I:3 (c) GATS is drafted in the present tense. The 'but for' test is the second possibility. The AB has stated that, in domestic taxation matters that may constitute prohibited subsidies, a 'but for' test may be used to assess a measure that is an exception to a general rule.[67] However, in determining the normative benchmark for comparison between situations in this way, the 'but for' test is applied to a domestic regulatory situation, and not to the relationship between the general rule and an exception in an international agreement. Moreover, the AB stressed that it had 'certain abiding reservations about applying any legal standard, such as this "but for" test, in the place of the actual treaty language'.[68] Using a 'but for' test would subject the governmental authority exception to market conditions beyond the regulating government's powers. Therefore, the link with governmental authority would be weakened and reduced to the commercial basis element. The scope of the governmental authority exception would be very narrow. Considering the

[65] R Adlung, 'Public Services and the GATS' (2006) 9 Journal of International Economic Law 455, 463.

[66] The 'but for' test can be summarised as 'the situation that would prevail but for the measures in question'. *United States – Tax Treatment for 'Foreign Sales Corporations'* WT/DS108/R, Panel report adopted 20 March 2000 para. 7.45.

[67] *US – FSC (Article 21.5 – EC) (AB)* para. 91.

[68] *United States – Tax Treatment for 'Foreign Sales Corporations'* WT/DS108/AB/R, AB report adopted 20 March 2000 para. 91.

otherwise broad scope of GATS, this would reduce the exception to practical irrelevance.

The third option, i.e. the situation created by the measure in the present time, means that a government, by fulfilling the two conditions set out above, may carve the supply of services out of the scope of GATS. If the interpretation of 'on a commercial basis' and 'in competition with' is sufficiently strict, there would appear to be little to hold against such an approach. Based on the interpretations set forth in the following sections, few services would qualify unless a government decides to intervene substantially. Fulfilling the two strict conditions would indicate that the government considers the measure at hand to be services supplied in the exercise of governmental authority. As will be established, this interpretation gives effect to the governmental authority exception without overstretching it. The criticism that such an approach allows governments to take services in and out of the scope of GATS would appear unfounded: there is no textual basis for a lock-in effect that would preclude a government from doing so, or a legal basis for fixing the scope of GATS in time. Legal certainty would not be impaired beyond what is acceptable from the perspective of a right to regulate. Similarly, the argument that the factual outcome of a GATS inconsistent measure creates a justification for the measure (e.g. that a measure eliminating competition would be justified *because* it eliminates competition) cannot be upheld. The governmental authority exception defines the scope of GATS, hence the measure is not a measure affecting trade in services falling within the scope of GATS. In the same sense, the fact that specific commitments have been scheduled does not mean, in my view, that a service covered by those commitments could not be supplied in the exercise of governmental authority.[69] This is the case for two reasons. First, the applicability of the governmental authority exception should be assessed before addressing any obligations under GATS. Second, the principle of effective treaty interpretation could only preclude this interpretation in cases where a scheduled commitment is deprived of any meaning by applying the governmental authority exception. The modification of the scope of a commitment through the application of the governmental authority exception would not be at odds with this principle. Moreover, even if a commitment would, at one moment in time, be deprived of meaning because of the application of the exception, this

---

[69] Marchetti and Mavroidis argue the opposite: Juan A Marchetti and Petros C Mavroidis, 'What Are the Main Challenges for the GATS Framework? Don't Talk About Revolution' (2004) 5 European Business Organization Law Review 511, 535.

does not necessarily render the commitment meaningless forever. The intervening regulator would need to make sure that the conditions for governmental authority remain fulfilled. If this is not the case, the specific commitment would reapply.

Of course, in order to safeguard the effectiveness of GATS, this approach must be combined with sufficiently clear and strict interpretations of 'on a commercial basis' and 'in competition with'.

1.2.1.2 The supply of a service 'on a commercial basis' Although it constitutes an interpretation of Article III:8 GATT 1994, the meaning of the term 'on a commercial basis' may be derived from the AB's interpretation of the term 'commercial resale' in *Canada – Renewable Energy*. Although a 'resale' focuses on the relationship between the buyer and the seller, the AB also addressed the meaning of 'commercial' from the perspective of the seller. The decisive element appears to be 'whether the transaction is oriented at generating a profit for the seller', based on the seller's long-term strategy.[70] Moreover, in earlier case law, it was noted that the ordinary meaning of the term 'commercial' included 'likely to make a profit',[71] not *make* a profit. Hence, loss-making by itself does not preclude a commercial basis. Additionally, there may be situations where the seller engages in a transaction without a profit-seeking intention but whilst acting in a self-interested manner.[72] Based on these distinctions, four situations may occur:

---

[70] *Canada – Certain Measures Affecting the Renewable Energy Generation Sector, Canada – Measures Relating to the Feed-In Tariff Program* WT/DS412/AB/R, WT/DS426/AB/R, AB report adopted 24 May 2013 paras 5.70–5.71. Based on the definition of 'juridical person' in Article XXVIII (l) GATS, it has been argued by Adlung that an element of strategic economic behaviour is sufficient to consider that a service is supplied on a commercial basis. However, as the author admits, such an interpretation blurs the line between this condition and the condition of 'in competition with'. The long-term profit-seeking intention may be reconcilable with an element of strategic economic behaviour. See Adlung, 'Public Services and the GATS' 462, especially footnote 20, and 463.

[71] *United States – Definitive Anti-Dumping and Countervailing Duties on Certain Products from China* WT/DS379/AB/R, AB report adopted 25 March 2011 para. 478 and *Canada – Measures Relating to Exports of Wheat and Treatment of Imported Grain* WT/DS276/R, Panel report adopted 27 September 2004 para. 6.84.

[72] *Canada – Renewable Energy (AB), Canada – Feed-In Tariff Program (AB)* para. 5.71.

a. Profit-making supply of a service.
b. Loss-making supply of a service supplied with a long-term profit-seeking intention from the service supplier.
c. Loss-making supply of a service supplied without a long-term profit-seeking intention but out of self-interest of the service supplier.
d. Loss-making supply of a service supplied without long-term profit-seeking intention nor out of self-interest of the service supplier.

Services supplied in situation a. are clearly supplied on a commercial basis,[73] whereas services supplied in situation d. are clearly not.[74] Further analysis is required regarding situations b. and c.

Despite the apparent focus on the service supplier in this categorisation, it should be stressed that one service may be supplied by a supplier on a commercial basis whilst another service may be supplied by the same supplier on a non-commercial basis.[75] One should make an analysis of both the specific service delivered and of the long-term profit-seeking intention of the service supplier,[76] but not of other services supplied by other service suppliers.

As concerns the second situation, which finds support in doctrine predating the AB's finding noted above,[77] it may be added that Article XXVIII (d) GATS defines 'commercial presence' in Mode 3 service

[73] Nonetheless, it may no longer be true that free services are incontestably not supplied on a commercial basis, considering the revenue model of many internet companies who supply free services to their users and make profits from e.g. the data they gather from their users. See Eric Leroux, 'What is a "Service Supplied in the Exercise of Governmental Authority" Under Article I:3(b) and (c) of the General Agreement on Trade in Services?' (2006) 40 Journal of World Trade 345, 354.

[74] I argue that it is irrelevant whether all other service suppliers in the same market do make profit. The conditions need to be fulfilled for a specific service and service supplier.

[75] Markus Krajewski, 'Public Services and Trade Liberalization: Mapping the Legal Framework' (2003) 6 Journal of International Economic Law 341, 351.

[76] See e.g. Marchetti and Mavroidis, 'What Are the Main Challenges for the GATS Framework? Don't Talk About Revolution' 530–531.

[77] Krajewski, *National Regulation and Trade Liberalization in Services* 68; J Anthony VanDuzer, 'Health, Education and Social Services in Canada: The Impact of the GATS' in John M Curtis and Dan Ciuriak (eds), *Trade Policy Research 2004* (Minister of Public Works and Government Studies Canada 2004) 378–383 and Leroux, 'What is a "Service Supplied in the Exercise of Governmental Authority" Under Article I:3(b) and (c) of the General Agreement on Trade in Services?' 349.

supply as 'any type of business or professional establishment'. Because businesses or professional establishments necessarily seek profit, the GATS concept of what is 'commercial' could imply (long-term) profitability.[78] Nonetheless, the question remains concerning what is to be understood as a long-term profit-seeking intention. National courts have sought to objectify the concept where it exists in national law by assessing, for example, what is the primary objective of the supplier. A service that is not supplied on a profit-seeking basis should not be generating private financial benefits. However, it could be promoting or achieving another purpose such as the alleviation of poverty, and in this sense the intention of the service supplier could play a role in assessing the long-term profit-seeking intention.[79] However, there should still be an objective element to determining the intention.[80] A factual analysis of a service supplier's business model and structure,[81] as well as the business model of the service itself, would be a likely starting point.

For the third situation, the key question is whether such services are supplied on an altogether commercial basis. In many cases, the supply of such a service could contribute to a long-term profit-seeking intention. For example, a lawyer providing free legal advice to an NGO may want to raise his profile, or the experience from working for the NGO may contribute to his skills as a lawyer. Alternatively, consider an exchange in which the lawyer provides free legal advice to his neighbour, who returns the favour through the provision of another free service. Such situations present potential problems from a trade perspective, as they are likely to be arranged on an informal basis. It suffices to restate that services supplied 'on a commercial basis' are services supplied with a profit, or services supplied with a long-term profit-seeking intention.

---

[78] Krajewski, 'Public Services and Trade Liberalization: Mapping the Legal Framework' 351; Leroux, 'What is a "Service Supplied in the Exercise of Governmental Authority" Under Article I:3(b) and (c) of the General Agreement on Trade in Services?' 349.

[79] VanDuzer, 'Health, Education and Social Services in Canada: The Impact of the GATS' 379–381.

[80] David Luff, 'Regulation of Health Services and International Trade Law' in Aaditya Mattoo and Pierre Sauvé (eds), *Domestic Regulation & Service Trade Liberalization* (World Bank & Oxford University Press 2003) 194.

[81] See e.g. the degree of autonomy for the management that supplies a service and the financial autonomy of the service supplier; Andrew Lang, 'The GATS and Regulatory Autonomy: A Case Study of Social Regulation of the Water Industry' (2004) 7 Journal of International Economic Law 801, 820.

1.2.1.3 The supply of a service 'in competition with one or more service suppliers' The second condition of the governmental authority exception requires that a service is not supplied 'in competition with' one or more service suppliers. For interpretational guidance, one may look to the Panel report in *Mexico – Telecoms*, in which the Panel gave meaning to the concept of 'anti-competitive practices' in Mexico's additional commitments on telecommunications under Article XVIII GATS. The Panel therefore turned to a dictionary definition of 'competition', i.e. 'rivalry in the market, striving for custom between those who have the same commodities to dispose of'.[82] This definition contains two conditions.

First, in order to have 'rivalry in the market', several service suppliers with the potential to supply the service should be targeting the same market.[83] As a result, it is not necessary that the consumer has an actual choice between service suppliers. For rivalry to exist in the market, at least two service suppliers would need to be able, practically, to supply the relevant service. For example, a service supplier already supplying the service abroad is likely to have the necessary expertise and means to be able to supply the service elsewhere. Merely theoretically, potential service suppliers should not be taken into account. A service supplier can demonstrate that it targets a market through facts, for example through a business case. Such an approach is in accordance with the AB's position that '[t]he word "competitive" must be distinguished from the words "competing" or "being in actual competition"', the former having a wider connotation, including potential competition, than the latter two.[84] A potential but in practical terms able service supplier is more than merely in a competitive relationship, without being in actual competition or actually competing. Similarly, the approach is in accordance with the Panel's finding in *Korea – Alcoholic Beverages* that potential competition extends to products which 'can reasonably be expected to become directly competitive in the near future'.[85]

---

[82] *Mexico – Telecoms (Panel)* para. 7.230; Marchetti and Mavroidis, 'What Are the Main Challenges for the GATS Framework? Don't Talk About Revolution' 533.

[83] Potential competitors have been previously taken into account in establishing whether a measure affects trade in services: *China – Electronic Payment Services (Panel)* para. 7.686.

[84] *United States – Transitional Safeguard Measure on Combed Cotton Yarn from Pakistan* WT/DS192/AB/R, AB report adopted 5 November 2001 para. 96.

[85] *Korea – Taxes on Alcoholic Beverages* WT/DS75/R, Panel report adopted 17 February 1999 para. 10.48.

Simply being an able service supplier that targets the relevant market is insufficient to fulfil the condition of rivalry in the market. Considering that governmental authority should be assessed in the situation created by the measure in the present time, at least two service suppliers would need to be legally able to supply the service in the relevant market. A governmental measure that effectively excludes all competition from the market would thus satisfy this condition. Deciding otherwise would limit the governmental authority exception to those services for which there is no potential competitor targeting the relevant market. In today's economy, the amount of services and markets that may meet this requirement is very small.

Second, 'those who have the same commodities to dispose of' indicates that the rivals should be in a competitive relationship.[86] There must be a degree of elasticity of substitution between the services.[87] This assessment requires a determination of the relevant services market in which the services are substitutable and, as such, could be said to be analogous to a likeness analysis. The test could be approached by applying concepts already used and accepted by national and international bodies. For example, the services' end-uses, their customer base, their price relationship including cross-price elasticity, and their respective distribution channels could be taken into account.[88] An interpretation of this condition on the basis of like service suppliers (supplying similar services in the relevant market),[89] would overly limit the range of potential competitors.[90] Moreover, this interpretation lacks a textual basis.

It should be noted, as addressed below in the context of 'likeness', that a different mode of supply between services does not necessarily determine the competitive relationship between those services. For example, the Panel in *China – Electronic Payment Services* stated that in

---

[86] That goods case law would be relevant *in casu* was noted in *China – Publications and Audiovisual Products (Panel)* footnote 620.

[87] Krajewski, 'Public Services and Trade Liberalization: Mapping the Legal Framework' 352–353.

[88] Inspiration can be drawn from competition law: Marchetti and Mavroidis, 'What Are the Main Challenges for the GATS Framework? Don't Talk About Revolution' 531–534; Leroux, 'What is a "Service Supplied in the Exercise of Governmental Authority" Under Article I:3(b) and (c) of the General Agreement on Trade in Services?' 368–384.

[89] Krajewski, *National Regulation and Trade Liberalization in Services* 70.

[90] Marchetti and Mavroidis, 'What Are the Main Challenges for the GATS Framework? Don't Talk About Revolution' 531; Adlung, 'Public Services and the GATS' 464.

the specific case at hand, the likeness analysis of Article XVII GATS would not differ according to whether the foreign service was supplied through Mode 1 or Mode 3.[91] By analogy, a domestic state monopoly could be in a competitive relationship with foreign commercial cross-border services suppliers.[92] However, the condition of rivalry in the market may not be fulfilled in such a case.

For both conditions, the determination of the relevant market is crucial. According to the AB, a panel's analysis of a benefit under the SCM Agreement must start with the determination of the relevant market. Only then can the correct price comparison be made in the market where services compete.[93] This reliance on the market is crucial. Therefore, an assessment of rivalry in the *actions* of a service supplier[94] does not take sufficient account of the relevant market. Similarly, a 'one-way conception' of competition that focuses on service suppliers 'who do not, themselves, engage in competition' may give insufficient weight to the market.[95] In this view, mere coexistence between those services which fall within the scope of the governmental authority exception and those services which do not, does not mean that the first service is supplied in competition with the second service. In my understanding, delineating the relevant market with sufficient precision alleviates the same concerns that trigger the foregoing interpretations. Two aspects play a role: (i) the relevant product market; and (ii) the relevant geographical market. First, according to the Panel in *Mexico – Telecoms*, the notion of demand substitution is central to the determination of the relevant market: if a consumer considers two products as substitutable, these products are part of the same market and the services should be practical alternatives.[96] The AB developed the notion of relevant market in the context of a benefit analysis under Article I:1 SCM Agreement and noted that consumer preference is not sufficient to establish the relevant market.[97]

---

91 *China – Electronic Payment Services (Panel)* para. 7.704.

92 Adlung, 'Public Services and the GATS' 464 and Krajewski, 'Patient Mobility Beyond Calais: Health Services Under WTO Law' 458–462.

93 *Canada – Renewable Energy (AB), Canada – Feed-In Tariff Program (AB)* para. 5.169.

94 Adlung, 'Public Services and the GATS' 465. Adlung, referring to VanDuzer, considers that 'as long as public universities or hospitals do not seek to poach students or patients, they cannot be deemed to be in competition'.

95 VanDuzer, 'Health, Education and Social Services in Canada: The Impact of the GATS' 390–395.

96 *Mexico – Telecoms (Panel)* para. 7.152.

97 *Canada – Renewable Energy (AB), Canada – Feed-In Tariff Program (AB)* para. 5.176.

An analysis and comparison of both demand-side and supply-side factors may be necessary, as may be considerations relating to the relevance of regulatory intervention.[98] Second, a factual assessment of the relevant geographical market should be made, taking into account the relevant product market.

1.2.1.4 The presence of governmental authority It has been argued that, in addition to the conditions that a service is supplied neither on a commercial basis nor in competition with other service suppliers, a third condition is implied by the text of the governmental authority exception. The reasoning goes that the meaning of 'services supplied in the exercise of governmental authority' in Article I:3 (b) GATS is not to be equated with the two conditions of Article I:3 (c) GATS.[99] The expression 'in the exercise of' could indicate that a service must also be delivered by the government or on its behalf for the governmental authority exception to apply.[100] Authority requires both command and control. Hence governmental action in a capacity that does not entail authority would not fall within the exception.[101]

Considering the text of the provision, which does not indicate that a third condition should be added, I do not agree. If a service is supplied neither on a commercial basis nor in competition with any other service supplier, a government will likely have intervened to fulfil these conditions. This intervention is probably the challenged measure under GATS. In my opinion, the governmental authority element is fulfilled through this intervention, whatever the subject of the government's intervention. A situation in which both conditions are fulfilled without any governmental intervention seems highly unlikely to be of any real economic relevance.

1.2.1.5 Public services, monopolies and universal service obligations

1.2.1.5.1 PUBLIC SERVICES A specific and sensitive issue in the context of the relatively limited governmental authority exception concerns public services. Although the abovementioned conditions are applicable,

---

[98] Ibid, paras 5.172–5.173 and 5.178.

[99] Krajewski, *National Regulation and Trade Liberalization in Services* 71; VanDuzer, 'Health, Education and Social Services in Canada: The Impact of the GATS' 393; Adlung, 'Public Services and the GATS' 465.

[100] VanDuzer, 'Health, Education and Social Services in Canada: The Impact of the GATS' 385.

[101] Zacharias, 'Article I GATS' 61.

and GATS does not contain a specific regime for public services, the issue nonetheless deserves further attention. Many governments use universal services obligations and public monopolies to ensure the supply of public services to their people. In the EU, public services or services of general (economic) interest, have been defined as 'a specific subset of services provided by or under the control of a public authority, because these services are considered "special" compared to other services'.[102] 'Special' refers to the fact that the services are supplied to pursue a public interest which is linked to governmental concerns such as social policies and distributional justice. For example, public services can be supplied on the basis of non-discriminatory access, and by charging reasonable prices for such services.[103] They include key governmental services in sensitive sectors such as health care, education and social security. Public services often appear in sectors with substantial and recognised market failures.[104] GATS does not contain an explicit reference to public services. However, as the agreement applies, essentially, to any service in any sector, it is also applicable to public services. Civil society actors have raised concerns that GATS fails to acknowledge differences in the nature, function and social relations of key public services because it makes no legal distinction between key public services and other services.[105] The European Parliament noted that 'the GATS agreement has given rise to widespread concern regarding […] its possible impact on public services and the regulation of services in general'.[106]

Aside from the potential applicability of the governmental authority exception, an examination of the practical impact of GATS presents two distinguishable situations.[107] First, the public service is supplied in a sector in which *no* specific commitments have been scheduled. In this

---

[102] Krajewski, 'Public Services and Trade Liberalization: Mapping the Legal Framework' 343 and 350.

[103] Ibid 344–345.

[104] Rupa Chanda, 'Social Services and the GATS: Key Issues and Concerns' (2003) 31 World Development 1997, 1997.

[105] Shawkat Alam, Pundarik Mukhopadhaya and David Randle, 'The General Agreement on Trade in Services (GATS), Water, and Human Rights from the Perspective of Developing Countries' (2011) 58 Netherlands International Law Review 43, 54–55 and the references there.

[106] European Parliament, Resolution of 12 March 2003 on the General Agreement on Trade in Services (GATS) within the WTO, including Cultural Diversity (P5_TA(2003)0087, 2003) preamble recital D.

[107] Marchetti and Mavroidis, 'What Are the Main Challenges for the GATS Framework? Don't Talk About Revolution' 535.

case, only the general obligations apply. The most important general obligation, the MFN obligation, does not preclude favouring domestic service suppliers over foreign ones. In this situation, there are few issues for public services.[108] Consequently, governments have appeared disinclined to schedule commitments in traditional public services sectors, in order to avoid accidentally subjecting public services to specific commitments. It is no coincidence that health and social services sectors contain the lowest number of scheduled commitments of almost all large sectors.[109] Another expression of this uncertainty is the 'conditioning' of Members' specific commitments so as to avoid public services falling within the scope of GATS.[110] The example of such a limitation in the EU, is addressed below. Other Members have listed sector-specific limitations to differentiate between 'public' and private parts of a sector. China, for example, has excluded national compulsory primary education from its primary education commitments.[111]

Second, the public service may be supplied in a sector in which specific commitments have been scheduled. In this case, the market access and national treatment obligations may apply and favouring domestic service suppliers may be irreconcilable with GATS commitments. Therefore, it is argued, the only practical issue is in the case of 'sloppy, imprecise scheduling'.[112] Taking into account the complexity and unforeseeable implications of GATS,[113] this may be a harsh analysis for many countries who undertook specific commitments in traditional public services sectors. The same may be said for technological and other evolutions which have changed public services supply beyond what was foreseeable at the time of scheduling. As stressed below, this highlights that careful drafting of the schedules of commitments is extremely important, especially considering the difficulties involved in the modification of Schedules.

---

[108] Adlung, 'The GATS Negotiations: Implications for Health and Social Services' 152.

[109] Chanda, 'Social Services and The GATS: Key Issues and Concerns' 2000; Adlung, 'The GATS Negotiations: Implications for Health and Social Services' 154; Adlung, 'Public Services and the GATS' 468.

[110] Adlung, 'Public Services and the GATS' 470.

[111] See ibid Table 2 at 477–478.

[112] Marchetti and Mavroidis, 'What Are the Main Challenges for the GATS Framework? Don't Talk About Revolution' 536.

[113] See above and Aaditya Mattoo, 'Services in a Development Round: Three Goals and Three Proposals' (2005) 39 Journal of World Trade 1223, 1224 and 1229.

Consequently, the applicability of the governmental authority exception is of most relevance where specific commitments have been scheduled with the potential to intervene in domestic public service regulation. I recall that public services are provided *by* or *under the control* of a public authority. Two specific, and interlinked, ways in which governments may pursue the distribution of public services merit more attention. Finally, the EU's use of GATS flexibilities for public services will be addressed.

1.2.1.5.2 MONOPOLIES OR EXCLUSIVE SERVICE SUPPLIERS SUPPLYING PUBLIC SERVICES Monopolies or exclusive service suppliers are often authorised or established by governments to provide public services, such as health or education services.[114] GATS contains specific disciplines on monopolies and exclusive service suppliers in Article VIII. It suffices here to highlight that, in principle, GATS applies to these service suppliers, unless the governmental authority exception applies. In the case of a legally established or authorised monopoly or exclusive service supplier, it seems that the service is by definition not supplied 'in competition with' another service supplier.[115] Similarly, the definition of exclusive service supplier in Article VIII:5 GATS requires that a Member 'substantially prevents competition among [the small number of suppliers authorised or established by the Member] in its territory'. The 'on a commercial basis' condition may be more difficult to satisfy. The first situation arises where the supplier is a private entity and supplies the services on a contractual basis through a type of private contract. This could be a concession, a right to exploitation or another type of contract. In these cases, the commercial basis may be difficult to deny, as these private operators are also commercial companies,[116] and they are unlikely to fulfil the required conditions. The second situation arises where the monopoly or exclusive service supplier is a public entity. A case-by-case analysis would be required.

Many former public monopolies and exclusive service suppliers that supplied public services have now been liberalised. A notable example is the telecommunications sector. In cases of partial liberalisation, the mere introduction of components of competitive or profitable behaviour may

---

[114] Adlung, 'Public Services and the GATS' 464.

[115] Marchetti and Mavroidis, 'What Are the Main Challenges for the GATS Framework? Don't Talk About Revolution' 537.

[116] Lang, 'The GATS and Regulatory Autonomy: A Case Study of Social Regulation of the Water Industry' 818–819; Adlung, 'Public Services and the GATS' 466–467.

change the analysis concerning the governmental authority exception.[117] For example, partial privatisation may mean that a public entity supplies services 'in competition with' private suppliers. A, perhaps unexpected, result is that the whole of the relevant service supplier's activity – including the non-privatised aspects of their service supply – could be brought within the scope of GATS.[118] In turn, this could trigger inconsistencies with the market access and national treatment obligations.

1.2.1.5.3 UNIVERSAL SERVICE OBLIGATIONS Governments may pursue the distribution of public services by imposing universal service obligations. Such obligations require a service supplier to provide basic service provisions to the whole population at an affordable rate. In the EU's Universal Service Directive, which addresses telecommunications, a universal service has been defined as a service 'available at the quality specified to all end-users in their territory, independently of geographical location, and, in the light of specific national conditions, at an affordable price'.[119] Telecommunications services are a textbook example of a sector in which universal service obligations are present. In GATS, the sector is subject to a plurilateral instrument, signed by over sixty Members, containing a set of specific commitments on telecommunications services.[120] This instrument, the Reference Paper on Basic Telecommunications, explicitly holds that:

> [a]ny Member has the right to define the kind of universal service obligation it wishes to maintain. Such obligations will not be regarded as anti-competitive per se, provided they are administered in a transparent, non-discriminatory and competitively neutral manner and are not more burdensome than necessary for the kind of universal service defined by the Member.

---

[117] Krajewski, 'Public Services and Trade Liberalization: Mapping the Legal Framework' 358.

[118] Debra Steger, *Dispute Settlement: World Trade Organization: 3.13 GATS* (United Nations Conference on Trade and Development Course on Dispute Settlement in International Trade, Investment and Intellectual Property, 2003) 9.

[119] [2002] OJ L108/33 Directive 2002/22/EC of the European Parliament and of the Council of 7 March 2002 on Universal Service and Users' Rights Relating to Electronic Communications Networks and Services Article 3.1. See, Markus Krajewski, 'Universal Service Provisions in International Agreements of the EU: From Derogation to Obligation?' in Erika Szyszczak et al. (eds), Developments in Services of General Interest (Springer 2011).

[120] Members party to the Reference Paper, including the EU, have listed it in their Schedule of specific commitments in the Additional Commitments column.

Non-discriminatory universal service obligations are not prohibited by GATS.[121] Discriminatory universal service obligations seem to be of little use from the perspective of public services provision. In sectors in which no specific commitments have been scheduled, they nonetheless remain available as long as the MFN obligation is complied with. If specific commitments have been scheduled, limitations yet allow policymakers to discriminate between domestic and foreign service suppliers concerning the universal service obligation.

In the context of the governmental authority exception, it may be questioned whether the imposition of a universal service obligation to a service supplier is not an indication that the service supplier supplies the service on a commercial basis. Consider a situation in which the service is not supplied in competition with another service supplier, for example by a monopolist. If that service supplier does not have a long-term profit seeking intention, why would a universal service obligation need to be imposed? Therefore, it is suggested that there would be few situations in which such a service is not supplied on a commercial basis.

1.2.1.5.4 THE EU'S USE OF GATS FLEXIBILITIES IN THE CASE OF PUBLIC SERVICES The EU negotiators were aware of the legal uncertainty surrounding the governmental authority exception. As noted, this is evident from the EU's care in modulating its obligations under the agreement. As concerns MFN, the EU's list of exemptions contains no mention of public services. This is unsurprising considering that there are few situations in which the MFN obligation would pose problems for public services policy. However, the Schedule of specific commitments does contain several notable aspects. First, the EU Schedule refers to universal service obligations in the context of the Reference Paper on Basic Telecommunications.

Second, although listed, some 'sensitive' public services sectors are subject to a relatively low level of specific commitments. For example, the health related and social services sector and the transport sector contain the lowest levels of specific commitments compared to all other sectors.[122] In so far as commitments have been scheduled, market access and national treatment obligations do apply. Consider, for example, higher education. Basic primary and secondary education provided by the

---

121 Marchetti and Mavroidis, 'What Are the Main Challenges for the GATS Framework? Don't Talk About Revolution' 537–538.

122 Felix Eschenbach and Bernard M Hoekman, *Services Policies in Transition Economies: On the EU and WTO as Commitment Mechanisms* (World Bank Policy Research Working Paper 3951, 2006) 23.

government is likely to fall within the scope of the governmental authority exception.[123] However, this may not be the case for certain aspects of higher education – a typical example of a partially liberalised services sector.[124] Higher education institutions often charge foreign students higher fees. Under certain interpretations of the 'on a commercial basis' condition, this could result in the conclusion that the education services supplied to foreign students are supplied on a commercial basis. This is not remedied by the fact that the profits may be used to cross-subsidise domestic students.[125] The EU Schedule reflects a cautious approach in this matter. It specifies that only privately funded services fall within the scope of the educational services sector. Consequently, the market access and national treatment obligations do not apply to publicly funded higher education services. In my example, foreign students may be charged higher fees. Privately funded educational services are covered by the specific commitments. Most EU Member States have made full commitments in Modes 1, 2 and 3 for such higher education services. Only a few Mode 4 commitments have been scheduled. This raises questions in the case of hybrid public-private financed educational services. The specific situation of a service supply would need to be evaluated on a case-by-case basis. A certain amount of private funding may change the publicly funded character of the institution.[126] This may impact on the applicability of the governmental authority exception and on the scope of the scheduled limitation.

Third, the Schedule contains a horizontal market access limitation on 'public utilities' for Mode 3 establishment. It states that 'services considered as public utilities at a national or local level may be subject to public monopolies or to exclusive rights granted to private operators'.[127] In an explanatory note to this limitation, it is explained that:

---

[123] Jasmin Tacoa-Vielma, 'Education Services' in WTO Secretariat (ed), *Guide to the GATS: An Overview of Issues for Further Liberalization of Trade in Services* (Kluwer Law International 2001) 232.

[124] Michael Moosberger, 'The GATS and Higher Education: Challenging the Nation State's Notion of the University' in Kern Alexander and Mads Andenas (eds), *The World Trade Organization and Trade in Services* (Martinus Nijhoff 2008).

[125] Krajewski, *National Regulation and Trade Liberalization in Services* 70.

[126] Krajewski, 'Public Services and Trade Liberalization: Mapping the Legal Framework' 361, at footnote 86.

[127] EU 2006 consolidated Schedule 306.

> Public utilities exist in sectors such as related scientific and technical consulting services, R&D services on social sciences and humanities, technical testing and analysis services, environmental services, health services, transport services and services auxiliary to all modes of transport. Exclusive rights on such services are often granted to private operators, for instance operators with concessions from public authorities, subject to specific service obligations. Given that public utilities often also exist at the sub-central level, detailed and exhaustive sector-specific scheduling is not practical. This limitation does not apply to telecommunications and to computer and related services.[128]

It should be noted that the listing of sectors is not exhaustive. The wording of the provision also indicates that it only covers legally established monopolies and exclusive service suppliers.[129]

The consequence of the limitation is that the market access obligation of Article XVI GATS does not apply to the establishment or authorisation of monopolies or exclusive service suppliers (in Mode 3). By virtue of Article XX:2 GATS, this also applies to the national treatment obligation in so far as the limitation is for a measure that is inconsistent with both Articles XVI and XVII GATS. Article XX:2 GATS, analysed below, notes that in such cases, a limitation shall be inscribed in the market access column but will also be considered to constitute a limitation to Article XVII, on national treatment. Hence, these monopoly or exclusive service rights may be granted without violating Article XVI or XVII GATS. It has been argued that this limitation indicates that the governmental authority exception has been interpreted narrowly by the EU.[130] However, in my opinion, the EU sought to clarify the position of its public utilities vis-à-vis its specific commitments for market access. Some questions with regard to the scope of the public utilities' limitation may nonetheless remain.[131] For example, the limitation undoubtedly applies to pre-existing monopolies and exclusive rights, but it is unclear whether this extends to future monopolies and exclusive rights. After all, Article VIII:4 GATS considers granting such rights to be a modification of the Schedule of specific commitments for which compensation is due. It has been argued that this means the limitation is not applicable to

---

[128] Ibid 306, footnote 3.

[129] These may or may not have been natural monopolies or exclusive service suppliers.

[130] Krajewski, 'Public Services and Trade Liberalization: Mapping the Legal Framework' 355.

[131] Adlung, 'Public Services and the GATS' 476.

future monopolies or exclusive service suppliers.[132] However, the wording of the limitation ('are' often granted, 'may' be subject) indicates the contrary.[133] Limitations in the Schedules are not just standstill limitations but allow measures to be taken *in the future*. Deciding otherwise would unduly limit the EU's regulatory autonomy. In my view, the application of Article VIII:4 GATS applies to situations in which *no* limitation has been scheduled. Another question is whether monopolies and exclusive rights envisaged but not yet in force at the time of scheduling are covered by the horizontal exemption.[134] In my opinion, these situations are covered for the same reasons as outlined above. Only in so far as the monopoly or exclusive rights fall outside of the limitation does the potential for a violation arise.

Within its outer limits, the EU negotiators are able to mould the 'public utilities' limitation as they see fit. The deliberate vagueness of the scope of the limitation could be considered a bargaining tactic: many services could be considered 'public utilities', and the EU's position vis-à-vis potential complaints is strengthened by the ambiguity of the wording and by the EU's refusal to list the relevant public utilities. In this sense, it becomes a strong defensive and offensive instrument. The downside to this approach is a lack of clarity as to the scope of the EU's commitments and the resulting regulatory autonomy.

1.2.2 Government procurement: a carve-out from the non-discrimination and market access obligations

Article XIII GATS on government procurement limits the scope of GATS *only* vis-à-vis the MFN, national treatment and market access obligations. According to the provision, these do not apply to laws, regulations or requirements governing government procurement of services, unless they are purchased with a view to commercial resale or use in commercial services sale.[135] Consequently, on the one hand, government procurement that *does not* fulfil these conditions is subject to all GATS obligations. On the other hand, government procurement that *does* fulfil the conditions is subject to all GATS obligations, except the abovementioned

---

[132] Ibid.

[133] Aaditya Mattoo, *Dealing with Monopolies and State Enterprises: WTO Rules for Goods and Services* (World Trade Organization Trade in Services Division Staff Working Paper TISD9801, 1997) 7.

[134] Adlung, 'Public Services and the GATS' 476.

[135] The last part of the provision seems to have been added to prevent governments from reselling services 'with a view to affording them a competitive edge over alternative supplies', ibid at note 28.

three. In any case, in addition to the applicable GATS obligations, the WTO's plurilateral Government Procurement Agreement (GPA) contains disciplines on procurement of services.[136] The EU is a party to this agreement which was renegotiated and entered into force on 6 April 2014.

2. THE SCOPE OF THE SELECTED EU RTAs FOR TRADE IN SERVICES

The scope of the services chapters of the selected EU RTAs differs from that of GATS. This is hardly surprising considering the greater possibility of excluding specific services sectors in bilateral talks over multilateral negotiations. In several ways, the scope is narrower compared to that of GATS, although in other ways it extends beyond the broad scope of GATS.

2.1 A Wider Scope

The scope of the services chapters of the selected EU RTAs is defined similarly to that of GATS, but with several distinct differences. In comparison to GATS, the emphasis lies on a differentiation based on the modes of supply, and, as a result, the term 'affecting' and its alternatives.

2.1.1 'Services' and 'supply of services'

Articles 108 EU-C&P and 77.12 EU-Georgia, which are carbon copies of Article I:3 (b) GATS, describe 'services' as any service in any sector, except services supplied in the exercise of governmental authority. Similarly, 'supply of a service', described in Article 108 EU-C&P in identical terms to Article XXVIII (b) GATS, includes the production, distribution, marketing, sale and delivery of a service. The EU-Singapore RTA does not contain such a description of services, although the definition of 'supply of a service' is included in Article 8.2 (j).

2.1.2 Modes of supply

2.1.2.1 Establishment A crucial formal difference between the selected EU RTAs[137] and GATS is the approach to modes of supply of

[136] See Article II.2 GPA.

[137] This structure of modes of supply and separate Schedules was introduced in the EU-Korea RTA. James Mathis and Eugenia Laurenza, 'Services and

services.[138] Articles 110 EU-C&P and 77.9 (a) EU-Georgia define 'establishment' as any type of business or professional establishment in any productive economic activity relating to the production of goods and supply of services through (i) the constitution, acquisition or maintenance of a juridical person (including capital participation for lasting economic links); or (ii) the creation or maintenance of a branch or representative office for the purpose of performing an economic activity.[139] This definition is wider than that of GATS Mode 3, i.e. commercial presence. Under GATS, the purpose of the establishment must be the supply of a service. GATS only applies to measures affecting trade in services, whilst Article 111 EU-C&P applies to all measures affecting establishment.[140] Additionally, the chapter falls under the title 'Trade in services, establishment and electronic commerce', indicating that establishment is not completely covered by trade in services.[141] This wider scope also explains why the definitions in the EU-C&P RTA and EU-Georgia DCFTA do not explicitly refer to Mode 3. As is the case in GATS, the disciplines cover both pre- and post-establishment phases,[142] and include services originating in the territory of establishment but delivered in the territory of another Member. From the perspective of regulatory autonomy, this approach can be criticised as the scope of the chapter on establishment may have an impact that is unexpected considering the commonplace equivalence of the terms 'Mode 3', 'commercial presence' and 'establishment' within the context of trade in services. Integrating

---

Investment in the EU – South Korea Free-Trade Area: Implications of a New Approach for GATS V Agreements and for Bilateral Investment Treaties' (2012) 13 The Journal of World Investment & Trade 157, 162–163.

[138] Although Article 8.2 (m) EU-Singapore RTA substantively replicates Article I:2 GATS in explaining the modes of supply, its chapter on cross-border trade in services nonetheless covers both Modes 1 and 2, as noted in Article 8.4 of the RTA.

[139] As per Articles 110 EU-C&P and 77.10 EU-Georgia, the term 'economic activity' does not include 'activities carried out in the exercise of governmental authority'.

[140] 'Measures of a Party affecting establishment' is explicitly defined as including 'measures with respect to all activities covered by the definition of establishment', thereby carefully avoiding limiting the scope to GATS Mode 3.

[141] The scope of establishment in the RTA perhaps bears closer resemblance to the scope of Articles 49 *juncto* 54 TFEU on the right of establishment, in so far as applicable to legal persons.

[142] Pierre Sauvé and Natasha Ward, *The EC-CARIFORUM Economic Partnership Agreement: Assessing the Outcome on Services and Investment* (European Centre for International Political Economy Paper, 2009) 12.

EU internal market law type definitions of establishment in the trade chapters of RTAs, which further contain GATS language and obligations, is confusing to say the least. The use of definitions which no longer require a link to services expands the investment-related aspects of Mode 3 *beyond* services. Applying GATS-type obligations to definitions that extend beyond the scope of GATS obfuscates the implications of these obligations.

At first sight, an almost identical approach to that in Articles 110 EU-C&P and 77.9 (a) EU-Georgia is followed in the EU-Singapore RTA. However, Article 8.8 (d) EU-Singapore notes that the economic activity should include, but not necessarily be limited to, supplying a service. This qualification would appear to limit the scope of the chapter on establishment in comparison to that of the EU-C&P RTA. Nonetheless, its scope would remain wider than that of GATS Mode 3.[143] Moreover, the limitation is unlikely to be of practical relevance: in today's world, it is easy to imagine that most undertakings active in a territory would, or could easily, supply *a* service, next to its perhaps non-services core business. If the establishment rules are sufficiently attractive, it would suffice for an undertaking to add the supply of one service to its activities in order to benefit from these rules.[144]

This wider scope based on the definition of establishment would be mitigated if the Schedules for establishment were limited to services. In such a case, the impact of the wider scope would be limited to ancillary establishment of activities in services sectors. A look at the Schedules reveals,[145] however, that this is not the case. In Annex VII Section B of the EU-C&P RTA, in addition to the expected services sectors, the following non-services sectors are listed: (i) agriculture, hunting, forestry; (ii) fishing and aquaculture; (iii) mining and quarrying; (iv) manufacturing; and (v) production, transmission and distribution on own

---

[143] Moreover, the EU-Singapore RTA contains a Chapter 9 on investment, which covers all establishment, with or without the provision of services.

[144] See National Board of Trade Sweden, *Everybody is in Services – The Impact of Servicification in Manufacturing on Trade and Trade Policy* (Kommerskollegium 2012:6, 2012); Sherry M Stephenson, 'Services and Global Value Chains' in World Economic Forum Global Agenda Council on the Global Trade System (ed), *The Shifting Geography of Global Value Chains: Implications for Developing Countries and Trade Policy* (World Economic Forum, 2012); and National Board of Trade Sweden, *Global Value Chains and Services – An Introduction* (Kommerskollegium 2013:1, 2013).

[145] This is a relatively consistent practice in EU RTAs that include Schedules for services liberalisation. See, for example, Annex IV-A EU-CARIFORUM; Annex 7-A-2 EU-Korea; Annex X EU-Central America.

account of electricity, gas, steam and hot water (excluding nuclear-based electricity generation). In addition to the W/120, on which GATS Schedules are usually based, (vi) services auxiliary to transport; and (vii) energy services are also added. Annex 8-A-2 of the EU-Singapore RTA contains the same services and non-services sectors and adds another services sector, 'other transport services'. In Annex XIV-A of the EU-Georgia DCFTA, the same sectors are found, with the addition of 'production, transmission and distribution of steam and hot water' (i.e. excluding 'for own account', which is a separately listed sector).

The importance of this finding must not be underestimated. Obligations applicable to 'establishment' (these are, *inter alia*, national treatment and market access obligations) are extended far beyond the scope of service suppliers. Looking from the perspective of GATS, this is quite unexpected. From the perspective of EU law, this is much less so. Nonetheless, as noted, the RTAs extend legal obligations and concepts that are designed to apply to establishment *in so far as linked to trade in services*, to establishment without the necessity of such a link. In so far as GATS Mode 3 already overlaps with the right of establishment – as a part of investment protection – the RTAs extend this overlap into the realm of establishment *tout court*. In summary, 'services are a part of what is being scheduled as an aspect of cross-border investment, but are no longer defining the scope of what is being committed'.[146] However, the question must be raised whether incorporating these non-services-related investment commitments in a way which appears to be based on GATS language and scheduling techniques is acceptable from the perspective of regulatory autonomy.[147] Certainly, in the context of, for example, Stabilisation and Association Agreements or the new generation of DCFTAs, it can be argued that the political incentive to extend (part of) the EU internal market to neighbouring countries is sufficiently strong to allow such an approach. However, in 'true' trade agreements, such as the EU-C&P or EU-Singapore RTAs, this is much less expected. Understanding this widening of the scope of GATS Mode 3 is key from the

[146] Mathis and Laurenza, 'Services and Investment in the EU – South Korea Free-Trade Area: Implications of a New Approach for GATS V Agreements and for Bilateral Investment Treaties' 158.

[147] Post scriptum: this may be why in CETA, there is no longer a chapter on 'establishment'. In that agreement, there are chapters for cross-border trade in services (i.e. GATS Modes 1 and 2, see below) and temporary presence of natural persons for business persons (i.e. a more narrow GATS Mode 4, see below), and an integrated chapter for investment that includes the 'establishment' as covered here.

perspective of regulatory autonomy, viewing the issue from the perspective of multilateral trade in services.

Finally, in addition to the above, Article 77.9 (b) EU-Georgia adds that establishment includes the right of natural persons to pursue economic activities as self-employed persons or by setting up undertakings which they effectively control. This addition widens the scope of the agreement's establishment provisions in two ways. First, including economic activities pursued by self-employed persons partially broadens the scope of establishment to include some services covered by GATS Mode 4. The overlap with the RTA alternative to Mode 4, i.e. temporary presence of natural persons for business purposes, is limited because, as addressed below, the latter is limited to specific categories of natural persons. Including such rights for natural persons is coherent with the right of establishment in EU law as provided for in Article 49 TFEU. Second, the explicit inclusion of undertakings set up and controlled by natural persons in the definition of establishment points at the difficulties in differentiating between Modes 3 and 4: commercial presence often requires the presence of natural persons.[148] In this case, it would seem that the entry of a natural person into a market, even with the intention of setting up an undertaking, precedes the setting up of the business. However, this situation would not be covered by GATS Mode 4, as it is more likely to be a matter of migration: at the moment of crossing the border, there is no 'international' service supply.[149] Hence, it is submitted that GATS would not apply. (Additionally, the temporary nature of Mode 4 services supply would exclude this situation from its scope.) If the natural person returns abroad and remotely remains in control, i.e. from outside the business's location, the situation may be covered by GATS Mode 3, but probably only in a post-establishment phase. In the DCFTA, this situation is covered by the chapter on establishment. Lastly, and this applies to both situations outlined above, the DCFTA goes further as it is not limited to the supply of services but includes any type of economic activity.

2.1.2.2 Cross-border trade in services Articles 117 EU-C&P, 8.4 EU-Singapore and 77.14 EU-Georgia define cross-border supply of

---

[148] Zacharias, 'Article I GATS' 53.

[149] Paragraph 1 of the GATS Annex on Movement of Natural Persons Supplying Services under the Agreement notes that it applies to measures affecting natural persons who are service suppliers of a Member in respect of the supply of a service. The latter condition would not be fulfilled in the example at hand.

services as encompassing both Mode 1 and Mode 2 supply of services. Although no explicit reference to GATS is made, the introduction of these terms through the use of the terms 'Mode 1' or 'Mode 2' clearly indicates an intent to interpret this as GATS Modes 1 and 2, as defined in Article I:2 (a) and (b) GATS. Combining these two modes of supply into one is perhaps unsurprising, as difficulties have arisen in GATS scholarship when trying to distinguish between Modes 1 and 2 – as noted above.

2.1.2.3 Temporary presence of natural persons for business purposes

The RTA alternative to GATS Mode 4 is 'temporary presence of natural persons for business purposes'. The definitions applied vis-à-vis this mode of supply of 'services' are very specific, setting out requirements for various categories of service suppliers to which the obligations apply. In the case of the EU-C&P RTA and the EU-Georgia DCFTA, these are key personnel, graduate trainees, business service sellers, contractual service suppliers, independent professionals and short-term visitors for business purposes. Definitions for these categories are inscribed in Articles 123 EU-C&P, 8.13 EU-Singapore and 88 EU-Georgia, corresponding largely with the definitions for Mode 4 in the EU's GATS Schedule. The maximum duration of the stay of the natural person depends on the category. For example, graduate trainees for ICT from Colombia or Peru may remain in the EU for up to three years. This limited scope reflects the EU's intention, as is also evident from its GATS commitments, discussed above, to use Mode 4 primarily to allow for the temporary presence of high-skilled workers. However, these definitions are not restricted to *services* for all covered categories of natural persons: nothing in the definitions of business visitors, graduate trainees, or intra-corporate transferees requires a link with the supply of services.[150] In the EU-Georgia DCFTA, Article 88.2 (c) defines 'business sellers' with explicit reference to trade in goods, which explains the change in terminology from 'business services sellers' in the EU-C&P RTA. Therefore, the scope of this 'mode of supply', as with establishment, extends beyond trade in services.

The obligations on temporary presence in the EU-C&P RTA only apply to listed sectors for contractual service suppliers, and independent professionals and short-term visitors for business purposes, as listed respectively in Articles 126.2–3, 127.2–3 and 128.1 EU-C&P. For

[150] Rudolf Adlung and Peter Morrison, 'Less than the GATS: "Negative Preferences" in Regional Services Agreements' (2010) 13 Journal of International Economic Law 1103, 1129.

business visitors, the listed activities for which the temporary stay is endeavoured to be facilitated do not appear to include activities that cannot be considered services. For key personnel and graduate trainees, the Schedule for establishment applies, including its reservations and the specific reservations for temporary presence of natural persons for business purposes in Annex IX. Thus, the broad scope of the establishment Schedules, including non-services sectors, is extended to these categories of natural persons. Similarly, in the EU-Georgia DCFTA, the obligations apply to sectors for which commitments (including reservations in separate Annexes) are made concerning establishment for key personnel, i.e. business visitors and intra-corporate transferees, and graduate trainees. For business sellers, commitments on cross-border service supply are also taken into account, again subject to specific reservations. All three categories of natural persons thus extend beyond the notion of service suppliers. Additionally, a separate Schedule is provided for contractual service suppliers. In Articles 8.13–8.15 EU-Singapore, only (i) key personnel and graduate trainees and (ii) business service sellers are covered. Again, the definitions of these categories are specific, and are limited to sectors for which specific commitments on establishment (both categories (i) and (ii)) or cross-border supply of services (only category (ii)) have been undertaken. For this RTA, too, the scope of natural persons covered by the commitments for key personnel and graduate trainees extends beyond service suppliers.

Considering the relatively narrow definitions for business visitors, graduate trainees, or intra-corporate transferees, and, in the case of the EU-Georgia DCFTA, business sellers, this broader scope may not be overly problematic. However, it appears symptomatic of the way in which traditional conceptions related to trade in *services* are being adapted in the EU's RTAs to cater for broader liberalisation. As with establishment, this broader scope constitutes a key understanding that must inform the following analysis of the obligations in the RTAs vis-à-vis the temporary presence of natural persons for business purposes.

2.1.3 Measures 'adopted or maintained by a Party', 'affecting' and 'concerning'

A 'measure' in the context of the services chapters includes any measure by a Party in any kind of form. Articles 108 EU-C&P, 8.2 (f) EU-Singapore and 77.2 EU-Georgia reproduce Article I:3 (a) GATS in comprising central, regional and local governments and authorities and non-governmental bodies in the exercise of powers delegated by such governments and authorities. Articles 118 EU-C&P, 8.3 EU-Singapore and 83 EU-Georgia mirror GATS, as these provisions apply to measures of the parties 'affecting' cross-border service supply. Here, 'affecting' should be interpreted identically to Article I:1 GATS. Where GATS only refers to measures 'by' Members, Articles 111 EU-C&P, 8.9 EU-Singapore and 78 EU-Georgia on establishment apply to measures that are 'adopted or maintained', highlighting that the RTA disciplines are not merely standstill provisions. The practical consequence of this wording is limited, as the key GATS disciplines also apply to existing measures.[151] Nonetheless, in combination with the potentially wide scope of the establishment chapters, as discussed in the previous section, this contributes to the forceful language of the establishment disciplines. Lastly, according to Articles 122 EU-C&P, 8.13 EU-Singapore and 88.1 EU-Georgia, all measures of a party 'concerning' entry and temporary stay of the specific categories of natural persons are covered by the relevant provisions. The use of the term 'concerning' instead of 'affecting' indicates a broader scope of these provisions.[152] Considering the already broad interpretation granted to 'affecting', it seems defensible that even measures which, in principle, affect other modes of supply could concern the entry and temporary stay of natural persons. For example, a measure that restricts cross-border trade in services may incentivise natural persons to cross the border in order to supply a service. Again, as concerns this term, the scope of application is broader than under GATS.

2.2 Exemptions from the Scope

2.2.1 Exemptions applicable to all modes of supply

The chapters on trade in services and establishment are limited by several explicit exemptions:

a. Articles 107.2 EU-C&P, 8.2 (d) EU-Singapore and 76.2 EU-Georgia exclude government procurement of services. However, Article 173 EU-C&P, 10.2 EU-Singapore and 142 EU-Georgia, which set out the scope of the respective chapters on government procurement, do include trade in services.
b. Articles 107.3 EU-C&P, 8.2 (a) EU-Singapore and 76.3 EU-Georgia exclude subsidies or grants, including government-supported loans, guarantees and insurance. This exemption is

---

[151] Article VI:5 GATS is an exception to this rule, see below.

[152] Angus Stevenson (ed) *Oxford Dictionary of English (Online Version)* (Oxford University Press 2014), where 'to concern' is defined, among other definitions, as 'to have relation or reference to; to refer to, relate to; to be about'.

notable considering the application of GATS to subsidies as measures affecting trade in services, in so far as specific commitments have been scheduled and no limitations are inscribed. This highlights the importance of subsidies as a policy instrument,[153] including the use of discriminatory subsidies.[154]

c. Articles 107.4 *juncto* 108 EU-C&P, 8.2 (b) EU-Singapore and 77 (l) EU-Georgia exclude services supplied in the exercise of governmental authority. The same conditions apply as under Article I:3 (c) GATS to establish governmental authority.[155] Considering the identical wording, it is submitted that the interpretation of the governmental authority exception in the RTAs should be identical to the one proposed in the context of Article I:2 GATS.

In addition to the governmental authority exception, the public utilities limitation in the EU's GATS Schedule is of paramount importance. The RTAs contain similar limitations. Annex VII Section B of the EU-C&P RTA, Appendix 8-A-2 of the EU-Singapore RTA and Annex XIV-A of the EU-Georgia DCFTA contain a public utilities limitation for establishment, that '[e]conomic activities considered as public utilities at a national or local level may be subject to public monopolies or to exclusive rights granted to private operators'. Interpretative footnote 6 to Appendix 8-A-2 EU-Singapore states:

---

153 This is also evident from the EU GATS Schedule, in which a horizontal Mode 3 national treatment limitation for subsidies is included. The limitation holds that eligibility for subsidies may be limited to juridical persons established within the territory of a Member State. Public sector services may be subsidised, and no commitment is undertaken for subsidies relating to research and development. For Mode 4, subsidies may be reserved for nationals of an EU Member State. EU 2006 consolidated Schedule 15–17.

154 Discriminatory subsidies are to be preferred over e.g. entry restrictions for foreign services and service suppliers because they can be better targeted. Brian Copeland and Aaditya Mattoo, 'The Basic Economics of Services Trade' in Aaditya Mattoo, Robert M Stern and Gianni Zanini (eds), *A Handbook of International Trade in Services* (Oxford University Press 2008) 116.

155 Annex XI to the EU-C&P RTA contains an Understanding concerning subparagraph (b) of the definition of 'services supplied in the exercise of governmental authority'. The Understanding only applies between the EU and Peru, and only relates to the definition of the governmental authority exception in so far as it applies to financial services. This Annex does not indicate that a different interpretation of the 'general' governmental authority exception is required. Article 10.1 (p) EU-Singapore, establishing the definition of 'privatised' in the chapter on government procurement, also mentions governmental authority without providing a different interpretation.

> Given that public utilities often also exist at the sub-central level, detailed and exhaustive sector-specific listing is not practical. To facilitate comprehension, specific footnotes in this list of commitments will indicate in an illustrative and non-exhaustive way those sectors where public utilities play a major role.

Footnote 201 to Annex VII Section B of the EU-C&P RTA is identical to the interpretative footnote 6 to Appendix 8-A-2 EU-Singapore, as is footnote 8 to Annex XIV-A of the EU-Georgia DCFTA.

In the case of the EU-Singapore RTA, as is the case under GATS, the public utilities limitation does not apply to telecommunications and computer and related services according to footnote 7. This is replicated in footnote 8 to Annex XIV-A of the EU-Georgia DCFTA, which is more elaborate and is identical to the EU's GATS limitation on public utilities. Hence, the public utilities limitation in the EU-C&P RTA is wider than that under GATS or under the EU-Singapore and EU-Georgia agreements, as it may also apply to telecommunications and computer and related services.

d. An extraordinary addition to the governmental authority exception can be found in Articles 167.2 EU-C&P and 134.3 EU-Georgia, which contain the general exceptions for the services and establishment chapters. These paragraphs do not contain an exception but rather a carve-out from the scope of these chapters. They state that the provisions of the respective title or chapter, including the annexes in which the Schedules of specific commitments are incorporated, shall not apply 'to activities in the territory of each Party, which are connected, even occasionally, with the exercise of official authority'. (In the EU-C&P RTA, this carve-out also applies to the title on current payments and movement of capital.) This carve-out, buried at the back of the services chapters in an additional paragraph to the well-known Articles XX GATT 1994 and XIV GATS-type general exceptions, is of utmost importance for regulatory autonomy. Although their wording is vague, the broad reach of the carve-out is immediately clear from its wording. Whereas two conditions need to be fulfilled for a measure to fall within the scope of the governmental authority exception, no such conditions apply here. In order to fall within the scope of the carve-out, it is merely required that activities are (i) connected, even if only occasionally, with (ii) the exercise of (iii) official authority.

First, it should be reiterated that, in the context of the governmental authority exception, no definition of 'governmental authority' is necessary to interpret that exception. However, as observed, some have noted that 'governmental authority' is a third condition for the application of the governmental authority exception – a submission which I refute. Governmental authority, albeit in the context of Article 1.1 (a) (1) SCM Agreement, has been interpreted as meaning 'the authority to perform governmental functions'.[156] The Panel in *US – Carbon Steel (India)* continued that:

> To determine whether an entity has governmental authority, an investigating authority must evaluate the core features of the entity and its relationship to government. Governmental control of the entity is relevant if that control is 'meaningful'.[157]

Meaningful control may be established through 'a combination of government shareholding plus other factors indicative of control'.[158] Similarly, the Panel in *China – Intellectual Property Rights* defined 'authority', in the context of Article 59 of the Agreement on Trade-Related Aspects of Intellectual Property Rights, as 'power or right to enforce obedience; moral or legal supremacy; right to command or give a final decision'.[159] From these interpretations, it seems as if 'authority' and 'governmental authority' are very alike concepts. Therefore, it is submitted that the term 'official authority' is merely used to distinguish between the governmental authority exception and the present carve-out. This is confirmed by the ordinary meaning of the term 'official', which includes 'Derived from, or having the sanction of, persons in office; authorized or supported by a government, organization, etc.'.[160]

---

[156] *United States – Countervailing Measures on Certain Hot-Rolled Carbon Steel Flat Products from India* WT/DS436/R, Panel report adopted 19 December 2014 para. 7.80, interpreting the *US – Anti-Dumping and Countervailing Duties (China) (AB)* paras 288, 290 and 317–319.

[157] *US – Carbon Steel (India) (Panel)* para. 7.80. Also see Zacharias, 'Article I GATS' 61, who argues that governmental authority requires 'command and control'.

[158] *US – Carbon Steel (India) (Panel)* para. 7.81; *United States – Countervailing Measures on Certain Hot-Rolled Carbon Steel Flat Products from India* WT/DS436/AB/R, AB report adopted 19 December 2014 para. 4.36.

[159] *China – Measures Affecting the Protection and Enforcement of Intellectual Property Rights* WT/DS362/R, Panel report adopted 20 March 2009 para. 7.236.

[160] Stevenson, *Oxford Dictionary of English (Online Version)*.

Second, the expression 'in the exercise of' could indicate that a service must also be delivered by the government or on its behalf.[161] This is confirmed by the ordinary meaning of the noun 'exercise', which includes 'The action of employing in its appropriate activity (an organ, a faculty, or power), of giving practical effect to (a right)'.[162]

Third, the carve-out applies to activities *connected*, even occasionally, with the exercise of official authority. The required nexus between the activity and the exercise of official authority is thus one of being 'connected'. The term 'in connection with' features in Articles I:1, II:1 (b), II:1 (c), V, the Ad Note to VII:1, VIII:1 (a), VIII:4, XIII:3 (a), the Ad Note to Article XIII:4, XV:5, and the Ad Note to Article XXXVII:1 (a) GATT 1994. In the context of these provisions, the term has been interpreted in WTO case law. The Panel in *China – Auto Parts* explained that the term 'in connection with' is broad language:

> Had the framers of the GATT considered the term 'on importation' as synonymous with the term 'in connection with importation', irrespective of the context in which these terms are laid out, they would have simply used one or the other not both.[163]

A fortiori, had the RTA negotiators wanted to limit the scope of the carve-out to activities in the exercise of official authority, they would not have chosen the broader language of 'in connection with'.[164] However, this Panel's reasoning would indicate that the activity that *is* the official authority is *not* excluded, as applying the carve-out does not state both 'in the exercise of official authority' and 'connected with the exercise of official authority', but only the latter. This interpretation leads to the result where services supplied in the exercise of governmental authority are excluded only if they fulfil the abovementioned conditions, whereas activities connected

---

161 VanDuzer, 'Health, Education and Social Services in Canada: The Impact of the GATS' 385.

162 Stevenson, *Oxford Dictionary of English (Online Version)*.

163 *China – Measures Affecting Imports of Automobile Parts* WT/DS339/R, WT/DS340/R, WT/DS342/R, Panel report adopted 12 January 2009 para. 7.177; see, similarly, *China – Measures Related to the Exportation of Various Raw Materials* WT/DS394/R / WT/DS395/R / WT/DS398/R, Panel report adopted 22 February 2012 paras 7.824–7.832 and 7.839.

164 'The other' could be considered to be the governmental authority exception.

with the exercise of official authority (but not *in the exercise of* governmental authority) are excluded without needing to fulfil these conditions. This outcome is quite unexpected. The Panels in *India – Autos* and *US – Poultry (China)* took a related approach, and explained that:

> 'in connection with importation' […] not only encompasses measures which directly relate to the process of importation but could also include those measures which relate to other aspects of the importation of a product or have an impact on actual importation.[165]

Again, *a fortiori*, this could mean that the carve-out for activities connected to official authority must be considered as a very broad carve-out, especially considering the addition of 'even occasionally'. In this reading, it includes the activities *in the exercise of* but also *in connection with the exercise of*. However, this broad interpretation raises the question of the relationship between the official authority carve-out and the governmental authority carve-out. It appears that there is no interpretation possible where the governmental authority exception is not entirely covered by the official authority carve-out. Considering the insertion of the official authority carve-out in the general exceptions provision, one wonders whether the governmental authority exception was merely left in the final text of the agreements as an additional safeguard for these services, or whether the negotiators foresaw another meaning for the official authority carve-out.

In summary, neither interpretation is fully satisfactory, but either way, the carve-out can be construed in a quite broad manner.

Finally, it is surprising that in the EU-Singapore RTA, no such carve-out can be found. Therefore, in the context of that agreement, the governmental authority exception continues to be of relevance.

e. Again, as is the case under GATS, Articles 107.6 EU-C&P, 8.4 EU-Singapore and 76.5 EU-Georgia exclude measures affecting natural persons seeking access to the employment market of a party and measures regarding citizenship, residence or permanent employment.

f. Whereas GATS does not explicitly exempt social security systems from the scope of its obligations, the governmental authority exception and the scheduled 'public utilities' limitation indicate that

[165] *India – Autos (Panel)* para. 7.257; *United States – Certain Measures Affecting Imports of Poultry from China* WT/DS392/R, Panel report adopted 25 October 2010 para. 7.410.

a substantial amount of services related to social security systems may, in the case of the EU, be excluded from scrutiny under GATS. Nonetheless, whether this is the case should be assessed on a case-by-case basis. The same approach was followed in the EU-Singapore RTA. This is not the case in the EU-C&P and EU-Georgia RTAs. Articles 167 EU-C&P and 134 EU-Georgia, comprising the general exceptions, contain an additional sub-paragraph addressing social security systems. The respective paragraphs 2 and 3 of these provisions state that the chapters on establishment and cross-border trade in services shall not apply to the respective social security systems of the parties. For the EU-C&P, this also applies to obligations on capital transactions. The importance of this exclusion should not be underestimated from the perspective of regulatory autonomy, as it takes away the legal uncertainty regarding the precise meaning of the governmental authority exception and the public utilities limitation vis-à-vis social security systems. The exact scope of the term 'social security system' remains unclear. GATS is the sole WTO agreement that explicitly references the term (system of) 'social security',[166] but it does not define the term. According to the *Oxford English Dictionary*, 'social security' means 'A state-run system providing financial support for people who are unemployed, sick, retired, or otherwise in need' and 'The money paid out under such a system'.[167] The suggested interpretation of this exclusion – confusingly included in an *exceptions* provision – is that measures that would fall within the scope of these chapters, are excluded only in so far as the contrary would burden the domestic social security system. This is the case because the Schedule contains commitments for health and social services that are privately funded. In order to give meaning to these commitments, the exclusion can only apply in so far as the term 'social security system' is restricted to the state-run aspects of the social security system and not applied, for example, to private operators who provide additional, but similar, services. A case-by-case analysis is nonetheless necessary, for instance where an obligatory service is provided by private enterprises.

---

[166] Paragraph 1 (b) (ii) of the Annex on Financial Services notes that the governmental authority exception should, in the context of financial services, be understood to include 'activities forming part of a statutory system of social security or public retirement plans'.

[167] Stevenson, *Oxford Dictionary of English (Online Version).*

g. The first paragraph of Articles 296 EU-C&P and 17.6 EU-Singapore states that the RTA shall only apply to taxation measures to the extent that such application is necessary to give effect to the provisions of the RTA. This exemption should be read together with the exceptions for taxation. The EU-Georgia DCFTA does not contain an equivalent provision.

With the exception of the exclusion for social security, most of these horizontal exclusions are mainly reminiscent of GATS, and are common exclusions in the services chapters of RTAs.[168] The exclusion of subsidies and grants is an important novelty from the perspective of regulatory autonomy. This exclusion may be considered exemplary in the sense that it preserves regulatory autonomy to a considerable extent, without compromising on legal certainty and transparency vis-à-vis other parties, and, as noted, on efficiency. The most notable exemption is the official authority carve-out in the EU-C&P and EU-Georgia RTAs, which appears to be a broader sibling to the governmental authority exception. In either interpretation proposed here it has the potential to exempt a much larger amount of services from the scope of the services chapters. From the perspective of regulatory autonomy, this carve-out clearly mitigates any additional constraints, compared to GATS, from the scope of the services chapters. This exclusion can be said to be an important GATS– provision.

2.2.2 Specific exemptions per mode of supply

Articles 111 (a)–(f) EU-C&P, 8.9 EU-Singapore and 78 EU-Georgia exempt several specific services sectors from the scope of the provisions on establishment, for example audio-visual services or services related to toxic waste. Articles 118 (a)–(c) EU-C&P, 8.3 EU-Singapore and 83 EU-Georgia contain fewer exemptions for cross-border trade in services (but those listed are substantively identical to the exemptions on establishment). In comparison to GATS, bilateral agreements need to cater only for the interests of the signatory parties. Hence, there is more potential to agree on excluding specific services from the scope of the agreement. In the case of GATS, a similar result in practical terms could be achieved by not scheduling specific commitments and by inscribing MFN exemptions (as the EU has done, for example for audio-visual services). Nonetheless, the exclusion of specific services offers both

---

[168] Federico Ortino, 'Services' in Simon Lester and Bryan Mercurio (eds), *Bilateral and Regional Trade Agreements: Commentary and Analysis* (Cambridge University Press 2009) 200–201.

greater legal certainty and ensures that the services are not subjected to *any* obligation. As explained above, under the GATS regime, certain obligations apply unconditionally.

From the perspective of regulatory autonomy, the importance of these exclusions is less systemically relevant than the horizontal exemptions. However, the EU's ability to negotiate these exemptions in a bilateral context in which GATS+ obligations arise, is important as it allows (relatively) specific defensive interests to be addressed. As noted, the benefit is legal certainty. The clear disadvantage is a less comprehensive scope, especially vis-à-vis obligations which are useful for trade liberalisation purposes but are less intrusive with regards to regulatory autonomy. The fragmentation of the international regulation of trade in services, which results from exempting specific services sectors, is to be discouraged for two reasons. First, the interests which lead to the exclusion of specific services may change over time, but it may prove difficult to renegotiate the exemptions. Second, although specific situations may justify an exemption, in most cases regulatory autonomy should be sufficiently preserved through the horizontal exemptions. For example, the goals of the 'cultural exception' for audio-visual services, i.e. the preservation of cultural pluralism, may well be achieved without excluding these services from the scope of the services chapters.[169]

[169] See Bregt Natens, 'Chronicle of a Death Foretold? The Cultural Exception for Audio-Visual Services in EU Trade Negotiations' (2014) 41 Legal Issues of Economic Integration 367.

4. Non-discrimination

1. NON-DISCRIMINATION OBLIGATIONS IN GATS

GATS contains two main non-discrimination obligations. The MFN obligation in Article II GATS, which applies to all measures covered by the agreement, is probably GATS' most important unconditional obligation. Article XVII GATS contains a national treatment obligation, which applies solely to sectors for which specific commitments have been scheduled. The case law addressing these obligations under GATS has focused on the national treatment obligation. Many of the interpretations of Article XVII GATS are directly relevant to Article II GATS. Therefore, national treatment is addressed first.

1.1 The National Treatment Obligation

1.1.1 The scope of the obligation

Article XVII:1 GATS requires Members to accord treatment no less favourable to services or service suppliers of any other Member than that treatment which it accords to its own similar services or service suppliers. The obligation applies to *all* measures affecting trade in services in sectors for which specific commitments have been scheduled, in so far as these commitments are not subject to scheduled limitations.

The scope of the national treatment obligation is not limited to *actual* service suppliers. The Panel in *EC – Bananas III* considered some *potential* service suppliers relevant to the assessment of the national treatment obligation: vertically integrated companies, which on the facts of *EC – Bananas III* are existing incumbents in the relevant *market*, are relevant potential service suppliers.[1] The AB did not address the issue of potential service suppliers explicitly, but narrowed the Panel's finding by referring only to *existing* banana companies. At the time, these companies did not supply the service. Nonetheless, they were clearly capable

[1] *European Communities – Regime for the Importation, Sale and Distribution of Bananas* WT/DS27/R, Panel report adopted 25 September 1997 para. 7.320.

of supplying the service. As such, the scope of the potential service suppliers which can be considered was limited.[2] It may be noted that this approach is similar to the above interpretation of the 'in competition with' condition in the context of the governmental authority exception. In *Canada – Autos*, the GATS-consistency of a measure granting import duty exemptions to a closed category of service suppliers was under scrutiny.[3] The Panel noted that *potential* competition suffices to establish less favourable treatment.[4] The AB did not uphold the Panel finding of less favourable treatment, albeit for unrelated reasons.[5] Taking into account potential service supplies could mean that potential service suppliers, even those lacking the capacity or ability to supply like services, can be like service suppliers to those who actually supply the service.[6] Still, these findings could have important repercussions for regulatory autonomy. If potential service suppliers have a right to non-discriminatory treatment, the scope of obligations as concerns regulations dealing with investment could be extended considerably, even if such regulations do not directly or predominantly deal with services.[7]

An important territorial limitation to the scope of GATS may be found in the 1993 and 2001 Scheduling Guidelines, which note that Article XVII GATS does not require a Member to extend treatment no less favourable to a service supplier located in the territory of another Member.[8] This applies only in so far as the measure entails *positive*

---

[2] *European Communities – Regime for the Importation, Sale and Distribution of Bananas* WT/DS27/AB/R, AB report adopted 25 September 1997, paras 223–227 as interpreted by Werner Zdouc, 'WTO Dispute Settlement Practice Relating to the General Agreement on Trade in Services' in Federico Ortino and Ernst-Ulrich Petersmann (eds), *The WTO Dispute Settlement System 1995–2003* (Kluwer Law International 2004) 400.

[3] *Canada – Certain Measures Affecting the Automotive Industry* WT/DS139/R, WT/DS142/R, Panel report adopted 19 June 2000 para. 10.246.

[4] Ibid para. 10.253, reversed by *Canada – Certain Measures Affecting the Automotive Industry* WT/DS139/AB/R, WT/DS142/AB/R, AB report adopted 19 June 2000 paras 172–174.

[5] *Canada – Autos (AB)* paras 181–182; see below.

[6] Zdouc, 'WTO Dispute Settlement Practice Relating to the General Agreement on Trade in Services' 400.

[7] Werner Zdouc, 'WTO Dispute Settlement Practice Relating to the GATS' (1999) 2 Journal of International Economic Law 295, 327.

[8] General Agreement on Tariffs and Trade, MTN.GNS/W/164, Scheduling of Initial Commitments in Trade in Services: Explanatory Note (3 September) para. 10; S/L/92 2001 Scheduling Guidelines para. 15.

action from the government.[9] As will be explained below, regardless of the mode of supply, a like service supplied by a like service supplier in the territory of the Member that enacts the measure, could claim that these fall within the national treatment obligation.

1.1.2 Likeness

The interpretation of 'likeness', a term found in various key WTO provisions, remains highly complex, although the concept has been interpreted repeatedly in WTO case law. Its relevance for regulatory autonomy is clear: 'the broader the WTO adjudicating bodies construe the concept of "likeness", the more intrusive the non-discrimination obligation becomes, which in turn intensifies the obligation's liberalizing effect'.[10] Moreover, the interpretation of 'likeness' is crucial for the scope of regulatory autonomy because Article XIV GATS, the general exceptions clause, does not include all legitimate policy objectives that may require distinctions between services and service suppliers: hence, a comprehensive analysis of likeness is necessary to avoid objectionable constraints on regulatory autonomy.[11]

1.1.2.1 Likeness in the national treatment and Most-Favoured-Nation obligations Both the MFN obligation of Article II GATS, addressed in the following section, and the national treatment obligation, contain a likeness test. The Panel in *EC – Bananas III*, addressing Article II GATS for the first time, turned to Article XVII GATS for interpretative guidance.[12] The AB, however, overruled the Panel and stated that, although not necessarily irrelevant, the 'Panel would have been on safer ground had it compared the MFN obligation in Article II of the GATS

---

[9] See P Poretti, *The Regulation of Subsidies Within the General Agreement on Trade in Services of the WTO: Problems and Prospects* (Kluwer 2009) 142; and, opposing, B De Meester and D Coppens, 'Mode 3 of the GATS: A Model for Disciplining Measures Affecting Investment Flows?' in Z Drabek and PC Mavroidis (eds), *Regulation of Foreign Investment: Challenges to International Harmonization* (World Scientific 2013) 136–137.

[10] Nicolas Diebold, *Non-Discrimination in International Trade in Services: 'Likenes' in WTO/GATS* (Cambridge University Press 2010) 2–3.

[11] Frieder Roessler, 'Increasing Market Access Under Regulatory Heterogeneity: The Strategies of the World Trade Organisation' in OECD (ed), *Regulatory Reform and International Market Openness* (OECD 1996) 121–122.

[12] See *EC – Bananas III (Panel)* para. 7.350; *Canada – Autos (Panel)* para. 10.247.

with the MFN and MFN-type obligations in the GATT 1994'.[13] Nonetheless, and although not necessarily contrary to the AB's findings, in the specific context of trade in services, it has been argued by several leading scholars that likeness in Articles II and XVII GATS should be interpreted identically.[14] Of course, the services and service suppliers that are to be compared differ, as the MFN obligation requires an assessment of the likeness of services and service suppliers *originating in different foreign countries*.[15] For the national treatment obligation, the relevant comparison is between domestic services and service suppliers, and foreign ones.

1.1.2.2 Likeness of services and/or of service suppliers? The likeness tests in Articles II and XVII GATS both make reference to treatment granted to 'like services and service suppliers'. These references demand an answer to a key question regarding GATS likeness: do the services *and* the service suppliers need to be like, or, is the likeness of one sufficient for both? The introduction of service suppliers into the likeness analysis has important repercussions, in comparison with the likeness analysis under GATT 1994. On the one hand, introducing service suppliers 'expands the *prohibitive* effect', as discrimination of foreign services suppliers is prohibited, on the other hand, 'it equally expands the *permissive* effect', as differences not related to the service but related to the service supplier, i.e. the 'production or process', 'can clearly justify at least certain forms of differential treatment'.[16]

The Panels in *EC – Bananas III* and *Canada – Autos* were the first to address likeness in GATS. In assessing whether the wording of the test constitutes a double requirement of likeness of both service *and* service supplier, these Panels stated respectively that 'at least to the extent that entities provide these like services, they are like service suppliers' and 'to the extent that the service suppliers concerned supply the same services,

---

13 *EC – Bananas III (AB)* para. 231.

14 Mitsuo Matsushita, Thomas J Schoenbaum and Petros C Mavroidis, *The World Trade Organization: Law, Practice and Policy* (2nd edn, Oxford University Press 2006) 620; Diebold, *Non-Discrimination in International Trade in Services: 'Likeness' in WTO/GATS* 139. Also see *EC – Bananas III (Panel)* para. 7.346, referring to its likeness findings under the assessment of Article XVII GATS.

15 *EC – Bananas III (Panel)* para. 6.94.

16 Joost Pauwelyn, 'The Unbearable Lightness of Likeness' in Marion Panizzon, Nicole Pohl and Pierre Sauvé (eds), *GATS and the Regulation of International Trade in Services* (Cambridge University Press 2008) 359 (emphasis original).

they should be considered 'like' for the purpose of this case'.[17] It must be stressed that, in both cases, the respondent did not claim that the services and service suppliers were unlike. As such, the interpretation of likeness was not a decisive issue.[18] However, the approach taken in these cases does appear circular, as it defines the likeness of the service supplier on the basis of the likeness of the service.[19] In a later case, the Panel's attention shifted focus towards the likeness of the service supplier, arguing that:

> when origin is the only factor on which a measure bases a difference of treatment between domestic service suppliers and foreign suppliers, the 'like service suppliers' requirement is met, provided there will, or can, be domestic and foreign suppliers that under the measure are the same in all material respects except for origin.[20]

In *China – Electronic Payments Services*, a more detailed analysis of likeness was undertaken. The Panel unsuccessfully asked the parties, the US and China, to provide the Panel with relevant criteria (i.e. factors other than origin) or an analytical framework to establish likeness.[21] The Panel also took the AB's earlier words of caution as to the transposition of trade in goods case law to trade in services into account.[22] The Panel assessed likeness by looking at the ordinary meaning of the words and the context of the phrase 'like services'. The Panel concluded that 'a likeness determination should be based on arguments and evidence that

---

[17] *EC – Bananas III (Panel)* para. 7.346; *Canada – Autos (Panel)* paras 10.247–10.248. This presumption that service suppliers are like if they supply like services is also evident in the 1997 article by A Mattoo, 'National Treatment in the GATS: Corner-Stone or Pandora's Box?' (1997) 31 Journal of World Trade 107, 133.

[18] Diebold, *Non-Discrimination in International Trade in Services: 'Likeness' in WTO/GATS* 196.

[19] Zdouc, 'WTO Dispute Settlement Practice Relating to the General Agreement on Trade in Services' 398.

[20] *China – Measures Affecting Trading Rights and Distribution Services for Certain Publications and Audiovisual Products* WT/DS363/R, Panel report adopted 19 January 2010 paras 7.975–7.976; confirmed in *China – Measures Affecting Electronic Payment Services* WT/DS413/R, Panel report adopted 31 August 2012 para. 7.695.

[21] *China – Electronic Payment Services (Panel)* para. 7.698.

[22] Ibid.

pertain to the competitive relationship of the services being compared'.[23] The Panel then turned to the likeness of the service suppliers. It noted that the analysis of the Panels in *EC – Bananas III* and *Canada – Autos*, on the automatic likeness of service suppliers where they provide like services, is to be read as a presumption.[24] In the specific circumstances of the case, the Panel found that the presumption did not hold.[25] The Panel held that it is for the complainant to raise a presumption that the services or service suppliers are 'essentially the same in competitive terms', and that the respondent may then seek to rebut this presumption.[26] Both for likeness of services and of service suppliers, the actual analysis of competitive relationship focused on the perceived competition between the domestic service and service supplier and the foreign service and service supplier, as well as on the service suppliers' descriptions of their business scope and the specific services they provide.[27]

In *Argentina – Financial Services*, the Panel followed the above guidance but needn't go into the relationship between the likeness of services and that of service suppliers because the distinction between domestic and foreign services and service suppliers was solely based on origin.[28]

The Panel's approach in *China – Electronic Payment Services* thus *distinguishes* between the likeness of services and that of service suppliers: it does not accept automatic likeness of the service suppliers if the services are like. This is of crucial importance for the issue of regulatory autonomy, as it creates leeway for governments to distinguish between different service suppliers who supply a like service.[29] This gives necessary weight to the importance of supplier regulation, which

---

[23] Ibid paras 7.699–7.702. The Panel conducted the analysis once, but referred to it for two further, distinct services which were at issue in the same case.

[24] Ibid para. 7.705.

[25] Ibid.

[26] Ibid paras 7.704 and 7.708.

[27] Ibid paras 7.703 and 7.706.

[28] *Argentina – Measures Relating to Trade in Goods and Services*, WT/DS453, Panel Report not yet adopted paras 7.165–7.185.

[29] Gaëtan Verhoosel, *National Treatment and WTO Dispute Settlement: Adjudicating the Boundaries of Regulatory Autonomy* (Hart 2002) 61; Kalypso Nicolaïdis and Joel P Trachtman, 'From Policed Regulation to Managed Recognition in GATS' in Pierre Sauvé and Robert M Stern (eds), *GATS 2000: New Directions in Services Trade Liberalization* (Brookings Institution 2000) 252–255.

can be taken into account when assessing likeness.[30] In terms of whether there should be a mutually dependent interpretation of likeness for services and service suppliers,[31] the Panel concluded that there should not be.

However, the Panel did not explicitly determine whether the likeness tests for services and for service suppliers is cumulative. It seems possible that a like service could be supplied by unlike service suppliers, as indicated by this Panel's approach.[32] Equally, it can be imagined that like service suppliers may supply unlike services. Henceforth, the question is whether a non-discrimination obligation could be violated if either the services, or the service suppliers, are unlike (but not both of these). Although several approaches have been presented in scholarship,[33] it will be necessary for future case law to clarify this issue. Whatever the relationship between likeness of services and of service suppliers, it seems clear that sufficient individual attention needs to be given to both – thereby giving deference to regulatory autonomy.[34] Nonetheless, drawing the line may prove impossible, and it is submitted that an overly artificial distinction should be avoided.[35] These considerations, together with the proposed differences for the assessment of likeness between services and service suppliers set out below, lead to the proposition that *both* services and service suppliers should be like.

1.1.2.3 The 'group' of services and service suppliers versus the 'like' services and service suppliers The following example, borrowed from an early, principal contribution on Article XVII GATS, demonstrates a

---

[30] Markus Krajewski, *National Regulation and Trade Liberalization in Services* (Kluwer Law International 2003) 106.

[31] See Diebold, *Non-Discrimination in International Trade in Services: 'Likeness' in WTO/GATS* 197–204.

[32] *China – Electronic Payment Services (Panel)* para. 7.705.

[33] They are (i) a cumulative test, (ii) an alternative test, which may be either a combined approach or a disjunctive approach, or (iii) a merged test. For an extensive overview, see Diebold, *Non-Discrimination in International Trade in Services: 'Likeness' in WTO/GATS* 204–219.

[34] As noted by Bart De Meester, 'Testing European Prudential Conditions for Banking Mergers in the Light of Most Favoured Nation in the GATS' (2008) 11 Journal of International Economic Law 609, 626 at footnote 68.

[35] Mireille Cossy, *Determining 'Likeness' under the GATS: Squaring the Circle?* (World Trade Organization Economic Research and Statistics Division Staff Working Paper ERSD-2006-08, 2006) 11–12.

crucial issue in the context of likeness:[36] a country making full national treatment commitments on 'passenger transportation services by road' subsequently imposes a higher tax on foreign suppliers of these services than on domestic ones. Almost all foreign suppliers are taxis and almost all domestic suppliers are buses. If a passenger transportation service by road is understood simply as 'a passenger transportation service by road', a tax on taxi services but not on bus services would violate Article XVII GATS because the tax causes a detrimental impact on foreign suppliers of passenger transportation services by road vis-à-vis like domestic service suppliers. The result is that 'the "likeness" criterion is immune to regulatory distinctions based on the precise type of passenger road transportation service'.[37] However, if the service is not 'passenger transportation by road', but 'taxi services', the foreign taxi service suppliers need to be compared to the domestic taxi service suppliers, who are in fact accorded the same treatment.

Therefore, the first step in the likeness analysis is the identification of the 'group' of services or service suppliers that are to be compared.[38] This aspect of the likeness analysis is obfuscated due to terminological issues: the term 'like product' is frequently applied to this first step.[39] It

[36] Mattoo, 'National Treatment in the GATS: Corner-Stone or Pandora's Box?' 122.

[37] Ibid.

[38] *European Communities – Anti-Dumping Measure on Farmed Salmon from Norway* WT/DS337/R, Panel report adopted 15 January 2008 para. 7.51, noting in the context Article 2.6 of the Anti-Dumping Agreement that: 'it must be known what the comparator is, before any assessment can be made as to whether another product is "identical" to or, in the absence of an identical product, "has characteristics closely resembling those of" the imported "product under consideration"'. Also see, implicitly, *European Communities – Measures Affecting Asbestos and Asbestos-Containing Products* WT/DS135/AB/R, AB report adopted 5 April 2001 para. 100, noting that the group of imported products must be compared with the group of like domestic products; *United States – Measures Affecting the Production and Sale of Clove Cigarettes* WT/DS406/R, Panel report adopted 24 April 2012 para. 7.124, dubbing the group of relevant products the 'like products'; *United States – Measures Affecting the Production and Sale of Clove Cigarettes* WT/DS406/AB/R, AB report adopted 24 April 2012 para. 192, referring to the 'universe of domestic products' (the issue was crucial in this report, see paras 191–200). I adopt the terminology 'group' as used by the AB in e.g. ibid and as used in James Flett, 'WTO Space for National Regulation: Requiem for a Diagonal Vector Test' (2013) 16 Journal of International Economic Law 37 46–47.

[39] Flett, 'WTO Space for National Regulation: Requiem for a Diagonal Vector Test' 47.

has been argued convincingly that the following, based on a goods context, applies equally to Article XVII GATS.[40] I see no reason why this could not also be extended to Article II GATS. In the context of an EU and US row over aircraft subsidies under the SCM Agreement, the AB has explained that a panel must assess:

> whether it was appropriate to examine all Airbus LCA [large civil aircraft] as a single 'subsidized product' and all Boeing LCA as a single 'like product' for purposes of its adverse effects inquiry. The Panel was also required to assess the European Communities' allegation that there are, in fact, five distinct product markets of Airbus and Boeing LCA, and should have reached a conclusion as to whether any of the parties' or a different 'product market' definition was appropriate for purposes of its displacement analysis.[41]

The AB continued, noting that the panel was obliged to define 'the relevant product market and the scope of the respondent's subsidized product that is in competition with the complainant's like product', on the basis of, *inter alia*, demand-side and supply-side substitutability, and cross-price elasticity.[42] In the context of Article III:4 GATT 1994, this relevant product market is said to ask 'a question about the relationships among the things that are reasonably to be considered together and collectively as "a product"'.[43] The product market may be construed more widely (with relatively heterogeneous things),[44] or more narrowly in a specific case.[45] For example, in establishing the 'like product' in the context of Article 2.1 of the Anti-Dumping Agreement, the Panel in *EC – Salmon (Norway)* noted that 'The mere fact that a dumping determination is ultimately made with respect to "a product" says nothing about the

---

[40] This is the central proposition in James Flett, 'National Treatment under the General Agreement on Trade in Services (GATS)' in Anselm Kamperman Sanders (ed), *The Principle of National Treatment in International Economic Law: Trade, Investment and Intellectual Property* (Edward Elgar Publishing 2014).

[41] *European Communities – Measures Affecting Trade in Large Civil Aircraft* WT/DS316/AB/R, AB report adopted 1 June 2011 para. 1131.

[42] Ibid para. 1134.

[43] Flett, 'WTO Space for National Regulation: Requiem for a Diagonal Vector Test' 46.

[44] By analogy, see *EC – Salmon (Norway) (Panel)* paras 7.53–7.59.

[45] Flett, 'WTO Space for National Regulation: Requiem for a Diagonal Vector Test' 46–47. Here, Flett argues that this actually is the 'accordion of likeness' from *Japan – Taxes on Alcoholic Beverages* WT/DS8/AB/R, AB report adopted 1 November 1996 20–21.

scope of the relevant product'.[46] A wider or narrower scope of the product market should not lead to different results as long as the same things are included from the domestic and import sides.[47] The complainant and respondent in a dispute can propose product markets. In the event of disagreement, a panel may employ competition-based criteria, in order to ensure that the product market is 'an appropriate basis'.[48] Care should nonetheless be taken;[49] as the Panel in *Korea – Alcohol Beverages* made clear, market definitions may differ between competition law and trade law.[50]

Admittedly, it is difficult to delineate this first step with the actual likeness analysis. According to the main proponent of this first-step approach, the actual 'likeness' analysis between the relevant groups is:

> the comparison between the treatment of the imported product and the treatment of the domestic product [which] requires the import and domestic categories to be described in terms that are identical in all respects. One cannot meaningfully test for de facto discrimination unless the data sets on each side of the comparison are objectively and even-handedly defined and compiled by reference to criteria that are identical in all respects.[51]

Although this approach should be kept in mind while assessing likeness, it has not been followed in GATS case law. For now therefore, it should simply serve as a reminder of the importance of delineating the groups of services or service suppliers that are to be compared. Undoubtedly, future case law should clarify this issue further, whether in a goods or a services context.

---

[46] *EC – Salmon (Norway) (Panel)* para. 7.48.

[47] Flett, 'WTO Space for National Regulation: Requiem for a Diagonal Vector Test' 46–47 and 88–89.

[48] Ibid 47–48. Also see Adrian Emch, 'Same Same But Different? Fiscal Discrimination in WTO Law and EU Law: What Are "Like" Products?' (2005) 32 Legal Issues of Economic Integration 369, 382–395 and 397.

[49] Jonell B Goco, 'Non-Discrimination, "Likeness", and Market Definition in World Trade Organization Jurisprudence' (2006) 40 Journal of World Trade 315, 332.

[50] *Korea – Taxes on Alcoholic Beverages* WT/DS75/R, Panel report adopted 17 February 1999 para. 10.81.

[51] Flett, 'WTO Space for National Regulation: Requiem for a Diagonal Vector Test' 47 (emphasis omitted).

1.1.2.4 Competitive likeness for services and competitive and policy likeness for service suppliers: balancing regulatory autonomy and trade liberalisation As noted in a leading contribution on likeness in GATS, and one can concur with this when reading the case law, neither panels nor the AB have needed to delve deeply into the issue of likeness. In the first two cases involving likeness, the respondents did not dispute the likeness of services and service suppliers, in the two subsequent cases, the assessment of likeness of service suppliers was relatively straightforward.[52] Consequently, the current approach to determining likeness in the case of Articles II and XVII GATS only appears to assess the competitive relationship between the services and service suppliers, and only in a relatively narrow sense. This may simply be because it was unnecessary for the panels to assess likeness in more detail, as 'the issue of "likeness" was not the critical element of the analysis'.[53] Hence, it has been sufficient for the likeness analysis to focus on a narrow notion of competitive relationship. However, this approach may be insufficient for cases where measures are, on the face of it, origin-neutral.[54]

The Panel in *Argentina – Financial Services* was presented with such a situation. As origin was not the only factor on which the different treatment was based, it considered a factor other than origin relevant to the likeness analysis.[55] The Panel held that this factor, perhaps surprisingly, is Argentina's regulatory concern of having access to tax information, especially in the context of the supply of a service by a supplier outside of the regulating Member's territory in Modes 1 and 2.[56] However, because Argentina's measure did not, in fact, clearly distinguish between countries for which it had access to tax information and others, the Panel concluded that it could not evaluate the impact of the factor other than origin. As a result, it found that the distinction between services and service suppliers was solely based on origin, and that they are therefore like.[57] This allowed the Panel to avoid further going into uncharted territory.

---

[52] Diebold, *Non-Discrimination in International Trade in Services: 'Likeness' in WTO/GATS* 195–196, to which one may add likeness in the case of *China – Electronic Payment Services (Panel)*.

[53] Diebold, *Non-Discrimination in International Trade in Services: 'Likeness' in WTO/GATS* 195.

[54] Peter Van den Bossche and Werner Zdouc, *The Law and Policy of the World Trade Organization* (3rd edn, Cambridge University Press 2013) 394.

[55] *Argentina – Financial Services (Panel)* paras 7.173 and 7.176.

[56] Ibid paras 7.176 and 7.179.

[57] Ibid paras 7.181 and 7.185.

A narrow focus on competitive relationships is problematic. The current case law is in line with the firm rejection of the 'aims and effects' test in the analysis of Articles II and XVII GATS by the AB.[58] A strict reading of this rejection results in a narrow base for the determination of likeness, which may miss out on important factors. This could lead to excessive liberalisation as compared to what is necessary to achieve the objective of these obligations: protecting the conditions of competition between domestic and foreign services and service suppliers.[59] However, as with GATT 1994 case law, the rejection of the aim and effects test should not be read as an outright rejection of *all* factors other than those taken into account in GATS case law thus far. A wider interpretation of likeness than one based solely on an analysis of competitive relationships needs to be considered; as in the case of likeness of services and service suppliers, such a restricted focus is of aggravated concern compared to what is the case for goods. If no differentiation can be made outside of narrow competitive relationships, than what added value is there in assessing the likeness of service suppliers in GATS?

There appear to be few situations in which like services would be supplied by service suppliers that are not in a competitive relationship. This may only be the case if the competitive relationship between the service suppliers is examined in a very wide sense. The undesirable outcome of that approach is, however, that the services supplied by a company that engages in sufficiently varied economic activities would be unlike a service supplied by a company that only supplies one type of service, even if, as concerns the actual supply of that service, the suppliers are identical. If a self-employed consultant with x years of experience and y educational background, supplies consultancy services, and a consultant working for a multi-national enterprise with the same experience and background, supplies a like service, these suppliers can, in my view, not be considered *not* like. This is not to say that the nature of the service supplier should not play a role, as explained below, but that a sole focus on competitive relationship is not the appropriate means for doing so. Therefore, the current narrow interpretation of likeness, focusing solely on competitive relationship, cannot be said to give meaning to all terms of the covered agreements.[60]

---

58 *EC – Bananas III (AB)* para. 241.

59 Cossy, *Determining 'Likeness' under the GATS: Squaring the Circle?* 38.

60 *United States – Standards for Reformulated and Conventional Gasoline* WT/DS2/AB/R, AB report adopted 20 May 1996 21.

As the AB has noted, case law from GATT 1994 may help to address this concern and inform the interpretation of likeness in the corresponding obligations under GATS.[61] This case law is useful, particularly as the likeness test under GATT 1994 has been the subject of much more rigorous interpretation. Whilst the focus of the GATT 1994 likeness case law remains on the competitive relationship between like products,[62] the test appears to be more refined. In the case of the national treatment obligation under Article III:4 GATT 1994, a 'mere economic analysis of the cross-price elasticity of demand' is insufficient, and "likeness" is a matter of judgement – qualitatively as well as quantitatively'.[63] The well-known case law on likeness in Article III:4 GATT 1994 may be summarised as taking into account:

> 101. […] four categories of 'characteristics' that the products involved might share: (i) the physical properties of the products; (ii) the extent to which the products are capable of serving the same or similar end-uses; (iii) the extent to which consumers perceive and treat the products as alternative means of performing particular functions in order to satisfy a particular want or demand; and (iv) the international classification of the products for tariff purposes.
>
> 102. These general criteria, or groupings of potentially shared characteristics, provide a framework for analyzing the 'likeness' of particular products on a case-by-case basis. These criteria are, it is well to bear in mind, simply tools to assist in the task of sorting and examining the relevant evidence.[64]

Processes and production methods (PPMs) may influence the physical properties of the product. If the PPM does not influence the physical properties of the product, it is a non-product-related process and production method (NPR-PPM).[65] Hence, the difference between PPMs and NPR-PPMs is that the latter 'do not affect the characteristics or properties of the products concerned'.[66] Although not directly relevant for the

---

[61] *EC – Bananas III (AB)* para. 231; *China – Publications and Audiovisual Products (Panel)* para. 7.975; *China – Electronic Payment Services (Panel)* para. 7.702.

[62] See e.g. *EC – Asbestos (AB)* para. 99.

[63] Van den Bossche and Zdouc, *The Law and Policy of the World Trade Organization* 388.

[64] *EC – Asbestos (AB)* paras 101–102.

[65] I also use this term for 'non-service-related' processes and production methods.

[66] Van den Bossche and Zdouc, *The Law and Policy of the World Trade Organization* 393.

determination of likeness,[67] it should be noted that NPR-PPMs play an increasing role in influencing consumer tastes and habits, thereby also influencing the likeness analysis.[68]

In future cases which require a more careful analysis of the likeness of services and service suppliers, an application of the GATT 1994 criteria to the context of trade in services must be considered. Transposing these conditions to the likeness of services, or, more importantly, of service suppliers,[69] leads to the following conclusions.

First, as concerns the *likeness of services*, the existing analytical framework of a narrow competitive basis appears warranted in the light of the GATT 1994 case law. The classification of services can be examined on the basis of the W/120 or the Central Product Classification (CPC), which includes services.[70] One applicable caveat is that the CPC is not based upon the competitive relationship of services (or service suppliers) as it was designed for statistical purposes.[71] The classification system may also be insufficiently refined.[72] Nonetheless, classification in the same sector may lead to a presumption of likeness.[73] Characteristics of the service (not 'physical' characteristics, considering the intangible nature of services),[74] end uses,[75] and consumer tastes and

---

[67] *United States – Restrictions on Imports of Tuna* DS21/R, GATT Panel report, 3 September 1991, unadopted, BISD 39S/155 para. 5.15.

[68] Diebold, *Non-Discrimination in International Trade in Services: 'Likeness' in WTO/GATS* 345; Van den Bossche and Zdouc, *The Law and Policy of the World Trade Organization* 393. See *Philippines – Taxes on Distilled Spirits* WT/DS396/AB/R, WT/DS403/AB/R, AB report adopted 20 January 2012 para. 132.

[69] As proposed by Diebold, *Non-Discrimination in International Trade in Services: 'Likeness' in WTO/GATS* 265–268.

[70] See *EC – Bananas III (Panel)* para. 7.322.

[71] Rüdiger Wolfrum, 'Article II GATS' in Rüdiger Wolfrum, Peter-Tobias Stoll and Clemens Feinäugle (eds), *Max Planck Commentaries on World Trade Law: WTO – Trade in Services*, vol 6 (Martinus Nijhoff 2008) 83.

[72] Mattoo, 'National Treatment in the GATS: Corner-Stone or Pandora's Box?' 128.

[73] *EC – Bananas III (Panel)* paras 7.287–7.293; Mattoo, 'National Treatment in the GATS: Corner-Stone or Pandora's Box?' 128.

[74] Cossy, *Determining 'Likeness' under the GATS: Squaring the Circle?* 335–336.

[75] Mattoo, 'National Treatment in the GATS: Corner-Stone or Pandora's Box?' 128; Zdouc, 'WTO Dispute Settlement Practice Relating to the General Agreement on Trade in Services' 395; Cossy, *Determining 'Likeness' under the GATS: Squaring the Circle?* 21.

habits[76] play a role in so far as they influence the competitive relationship between the services. Although more of an issue for national treatment than for MFN, the method of supply of a service could also be a crucial element in the context of properties, nature and quality of a service, and could also influence consumer tastes and habits.[77] This issue of methods of supply is examined in further detail below. In summary, for services, I adhere to the notion of 'competitive likeness' or 'market likeness'.[78]

Second, for the *likeness of service suppliers*, the use of the aforementioned criteria becomes more problematic. The use of classification instruments has been criticised[79] for leading to the approach in, for example, *EC – Bananas III* that the likeness of the service necessarily implies the likeness of the suppliers. Focusing too strictly on the general characteristics of the service supplier, such as their activities, equipment, types of employee and marketing stages,[80] may lead to a situation where 'the existence of *like* suppliers would become a theoretical construct which could hardly be found in the real world'.[81] End uses appear to be less relevant for assessing the likeness of the service supplier, as compared to for the likeness of services.

It has been argued that consumers' tastes and habits should play a key role in the establishment of likeness of service suppliers.[82] A consumer-oriented approach to determining the competitive relationship of services

---

[76] Krajewski, *National Regulation and Trade Liberalization in Services* 99; Cossy, *Determining 'Likeness' under the GATS: Squaring the Circle?* 21; Diebold, *Non-Discrimination in International Trade in Services: 'Likeness' in WTO/GATS* 262–264. It is true, as noted by Zdouc, 'WTO Dispute Settlement Practice Relating to the General Agreement on Trade in Services' 395–396, that this criterion would have less impact where the service does not require close interaction between the consumer and the service supplier.

[77] Diebold, *Non-Discrimination in International Trade in Services: 'Likeness' in WTO/GATS* 252.

[78] These terms are used by Amelia Porges and Joel P Trachtman, 'Robert Hudec and Domestic Regulation: The Resurrection of Aim and Effects' (2003) 37 Journal of World Trade 783, 785; Petros C Mavroidis, 'Driftin' too Far from Shore – Why the Test for Compliance with the TBT Agreement Developed by the WTO Appellate Body is Wrong, and What Should the AB Have Done Instead' (2013) 12 World Trade Review 509.

[79] Cossy, *Determining 'Likeness' under the GATS: Squaring the Circle?* 17.

[80] As argued by the US in *EC – Bananas III (Panel)* para. 4.667.

[81] Zdouc, 'WTO Dispute Settlement Practice Relating to the GATS' 333 (emphasis original).

[82] Krajewski, *National Regulation and Trade Liberalization in Services* 99; Cossy, *Determining 'Likeness' under the GATS: Squaring the Circle?* 21, who notes that end use and, to a lesser extent, consumer tastes and habits are most

and service suppliers requires many more factors, besides the aforementioned three, to be taken into account. These factors include evidence which has been taken into account in past case law, such as: marketing studies, price differences, distribution channels, sales points, statements by national authorities, evidence from third markets and health risks.[83] However, an overemphasis on consumer tastes and habits risks that consumers are to bear too vast a responsibility.[84] Moreover, there is a danger that (governmental) information campaigns, whether their basis is correct or not, could influence consumers' tastes and habits and have a bearing on outcomes regarding likeness. This issue is much more prevalent in the case of services as compared to the case of goods. Consider the vast information asymmetries on, for example, the quality of services and service suppliers.[85] It must also be recalled that consumer tastes and habits are but one of the relevant elements that need to be taken into account when assessing likeness. Therefore, although it has some clear moral benefits, the suggestion that a panel would accept that services or service suppliers are not like *because* one construction service is provided through child labour and the other by an adult, seems unlikely.[86] In a particular context, a panel may find that such services or service suppliers are not like, but would perhaps do so due to different reasons:

> if tastes and perceptions bear directly on the service, the characteristics and qualities of the suppliers are likely to be an important element in shaping these tastes and perceptions. For example, the particular qualifications of certain suppliers may make them like or unlike from a consumer's point of view.[87]

This approach links consumer tastes and habits to characteristics and qualities of the service supplier. I would add that these characteristics and

---

relevant; Diebold, *Non-Discrimination in International Trade in Services: 'Likeness' in WTO/GATS* 262–264.

83 Diebold, *Non-Discrimination in International Trade in Services: 'Likeness' in WTO/GATS* 264.

84 Similarly, see De Meester, 'Testing European Prudential Conditions for Banking Mergers in the Light of Most Favoured Nation in the GATS' 630.

85 Pierre Sauvé and Robert M Stern, 'New Directions in Services Trade Liberalization: An Overview' in Pierre Sauvé and Robert M Stern (eds), *GATS 2000: New Directions in Services Trade Liberalization* (Brookings Institution 2000), 15.

86 Diebold, *Non-Discrimination in International Trade in Services: 'Likeness' in WTO/GATS* 347.

87 Cossy, *Determining 'Likeness' under the GATS: Squaring the Circle?* 22.

qualities need to be related to the supply of the service. Returning to the consultancy services example, the relevant characteristics and qualities would be those that influence the service itself, not those of the supplier in general. This approach mitigates the concerns raised by the US in *EC – Bananas III*.

Combining an assessment of consumer tastes and habits, and the characteristics of the service supplier, *in so far as they are relevant* to the supply of the service, appears to be the most suitable way to determine the likeness of two service suppliers. In both criteria, NPR-PPMs have a place. It has been noted that the role of NPR-PPMs in determining likeness of *services* is limited, considering that services are often produced and consumed at the same time.[88] However, it has also been stated that their role is more important in determining the likeness of the *service suppliers*, which requires an assessment of some process methods.[89] The issue is crucial for regulatory autonomy, as a 'true PPM-measure pursues primarily policy goals unrelated to trade. Most of the time, the measure is aimed at subjects such as labour standards, human rights, environmental protection or animal welfare'.[90] In many cases, such measures are likely to be *NPR*-PPMs. In the context of GATS, the issue is perhaps less contentious as trade in services entails fewer extraterritorial effects: whilst process and production of a service supplied through Modes 1 and 2 may still be foreign, in the case of Modes 3 and 4 the services occur on the territory of the importing Member.[91] Therefore, the regulation of the service can be subjected to domestic regulatory measures for Modes 3 and 4. Consequently, PPMs seem to play an important role in the determination of the likeness of the service supplier (as the relative importance of the characteristics of the service supplier is greater than with goods),[92] whilst NPR-PPMs may be more relevant than under GATT 1994 case law, considering the more

---

[88] Markus Krajewski and Maika Engelke, 'Article XVII GATS' in Rüdiger Wolfrum, Peter-Tobias Stoll and Clemens Feinäugle (eds), *Max Planck Commentaries on World Trade Law: WTO – Trade in Services*, vol 6 (Martinus Nijhoff 2008), 406.

[89] Wolfrum, 'Article II GATS' 84.

[90] Diebold, *Non-Discrimination in International Trade in Services: 'Likeness' in WTO/GATS* 339.

[91] Nicolaïdis and Trachtman, 'From Policed Regulation to Managed Recognition in GATS' 253.

[92] Pauwelyn, 'The Unbearable Lightness of Likeness' 359.

limited concerns on extraterritoriality for Modes 3 and 4,[93] and the requirement of addressing the likeness of the service supplier for all four modes of supply. The likeness of the service supplier is determined by consumer tastes and habits and the characteristics of the service supplier, both of which (but especially the former) may be influenced by taking NPR-PPMs into account.

The abovementioned finding of the Panel in *Argentina – Financial Services* that the regulatory concern on tax exchange information is relevant to the likeness analysis is in line with this argument. To bring it in line with the case law, the Panel further framed its finding by pointing out that both parties agree that the *competitive relationship* between services and service suppliers was strongly affected depending on whether the suppliers are located in a jurisdiction that exchanges tax information or not.[94] However, the Panel did not make the link with consumer tastes and habits or the characteristics of the service supplier but rather applied AB case law on Article 2.1 TBT Agreement to its likeness analysis.[95] In my view, although I agree with its outcome, this reasoning is incorrect for the reasons explained in the previous paragraph. At the time of writing, Argentina had appealed this finding of the Panel before the AB.

In summary, for the likeness of service suppliers, I argue in favour of indirectly taking some aspects of 'regulatory likeness' or 'policy likeness' into account,[96] in addition to the more narrow 'competitive likeness' or 'market likeness'. This may differ from the competitive likeness approach that dominates GATT 1994 case law, but this difference may be less significant than it first appears. Consider the case law on likeness in Article 2.1 TBT Agreement, where the AB noted that 'the regulatory concerns that underlie a measure may be considered to the extent that they have an impact on the competitive relationship'.[97] The role of regulatory concern is more significant as concerns the likeness of service

---

[93] For Modes 1 and 2, consumers may well distinguish between services on the basis of the foreign service suppliers' behaviour vis-à-vis that of domestic service suppliers in their respective home countries. This entails extraterritorial effects.

[94] *Argentina – Financial Services (Panel)* para. 7.180.

[95] Ibid paras 7.176–7.179.

[96] This approach is in line with *US – Clove Cigarettes (AB)* paras 117–119.

[97] Ibid and 156. In para. 120, the AB explains that the likeness analysis under Article III:4 GATT 1994 is relevant to that in Article 2.1 TBT Agreement. As with the analysis of less favourable treatment, this explanation would also appear to apply *vice versa*.

suppliers, as compared to the likeness of services. Such a difference is justified. First, the text of Articles II and XVII GATS requires an assessment of the likeness of the services *and* of the service suppliers. A narrow interpretation of competitive likeness cannot give sufficient weight to the likeness of service suppliers. Second, a wide interpretation of competitive likeness, as proposed by the US in *EC – Bananas III* would also lead to unsatisfactory results. Therefore, the likeness of service suppliers should be assessed on the basis of their characteristics in so far as they are relevant to the supply of the service, and on the basis of consumer tastes and habits. For both criteria, PPMs and NPR-PPMs play an inevitable role. The regulation of the service supplier thereby comes within the ambit of the likeness analysis: the competitive likeness is supplemented by some aspects of regulatory likeness.

1.1.2.5 Likeness across modes of supply or methods of supply Finally, the influence of modes of supply on likeness needs to be mentioned. This issue was already raised in 1996 by the Secretariat, which noted that:

> The text of Article XVII does not suggest that the mode of supply is a consideration in defining 'likeness' of a service: different modes of supply could be used to provide a 'like' service. The structure of the schedules, however, implies that a Member's commitments are mode-specific, i.e. a Member making a commitment to provide national treatment, does so within a specific mode but is allowed to discriminate between the same service supplied by different modes.[98]

Subsequently, the Panel in *Canada – Autos* stated that, for the purposes of the case, 'services supplied in Canada through modes 3 and 4 and those supplied from the territory of other Members through modes 1 and 2 are "like" services'.[99] In *US – Gambling*, this matter was addressed extensively by the parties: in essence, Antigua and Barbuda claimed that remote gambling services are like land-based gambling services, while the US opposed this view.[100] However, these arguments were left unaddressed by the Panel, which exercised judicial economy as to Article XVII GATS. It seems that, for now, the Panel in *Canada – Autos* has

---

98 S/WPGR/9, Subsidies and Trade in Services (Note by the Secretariat 6 March 1996) para. 28.

99 *Canada – Autos (Panel)* para. 10.307. The AB did not address the finding.

100 *United States – Measures Affecting the Cross-Border Supply of Gambling and Betting Services* WT/DS285/R, Panel report adopted 20 April 2005 paras 3.148–3.220.

established the idea that modes of supply do not *in se* play a role in determining likeness.

As noted by the Secretariat, accepting likeness across modes in such a manner may raise questions regarding the value of modal commitments.[101] It has been argued that the result of accepting likeness across methods of supply may limit real-life regulatory needs:

> [S]ervices supplied through the Internet for instance, whether cross-border or within the same territory, would have to be subject to the same regulation as services provided by commercial establishment or physical persons having a direct contact with the consumer ('face to face').[102]

Taking a step back, the issue may not be as pressing as it first seems. In the case of national treatment, the relevant comparison for likeness is between domestic and foreign service suppliers. The former do not fall within the definitions of modes of supply in GATS. Thus, in the context of national treatment, likeness across modes is perhaps rather irrelevant a concept, as it could never serve to illustrate likeness between foreign and domestic services and service suppliers.[103] This does not hold true in the MFN context,[104] as indicated by the Panel's reasoning in *Canada – Autos*. However, in such cases, the relevance of the mode of supply *in se* is still limited, and the concept 'method of supply' may be more appealing. The *method* of supply of a service is, for example, face-to-face or through the internet.[105] Of course, this does relate to the *mode* of supply, but it is a more useful proxy to assess an impact on likeness. The mode of supply is not necessarily the same as the method of supply, which is potentially characterised in more detail. Equally, the method of supply may also play a role in determining likeness under the national treatment obligation, as a domestic service *is* supplied through a *method* of supply.

---

[101] Krajewski and Engelke, 'Article XVII GATS' 405.

[102] Cossy, *Determining 'Likeness' under the GATS: Squaring the Circle?* 14.

[103] Ibid 14–15.

[104] Wolfrum, 'Article II GATS' 84.

[105] Cossy, *Determining 'Likeness' under the GATS: Squaring the Circle?* 15; Krajewski and Engelke, 'Article XVII GATS' 405. See a similar distinction between 'modes of supply' and 'means of supply' in *US – Gambling (Panel)* paras 6.362–6.363, 6.368–6.370 and 6.376–6.378. In para. 6.285, the Panel noted that 'mode 1 under the GATS encompasses all possible means of supplying services from the territory of one WTO Member into the territory of another WTO Member'.

Therefore, I agree that the crux of the matter is whether the method of supply 'should, as such, play a role in the determination of likeness'.[106] The *mode* of supply is *in se* not relevant. However, in my view, the *method* of supply is relevant: the end use of services supplied through different methods of supply, the classification of the service, the characteristics of service and service supplier, and the consumer tastes and habits concerning both the service and the service supplier, may all differ. (Note that the method of supply has been said to be comparable to the method of production.[107]) Generally speaking, there will not be a full competitive relationship between services supplied through different methods of supply.[108] This does not entail unexpected liberalisation, or an overstretching of the obligation,[109] as the Schedules still limit the scope of the national treatment obligation:[110] only in so far as commitments have been made and no conditions have been scheduled, can the national treatment apply. Taking the method of supply into account when assessing likeness does not alter this. Equally, for the MFN obligation, it appears that the mode of supply is not determinative of the scope of that obligation, considering the lack of a textual basis for arguing so.

This interpretation addresses the two questions raised with respect to modality and likeness. The first question asks 'whether Members can explicitly retain the right to discriminate between modes'.[111] This question raises doubts as regards the value of commitments if a Member may, for example, grant a subsidy to a national service supplier only after according full Mode 1 market access and national treatment; this measure would modify the conditions of competition vis-à-vis the foreign service

---

[106] Cossy, *Determining 'Likeness' under the GATS: Squaring the Circle?* 14, 15.

[107] Nicolas Diebold, 'The Morals and Order Exceptions in WTO Law: Balancing the Toothless Tiger and the Undermining Mole' (2008) 11 Journal of International Economic Law 43, 70.

[108] Krajewski and Engelke, 'Article XVII GATS' 405–406.

[109] Zdouc, 'WTO Dispute Settlement Practice Relating to the General Agreement on Trade in Services' 402.

[110] For example, if a Member limits market access in accordance with the type of legal entity of the foreign service supplier through a limitation on Article XVI:2 (e) GATS, it may still prohibit service supply through a subsidiary and a branch, thereby influencing the likeness analysis and thus the scope of the national treatment obligation. Mattoo, 'National Treatment in the GATS: Corner-Stone or Pandora's Box?' 133.

[111] Ibid.

suppliers.[112] By contrast, if the *method* of supply is the relevant proxy, the above example may be said to constitute a national treatment violation in so far as the domestic and foreign service supplier are like, taking into account, *inter alia*, the difference between the service supplied through Mode 1 and by the domestic service supplier. If both suppliers provide the service through, for example, telephone communication, the services may well be like and the measure could violate the national treatment obligation if it modifies the conditions of competition to the detriment of the foreign service supplier.

The second, related, question raised, is 'whether Members who have made a full non-discriminatory commitment, can, nevertheless, apply different standards of treatment to different modes'.[113] This question arises where a Member makes full commitments on national treatment in several Modes of supply, and asks 'whether nominally identical commitments translate into effective equality of treatment'.[114] The example given by two authors concerns a subsidy granted to domestic services. Foreign service suppliers under Modes 3 and 4 could claim that the subsidy should be extended to them, which would also affect services supplied through Modes 1 and 2. The question is whether these service suppliers could claim access to the subsidy.[115] Applying the above interpretation once again, the likeness of the services, taking into account the method of supply, seems to lead to the most acceptable outcome.

1.1.2.6 Conclusion In summary, first, this section established that likeness in the national treatment and MFN obligations should be interpreted identically. Second, it proposed that, under GATS, both services and service suppliers should be like. Deciding otherwise would mean regulators could not distinguish between service suppliers who supply like services. Considering the importance of the likeness of the service supplier from a regulatory perspective, for example with regard to information asymmetries, would overly constrain regulatory autonomy. Third, this section pointed at the importance of the group of like services or service suppliers. In GATT 1994 case law, this issue received limited

---

112 Patrick Low and Aaditya Mattoo, 'Is There a Better Way? Alternative Approaches to Liberalization Under the GATS' in Pierre Sauvé and Robert M Stern (eds), *GATS 2000: New Directions in Services Trade Liberalization* (Brookings Institution 2000) 453.

113 Mattoo, 'National Treatment in the GATS: Corner-Stone or Pandora's Box?' 119.

114 Ibid 120.

115 Ibid.

attention. However, the delineation of the groups which are to be compared has a direct influence on the outcome of the competitive relationship analysis. For now, as this issue is yet to be addressed in GATS case law, it is merely proposed that the issue should not be overlooked. Fourth, this section discussed, in some detail, how likeness of services and likeness of service suppliers could be assessed. Whereas likeness of services follows the GATT 1994 approach of 'competitive likeness' or 'market likeness', the likeness of service suppliers should not be limited to such concerns. In addition to the competitive likeness elements, I argue in favour of taking into account some aspects of 'regulatory likeness' or 'policy likeness' indirectly. This approach is consistent with existing case law and does not overly constrain regulatory autonomy. Moreover, it creates some important wiggle room for regulators, who may distinguish between service suppliers on the basis of consumer tastes and habits, and the characteristics of the service supplier in so far as is relevant to the supply of the service. In practice, this could mean that, in certain circumstances, a regulator could distinguish between service suppliers on the basis of the service supplier's experience, knowledge of languages or whether the mother company has met certain requirements. Finally, I claim that the method of supply should be taken into account when assessing likeness, but that the mode of supply should not *in se* play a role: cross-modal likeness is possible.

1.1.3 Less favourable treatment[116]

1.1.3.1 Less favourable treatment in the national treatment and Most-Favoured-Nation obligations Aside from the requirement of having like services and service suppliers, the text of both Articles II and XVII GATS contain a similar requirement vis-à-vis the treatment granted to foreign services and service suppliers. For national treatment, such treatment should be no less favourable than that accorded to domestic services and service suppliers. Similarly, for MFN, such treatment should be no less favourable than that accorded to the like services and service suppliers of any other country.[117] As was the case for likeness, the interpretation of the less favourable treatment standard appears to be

---

[116] This section draws from Bregt Natens and Dylan Geraets, 'Modification of the Conditions of Competition for Goods and Services: The Side-track that Never Was' 12 Manchester Journal of International Economic Law 57.

[117] In *EC – Bananas III (Panel)* para. 6.94, the likeness and less favourable treatment conditions were explicitly set out as conditions necessary for establishing a violation of the MFN obligation.

relevant to Articles II and XVII GATS. However, whereas Article II GATS simply states that a Member may not accord treatment no less favourable than that it accords to like services and service suppliers of any other country, Article XVII GATS is more elaborate. In relevant part, Article XVII GATS reads that:

> 1. [...] each Member shall accord to services and service suppliers of any other Member, in respect of all measures affecting the supply of services, treatment no less favourable than that it accords to its own like services and service suppliers.[*]
>
> 2. A Member may meet the requirement of paragraph 1 by according to services and service suppliers of any other Member, either formally identical treatment or formally different treatment to that it accords to its own like services and service suppliers.
>
> 3. Formally identical or formally different treatment shall be considered to be less favourable if it modifies the conditions of competition in favour of services or service suppliers of the Member compared to like services or service suppliers of any other Member.
>
> [*] Specific commitments assumed under this Article shall not be construed to require any Member to compensate for any inherent competitive disadvantages which result from the foreign character of the relevant services or service suppliers.

In respect of these textual differences, the Panel in *EC – Bananas III* noted that paragraphs 2 and 3 of Article XVII GATS clarify and reinforce the less favourable treatment standard. Further, the Panel held that these paragraphs did not justify giving a different ordinary meaning to the term 'treatment no less favourable' in the MFN and national treatment provisions.[118] These textual differences merely 'serve the purpose of codifying' the interpretation of less favourable treatment. This codified interpretation sees the less favourable treatment standard as requiring the provision of conditions of competition which are no less favourable, regardless of whether this is achieved through the application of formally identical or formally different measures. Furthermore, the second and third paragraphs 'do not impose new obligations on Members additional to those contained in paragraph 1'.[119] The AB, however, nuanced this

---

118 Ibid para. 7.301.

119 Ibid. Also see Zdouc, 'WTO Dispute Settlement Practice Relating to the General Agreement on Trade in Services' 404–405 with references to the GATT Panels that served as inspiration, i.e. Italian Discrimination Against Imported Agricultural Machinery L/833, GATT Panel report, adopted 23 October 1958, BISD 7S/60 para. 12 (from which Article XVII:3 GATS was derived); United States Section 337 of the Tariff Act of 1930 L/6439, GATT Panel report, adopted

position, stating that interpretations of less favourable treatment under Article XVII GATS or Article III GATT 1994 are 'not necessarily relevant to the interpretation' of the same term in the context of Article II GATS.[120] This view finds some support in light of the different objectives of an MFN obligation (non-discrimination between services or service suppliers of third Members) and a national treatment obligation (non-discrimination between domestic and foreign services or service suppliers).[121] However, the textual differences do not mean that the less favourable treatment condition must be interpreted differently.[122] In essence, the less favourable treatment aspect of both obligations is breached when a measure creates less favourable conditions of competition.[123] This is unsurprising considering the importance of this concept in GATT 1994 case law on less favourable treatment, and the explicit link in case law on Article XVII GATS to the national treatment obligation in Article III:4 GATT 1994. In my view, the interpretations of Articles III:4 GATT, XVII GATS, and, as noted above, Article II GATS,[124] coincide as concerns the less favourable treatment condition.

A notable point of difference between goods and services, as noted above concerning likeness, is the relationship between the less favourable treatment of the services and that of the service suppliers. Often, these two factors will coincide. However, in cases where they do not, an important question arises. Namely, is it sufficient that there is a modification of the like foreign service supplier's conditions of competition even if this not the case for the like service (and *vice versa*)? The use of the word 'or' in Article XVII:3 GATS indicates an affirmative answer, in so far as both services and service suppliers are like. Consequentially, subject to the approach taken under the likeness condition, the scope of the less favourable treatment condition in Article XVII GATS may be wider than is the case for trade in goods.[125]

---

7 November 1989, BISD 36S/345 para. 5.11 (which served as inspiration for Article XVII:2 GATS).

[120] *EC – Bananas III (AB)* para. 231.

[121] Wolfrum, 'Article II GATS' 88.

[122] Zdouc, 'WTO Dispute Settlement Practice Relating to the General Agreement on Trade in Services' 415, interpreting *EC – Bananas III (AB)* para. 233.

[123] *EC – Bananas III (Panel)* para. 7.301.

[124] Zdouc, 'WTO Dispute Settlement Practice Relating to the General Agreement on Trade in Services' 416.

[125] Ibid.

1.1.3.2 A modification of the conditions of competition Essentially, GATS case law interpreted the less favourable treatment criterion as assessing whether the measure *modifies the conditions of competition.* The centrality of 'modification of the conditions of competition' to the less favourable treatment condition is apparent from the GATT 1947-era Panel report on *US – Section 337* onwards, with the Panel noting that the less favourable treatment condition 'calls for effective equality of opportunities for imported products'.[126] The impacts of the measure on the equality of competitive conditions 'are, first and foremost, those that are discernible from the design, structure, and expected operation of the measure'.[127] In summary, as Geraets and Natens have argued elsewhere:

> conditions of competition are the overall framework of governmental measures (laws, regulations and requirements) that impact the internal sale, offering for sale, purchase, transportation, distribution or use of goods or services. A [modification of the conditions of competition] occurs when a measure causes a change in the overall framework of governmental measures and that change results in an alteration in the competitive opportunities between foreign and domestic products or services.[128]

In the context of GATS, the Panel in *China – Electronic Payment Services* stated that, provided all other conditions of Article XVII GATS are fulfilled, there is less favourable treatment 'if and only if such treatment modifies the conditions of competition to their detriment'.[129] Thus, at least according to this Panel, the scope of less favourable treatment in Article XVII GATS does not extend beyond a modification of the conditions of competition, which is a necessary condition for the establishment of less favourable treatment. Equally, it would also appear to be a sufficient condition. In *EC – Seal Products*, the AB rejected 'the proposition that the detrimental impact of a measure on competitive opportunities for like imported products is not dispositive for the

---

126 US – Section 337 Tariff Act (GATT Panel) para. 5.11.

127 *Thailand – Customs and Fiscal Measures on Cigarettes from the Philippines* WT/DS371/AB/R, AB report adopted 15 July 2011 para. 130. Also see *Canada – Certain Measures Concerning Periodicals* WT/DS31/AB/R, AB report adopted 30 July 1997 para. 30.

128 Natens and Geraets, 'Modification of the Conditions of Competition for Goods and Services: The Side-track that Never Was', at the end of section 1.

129 *China – Electronic Payment Services (Panel)* para. 7.687.

purposes of establishing a violation of Article III:4'.[130] On the contrary, Natens and Geraets have argued elsewhere that as soon as a governmental measure results in a modification of the conditions of competition that has a detrimental impact on imported (products or) services, the measure accords less favourable treatment. The sole exception to this is a case with no 'genuine relationship' between the measure and the adverse impact.[131] This requirement has been part of the GATT 1994 case law since *US – Gasoline*, where the Panel clarified that the relevant conditions of competition are those 'established by government measures and would not therefore include factors such as the "flexibility of individual producers" in this case'.[132] Indeed, footnote 10 to Article XVII GATS also reflects this requirement: if the conditions of competition are modified due to inherent competitive disadvantages of the foreign service provided, there is no less favourable treatment. Thus, there appears to be no room for regulatory motives or considerations in assessing the less favourable treatment condition in the national treatment and MFN obligations in GATS. This is in line with the AB's rejection of the aims and effects test, which also applies vis-à-vis the assessment of whether a measure modifies the conditions of competition.[133] A recent compliance Panel in *US – COOL* followed the AB's approach. In doing so, it rejected the US' argument that a detrimental impact on competitive conditions is insufficient for establishing less favourable treatment, and consequently stated that there is no room for an assessment of legitimate regulatory distinctions in the context of Article III:4 GATT 1994.[134] The result is

---

[130] *European Communities – Measures Prohibiting the Importation and Marketing of Seal Products* WT/DS400/AB/R, AB report adopted 18 June 2014 para. 5.110.

[131] See *United States – Certain Country of Origin Labelling (COOL) Requirements* WT/DS384/AB/R, WT/DS386/AB/R, AB report adopted 23 July 2012 para. 270.

[132] *United States – Standards for Reformulated and Conventional Gasoline* WT/DS2/R, Panel report adopted 20 May 1996 para. 6.25. Geraets and I argue that the AB's finding in *Dominican Republic – Measures Affecting the Importation and Internal Sale of Cigarettes* WT/DS302/AB/R, AB report adopted 19 May 2005 para. 96 is merely another restatement of the 'genuine relationship' requirement. Similarly, one can argue that the Panel's statement in *European Communities – Measures Affecting the Approval and Marketing of Biotech Products* WT/DS293/R, Panel report adopted 21 November 2006 para. 7.2514 can be read in the same way.

[133] *EC – Bananas III (AB)* para. 243.

[134] *United States – Certain Country of Origin Labelling (COOL) Requirements (Recourse to Article 21.5 of the DSU by Canada and Mexico)* WT/DS384/

that a legitimate regulatory distinction between like services and service suppliers that has a trade impact would need to be justified under an exception provision.

A close examination of the case law on less favourable treatment in GATS clarifies the manner in which the less favourable treatment condition is being shaped in the context of services. (In support of the argument that less favourable treatment in the MFN and national treatment obligations needs to be interpreted consistently, this survey also highlights that panels do not appear to put a particular emphasis on paragraphs 2 and 3 of Article XVII GATS.) At the outset, it may be noted that Article XVII:2 GATS has been interpreted as explicitly including *de facto* discrimination, aside from *de jure* discrimination, in the national treatment obligation.[135] This applies equally to the MFN obligation, as deciding otherwise would make it too easy to 'devise discriminatory measures aimed at circumventing the basic purpose' of Article II GATS.[136] Hence, *de facto* discriminatory measures may *not* lead to a modification of the conditions of competition to the detriment of either foreign services and service suppliers, or the services or service suppliers of any third country. Note however that a close reading of Article XVII GATS also indicates that a Member may *comply* with the national treatment obligation through granting both different and identical treatment.[137] Thus, formally different treatment may explicitly differentiate on the basis of origin, so long as this does not constitute discrimination.[138]

In *EC – Bananas III*, the Panel and the AB considered that as licence transferees were 'most often' foreign service suppliers and licence sellers were 'usually' domestic service suppliers, foreign service suppliers were 'subject to less favourable conditions of competition in their ability to compete in the [relevant] services market'.[139] It may be noted that, when the licensing system under scrutiny had been introduced, the EU had stated that the purpose of the measure was the cross-subsidisation of Category B service suppliers.[140] This analysis was not countered by

---

RW, WT/DS386/RW, Panel report circulated 20 October 2014, not yet adopted paras 7.621 and 7.625.

135 S/L/92 2001 Scheduling Guidelines para. 13.

136 *EC – Bananas III (AB)* para. 234; *Canada – Autos (AB)* para. 141.

137 *China – Publications and Audiovisual Products (Panel)* para. 7.1130.

138 *Korea – Measures Affecting Imports of Fresh, Chilled and Frozen Beef* WT/DS161/AB/R, AB report adopted 10 January 2001 para. 144; Flett, 'WTO Space for National Regulation: Requiem for a Diagonal Vector Test' 54–55.

139 *EC – Bananas III (Panel)* para. 7.336.

140 Ibid para. 7.352.

factual evidence, which pointed at a lack of significant change in market share.[141] A similar situation was addressed in *Canada – Autos*, where the origin-neutral measure provided an incentive for manufacturers to purchase domestic services, thus modifying the conditions of competition.[142] These findings indicate that, for an assessment of the detrimental impact of the measure, it suffices that foreign services and service providers are 'usually' disfavoured.

Furthermore, in *Canada – Autos*, the AB noted that, where a measure directly regulates *goods*, a panel must analyse the detrimental impact of a measure on a service supplier *in their capacity as service supplier*. This is so even if the service supplier is, in a different capacity, also experiencing the detrimental impact of the measure as a manufacturer of goods.[143] This finding seems to have limited the scope of *de facto* discrimination under the national treatment obligation,[144] or, at least to have clarified the overlap between Articles III:4 GATT 1994 and XVII GATS in situations where the measure affects both goods and services.

At issue in *China – Publications and Audiovisual Products* were *de jure* discriminatory measures. The Panel noted that, considering the measure excluded the foreign service suppliers at hand, the conditions of competition were modified 'in the most radical way', i.e. by eliminating all foreign competition and depriving foreign service suppliers of any opportunity to compete.[145] Regarding another measure, according to which foreign service suppliers were subjected to a maximum 30-year operating term whilst domestic service suppliers were not, the Panel held that GATT 1994 case law on less favourable treatment in national treatment was relevant. Indeed, both obligations required 'an analysis of the effects of a measure on conditions of competition'.[146] Consequently, the Panel argued, LFT must be assessed through 'careful analysis of the measure and the market', the main concern being whether the measure 'unfavourably modifies "conditions of competition" to the detriment' of

---

[141] Ibid para. 7.337. Concerning related measures, the Panel confirmed this finding in paras 7.363–7.366, 7.378–7.379 and 7.392. This was reconfirmed in *EC – Bananas III (AB)* paras 244, 246 and 248.

[142] *Canada – Autos (Panel)* para. 10.307. This finding was not appealed.

[143] *Canada – Autos (AB)* para. 181.

[144] Zdouc, 'WTO Dispute Settlement Practice Relating to the General Agreement on Trade in Services' 410.

[145] *China – Publications and Audiovisual Products (Panel)* para. 7.979. Regarding other measures at issue with similar *de jure* discriminations, the Panel reiterates its finding in paras 7.996, 7.1073, 7.1094, 7.1421.

[146] Ibid paras 7.1131–7.1132.

foreign service suppliers.[147] The Panel then applied this test and found, first, that the measure 'could impose significant costs' on the foreign service supplier. Second, although the costs and the risk of service interruptions were only likely to materialise towards the end of the 30-year operating term, this could *potentially* affect conditions of competition, especially for those service suppliers looking to provide the services for a period longer than 30 years.[148] The Panel concluded that the discriminatory measure had 'implications in the marketplace' and, as no limitation was scheduled in this regard, the measure violated Article XVII GATS.[149]

Similarly, in *China – Electronic Payment Services*, the Panel found that the measures under scrutiny resulted in formally different treatment between domestic and foreign service suppliers.[150] The Panel found *inter alia* that there had been a modification of the conditions of competition on the basis that payment cards, in certain circumstances, were required to feature the domestic electronic payment service provider's logo, both prominently and for free. This had raised the profile of that domestic service supplier and had modified the conditions of competition.[151] Similarly, one-way-only interoperability requirements modify the conditions of competition in favour of domestic service suppliers. Foreign service suppliers would need to incur both time and cost to remedy this disadvantage.[152] Other related measures also indicated a modification of the conditions of competition. For example, foreign services could be denied by merchants and acquirers while the like domestic service could not be denied.[153]

The findings in both Chinese cases highlight that a formally different, i.e. *de jure* discriminatory, measure will modify the conditions of competition even if the detrimental impact is both future and uncertain. Thus, foreign services *or* service suppliers may *not* be subjected to treatment that *could, in the future*, increase costs or risks, or *could* induce consumer disfavour. In other words, a potential disparate impact suffices

---

[147] Ibid para. 7.1131, citing *US – FSC (Article 21.5 – EC) (AB)* paras 215 and 221, and 7.1136.

[148] *China – Publications and Audiovisual Products (Panel)* paras 7.1136–7.1138.

[149] Ibid para. 7.1139. The Panel reiterates this finding, as concerns a similar measure, in para. 7.1425.

[150] *China – Electronic Payment Services (Panel)* paras 7.694 and 7.720.

[151] Ibid para. 7.712.

[152] Ibid paras 7.714 and 7.738.

[153] Ibid paras 7.725 and 7.736.

to establish less favourable treatment. Although there is no reason to second-guess the Panel's conclusions in both cases, this interpretation of a modification of the conditions of competition seems to leave very little room for domestic regulators to grant treatment no less favourable through *formally different* treatment.

The Panel in *Argentina – Financial Services* was confronted with such a situation.[154] It found through an extensive interpretative exercise that the context of GATS, which includes *inter alia* references to the right to regulate in its preamble and to service *suppliers*, indicates that the regulatory framework in which service suppliers operate was relevant to its analysis of less favourable treatment.[155] The Panel invoked the AB's abovementioned findings in *Thailand – Cigarettes* and, in the context of the TBT Agreement, in *US – COOL*.[156] The Panel subsequently found that the measure preliminarily accorded less favourable treatment because it modified the conditions of competition to the detriment of certain foreign services and service suppliers. However, this finding could be rebutted on the basis of the regulatory distinction between countries that do share tax information and those that do not. In the present case, the presumption was upheld because the difference in treatment between services and service suppliers was *not* based on the purported regulatory distinction. Specifically, the issue was that Argentina did not *actually* base the treatment on whether it had access to the said tax information, although the measure purported that this regulatory distinction led to the difference in treatment. It therefore violated the MFN obligation.[157] It is clear from the above analysis that I disagree with the Panel's approach in light of the case law. Nonetheless, this case may force the AB to finally pronounce on the issue as, at the time of writing, Panama appealed this finding.

The Panel in *Argentina – Financial Services* was further asked to rule on a national treatment claim. In this respect, it noted that the measures aimed at levelling the playing field between services and service suppliers which originated in countries that exchanged tax information and those that didn't. It found no modification of the conditions of competition in favour or Argentine services and service suppliers. Rather, the

---

154 *Argentina – Financial Services (Panel)* para. 7.273.

155 Ibid paras 7.209–7.233 for MFN and 7.505 for national treatment.

156 Ibid para. 7.235.

157 Ibid paras 7.287–7.292, 7.301, 7.309, 7.319, 7.329, 7.339, 7.351 and 7.360.

measures were 'designed precisely to guarantee' the competitive relationship.[158] This finding deserves praise and highlights the limits to the stringent case law on modification of conditions of competition in the specific situation of harmful tax competition between countries – as recognised by the OECD and the G-20.[159]

1.1.3.3 The disparate impact test as the standard of less favourable treatment A modification of the conditions of competition is instructive for a finding of less favourable treatment. A detrimental impact on foreign services and service suppliers in comparison to like domestic services and service suppliers leads to a finding that there is such a modification. There is a clear tendency to reach such a finding by applying the 'disparate impact test' or asymmetric impact test.[160] According to the disparate impact test, there is a modification of the conditions of competition if a larger percentage of foreign services and service suppliers are accorded less favourable treatment in comparison to the same group, based on market conditions and competitive relationships, of the like domestic services and service suppliers.[161] The determination of the 'group' constituting 'the' service or 'the' service supplier (which is then to be compared with the same 'group' in the 'likeness' assessment) is crucial. It is not sufficient to find a *single* foreign service and service provider that is treated less favourably than a *single* like domestic service and service supplier: the group of foreign services and service suppliers must be accorded less favourable treatment than the group of like domestic services and service suppliers.[162] In other words, the 'like imports bear a heavier overall burden than the like domestic products'.[163]

---

158 Ibid paras 7.514–7.516 and 7.521.

159 Ibid paras 7.509–7.515.

160 See Diebold, *Non-Discrimination in International Trade in Services: 'Likeness' in WTO/GATS* 98; Nicolas Diebold, 'Standards of Nondiscrimination in International Economic Law' (2011) 60 International and Comparative Law Quarterly 831, 843 argues that the case law on Article III:4 GATT 1994 has moved in the direction of the asymmetric impact test.

161 Diebold, *Non-Discrimination in International Trade in Services: 'Likeness' in WTO/GATS* 95.

162 Porges and Trachtman, 'Robert Hudec and Domestic Regulation: The Resurrection of Aim and Effects' 796.

163 Lothar Ehring, 'De Facto Discrimination in World Trade Law: National and Most-Favoured-Nation-Treatment or Equal Treatment?' (2002) 36 Journal of World Trade 921, 925.

In *EC – Bananas III*, both the AB and the Panel made use of this approach, both for the MFN and the national treatment violations.[164]

This disparate impact test can be contrasted to the 'diagonal (vector) test', according to which there is less favourable treatment whenever a *single* foreign service or service supplier is treated less favourably than *any* like domestic service or service supplier.[165] Such an approach does not require comparing the groups of domestic and imported services or service suppliers.[166] The diagonal test places a greater constraint on regulatory autonomy as compared to the disparate impact test. It has been argued that the disparate impact test is:

> a restriction on the concept of discrimination itself that should put a needed brake on the creeping WTO regulation of domestic intervention. In some way, it may become the functional equivalent of the Keck ruling by the [Court of Justice of the European Union] in that both rulings, after a period of broadly interpreting trade disciplines, impose certain limits that preserve the regulatory autonomy of states.[167]

Moreover, this test indeed results in a 'greater flexibility for objective distinctions between products'.[168]

In the few GATS disputes thus far, panels have not yet had to deal with difficult examples of the disparate impact assessment. Future case law will have to clarify the extent to which the services context plays a role in determining how the disparate impact test is interpreted. For example, the timeframe for assessing the modification of the conditions of competition is relevant, i.e. whether to assess the modification in the short term (in which case there would be more chance of finding a violation) or the long term (taking into account that service suppliers are free to

---

[164] *EC – Bananas III (Panel)* paras 7.332–7.338, 7.349, 7.363–7.368, 7.384, 7.392–7.393 and 7.396; *EC – Bananas III (AB)* paras 229–234, 243–244 and 246; Ehring, 'De Facto Discrimination in World Trade Law: National and Most-Favoured-Nation-Treatment or Equal Treatment?' 934–935.

[165] Diebold, *Non-Discrimination in International Trade in Services: 'Likeness' in WTO/GATS* 94. For thorough criticism of this test, see Ehring, 'De Facto Discrimination in World Trade Law: National and Most-Favoured-Nation-Treatment or Equal Treatment?'.

[166] Ehring, 'De Facto Discrimination in World Trade Law: National and Most-Favoured-Nation-Treatment or Equal Treatment?' 946.

[167] Joost Pauwelyn, 'Recent Books on Trade and Environment: GATT Phantoms Still Haunt the WTO' (2004) 15 European Journal of International Law 575, 583.

[168] Ehring, 'De Facto Discrimination in World Trade Law: National and Most-Favoured-Nation-Treatment or Equal Treatment?' 953.

adapt to the new rules, in which case there is less chance of a modification of the conditions of competition).[169]

1.1.4 Constraints on regulatory autonomy

The interpretation of 'likeness' and 'less favourable treatment' is crucial in assessing the constraints on regulatory autonomy that result from the national treatment obligation.[170] A first issue is the relevance of the 'regulatory purpose' of the measure, i.e. whether it pursues a legitimate policy. It has been noted that a strict denunciation of taking legitimate policies into account when assessing a measure's compliance with non-discrimination obligations in GATS may 'undermine sovereign regulatory powers' to a larger degree than is the case for trade in goods. Indeed, a much greater range of regulations have the potential to affect service suppliers as compared to suppliers of goods.[171] Disciplines on trade in services have the potential to encroach on socially delicate matters, and information asymmetries related to *inter alia* the intangible nature of services often require substantial regulatory intervention. Nonetheless, in my view, the door for taking 'regulatory' elements into account in the analysis of less favourable treatment has been shut completely by the AB in *EC – Seal Products*. Regardless of its regulatory purpose, if a governmental measure has a negative impact on the competitive opportunities of foreign services and service suppliers as compared to the group of like domestic services or service suppliers, this will amount to a finding of a modification of the conditions of competition and therefore to less favourable treatment. The sole exception is

---

[169] Flett, 'National Treatment under the General Agreement on Trade in Services (GATS)' 76–77.

[170] Diebold, *Non-Discrimination in International Trade in Services: 'Likeness' in WTO/GATS* 94–96 draws up a matrix of the potential constraints on regulatory autonomy that result from different interpretations of likeness and less favourable treatment. This table illustrates the interaction of different interpretations of both conditions vis-à-vis the overall constraints on regulatory autonomy from the national treatment and MFN obligations. This approach differs from that in Pauwelyn, 'The Unbearable Lightness of Likeness' 363, who considers the likeness test only the trigger for the actual analysis of less favourable treatment. Under the disparate impact test, the scope of likeness is however relevant, as the impact on the group of like services and service suppliers is to be compared: the wider the group, the more chances of having a disparate detrimental impact vis-à-vis foreign services and service suppliers. I therefore follow Diebold, not Pauwelyn.

[171] Zdouc, 'WTO Dispute Settlement Practice Relating to the GATS' 342.

the requirement that there must be a genuine relationship between the measure and the detrimental impact.

The current approach towards less favourable treatment in GATT 1994 case law, read in conjunction with the limited GATS case law,[172] considerably constrains regulatory autonomy. This is because the sole relevant factor for establishing a violation is whether economic market conditions have been altered. The wide interpretation of such an alteration, i.e. that a modification of the conditions of competition appears to be found quite easily, strengthens these concerns. The trend towards a purely market-based assessment of less favourable treatment (i.e., an approach in which regulatory concerns do not play any role) is extremely problematic from a regulatory autonomy perspective. Indeed, the result of such an approach is that a regulator does not have any leeway to distinguish between domestic and foreign services and service suppliers under the less favourable treatment test. Nonetheless, these concerns may be mitigated by applying the disparate impact test. In contrast to the diagonal vector test, before it can be concluded that there has been a modification of the conditions of competition, the disparate impact test requires that a real detrimental impact on foreign services and service suppliers has resulted from the measure.

However, the condition of less favourable treatment is but one element of a larger picture, encompassing a number of tests and conditions. Therefore, if it is true that 'elements having to do with the "aims and effects" doctrine' are reappearing in the assessment of non-discrimination obligations,[173] this will also be true for the likeness analysis. I have argued in favour of a GATT-1994-like 'competitive likeness' approach for services. A crucial contextual difference between GATT 1994 and GATS is the likeness of service suppliers. Assessing the likeness of service suppliers on the basis of the above argumentation allows for some wiggle room for regulators. Taking into account consumer habits and preferences and the characteristics of the service supplier in so far as this is relevant for the supply of the service, allows for some form of 'regulatory

---

[172] In *EC – Bananas III*, a *de facto* discriminatory measure was assessed in a manner that can be classified as following the disparate impact test. See Zdouc, 'WTO Dispute Settlement Practice Relating to the General Agreement on Trade in Services' 408–409.

[173] Eric Leroux, 'Eleven Years of GATS Case Law: What Have We Learned?' (2007) 10 Journal of International Economic Law 749, 782.

likeness' in addition to 'competitive likeness'. The consequence is that, to some extent, regulatory measures may contribute to a finding of 'unlikeness'.[174]

Finally, it must be recalled that the scope of the national treatment obligation is limited: it is a conditional obligation dependant on whether a Member has scheduled specific commitments and is subject to any limitations therein.

1.2 The Most-Favoured-Nation Obligation

The MFN obligation of Article II GATS is a general principle of non-discrimination, based on the principle of reciprocity. Its primary purpose is to 'ensure all WTO Members equality of opportunity' for services and services suppliers.[175] The MFN obligation is the most important of GATS' unconditional obligations and applies to any measure covered by GATS.[176] Hence, it could be said that the liberalisation effect of MFN is 'more momentous' than the national treatment obligation.[177] According to Article II:1 GATS, (i) for measures covered by the obligation, a Member must, (ii) immediately and unconditionally, (iii) accord treatment no less favourable, whether *de jure* or *de facto*,[178] to services and service suppliers of a Member, (iv) than to like services or service suppliers of any other country. Consequently, it does not prohibit treating *domestic* services and service suppliers more favourably than *foreign* ones but solely proscribes discrimination between foreign services and service suppliers. Nonetheless, the MFN obligation results in substantial, albeit not necessarily straightforward, constraints on regulatory autonomy. To assess such constraints, the legal tests which are applied to establish a violation of Article II GATS should be examined.[179]

---

[174] Nonetheless, I do not agree with Donald H Regan, 'Regulatory Purpose and "Like Products" in Article III:4 of the GATT (With Additional Remarks on Article III:2)' (2002) 36 Journal of World Trade 443, who sees a much broader role for regulatory purpose in the likeness analysis.

[175] Van den Bossche and Zdouc, *The Law and Policy of the World Trade Organization* 318.

[176] *EC – Bananas III (Panel)* para. 7.298; Wolfrum, 'Article II GATS' 77.

[177] Zdouc, 'WTO Dispute Settlement Practice Relating to the General Agreement on Trade in Services' 395.

[178] *EC – Bananas III (AB)* para. 234; *Canada – Autos (AB)* para. 141.

[179] Zdouc, 'WTO Dispute Settlement Practice Relating to the General Agreement on Trade in Services' 417.

1.2.1 The scope of the obligation

Article II:1 GATS expressly states that the obligation applies to 'any measure covered by this agreement'. Only measures that are listed in a Member's List of MFN Exemptions (and measures covered by the frontier zones provision) are exempted.[180] In comparison to the MFN obligation in Article I GATT 1994, on the one hand, Article II GATS has a broader scope because it applies to all measures affecting trade in services, and to services and service suppliers alike.[181] The more favourable treatment accorded to the services or service suppliers of any *country*, even if that country is not a WTO Member, needs to be extended to other Members.[182] Moreover, as a result of GATS' broad scope, which also includes some aspects of the movement of capital and labour, the scope of its MFN obligation is wider than is the case for goods under GATT 1994.[183] Contrary to Article I GATT 1994, the MFN obligation in GATS is defined solely 'in terms of treatment of foreign services and service suppliers'. However, this does not exclude measures that affect exports of foreign service suppliers established under Mode 3.[184] Nonetheless, Members may discriminate between different export destinations and between recipients on the basis of their nationality.[185] In practice, this gap in the scope of the GATS MFN obligation does not appear to cause trade frictions.[186] This does not mean that, for domestically established foreign suppliers and their services – i.e. Mode 3 service suppliers – the MFN obligation would not apply: a Member may not discriminate *between* domestically established foreign service suppliers, and this is also true for measures affecting these service suppliers'

---

[180] Article II:2 GATS and the GATS Annex on Article II Exemptions.

[181] Zdouc, 'WTO Dispute Settlement Practice Relating to the General Agreement on Trade in Services' 383.

[182] R Adlung, 'Export Policies and the General Agreement on Trade in Services' (2015) 18 Journal of International Economic Law 487, 493.

[183] Rudolf Adlung and Antonia Carzaniga, 'MFN Exemptions under the General Agreement on Trade in Services: Grandfathers Striving for Immortality?' (2009) 12 Journal of International Economic Law 357, 359.

[184] Adlung, 'Export Policies and the General Agreement on Trade in Services' 493–494. See, to the contrary, Aaditya Mattoo, *Dealing with Monopolies and State Enterprises: WTO Rules for Goods and Services* (World Trade Organization Trade in Services Division Staff Working Paper TISD9801, 1997) 5.

[185] Adlung, 'Export Policies and the General Agreement on Trade in Services' 500.

[186] Ibid.

exports.[187] Moreover, as noted, the MFN obligation applies to both the pre- and post-establishment phases in the case of Mode 3.[188]

1.2.2 Immediately and unconditionally

Article II:1 GATS specifies that each Member shall immediately and unconditionally grant treatment no less favourable to like services and service suppliers. This condition has not been interpreted in GATS case law.[189] However, the phrase 'shall be accorded immediately and unconditionally', has been interpreted in the context of the MFN obligation in Article I:1 GATT 1994. The AB has clarified that 'unconditional' does not mean that *no* conditions may be attached to the advantage (the MFN obligation under GATT 1994 is wider than prohibiting less favourable treatment) but that conditions that have a detrimental impact on the competitive opportunities of like products are prohibited.[190] 'Unconditionally' does require that the extension of the treatment is not 'made subject to conditions with respect to the situation or conduct of those countries'.[191]

1.2.3 Likeness

The likeness criterion has been addressed above. It was argued that the likeness criterion applies to national treatment and MFN in an identical manner, with the exception of the services and service suppliers which need to be compared.

1.2.4 Treatment no less favourable

The less favourable treatment condition has also been addressed above; it applies to national treatment and MFN obligations identically.

---

[187] Ibid 494.

[188] *China – Publications and Audiovisual Products (Panel)* para. 7.974; Pierre Sauvé and Christopher Wilkie, 'Investment Liberalization in GATS' in Pierre Sauvé and Robert M Stern (eds), *GATS 2000: New Directions in Services Trade Liberalization* (Brookings Institution 2000) 348; Martín Molinuevo, *Protecting Investment in Services: Investor-State Arbitration Versus WTO Dispute Settlement* (Wolters Kluwer 2012) 80–82 and 94–103.

[189] *Argentina – Financial Services (Panel)* para. 7.263.

[190] *EC – Seal Products (AB)* paras 5.88 and 5.93, clarifying *Canada – Autos (AB)* para. 76.

[191] *United States – Certain Measures Affecting Imports of Poultry from China* WT/DS392/R, Panel report adopted 25 October 2010 para. 7.436.

1.2.5 Exceptions to the Most-Favoured-Nation obligation[192]

1.2.5.1 The List of Most-Favoured-Nation Exemptions The second paragraph of Article II GATS contains the legal basis for Members' Lists of MFN Exemptions. MFN exemptions can either allow more favourable treatment or contain 'targeted denials' of less favourable treatment.[193] MFN exemptions had to be listed at the time of conclusion of GATS in the Annex on Article II Exemptions. Acceding Members can also adopt a list of MFN Exemptions.[194] Although, supposedly, the exemptions only apply to measures that existed at the entry into force of the agreement, some future exemptions 'were presented as existing ones'.[195] Paragraph 6 of the Annex on Article II Exemptions provides that, in principle, the exemptions were to become extinct after a maximum of ten years. In reality, many exemptions seem to have been scheduled indefinitely.[196] Legally speaking, this raises questions regarding the WTO compatibility of such indefinite exemptions. Considering that so many exemptions are scheduled indefinitely, there is perhaps little risk that a case will be brought; a similar situation exists regarding the WTO compatibility of RTAs. However, if the economic relevance of a specific MFN exemption were sufficiently large, it is not unthinkable that a Member with no (or relatively unimportant) MFN exemptions in its own List, would bring up such an argument.

In total, over 90 Members listed almost 500 measures in their lists of MFN Exemptions.[197] Just over half of all exemptions apply to audio-visual services and maritime, air and road transport services, which are

---

[192] The specific exception for the MFN obligation in Article XIV (e) GATS is addressed in the section on the general exceptions, due to the integrated approach of that provision in subparagraphs (a)–(e).

[193] Adlung and Carzaniga, 'MFN Exemptions under the General Agreement on Trade in Services: Grandfathers Striving for Immortality?' 358.

[194] See GATS/EL/135, The People's Republic of China: Final List of Article II (MFN) Exemptions (14 February 2002).

[195] Wolfrum, 'Article II GATS' 90.

[196] This is the case for 425 out of 491 MFN exemptions. Adlung and Carzaniga, 'MFN Exemptions under the General Agreement on Trade in Services: Grandfathers Striving for Immortality?' 373. Also see the EU's list of exemptions: GATS/EL/31, European Communities and Their Member States: Final List of Article II (MFN) Exemptions (15 April 1994), which contains 26 exemptions scheduled for an indefinite period of time.

[197] Adlung and Carzaniga, 'MFN Exemptions under the General Agreement on Trade in Services: Grandfathers Striving for Immortality?' 360. For a sectoral overview of MFN exemptions, see p. 371. For a temporal overview of the duration of MFN exemptions, see p. 373.

sectors in which few GATS commitments have been made. About one fifth of all exemptions apply horizontally, i.e. to all sectors.[198] Exemptions are mostly listed (i) due to reciprocity: Members state that the exemptions are 'needed to achieve equal access or treatment in foreign markets' or 'necessary to respond to unfair practices abroad', or (ii) due to preferential treatment accorded to other Members as a result of bi- or plurilateral agreements.[199]

The EU List of MFN Exemptions contains nine horizontal exemptions. Only three of these exemptions apply to all EU Member States. These exemptions address the progressive liberalisation between the EU and Switzerland, San Marino, Monaco, Andorra and Vatican City State. They also address work permits for seasonal workers from states in Central Eastern and South-Eastern Europe and in the Mediterranean Basin. The List further contains 19 sector-specific exemptions. Eight exemptions relate to: (i) audio-visual services (highlighting this sector's sensitive nature) and three exemptions relate to; (ii) publishing. The other sectors for which an exemption is listed are: (iii) road transport; and (iv) internal waterways transport (each with two listings); (v) computerised reservation systems and air transport sales and marketing services; (vi) rental and leasing of ships; and (vii) direct non-life insurance and financial services. Not all exemptions apply to all EU Member States, as some Member States, such as France and Italy, have negotiated specific exemptions. Likewise, not all exemptions address all third countries. In some cases, the beneficiary third countries for which the exemption applies are listed. For instance, an indefinite MFN exemption is listed for the production and distribution of cinematographic works and television programmes in Nordic countries. This exempts Denmark from an obligation to extend the treatment accorded to Finland, Norway, Sweden and Iceland – both EU Member States and non-EU Member States – regarding benefits provided in conformity with support programmes that enhance the production and distribution to third countries of audio-visual works produced in Nordic countries. The rationale for this exemption is the preservation and promotion of regional identity.

---

198 OECD Working Party of the Trade Committee, Trade in Services: A Roadmap to MFN Exemptions (TD/TC/WP(2001)25/FINAL, 2001) 11 and 13–14. See Laura Altinger and Alice Enders, 'The Scope and Depth of GATS Commitments' (1996) 19 The World Economy 307, 324 for a table of sectoral coverage of MFN exemptions.

199 These two categories cater for 37 per cent and 55 per cent of all MFN exemptions respectively. OECD Working Party of the Trade Committee, Trade in Services: A Roadmap to MFN Exemptions 23–26.

1.2.5.2 Frontier zones Article II:3 GATS exempts Members from extending more favourable treatment to all other Members if such treatment is accorded to facilitate an exchange of services that are both locally produced and consumed in order to facilitate exchanges limited to contiguous frontier zones. This exemption only applies to adjacent countries. Article II:3 GATS has never been addressed in WTO dispute settlement and can be considered of minor importance. Moreover, its relevance for regulatory autonomy seems to be non-existent.

1.2.5.3 Least-developed countries The importance of development is evident from the GATS preamble,[200] and reflected in Article IV GATS. Most relevant for the purposes of this book, paragraph 3 of Article IV GATS 'almost certainly creates an exemption' from the MFN obligation.[201] Indeed, regarding the negotiation of specific commitments, least-developed countries can show restraint in opening up their services sectors whilst developed countries should refrain from pursuing overly aggressive commitments from services sectors.[202] A waiver, allowing developed and developing countries to deviate from their MFN obligations to grant preferential treatment to all least-developed countries was adopted in 2011, and is being operationalised at the time of writing. From the perspective of regulatory autonomy, this exception is of limited importance.

1.2.5.4 Economic integration exceptions The existence of RTAs is at first sight irreconcilable with the MFN principle: the preferential liberalisation in RTAs unquestionably erodes the MFN obligation. As put succinctly by one author: 'In the absence of "open clubs", PTAs are per construction antithetical to the idea of non-discriminatory trade, the cornerstone of the [WTO] edifice'.[203] The result of the proliferation is that MFN treatment may have become 'LFN', or Least-Favoured-Nation

---

[200] GATS preamble, fourth to sixth recital.

[201] Mary E Footer and Carol George, 'The General Agreement on Trade in Services' in Patrick FJ Macrory, Arthur E Appleton and Michael G Plummer (eds), *The World Trade Organization: Legal, Economic and Political Analysis*, vol 1 (Springer 2005) 833.

[202] TN/S/13, Modalities for the Special Treatment for Least-Developed Country Members in the Negotiations on Trade in Services (Adopted by the Council for Trade in Services 5 September 2003) para. 4.

[203] Petros C Mavroidis, 'If I Don't Do It, Somebody Else Will (Or Won't): Testing the Compliance of Preferential Trade Agreements With the Multilateral Rules' (2006) 40 Journal of World Trade 187, 187.

treatment.[204] Nonetheless, WTO law allows such deviation from the MFN principle. Both GATT 1994, in Article XXIV, and GATS, in Articles V and V bis, contain economic integration exceptions.

1.2.5.4.1 REGIONAL ECONOMIC INTEGRATION AGREEMENTS In order to qualify for Article V GATS, which contains an exception from the MFN obligation for EIAs, the two conditions of Article V:1 GATS must be fulfilled. These conditions 'allow for ambitious liberalization to take place at a regional level, while at the same time guarding against undermining the MFN obligation by engaging in minor preferential arrangements'.[205]

a. First, the agreement must have substantial sectoral coverage. This condition should, according to footnote 1 to Article V:1 GATS, be understood in terms of the number of sectors and volume of trade affected, and should not *a priori* exclude a mode of supply.[206]
b. Second, the RTA must provide for the absence or elimination of substantially all discriminatory measures in the sense of the national treatment obligation through the elimination of existing discriminatory measures and/or the prohibition of new such measures *within* the EIA.[207] This condition is referred to as the internal trade requirement.[208] The elimination of substantially all discrimination needs to be fulfilled either at the time of entry into force of the EIA or on the basis of a reasonable time-frame. The requirement does not apply to measures permitted under Articles XI, XII, XIV and XIV bis GATS.

   In order to assess whether 'substantially all' discrimination is eliminated, the relationship between the agreement and a wider process of economic integration or trade liberalisation among the

[204] A term coined by Bhagwati, noting that, in 2008, the EU applied its MFN tariffs to only six countries (Australia, New Zealand, Canada, Japan, Taiwan Province of China and the United States) whilst all other states enjoy more favourable tariffs. Jagdish Bhagwati, 'Termites in the Trade System' (2008) 4 Asia-Pacific Trade and Investment Review 3, 7.

[205] *Canada – Autos (Panel)* para. 10.271.

[206] See Sherry M Stephenson, 'GATS and Regional Integration' in Pierre Sauvé and Robert M Stern (eds), *GATS 2000: New Directions in Services Trade Liberalization* (Brookings Institution 2000) 514–517.

[207] See ibid 517–519.

[208] Yoeri Devuyst and Asja Serdarevic, 'The World Trade Organization and Regional Trade Agreements: Bridging the Constitutional Credibility Gap' (2007–2008) 18 Duke Journal of Comparative & International Law 1, 20.

parties to the EIA may considered. The scope of the term, which aims to avoid RTAs that grant preferential treatment to a limited number of services and service suppliers which would disintegrate the global economy, has been subject to disagreement between Members.[209] The AB has clarified that 'substantially' means considerably more than 'some', but is not the same as 'all'.[210] The Panel in *Canada – Autos* noted that a measure that grants more favourable treatment to one party to an RTA as compared to another party, or to some service suppliers in an RTA but not to other service suppliers, is inconsistent with the obligation to eliminate substantially all discrimination.[211] This ruling 'imposes an obligation on the PTA partners to ensure MFN treatment to all parties to the PTA'.[212] However, the Panel seems to accord very little meaning to the term 'substantially' all discrimination: in plurilateral agreements, it is possible that specific concessions are made vis-à-vis one party but not to other parties, or for some service suppliers but not for others. Contrary to what the Panel seems to suggest, the internal trade requirement does not forbid such practices. A more nuanced interpretation is appropriate in light of the text of the provision.[213]

c. A third condition is the external trade requirement,[214] found in Article V:4 GATS. It requires that the EIA does not raise the overall level of barriers to trade in services within the respective sectors or subsectors compared to the level applicable prior to the EIA in respect of any Member *outside* the EIA.[215]
d. Article V:7 requires, as a fourth condition, notification to the Council for Trade in Services (CTS). (Under the guidance of the General Council, this WTO body is responsible for overseeing

---

209 Ibid 28.

210 *Turkey – Restrictions on Imports of Textile and Clothing Products* WT/DS34/AB/R, AB report adopted 19 November 1999 paras 48–49.

211 *Canada – Autos (Panel)* paras 10.269–10.271.

212 Md Rizwanul Islam and Shawkat Alam, 'Preferential Trade Agreements and the Scope of GATT Article XXIV, GATS Article V and the Enabling Clause: An Appraisal of GATT/WTO Jurisprudence' (2009) 56 Netherlands International Law Review 1, 26.

213 Heng Wang, 'The Interpretation of GATS Disciplines on Economic Integration: GATS Commitments as a Threshold?' (2012) 46 Journal of World Trade 397, 419.

214 Devuyst and Serdarevic, 'The World Trade Organization and Regional Trade Agreements: Bridging the Constitutional Credibility Gap' 20.

215 See Stephenson, 'GATS and Regional Integration' 519–520.

the functioning of GATS.) However, since the 2006 Decision on the Transparency Mechanism for RTAs by the General Council, it is now the Committee on Regional Trade Agreements (CRTA) which is to be notified.[216] Notably, the 2006 Decision shifts the focus from a 'legal examination' to the mere 'consideration' of RTAs.[217] In practice, notification often occurs after entry into force of the RTA, the Members having 'concealed their integration propositions from surveillance' by the CRTA.[218] Other agreements have not been notified at all.[219]

These conditions apply to the WTO legality of an RTA as a whole. To justify a WTO-inconsistent measure that is part of an RTA, the AB has ruled that the measure must have been introduced upon the formation of the RTA (which fulfils the above conditions) and that the RTA would have been prevented without it.[220]

The Panel in *Canada – Autos* explicitly referred to Article V as an exception *to the MFN obligation*.[221] However, the AB has been said to have accepted in *Turkey – Textiles*[222] that Article XXIV GATT 1994 is

---

216 WT/L/671, Transparency Mechanism for Regional Trade Agreements (Adopted by the General Council 14 December 2006).

217 Sherzod Shadikhodjaev, 'Checking RTA Compatibility with Global Trade Rules: WTO Litigation Practice and Implications from the Transparency Mechanism for RTAs' (2011) 45 Journal of World Trade 529, 538–539.

218 Richard Senti, 'Regional Trade Agreements in the World Trade Order' in Christoph Herrmann and Jörg Philipp Terhechte (eds), *European Yearbook of International Economic Law*, vol 1 (Springer Verlag 2010) 239–240.

219 Shintaro Hamanaka, 'Finding Non-notified Trade Agreements to the WTO: Preliminary Investigation in Asia-Pacific' (2014) 48 Journal of World Trade 1077. The issue is known to the CRTA: WT/REG/W/75/Rev.1, List of RTAs Which Have Appeared in Factual Presentations (Issued up to 1 July 2013) and Have Not Yet Been Notified to the WTO. The list contains 53 RTAs, none of which includes the EU as a party.

220 *Turkey – Textiles (AB)* para. 58. In the view of the AB, this also applies between RTA members: *Peru – Additional Duty on Imports of Certain Agricultural Products* WT/DS457/AB/R, AB report adopted 31 July 2015 paras 5.112–5.113.

221 *Canada – Autos (Panel)* para. 10.271.

222 *Turkey – Textiles (AB)* para. 65. The Panel had found that a violation of Articles XI and XIII GATT 1994 could not be justified under Article XXIV GATT 1994. *Turkey – Restrictions on Imports of Textile and Clothing Products WT/DS34/R*, Panel report adopted 19 November 1999 paras 9.86 and 9.188–9.189.

not solely an exception to the MFN obligation.[223] Accordingly, under Article XXIV GATT 1994, Members could perhaps justify a measure that violates an obligation other than the MFN obligation, such as Article XI GATT 1994 on quantitative restrictions (as was attempted by Turkey in the aforementioned case). The issue may be of limited relevance as the case at hand addressed a customs union, with a common external policy in the context of which Articles XI and XIII GATT 1994 type measures were relevant. It may be said that this kind of EIA is the exception rather than the rule.[224]

Clearly, the practical relevance of Article V GATS, in so far as it allows for EIAs, is very large.[225] However, the interpretation of the conditions under which such agreements are allowed, is not very important, as their implementation is not stringent. Considering that all Members pursue integration agreements, there is a fear that bringing a claim will backfire – as such, the current *status quo* is unlikely to change.[226] It seems that, instead of being an exception, '*A right to PTA* has de facto emerged and this right is hardly put into question anymore' and disciplining RTAs is 'not an enterprise worth pursuing neither for intellectual nor for political reasons'.[227] This is reinforced by the finding that some deeper integration aspects of RTAs, notably regulatory policies, are designed and applied on an MFN basis.[228] The fact that some GATS–provisions may be included in the RTA does not alter this finding,

---

[223] Peter Hilpold, 'Regional Integration According to Article XXIV GATT – Between Law and Politics' (2003) 7 Max Planck Yearbook of United Nations Law Online 219, 246; Devuyst and Serdarevic, 'The World Trade Organization and Regional Trade Agreements: Bridging the Constitutional Credibility Gap' 20. Also see *Peru – Agricultural Products (AB)* para. 5.112.

[224] James Mathis, 'WTO, Turkey – Restrictions on Imports of Textile and Clothing Products' (2000) 27 Legal Issues of Economic Integration 103, 113.

[225] See TN Srinavasan, 'Nondiscrimination in GATT/WTO: Was There Anything to Begin with and is There Anything Left?' (2005) 4 World Trade Review 69. Here, in light of the proliferation of RTAs, it is argued that these exceptions have reduced the relevance of non-discrimination in WTO law.

[226] Mavroidis, 'If I Don't Do It, Somebody Else Will (Or Won't): Testing the Compliance of Preferential Trade Agreements With the Multilateral Rules' 187–188. For a more comprehensive analysis of why Members have not challenged more RTAs, see 208–213.

[227] Petros C Mavroidis, 'WTO and PTAs: A Preference for Multilateralism? (or, the Dog That Tried to Stop the Bus)' (2010) 44 Journal of World Trade 1145, 1150–1152 (emphasis original).

[228] James Mathis, 'Regulatory Regionalism in the WTO – Are "Deep Integration" Processes Compatible with the Multilateral Trading System?' in

although these provisions may provide evidence of a violation of Article V GATS, as well.[229] In summary, RTAs can in practice be concluded without much risk, especially if the parties are willing to respect the ground rules.

1.2.5.4.2 LABOUR MARKET INTEGRATION AGREEMENTS In a similar vein to EIAs, Article V bis GATS allows Members to become a party to an agreement establishing full integration of the labour markets between or among the parties to such an agreement. Describing full integration, footnote 2 to the article explains that:

> Typically, such integration provides citizens of the parties concerned with a right of free entry to the employment markets of the parties and includes measures concerning conditions of pay, other conditions of employment and social benefits.

In order to qualify for the exception, the labour market integration agreement must exempt citizens of the parties to the agreement from requirements concerning residency and work permits. The agreement must also be notified to the CTS. The relevance of Article V bis is limited; labour market integration agreements are rare in international (economic) law.[230]

1.2.5.5 Recognition Although little used in practice,[231] recognition of the education and other qualifications of service suppliers of other Members can greatly support the liberalisation of trade in services. Article VII GATS therefore addresses the recognition by one Member of the education or experience obtained, requirements met, or licences or

---

Simon Lester, Bryan Mercurio and Lorand Bartels (eds), *Bilateral and Regional Trade Agreements: Commentary and Analysis* (Cambridge University Press 2015).

229 Adlung R and Morrison P, 'Less than the GATS: "Negative Preferences" in Regional Services Agreements' (2010) 13 Journal of International Economic Law 1103, 1109–1117.

230 Jürgen Bast, 'Article V bis GATS' in Rüdiger Wolfrum, Peter-Tobias Stoll and Clemens Feinäugle (eds), *Max Planck Commentaries on World Trade Law: WTO – Trade in Services*, vol 6 (Martinus Nijhoff 2008) 153. One example is the integration of Scandinavian labour markets, even though Norway is not an EU Member State.

231 Americo Beviglia Zampetti, 'Market Access Through Mutual Recognition: The Promise and Limits of GATS Article VII' in Pierre Sauvé and Robert M Stern (eds), *GATS 2000: New Directions in Services Trade Liberalization* (Brookings Institution 2000) 293–298.

certifications granted in a particular country for the purposes of the fulfilment, in whole or in part, of the Member's standards or criteria for the authorisation, licensing or certification of services suppliers. The recognition can be autonomous or mutual. It is clear that there is no obligation of recognition in GATS. Paragraph 1 of Article VII allows such recognition vis-à-vis a *particular* Member, as an exception to the MFN obligation.[232] To remedy trade diversion from such discrimination,[233] certain conditions must be fulfilled. Aside from transparency obligations related to recognition, Article VII GATS contains three obligations.

First, Article VII:2 GATS obliges Members who are party to an existing or future recognition agreement or arrangement to afford adequate opportunity for other Members to negotiate their accession to the agreement or arrangement, or to negotiate comparable ones. In the case of autonomous recognition, the Member shall afford adequate opportunity for other Members to demonstrate that education, experience, licences or certifications obtained, or requirements met in the latter Member's territory should be recognised. 'Adequate opportunity' has been said to require 'at least a general willingness to include other WTO Members in the recognition processes'.[234]

Second, Article VII:3 GATS states that a Member shall not accord recognition in a manner which would constitute a means of discrimination between countries in the application of its standards or criteria for the authorisation, licensing or certification of services suppliers, or a disguised restriction on trade in services. It has been argued that 'likeness' is useful to understand the scope of this non-discrimination requirement.[235]

Third, Article VII:5 GATS adds that wherever appropriate, recognition should be based on multilaterally agreed criteria. Additionally, Members must work in cooperation with relevant intergovernmental and non-governmental organisations to establish and adopt common international standards and criteria for recognition.

From the perspective of regulatory autonomy, mutual recognition agreements touch upon a:

---

[232] Ibid 298–301; Van den Bossche and Zdouc, *The Law and Policy of the World Trade Organization* 536.

[233] Markus Krajewski, 'Article VII GATS' in Rüdiger Wolfrum, Peter-Tobias Stoll and Clemens Feinäugle (eds), *Max Planck Commentaries on World Trade Law: WTO – Trade in Services*, vol 6 (Martinus Nijhoff 2008) 199.

[234] Krajewski, 'Article VII GATS' 201.

[235] Ibid 202–203.

> fundamental tension which is at the heart of this whole debate, that between the trade culture which emphasises openness and competition and the regulatory culture which emphasise[s] the need for constraints on such competition and the collective responsibility for mitigating the potentially harmful effects of markets.[236]

Education, training systems and licensing requirements are opaque and complex. As such, the trust to conclude mutual recognition agreements whilst maintaining collective responsibility cannot be fostered without case-by-case institutional learning. Concluding mutual recognition agreements without such learning risks lowering professional standards.[237] It is therefore unsurprising that the potential of mutual recognition agreements is greatest in the context of countries with similar relevant regulatory regimes.[238] The lowering of professional standards may also occur where the requirements in a recognition agreement cannot be altered, or have to be based on international standards or broadly applicable requirements. Members would want to preserve their regulatory autonomy to modify the requirements for a number of reasons, for example changed policy objectives.[239] The obligations for mutual recognition agreements set forth by GATS do not appear problematic in these settings. They do not constrain regulatory autonomy but reduce constraints resulting from the MFN obligation.

Moreover, legal questions remain: (i) regarding the scope of the obligation: Article VII:2 GATS does not apply to agreements between professional associations;[240] and (ii) regarding the meaning of 'mutual recognition'.[241] It is also unclear whether, *ratione temporis*, recognition

---

[236] Kalypso Nicolaïdis, 'Managed Mutual Recognition: The New Approach to the Liberalization of Professional Services' in OECD (ed), *Liberalization of Trade in Professional Services* (OECD Publications 1997) para. 10 <http://users.ox.ac.uk/~ssfc0041/managemr.htm>.

[237] Ibid.

[238] Aaditya Mattoo and Pierre Sauvé, 'Domestic Regulation and Trade in Services: Looking Ahead' in Aaditya Mattoo and Pierre Sauvé (eds), *Domestic Regulation and Service Trade Liberalization* (World Bank & Oxford University Press 2003) 228–229.

[239] Beviglia Zampetti, 'Market Access Through Mutual Recognition: The Promise and Limits of GATS Article VII' 302.

[240] Ibid 299; Krajewski, 'Article VII GATS' 201.

[241] Beviglia Zampetti, 'Market Access Through Mutual Recognition: The Promise and Limits of GATS Article VII' 298–301.

agreements negotiated in the context of RTAs fall under Article VII GATS or under the regional economic integration exception of Article V GATS.[242]

1.2.6 Constraints on regulatory autonomy

The unconditional application of the MFN obligation in GATS affirms the central character of this non-discrimination principle. The constraints on regulatory autonomy need to be assessed on two levels. First, how does the MFN principle constrain regulatory autonomy in general, i.e. are there unexpected constraints on regulatory autonomy that follow from the understanding that a regulator cannot discriminate between domestic and foreign services or service suppliers? Second, what does interpretation of the legal tests for the MFN obligation mean for regulatory autonomy? In assessing regulatory autonomy constraints, the three specific exceptions to the MFN obligation addressed below need to be taken into account. These are: an exception for frontier zones in Article II:3 GATS; an exception for EIAs such as RTAs in Article V GATS; and an exception for recognition measures in Article VII GATS.

1.2.6.1 Constraints resulting from the Most-Favoured-Nation principle

An MFN obligation does not prevent a Member from treating *domestic* services or service suppliers more favourably than *foreign* ones. Consequently, at first sight, the impact of the MFN obligation on regulatory autonomy 'seems relatively minor' as, usually, a difference in treatment is created by differentiating between domestic and foreign services or service suppliers.[243] However, it may be in the interest of domestic legislators to introduce regulations which appear difficult to reconcile with the MFN obligation,[244] for example where one country's educational system for a specific service supplier is very similar to the domestic one. Further, the obligation discourages granting beneficial treatment to third states, as such treatment must be extended to all third Members.[245] In this sense, MFN is an instrument to multilateralise the reduction of barriers to

242 Carsten Fink and Marion Jansen, 'Services Provisions in Regional Trade Agreements: Stumbling or Building Blocks for Multilateral Liberalization?' (Conference on Multilateralising Regionalism, Geneva, 10–12 September 2007) 22.

243 Krajewski, *National Regulation and Trade Liberalization in Services* 122–123.

244 Adlung and Carzaniga, 'MFN Exemptions under the General Agreement on Trade in Services: Grandfathers Striving for Immortality?' 359.

245 Wolfrum, 'Article II GATS' 76.

trade in services.[246] This may result in constraints on regulatory autonomy: consider, for example, the differences between two foreign service suppliers as concerns their respective professional cultures or legal protection for consumers. Moreover, in two specific situations of more favourable treatment granted to specific Members, the MFN obligation may play an unexpected role. These two situations are discussed below.

1.2.6.1.1 BILATERAL INVESTMENT TREATIES VIOLATE THE MOST-FAVOURED-NATION OBLIGATION The scope of the MFN obligation may have repercussions for bilateral investment treaties (BITs). As noted, GATS Mode 3 covers certain aspects of foreign investment. Further, the potential of services liberalisation to promote investment through establishment is significant; 'presence-impeding' measures in investment are very often linked to services.[247] However, countries around the world have concluded BITs, which often afford more favourable treatment to investors from BIT parties than to other investors. According to UNCTAD, there were 2,857 BITs in force in 2013.[248] A vast number of BITs have been concluded by the EU Member States.[249] Notably, the EU only gained the exclusive competence with respect to investment at the entry into force of the Lisbon Treaty.[250] Benefits differ from BIT to BIT, and no Member has concluded BITs with all other Members.[251] In so far as these BITs cover trade in services, they are measures to which GATS applies. Consequently, the GATS MFN obligation applies to BITs.

---

[246] Zdouc, 'WTO Dispute Settlement Practice Relating to the General Agreement on Trade in Services' 382.

[247] Sauvé and Wilkie, 'Investment Liberalization in GATS' 346.

[248] UNCTAD, Global Value Chains: Investment and Trade for Development (World Investment Report, 2013) 101–102.

[249] The list in the EU's Official Journal is 96 pages long. See [2013] OJ C131/2, 8 May 2013, List of the Bilateral Investment Agreements Referred to in Article 4(1) of Regulation (EU) No 1219/2012 of the European Parliament and of the Council Establishing Transitional Arrangements for Bilateral Investment Agreements between Member States and Third Countries.

[250] By virtue of Article 207 TFEU.

[251] Federico Ortino and Audley Sheppard, 'International Agreements Covering Foreign Investment in Services: Patterns and Linkages' in Lorand Bartels and Federico Ortino (eds), Regional Trade Agreements and the WTO Legal System (Oxford University Press 2006) 204 and 206; Federico Ortino, 'The Principle of Non-Discrimination and its Exceptions in GATS: Selected Legal Issues' in Kern Alexander and Mads Andenas (eds), The World Trade Organization and Trade in Services (Marinus Nijhoff 2008) 194.

First, a BIT may violate the MFN obligation if it contains a measure, covered by GATS, which immediately and unconditionally accords less favourable treatment to services and service suppliers of one Member, i.e. the BIT party, as compared to that which it accords to like services or service suppliers of any other Member. As noted above, the scope of GATS is very broad, and there are no indications that BITs themselves, or their ratification and incorporation into the domestic legal order, would be exempt from this scope.[252] Second, services and service suppliers covered by a BIT must be considered 'like' those which are not covered. As noted, when the 'services in question in a particular case are essentially or generally the same in competitive terms', they are like.[253] There is ample opportunity for services and service suppliers covered by a BIT to be like those which are not covered. As noted, regarding the likeness of service suppliers, the Panels in *China – Electronic Payment Services* and *China – Publications and Audiovisual Products* held that, when origin is the only factor upon which a measure bases a difference of treatment between domestic service suppliers and foreign suppliers, the service suppliers are like.[254] It is the BIT itself which introduces such an origin-based discrimination.[255] In general, it seems that the existence of a BIT between two Members does not make the services provided by an investor from a party to the BIT, or the investor himself, unlike an investor or his services from another Member. Third, the treatment awarded to investors from parties which are not BIT parties must be less favourable than investors from parties to the agreement. Some illustrations serve to highlight the range of BIT provisions which may afford less favourable treatment to non-parties: the possibility for investors of parties to a BIT to make use of an investor-state dispute settlement (ISDS) mechanism may upset the competitive relationship between the service suppliers, as may other investment protection and liberalisation provisions such as commitment to fair and equitable treatment or

---

[252] Ortino and Sheppard, 'International Agreements Covering Foreign Investment in Services: Patterns and Linkages' 206–208; Ortino, 'The Principle of Non-Discrimination and its Exceptions in GATS: Selected Legal Issues' 195–197.

[253] *China – Electronic Payment Services (Panel)* para. 7.702.

[254] *China – Publications and Audiovisual Products (Panel)* para. 7.975. Also see *China – Electronic Payment Services (Panel)* para. 7.695.

[255] Ortino, 'The Principle of Non-Discrimination and its Exceptions in GATS: Selected Legal Issues' 198.

guarantees against expropriation.[256] The economic integration exception of Article V does not appear to exclude BITs from the scope of the MFN obligation: most BITs are unlikely to satisfy the conditions of that provision.[257] Consequently, the more favourable treatment accorded to the BIT partner would need to be extended to all other WTO Members on an MFN basis.[258] This may however *not* be the case for encompassing RTAs that include services and investment disciplines, as these agreements may satisfy the conditions of Article V more easily.

The preceding analysis is, perhaps, not straightforward. However, it does not appear to be far-fetched. Indeed, this issue has been discussed by Korea and Japan during negotiations concerning a BIT.[259] It has also been said that this understanding may have chilled negotiators' will to conclude the failed negotiations for a Multilateral Agreement on Investment (MAI).[260] Significantly, several Members have listed MFN exemptions for Mode 3 referring to BITs with non-specified partner countries.[261] (As noted, in so far as an MFN exemption applies to BITs

---

[256] Ortino and Sheppard, 'International Agreements Covering Foreign Investment in Services: Patterns and Linkages' 209–210; Rudolf Adlung and Martín Molinuevo, 'Bilateralism in Services Trade: Is There Fire Behind the (BIT-)Smoke?' (2008) 11 Journal of International Economic Law 365, 392.

[257] Ortino and Sheppard, 'International Agreements Covering Foreign Investment in Services: Patterns and Linkages' 205 and 210–214; Adlung and Molinuevo, 'Bilateralism in Services Trade: Is There Fire Behind the (BIT-) Smoke?' 393; Ortino, 'The Principle of Non-Discrimination and its Exceptions in GATS: Selected Legal Issues' 193.

[258] This issue has been raised by several scholars: Yong-Shik Lee, 'Bilateralism under the World Trade Organization' (2006) 26 Northwestern Journal of International Law and Business 357, 368–369; Ortino and Sheppard, 'International Agreements Covering Foreign Investment in Services: Patterns and Linkages' 205 and 210–214; Adlung and Molinuevo, 'Bilateralism in Services Trade: Is There Fire Behind the (BIT-)Smoke?' 392; Ortino, 'The Principle of Non-Discrimination and its Exceptions in GATS: Selected Legal Issues' 193; Ramon Torrent, 'The Contradictory Overlapping of National, EU, Bilateral, and Multilateral Rules on Foreign Direct Investment: Who is Guilty of Such a Mess?' (2010) 34 Fordham International Law Journal 1377, 1391–1393.

[259] Lee, 'Bilateralism under the World Trade Organization' 369.

[260] Sauvé and Wilkie, 'Investment Liberalization in GATS' 347. The MAI negotiations were conducted in the seat of the Organisation for Economic Co-operation and Development (OECD).

[261] Adlung and Molinuevo, 'Bilateralism in Services Trade: Is There Fire Behind the (BIT-)Smoke?' 395; Adlung and Carzaniga, 'MFN Exemptions under the General Agreement on Trade in Services: Grandfathers Striving for Immortality?' 372.

which were not existent at the time of entry into force of GATS, such an approach may not be consistent with the wording of Article II:2 GATS, which states that Members may only *maintain* a measure inconsistent with the obligation.[262]) The EU's List of MFN Exemptions contains an entry for measures based on existing or future bilateral agreements between the EU and certain Member States on the one hand, and San Marino, Monaco, Andorra and Vatican City State on the other hand. The exemption applies to the right of establishment for juridical and natural persons (and for waiving the requirements of work permits for natural persons supplying services). According to the List, the conditions creating the need for the exemption are the geographical situation of, and the historical, economic and cultural links between, the EU Member States and the countries and principalities concerned.[263] Nonetheless, it is clear that the limited scope of this exemption does not cover all BITs.

There has not yet been a dispute regarding the alleged non-compliance of a BIT with the MFN obligation. More generally, this may be linked to the very limited attention afforded to regional integration in WTO dispute settlement. One reason for the lack of complaints regarding the WTO (non)compliance of RTAs and BITs is likely to be the fact that all Members are engaged in such agreements. Consequently, there could be a fear of opening a floodgate of claims. Further, such a claim could destabilise the complex relationship between the WTO and regional EIAs, whether RTAs or BITs. Nonetheless, legally speaking, 'investment treaties effectively provide for open regionalism' in the economically crucial Mode 3 services supply, as benefits need to be extended on an MFN basis.[264] It is likely that not all actors are fully aware of their obligations in this area. From the perspective of regulatory autonomy, this application of the MFN obligation to BITs is crucial: the current 'dispute peace' may, at any time, escalate into a trade row. If there appear to be no possibilities for a panel to refute the claim that a BIT is inconsistent with the MFN obligation, the benefits flowing from many BITs may need to be multilateralised. Clearly, this would go far beyond

---

[262] Adlung and Molinuevo, 'Bilateralism in Services Trade: Is There Fire Behind the (BIT-)Smoke?' 395–396. The authors note that this issue depends on 'whether investment treaties can be considered to constitute one single measure and their extension by the same Member to new BIT-partners as its continuation, despite variations in sector and policy scope'.

[263] GATS/EL/31, European Communities and Their Member States: Final List of Article II (MFN) Exemptions (15 April 1994) 10.

[264] Adlung and Molinuevo, 'Bilateralism in Services Trade: Is There Fire Behind the (BIT-)Smoke?' 402–403.

the intentions of the BIT negotiators (and potentially also beyond the expectations of the GATS negotiators). The integration of BITs into fully fledged RTAs appears to be the best (and only) strategy for ensuring compliance with the MFN obligation of Article II GATS.

1.2.6.1.2 MOST-FAVOURED-NATION OBLIGATIONS IN RTAs VIOLATE THE MOST-FAVOURED-NATION OBLIGATION IN GATS As noted, many RTAs seem to meet the conditions set out in the Article V GATS regional integration exception as concerns their coverage of trade in services. However, consider the case of an MFN obligation in the services chapter of an RTA: such a provision generally requires the extension of preferential treatment provided for in another RTA to the other party to the RTA that contains the MFN obligation.[265] It has been argued by one author that these MFN clauses in RTAs violate the MFN obligation in Article II GATS (they are measures that afford more favourable treatment to the services and service suppliers of the signatory state than to those of other states) and do not satisfy the conditions of GATS' economic integration exception found in Article V.[266] This is the case because these MFN obligations 'detract from the WTO's aim of expanding the trade in goods and services in the world through the elimination of discriminatory treatment in international trade relations'.[267] More specifically, liberalisation resulting from the MFN clause in an EIA 'provides durable advantages to the service providers from the EIA parties and excludes the service providers from third countries from the EIA party's market'.[268] The exclusionary effect of the MFN clause thus raises the overall level of barriers to trade in services with third countries in comparison to the pre-EIA level. It is argued that this means an EIA with such an MFN obligation violates Article V:4 GATS.[269]

Moreover, it has been argued that, in *Turkey – Textiles*, the AB introduced a necessity requirement for measures which violate GATT 1994 and which Members seek to justify under the regional integration

---

[265] If A and B conclude an RTA with an MFN clause for services, and A subsequently concludes an RTA with C in which more preferential terms are negotiated, the MFN clause between A and B will grant the same more preferential treatment (granted to C) to B.

[266] Jong Bum Kim, 'Entrenchment of Regionalism: WTO Legality of MFN Clauses in Preferential Trade Agreements for Goods and Services' (2014) 13 World Trade Review 443, 465–469.

[267] Ibid 470.

[268] Ibid 469.

[269] Ibid 469–470.

exception of Article XXIV GATT 1994.[270] Although it is unclear whether this requirement applies to GATS, it may be that the measure must be necessary for the formation of the EIA.[271] It was therefore stated that, instead of an MFN obligation, the parties to the RTA could already include anticipated future trade liberalisation with third countries, or may opt for an 'MFN-consultation clause that is effective only within "a reasonable time-frame" after the enactment of the EIA and that results in trade liberalization during that time-frame'.[272] This position cannot be sustained. For example, the first proposition is not reasonably available in that it ignores the gradual liberalisation process that characterises preferential liberalisation. It asks negotiators to look into the future. The second proposition does not have the same effect as an MFN obligation in an RTA; it cannot be considered a genuine alternative. Nonetheless, based on the former proposition, RTAs with these MFN clauses may not be permissible and therefore may violate Article II GATS.

A similar argument was raised by the Secretariat in 1993 as concerns investor-state dispute settlement clauses in BITs, which may grant more favourable treatment to service suppliers benefiting from such dispute settlement vis-à-vis those service suppliers from Members who do not have a BIT with such clauses.[273]

1.2.6.2 Constraints from the interpretation of the Most-Favoured-Nation obligation The constraints on regulatory autonomy resulting from the MFN obligation are very similar to those resulting from the national treatment obligation: likeness and less favourable treatment have been interpreted very similarly in each obligation. However, the importance of exact interpretation may be greater in the case of the MFN obligation, considering this obligation's unconditional nature. Nonetheless, as noted,

---

270 *Turkey – Textiles (AB)* para. 46; Sungjoon Cho, 'Breaking the Barrier between Regionalism and Multilateralism: A New Perspective on Trade Regionalism' (2001) 42 Harvard International Law Journal 419, 448; Joel P Trachtman, 'Toward Open Recognition: Standardization and Regional Integration under Article XXIV of GATT' (2003) 6 Journal of International Economic Law 459, 475–476.

271 Adrian Emch, 'Services Regionalism in the WTO: China's Trade Agreements with Hong Kong and Macao in the light of Article V(6) GATS' (2006) 33 Legal Issues of Economic Integration 351, 361–363.

272 Bum Kim, 'Entrenchment of Regionalism: WTO Legality of MFN Clauses in Preferential Trade Agreements for Goods and Services' 469, 469.

273 General Agreement on Tariffs and Trade, MTN.GNS/W/177/Rev.1, Issues Relating to the Scope of the General Agreement on Trade in Services: Note by the Secretariat (4 November) (1993) paras 12–13.

it should be stressed that – beyond the two examples explored in the previous section – there are unlikely to be many practical situations in which foreign services and service suppliers need to be accorded less favourable treatment in comparison to *other* foreign services and service suppliers and which are not covered by the exceptions to the obligation or the List of MFN exemptions.[274] Therefore, the most poignant constraints on regulatory autonomy from the MFN obligation are not related to the interpretation of the obligation's inherent legal tests.

2. NON-DISCRIMINATION OBLIGATIONS IN THE SELECTED EU RTAs

2.1 National Treatment Obligations, and One Most-Favoured-Nation Obligation, for Establishment

2.1.1 National treatment for establishment in the EU-Colombia & Peru RTA

As concerns establishment, Article 113.1 EU-C&P contains the national treatment obligation applicable to Colombia, whilst paragraph 2 of the Article contains the provision, applicable to Peru. The corresponding national treatment obligation, applicable to the EU, is found in Article 113.3 EU-C&P. The reason for splitting the national treatment obligation in this way lies in the slight difference in wording. The national treatment obligation applicable to the EU and Colombia uses GATS terminology, whilst the obligation applicable to Peru covers treatment granted in *like circumstances* to Peruvian establishments and investors, rather than to like establishments or investors directly. Interpretative footnotes 26 and 27 clarify that Colombia has agreed to the term 'like circumstances' in other agreements, whilst Peru's obligations under the RTA do not limit the enforceability of rights under Article XVII GATS, especially as concerns 'like services and service suppliers'. Paragraph 4 adds footnote 10 to Article XVII GATS to the RTA in respect of all parties, stating that the specific commitments assumed under the national treatment obligation shall not be construed to require any party to compensate for

---

[274] During the GATS negotiations, Members had considered that the MFN obligation contained sufficient flexibility. For example, the List of MFN exemptions could be used to mitigate constraints on regulatory autonomy which were too stringent. Zdouc, 'WTO Dispute Settlement Practice Relating to the General Agreement on Trade in Services' 402–403.

inherent competitive disadvantages which result from the foreign character of the relevant investors.

The national treatment obligation that is applicable to the EU reads, in full:

> In the sectors for which market access commitments are listed in Annex VII (List of Commitments on Establishment) by the EU Party, and subject to any conditions and qualifications set out therein, the EU Party, with respect to all measures affecting establishment, shall grant to establishments and investors of the signatory Andean Countries treatment no less favourable than that it accords to its own like establishments and investors.

The national treatment obligation differs from Article XVII:1 GATS in three ways. First, the obligation refers to 'market access commitments'. As noted, this is because the Schedule only contains market access commitments, which are also considered as commitments for national treatment.

Second, the scope of the obligation differs. Whilst Article XVII GATS applies to measures affecting trade in services, the national treatment obligation in the establishment chapter is logically limited to measures affecting establishment – note that the scope of the *chapter* on establishment applies to measures adopted or maintained by the parties affecting establishment. Recall that the definition of establishment in the EU-C&P RTA is wider than GATS Mode 3, as Article 111 EU-C&P applies to all measures affecting establishment (regardless of a link to services). Therefore, the scope of the national treatment obligation is considerably wider than is the case for Mode 3 of GATS. This finding is strongly reinforced by the scheduling of commitments for non-services sectors.[275] Some EU Member States have scheduled limitations on investment for all sectors, although this approach is not used often.[276] As a result of these commitments and the scope of the national treatment obligation, a national treatment obligation applies to investment through establishment, in almost any sector, regardless of a link to services supply. The

---

[275] Examples include: agriculture, hunting and forestry; fishing and aquaculture; mining and quarrying; manufacturing; and the production, transmission and distribution on own account of electricity, gas, steam and hot water.

[276] For example, Annex VII Section B EU-C&P RTA contains the following horizontal reservation: 'Investment in Spain by foreign government and foreign public entities (which tends to imply, besides economic, also non-economic interests to entity's part), directly or through companies or other entities controlled directly or indirectly by foreign governments, needs prior authorization by the government'.

only limitations are: (i) scheduled horizontal and sectoral limitations, which are limited for the non-services sectors; and (ii) the carve-outs from the scope of the establishment chapter.

Third, rather than to domestic like services and service suppliers, as is the case under GATS, the 'treatment no less favourable' must be granted to like establishments and investors. Once again, the phrase 'establishments and investors' raises the question of whether both the establishment and the investor need to be like, or whether the likeness of either one or the other suffices. 'Investor of a party' is defined in Article 110 EU-C&P as:

> any natural or juridical person of that Party that seeks, through concrete actions to perform, is performing or has performed an economic activity in another Party through setting up an establishment.

This definition also includes *potential* investors, so long as they are undertaking concrete actions. This may be considered a clarification of the AB's approach in *EC – Bananas III*, where the AB took into account banana companies that did not, at the time, supply the service, but nonetheless had the capacity to do so.[277] Under the EU-C&P RTA, the investor is required to have taken concrete actions, this is a step beyond merely being able to provide the service.

Regardless of these differences, it is submitted that the interpretations of 'likeness' and 'less favourable treatment' as set out for Article XVII GATS applies *mutatis mutandis* to the EU-C&P RTA. It is true that Article 113 EU-C&P does not contain equivalents to paragraphs 2 and 3 of Article XVII GATS. However, as submitted above, these paragraphs are merely codifications of prior GATT 1994 case law on non-discrimination and do not substantially influence the interpretation of the provision. Neither does the wider scope of the obligation here, as compared to under GATS Mode 3, indicate that another interpretation should be given to 'likeness' or 'less favourable treatment' in Article 113 EU-C&P. Considering the identical wording of the obligation in the RTA to Article XVII:1 GATS (and the inclusion of footnote 10 to Article XVII GATS in Article 113.4 EU-C&P), it seems that the parties would have intended to extend the national treatment obligation to establishment in goods sectors.

---

[277] *EC – Bananas III (AB)* paras 223–227 as interpreted by Zdouc, 'WTO Dispute Settlement Practice Relating to the General Agreement on Trade in Services' 400.

The third difference between Article XVII GATS and 113 EU-C&P raises further questions regarding likeness: should the likeness analysis for services and service suppliers differ from that for establishments and investors? The differences between services and service suppliers on the one hand and establishments and investors on the other are – for the purposes of establishing likeness – limited. Establishments *are* services and investors *are* service suppliers under Mode 3, if these establishments are made by the investors for the purpose of supplying a service.[278] Hence, the scope is wider only when the investors set up an establishment for the purpose of another economic activity, linked to the committed non-services sectors in the Schedule. This widening of the scope, but based on the same context and text as under Article XVII GATS, does not require a different interpretation of likeness to the one argued for under GATS. The elements of 'policy likeness' suggested for service suppliers could be transposed to investors outside services sectors without foreseeable problems. Finally, I see no reason to interpret less favourable treatment for establishments and investors differently to less favourable treatment under Article XVII GATS.

2.1.2 Non-discrimination for establishment in the EU-Singapore RTA

2.1.2.1 National treatment obligation The national treatment obligation for establishment in the EU-Singapore RTA is included in Article 8.11. The provision applies to all parties to the RTA. It is reminiscent of Article XVII GATS, including the latter's paragraphs 2 and 3, and footnote 10 is integrated in a fourth paragraph. Footnote 14 to the provision adds that the national treatment obligation applies equally to measures regulating the composition of boards of directors of an establishment. This is said to include nationality and residency requirements. Article 8.11 EU-Singapore refers to the Schedule of specific commitments, which contains merged limitations for market access and national treatment. The national treatment obligation applies to measures affecting establishment, in all economic activities.[279] As noted, for this agreement, the economic activity should include, but not be limited to, supplying a service.[280] Therefore, although, like the EU-C&P RTA, the Schedule contains commitments for non-services sectors, the national treatment obligation for establishment has a narrower scope than under the

---

[278] See the definition of 'commercial presence' in Article XXVIII (d) GATS.

[279] With the exception of measures excluded from the scope of the chapter on establishment, see above.

[280] Article 8.8 (d) EU-Singapore.

EU-C&P RTA. This may be attributed to the existence of a dedicated chapter on investment protection in the EU-Singapore RTA. Nonetheless, the scope of this national treatment obligation is perhaps wider than under GATS Mode 3, as there are few economic activities in today's economies in which *no* service is supplied, or could easily be supplied.

The beneficiaries of the national treatment obligation in the EU-Singapore RTA are 'like establishments and entrepreneurs'. The difference in terminology as compared to Article 120 EU-C&P's 'investors' seems notable. However, the relevant Schedule, in Annex 8-A-2 EU-Singapore, refers to investors, not entrepreneurs. Preambular paragraph 7 to that Annex notes that 'investor' in the Schedule 'shall be understood as the term of "entrepreneur" defined in paragraph (c) of Article 8.8'. That provision states that 'entrepreneur' means 'any person of a Party that seeks to perform or performs an economic activity through establishment'. Comparing this definition to the one of 'investor' in the EU-C&P RTA, the main difference appears to be that investors that have performed but stopped performing an economic activity are not covered under the establishment chapter of the EU-Singapore RTA. This appears to indicate that national treatment need not be accorded if there is no longer an economic activity performed through the establishment.

For the same reasons as noted above, the differences between Article XVII GATS, the national treatment obligation under the EU-C&P RTA and the provision at hand in the EU-Singapore RTA do not indicate that the interpretation of 'likeness' and 'less favourable treatment' in Article XVII GATS need to be deviated from. This conclusion is strengthened by the fact that Article 8.11 EU-Singapore resembles Article XVII GATS even more closely than Article 113 EU-C&P. Further, the scope of Article 8.11 EU-Singapore is narrower than that of Article 113 EU-C&P and is more in line with that of Article XVII GATS.

2.1.2.2 An additional wide non-discrimination obligation In addition to the national treatment obligation, Article 8.12.2 EU-Singapore, part of the chapter's provision on the Schedule of specific commitments, contains a wide non-discrimination obligation. Article 8.12.2 EU-Singapore states that:

> Neither Party may adopt new or more discriminatory measures with regard to establishments and entrepreneurs of the other Party in relation to the specific commitments undertaken in conformity with paragraph 1.

Paragraph 1 of this Article explains that the Schedules contain the commitments for which establishment is liberalised.

Four elements of the *scope* of Article 8.12.2 EU-Singapore stand out. First, the obligation contains a standstill obligation for discriminatory measures with regard to establishments and entrepreneurs of the other party. As this obligation only applies to new measures or more discriminatory, i.e. altered, measures, its reach is narrower than that of the national treatment obligation. Second, the use of the term 'establishments and entrepreneurs', in combination with the scope of GATS Mode 3 in this regard, indicates that both pre- and post-establishment phases are covered. This also applies to the national treatment obligation. Third, Article 8.12.2 EU-Singapore applies 'with regard to establishments and entrepreneurs', whereas the national treatment obligation for establishment in the EU-Singapore RTA applies 'with respect to all measures affecting establishment'. Therefore, it seems Article 8.12.2 EU-Singapore would apply even where the measure does not *affect* establishment. However, considering the broad interpretation of 'affecting', there is perhaps little that would not be covered by 'affecting'. Fourth, unlike the national treatment obligation, the obligation does not state that it applies to sectors *inscribed* in the Schedule. Instead, it applies to establishments and entrepreneurs 'in relation to' the specific commitments, undertaken in conformity with Article 8.12.1 EU-Singapore. The addition of the latter sentence indicates that, in essence, the limitations inscribed in the Schedule apply. However, the term 'in relation to the specific commitments' should be interpreted as having a broader meaning than 'in the sectors inscribed in the Schedule'. As noted, with regard to the difference between 'on importation' and 'in connection with importation', the Panel in *China – Auto Parts* stated that:

> Had the framers of the GATT considered the term 'on importation' as synonymous with the term 'in connection with importation', irrespective of the context in which these terms are laid out, they would have simply used one or the other not both.[281]

The AB, in interpreting the term 'in relation to' in the context of Article 14 (d) SCM Agreement, noted that:

> the phrase 'in relation to' implies a comparative exercise, but its meaning is not limited to 'in comparison with'. The phrase 'in relation to' has a meaning

[281] *China – Measures Affecting Imports of Automobile Parts* WT/DS339/R, WT/DS340/R, WT/DS342/R, Panel report adopted 12 January 2009 para. 7.177; see, similarly, *China – Measures Related to the Exportation of Various Raw Materials* WT/DS394/R / WT/DS395/R / WT/DS398/R, Panel report adopted 22 February 2012 paras 7.824–7.832 and 7.839.

> similar to the phrases 'as regards' and 'with respect to'. These phrases [...] may imply a broader sense of 'relation, connection, reference'.[282]

In the context of Article 8.12.2 EU-Singapore, this comparative exercise is linked to the commitments in the Schedule for establishment. In comparison to those commitments, Article 8.12.2 EU-Singapore applies not only where the measure does fall squarely within the scope of the commitment, but also where there is a mere relation, connection or reference to the obligation. In this sense, the scope of the obligation is substantially wider than that of the national treatment obligation. Figure 4.1 summarises the relationship between the scope of the national treatment obligation and the additional wide non-discrimination obligation for establishment in the EU-Singapore RTA.

As compared to the national treatment obligation in Article 8.11 EU-Singapore, the wide non-discrimination obligation in Article 8.12.2 of that agreement also has a different standard for discrimination. First, this standard does not require that domestic and foreign establishments or entrepreneurs are like. The absence of a likeness requirement substantially extends the reach of the obligation: any discrimination between foreign and domestic entrepreneurs or establishments would suffice, regardless of the competitive relationship between the entrepreneurs or establishments.

Second, the standard set by Article 8.12.2 EU-Singapore does not require that the discrimination leads to less favourable treatment of the foreign establishment or entrepreneur. Therefore, Article 8.12.2 EU-Singapore disciplines discrimination whether or not such discrimination accords less favourable treatment. This discrimination could constitute: (i) *de jure* discrimination that does not accord less favourable

---

[282] *United States – Final Countervailing Duty Determination with Respect to Certain Softwood Lumber from Canada* WT/DS257/AB/R, AB report adopted 17 February 2004 paras 88–89; confirmed in *United States – Countervailing Measures on Certain Hot-Rolled Carbon Steel Flat Products from India* WT/DS436/AB/R, AB report adopted 19 December 2014 para. 4.149. At footnote 107 to paragraph 89 in *US – Softwood Lumber IV*, the AB recognises that the meaning of the term 'in relation to' may vary according to the context. It is submitted that the AB's abovementioned finding applies to the meaning of the term 'in relation to' in the context of Article 8.12.2 EU-Singapore. The alternative meaning suggested by the AB in a different context, i.e. that of Article 15.6 SCM Agreement, is not applicable in casu: '"the amount of subsidization established in relation to the imports from each country is more than de minimis". In this provision, the phrase "in relation to" is not used in the sense of "in comparison with" but rather in the sense of "in proportion to".'

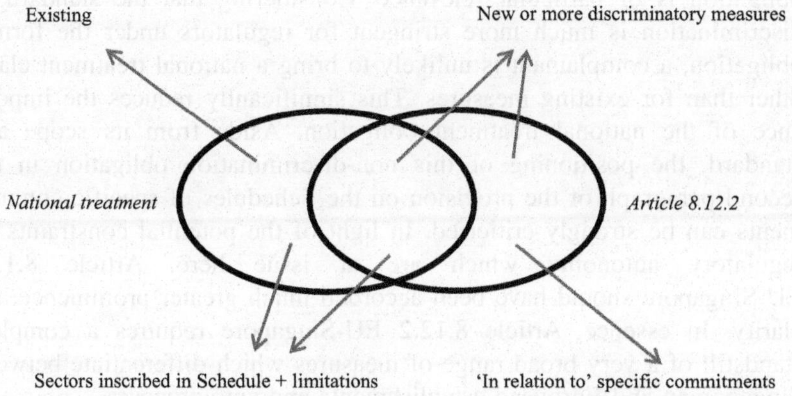

Figure 4.1 The scope of non-discrimination obligations for establishment in the EU-Singapore RTA

treatment – i.e. it prohibits formally different treatment; and (ii) *de facto* discrimination that does not accord less favourable treatment. From a WTO law perspective, the prohibition of the former type of discrimination means that no difference in treatment whatsoever can be accorded as regards the establishment or operation of juridical persons. (This can be said to mean that Article XVII:2 GATS does not apply, as formally different treatment would violate this provision.) The latter type of discrimination, however, can be considerably more difficult to delineate. The language can be interpreted to signify a diagonal vector test whereby the best treatment granted to *any* one domestic entrepreneur or establishment (recall the absence of the requirement of likeness) must be granted to *all* foreign entrepreneurs or establishments.

These findings substantially constrain regulatory autonomy, as the 'safety valves' of likeness and the disparate impact test for less favourable treatment are not present. Such an approach is reminiscent of EU internal market law: for example, Articles 49 and 56 TFEU, on establishment and services respectively, contain, *inter alia*, non-discrimination obligations absent a likeness element.[283] From a GATS perspective, this type of non-discrimination is surprising. The relationship between this additional wide non-discrimination obligation and the national treatment

---

283 See Catherine Barnard, *The Subtantive Law of the EU: The Four Freedoms* (3rd edn, Oxford University Press 2010) 333–335 for the right of establishment and 373–376 for services.

obligation is of particular relevance. Considering that the standard of discrimination is much more stringent for regulators under the former obligation, a complainant is unlikely to bring a national treatment claim other than for existing measures. This significantly reduces the importance of the national treatment obligation. Aside from its scope and standard, the positioning of this non-discrimination obligation in the second paragraph of the provision on the Schedules of specific commitments can be strongly criticised. In light of the potential constraints on regulatory autonomy which are at issue here, Article 8.12.2 EU-Singapore should have been accorded much greater prominence and clarity. In essence, Article 8.12.2 EU-Singapore requires a complete standstill of a very broad range of measures which differentiate between Singaporean and European establishments and entrepreneurs.

2.1.3 Non-discrimination for establishment in the EU-Georgia DCFTA

2.1.3.1 National treatment and Most-Favoured-Nation obligations As concerns establishment in the EU-Georgia DCFTA, the national treatment obligation is integrated with an MFN obligation in Article 79. By way of contrast, the EU-C&P and EU-Singapore RTAs do not contain MFN obligations for establishment.[284] As in the case of the EU-C&P RTA, separate paragraphs of the obligation apply to Georgia and to the EU. However, with the exception of the reference to the relevant Annex containing reservations to the negative list, these obligations are identical. The non-discrimination obligation applicable to the EU reads as follows:

> 2. Subject to reservations listed in Annex XIV-A to this Agreement, the Union shall grant, upon entry into force of this Agreement:
>   (a) as regards the establishment of subsidiaries, branches and representative offices of juridical persons of Georgia: treatment no less favourable than that accorded to its own juridical persons, their branches and representative offices; or to subsidiaries, branches and representative offices of any third country's juridical persons, whichever is the better;
>   (b) as regards the operation of subsidiaries, branches and representative offices of juridical persons of Georgia in the Union, once established: treatment no less favourable than that accorded to its own juridical persons, their branches and representative offices; or to subsidiaries,

[284] Other EU RTAs do contain MFN obligations for services. See Articles 7.8 and 7.14 EU-Korea and Articles 70 and 79 EU-CARIFORUM.

branches and representative offices of any third country's juridical persons, whichever is the better[†].

[†] This obligation does not extend to the investment protection provisions not covered by this chapter, including provisions relating to investor-to-state dispute settlement procedures, as found in other agreements.

This type of integrated non-discrimination obligation is found in several EU Stabilisation and Association Agreements.[285] It is also reminiscent of Article 2.1 TBT Agreement. The AB has clarified that violations of the MFN obligation or national treatment obligation in Article 2.1 TBT Agreement are subject to the same conditions as each other. It is only the comparator which differs (i.e. products of a third country for the MFN obligation and domestic products for the national treatment obligation).[286] As the AB has noted on a number of occasions, all applicable provisions of a treaty, *in casu* the WTO Agreement of which all covered agreements (such as the GATT 1994 and the TBT Agreement) are part, must be interpreted 'in a way that gives meaning to *all* of them, harmoniously'.[287] Nonetheless, this does not mean that identical meanings should be given to Articles I:1 and III:4 GATT 1994 on the one hand and Article 2.1 TBT Agreement on the other hand.[288] The difference in interpretation between Articles III:4 GATT 1994 and 2.1 TBT Agreement, a contentious subject in the *EC – Seal Products* dispute, may give the impression that Article 79 EU-Georgia should be interpreted differently from the national treatment obligation in the EU-C&P and EU-Singapore RTAs. However, the AB explained that it is the *context* of the TBT Agreement that is defining for the different interpretation of Article 2.1 TBT Agreement in comparison to Article III:4 GATT 1994.[289]

This requirement of harmonious interpretation, referred to by the AB as the 'principle of coherent and consistent interpretation',[290] thus applies

[285] See Articles 48 EU-Macedonia, 53 EU-Montenegro, 53 EU-Serbia, 50 EU-Albania and 51 EU-Bosnia-Herzegovina.

[286] *United States – Measures Concerning the Importation, Marketing and Sale of Tuna and Tuna Products* WT/DS381/AB/R, AB report adopted 13 June 2012 paras 202 and 229; *US – COOL (AB)* para. 267.

[287] *Argentina – Safeguard Measures on Imports of Footwear* WT/DS121/AB/R, AB report adopted 12 January 2000 para. 81 (emphasis original).

[288] *EC – Seal Products (AB)* para. 5.123.

[289] *US – Clove Cigarettes (AB)* paras 109 and 181. Also see *United States – Measures Concerning the Importation, Marketing and Sale of Tuna and Tuna Products* WT/DS381/AB/R, AB report adopted 13 June 2012 para. 212; *US – COOL (AB)* para. 268; *EC – Seal Products (AB)* para. 5.124.

[290] *EC – Seal Products (AB)* para. 5.123.

within a treaty, and takes into account the *context* of the provision. Of course, the EU-C&P and EU-Singapore RTAs are not part of the same treaty as the EU-Georgia DCFTA. However, the latter agreement contains a further national treatment obligation for services. Article 85 EU-Georgia, discussed below, reiterates Article XVII GATS. Considering that there is no relevant difference in the context between Articles 79 and 85 EU-Georgia, in contrast to what is the case with Articles III:4 GATT 1994 and 2.1 TBT Agreement, it is submitted that both provisions in the RTAs should be interpreted harmoniously, which, *in casu*, means in the same way. Based on the presumption of WTO consistent interpretation, Article 79 EU-Georgia should be interpreted in a way largely coinciding with the interpretation of Article XVII GATS and thus also the national treatment obligations for establishment in the EU-C&P and EU-Singapore RTAs.

Nonetheless, as with the obligations in the previous two sections, there are differences between Article XVII GATS and Article 79 EU-Georgia which may influence the interpretation of the latter provision. The three differences discussed in the previous two sections are addressed in this section, this time in the context of the EU-Georgia DCFTA. First, Annex XIV-A to the EU-Georgia DCFTA contains the EU's commitments for establishment. As noted, in contrast to previous EU practice, the provisions on establishment in this agreement apply to commitments made on the basis of a negative list and can hence be seen as more sweeping. This broader scope does not influence the interpretation of Article 79, as a different scheduling technique does not necessarily lead to different levels of commitment.[291] Indeed, GATS also allows for negative listing,[292] and, just as the interpretation of Article XVII GATS should not depend on the scheduling technique, neither should the interpretation of Article 79 EU-Georgia. Second, the scope of the term 'establishment' under the EU-Georgia DCFTA differs from that under Mode 3 GATS. As noted above, and reiterated for the EU-C&P RTA, it includes establishment for any economic activity, and the commitments include non-services sectors. The scope is widened even further by way of the inclusion of natural persons pursuing economic activities as self-employed persons or setting up undertakings which they effectively control. However, the beneficiaries of Article 79 EU-Georgia are defined as 'subsidiaries, branches and representative offices of juridical persons

[291] Rudolf Adlung and Hamid Mamdouh, *How to Design Trade Agreements in Services: Top Down or Bottom Up?* (World Trade Organization Economic Research and Statistics Division Staff Working Paper ERSD-2013-08, 2013) 17.

[292] Ibid.

of Georgia',[293] and the definitions of these types of establishment are limited to juridical persons as well.[294] Therefore, the extension of the 'establishment' concept to natural persons does not apply to this non-discrimination obligation. In conclusion, neither difference gives rise to an interpretation different to that under Article XVII GATS.

The same cannot be said regarding the third difference highlighted in the analysis of the national treatment obligations in the EU-C&P and EU-Singapore RTAs. As noted, the beneficiaries of the non-discrimination obligation are the subsidiaries, branches and representative offices of juridical persons of Georgia. However, there is no requirement that these are 'like' subsidiaries, branches and representative offices of juridical persons of the EU (for the national treatment obligation), or of any other country (for the MFN obligation). If, as submitted, the less favourable treatment condition is to be interpreted in accordance with WTO case law,[295] there is no room for regulatory considerations in the assessment of less favourable treatment. Significantly, under such an interpretation, the likeness analysis cannot be used in Article 79 EU-Georgia to mitigate potentially unwanted results of the less favourable treatment assessment. This interpretation would indicate that the national treatment and MFN obligations for establishment in the EU-Georgia DCFTA are wider than their GATS counterparts. The obligations would thus establish a baseline that does not allow any discrimination that (potentially) modifies the conditions of competition to the detriment of Georgian subsidiaries, branches and representative offices in comparison to any other subsidiaries, branches and representative offices. In this context, the obligations contained in Article 79 EU-Georgia have the potential to constrain regulatory autonomy considerably further than the obligations contained in Articles XVII and II GATS.

The absence of likeness could be considered to constitute a difference in context, similar to the absence of general exceptions in Article 2.1 TBT Agreement. This difference could be considered to be sufficient to interpret less favourable treatment differently. However, considering the

---

[293] Notably, this differs from 'establishments and investors' in the EU-C&P RTA and 'establishments and entrepreneurs' in the EU-Singapore RTA.

[294] See the definitions in Articles 77 (d), (e), (f) and (g) EU-Georgia.

[295] The result may even be the same if the interpretational rule in the agreement is followed, i.e. that relevant WTO DSB interpretations shall be taken into account (whether the obligation that is being interpreted is identical to GATS or not).

objective of integrating Georgia in the EU internal market,[296] the wider scope of the non-discrimination obligation for establishment seems intentional. Moreover, the approach in Article 79 EU-Georgia seems to be in line with EU law, for example Articles 49 TFEU on establishment and 56 TFEU on services which contain, *inter alia*, a non-discrimination obligation without a likeness element.[297] Therefore, it is submitted that the interpretation of less favourable treatment under Articles XVII and II GATS should be transposed to Article 79 EU-Georgia.

A fourth difference as compared to Article XVII GATS, and as compared to the relevant provisions of the EU-C&P and EU-Singapore RTAs, is that Article 79.2 EU-Georgia DCFTA, is split into two subparagraphs. The first focuses on the actual establishment, i.e. pre-establishment, and the second focuses on the operation, i.e. post-establishment, of subsidiaries, branches and representative offices. The GATS definition of Mode 3 incorporates both pre- and post-establishment phases, and the national treatment and MFN obligations therefore apply to both. Thus, this addition to Article 79 EU-Georgia merely clarifies what has been submitted as the correct interpretation of the scope of GATS Mode 3.

2.1.3.2 Implications of the Most-Favoured-Nation obligation The MFN aspect of the Article 79.2 EU-Georgia obligation has greater consequences for regulatory autonomy than the national treatment aspect of this obligation. Notably, this MFN obligation contains no limiting language and therefore applies to *any* more favourable treatment granted to any country.[298] Moreover, Annex XIV-A, containing the relevant commitments for the EU, does not exclude economic integration agreements from the scope of the MFN obligation. It does not have a regional

---

296 Article 1.2 (h) EU-Georgia.

297 See Barnard, *The Subtantive Law of the EU: The Four Freedoms* 333–335 for the right of establishment and 373–376 for services.

298 Compare to e.g. Article 70 EU-CARIFORUM, which does not apply to treatment granted under:

a. RTAs concluded prior to signature of the EU-CARIFORUM RTA.
b. RTAs that create internal markets.
c. RTAs that require parties to 'significantly approximate their legislation with a view to removing non-discriminatory obstacles to commercial presence and to trade in services'.
d. Recognition measures regarding qualifications, licences or prudential measures in accordance with Article VII of the GATS.
e. International agreements or arrangements relating to taxation.
f. Measures listed in the List of MFN Exemptions under GATS.

integration exception such as the one in Article V GATS. As a result, the MFN obligation has an unfettered multiplying effect vis-à-vis (existing and) future treatment granted to subsidiaries, branches and representative offices of juridical persons of other countries that is more favourable. Such treatment must be extended to the same Georgian economic actors, in so far as they are covered by Article 79 EU-Georgia (i.e. subject to the limitations to the scope of the provision and in the Schedule). Therefore, the MFN obligation seeks to ensure the unfettered liberalisation of trade in services. Further, recall the absence of a likeness requirement. Taken together, these factors make it easy for the MFN obligation to be triggered, a situation which may have systemic implications for the regulation of international trade.[299] From the perspective of each party's economic actors, the inclusion means that they will always have the most preferential treatment.[300] Moreover, at a systemic level, such an MFN clause 'serves to soften discrimination' that results from RTAs and reduces discrimination in future RTAs.[301] The downside is a reduced bargaining position in future RTAs as the negotiating partner's economic actors will not get *more* favourable treatment than that granted to the beneficiaries of MFN obligations in prior RTAs.[302] For the EU, these concerns are limited considering the economic size of Georgia. However, the impact of such MFN obligations in RTAs with large economies could be substantial.[303]

---

[299] It has been noted that for developing countries such an unfettered MFN obligation could be problematic as it entails 'contracting away' future rights. See Claude Chase, 'MFN in the CARIFORUM-EC Economic Partnership Agreement: Policy Blunder or Legal Inconsistency?' (2011) 38 Legal Issues of Economic Integration 189, especially at 195. Here, Chase argues that the limitations negotiated by the CARIFORUM countries are sufficient to reject the criticism on the inclusion of the MFN obligation.

[300] Fink and Jansen, 'Services Provisions in Regional Trade Agreements: Stumbling or Building Blocks for Multilateral Liberalization?' 17.

[301] Ibid 12; Iza Lejárraga, *Deep Provisions in Regional Trade Agreements: How Multilateral-friendly? An Overview of OECD Findings* (OECD Trade Policy Papers N°168, 2014) 35.

[302] Fink and Jansen, 'Services Provisions in Regional Trade Agreements: Stumbling or Building Blocks for Multilateral Liberalization?' 17.

[303] In the CETA draft, published 26 September 2014, in Article X-04, there is an MFN obligation for cross-border trade in services that is only limited for recognition measures. For an analysis of MFN in CETA (focusing on investment, but the analysis may be extended to cross-border trade in services) predating the draft, see Lawrence L Herman, *Who Else Benefits from CETA? Some Implications of 'Most-Favoured Nation' Treatment* (CD Howe Institute Essential Policy Intelligence E-Brief, 2013) 4–6.

2.1.3.3 An additional wide non-discrimination obligation In addition to the national treatment and MFN obligations, paragraph 3 to Article 79 EU-Georgia contains an additional non-discrimination obligation. Reminiscent of the abovementioned non-discrimination obligation in the EU-Singapore RTA, it states that the parties may not adopt measures that introduce discrimination, as regards the establishment or operation of juridical persons of the other party, in comparison with their own juridical persons. The obligation is limited by the reservations in Annex XIV-A to the EU-Georgia DCFTA, which contains the reservations for the national treatment and MFN obligations. Article 79.3 EU-Georgia is thus a national treatment-type standstill provision for pre- and post-establishment. In contrast to Article 8.12.2 EU-Singapore, the scope of Article 79.3 EU-Georgia appears to be narrower than that of the national treatment obligation in Article 79.2 EU-Georgia, as there is no similar wording to 'in relation to'. Moreover, arguably, Article 79.3 EU-Georgia does not apply to alterations of existing measures which introduce discrimination or are more discriminatory compared to the original measure.

In addition to having a narrower scope to that of the national treatment obligation, the additional wide non-discrimination obligation in Article 79.3 EU-Georgia has a different standard for discrimination. Indeed, considering that its scope falls fully within that of the national treatment obligation, the standard of discrimination in the Article 79.3 EU-Georgia meaning must, logically, extend beyond that which is covered by the national treatment obligation in Article 79.2 EU-Georgia. As was the case under the EU-Singapore wide non-discrimination obligation, this EU-Georgia DCFTA obligation prohibits discrimination absent any requirement that the discrimination leads to less favourable treatment. Further, as is also the case under the national treatment and MFN obligations in the EU-Georgia DCFTA, the prohibition of discrimination does not contain any requirement of likeness. Thus, in order for this obligation to have any meaningful effect, it must discipline discrimination that does not accord less favourable treatment (as such discrimination would already be covered by the national treatment obligation). The introduction of such discrimination is prohibited. As noted, this means that no formal difference in treatment can be accorded whatsoever as regards the establishment or operation of juridical persons. It also means that a diagonal vector test applies, whereby the best treatment granted to *any* one domestic juridical person (recall the absence of the requirement of likeness) as regards their establishment or operation must be granted to *all* foreign juridical persons.

As explained in the context of Article 8.12.2 EU-Singapore, these findings indicate substantial constraints on regulatory autonomy, as the 'safety valves' of likeness and the disparate impact test for less favourable treatment are not present. The fact that the scope of Article 79.3 EU-Georgia falls within the scope of the national treatment obligation appears to mitigate these concerns to some extent. However, the negative listing approach in the EU-Georgia DCFTA means that this obligation applies to *all* sectors (which includes non-services sectors, as explained when assessing the scope of 'establishment'), except for any scheduled reservations (which also delineate the scope of Article 8.12.2 EU-Singapore). Therefore, in practice, the difference in scope between Articles 8.12.2 EU-Singapore and 79.3 EU-Georgia may be quite limited. Finally, it is notable that this additional wide non-discrimination obligation has been inserted into the same provision as the national treatment and MFN obligations. From the perspective of legal certainty and transparency, this situation is preferable as compared to the EU-Singapore RTA.

2.1.3.4 A specific exception for the non-discrimination obligations It should be mentioned that Article 82 EU-Georgia contains an exception to the national treatment and MFN obligations for establishment, as well as to the additional prohibition of discrimination. The exception applies to measures concerning both the establishment and the operation of branches or representative offices of juridical persons of the other party that are not incorporated in the territory of the first party. In such cases, the non-discrimination obligations do not prevent a party from applying rules that are justified by legal or technical differences between the abovementioned branches and representative offices as compared to branches and representative offices of juridical persons that are incorporated in the territory of the party.[304] The difference in treatment must not go beyond what is strictly necessary as a result of these legal or technical differences.[305] The term 'legal or technical differences' is not further

---

[304] For financial services, this exception may also be invoked for prudential reasons.

[305] An almost identical obligation can be found in, e.g., Articles 35 EU-Algeria, 54 EU-Bosnia Herzegovina, 52 EU-Croatia, 36 EU-Jordan, 51 EU-Macedonia, 56 EU-Montenegro, 56 EU-Serbia. Similarly, Article 24 of the EFTA Convention contains a national treatment obligation that is limited by an exception almost identical to Article 82 EU-Georgia.

clarified,[306] and no guidance for its interpretation can be found in WTO case law. However, the inclusion of the term 'strictly necessary' indicates that the exception is not intended to be given a broad reach, especially in light of the already strict requirements needed to satisfy the necessity condition in Article XIV GATS.[307] Considering that 'necessity' has such a distinct meaning in WTO case law, it is submitted that this accepted meaning should be used to interpret the term 'strictly necessary' here.

2.1.3.5 Neither obligation nor exception: mutual recognition between the parties Article 96 EU-Georgia contains provisions on mutual recognition, which, in contrast to GATS,[308] cannot be considered an exception to the MFN obligation as it only applies between the parties to the DCFTA. For the sake of completeness, even though the provision does not contain any obligations, it is worth noting that paragraph 1 of Article 96 states that nothing in the relevant chapter, i.e. the chapter on establishment, trade in services and electronic commerce, is to *prevent* a party from requiring that natural persons must possess certain qualifications and/or professional experience. Especially in comparison to Article VII:1 GATS, it is notable that the agreement's provision on mutual recognition commences with this statement. The remainder of Article 96 provides for an elaborate procedure in which the Association Committee in Trade, established by the DCFTA, must review recommendations by professional bodies. Only after an assessment, *inter alia*, of the economic value of a potential mutual recognition agreement, shall the Association Committee in Trade 'establish the necessary steps to negotiate' a mutual recognition agreement. Finally, Article 96.5 EU-Georgia adds that such an agreement must be in conformity with GATS, especially Article VII.

It may be noted that Articles 129 EU-Colombia & Peru and 8.16 EU-Singapore contain very similar provisions on mutual recognition. The 'soft' wording of these provisions can be said to demonstrate the 'lack of any real conviction in EU efforts to include mutual recognition in its FTAs'.[309]

---

[306] None of the agreements mentioned in the previous footnote clarify the meaning of the terms.

[307] See below.

[308] For this reason, mutual recognition is addressed briefly here.

[309] Stephen Woolcock, *European Union Policy Towards Free Trade Agreements* (ECIPE Working Paper 03/2007, 2007) 8.

2.2 National Treatment and a Wide Non-discrimination Obligation for Cross-border Supply of Services

Article 120 EU-C&P contains the national treatment obligation for cross-border supply of services. As with the national treatment obligation for establishment, different terminology applies to Peru: the treatment may not be less favourable than that treatment which Peru accords in like circumstances to its own services and service suppliers.[310] In the case of the EU and Colombia, the obligation refers to treatment no less favourable than that which the EU or Colombia accord to their own like services and service suppliers. The rest of the obligation duplicates Article 113 EU-C&P. Interpretative footnote 10 to Article XVII GATS is reiterated in paragraph 4 of Article 120. As noted with regard to the national treatment obligation for establishment, only market access commitments are referenced and the scope is limited to cross-border trade in services. The beneficiaries of the obligation are like services and service suppliers, as under GATS. There are no indications that Article 120 EU-C&P should be interpreted differently to Article XVII GATS.

A national treatment obligation for cross-border trade in services is also included in Article 8.6 EU-Singapore. Other than referring to the parties to the RTA and the scope being limited to cross-border trade in services, this provision replicates Article XVII GATS. Once again, footnote 10 to that provision is included here as a fourth paragraph. In addition to the national treatment obligation, Article 8.7.2 EU-Singapore also contains a wide non-discrimination obligation, identical to the one discussed with regard to establishment. The inclusion of this obligation for cross-border trade in services is notable, considering the lack of an equivalent provision in the other two EU RTAs.

In contrast to the case for establishment, the EU-Georgia DCFTA does not contain an integrated national treatment and MFN obligation, but merely a national treatment obligation. Substantially, Article 85 EU-Georgia is identical to Article 8.6 EU-Singapore. The interpretation of national treatment in GATS should also apply to both of these provisions. There is no wide non-discrimination obligation for cross-border trade in services in the EU-Georgia DCFTA.

---

[310] Footnote 30 to Article 120.2 EU-C&P reiterates that the rights for the services and service suppliers of the EU, especially from the term 'like services and service suppliers' in Article XVII GATS vis-à-vis Peru, remain fully enforceable within the framework of the WTO.

2.3 Non-discrimination for Temporary Presence of Natural Persons for Business Purposes

In addition to paragraph 1, which allows foreign investors to employ certain types of foreign natural persons, albeit subject to restrictions,[311] Article 124.2 EU-C&P adds a non-discrimination obligation. The obligation applies to all sectors for which commitments have been inscribed in Annex VII, which contains the Schedule for establishment. The limitations in this Schedule do not apply. However, the Schedule in Annex VII is limited by Annex IX, which contains reservations regarding the temporary presence of natural persons for business purposes. Thus, for commitments in Annex VII, in so far as they are not limited by Annex IX, as concerns key personnel (i.e. business visitors and intra-corporate transferees) and graduate trainees of another party:

> the measures which a Party shall not maintain or adopt [...] are defined as discriminatory limitations and as limitations on the total number of natural persons that an investor may employ as key personnel and graduate trainees in a specific sector in the form of numerical quotas or a requirement of an economic needs test.[312]

As such, Article 124.2 EU-C&P contains two obligations: (i) a prohibition of discriminatory limitations; and (ii) a prohibition of limitations on the total number of natural persons that an investor may employ as key personnel and graduate trainees in a specific sector in the form of numerical quotas or a requirement of an economic needs test.[313] The first

---

[311] These are temporal restrictions, but also limitations: Article 124.1 only applies to sectors liberalised in the establishment Schedules (in Annex VII), subject to any reservations in that Schedule or in Annex IX, which contains reservations regarding the temporary presence of natural persons for business purposes.

Similar obligations for allowing entry apply to business services sellers (Article 125 EU-C&P), contractual service suppliers (Article 126 EU-C&P) and independent professionals (Article 127 EU-C&P). The right of entry is dependent on conditions, including, for contractual service suppliers and independent professionals, those conditions specified in Annex IX on the temporary presence of natural persons for business purposes.

[312] Preambular paragraph 3 to the EU Schedule in Annex IX of the EU-C&P RTA clarifies that commitments on key personnel and graduate trainees do not apply if the intent or effect of such temporary presence 'is to interfere with or otherwise affect the outcome of any labour/management dispute or negotiation'.

[313] The second obligation must be as noted above; the sentence does not make sense if read otherwise.

is a general non-discrimination obligation; the second is a market access type obligation. Both obligations are addressed below.

The non-discrimination obligation is notable for two reasons. First, its scope extends beyond services because it refers back to the Schedule for establishment, which include non-services sectors. This is also evident from the specific limitations in Annex IX, which contains a limitation for the 'manufacturing' sector. The concerns raised above therefore apply *mutatis mutandis*, with the *caveat* that, here, the scope is limited to key personnel and graduate trainees.

Second, the non-discrimination obligation amounts to a prohibition of introducing or maintaining 'discriminatory limitations'. In the case of Article 124 EU-C&P, the limitation must concern the entry and temporary stay in its territory of key personnel and graduate trainees.[314] Thus, the prohibition only applies to limitations on the entry and temporary stay of these categories of natural persons, not to any other aspect related to the service or supplier. However, it is unclear from the text of the provision (i.e. '*any*' foreign key personnel and graduate trainees) who should be assessed for discrimination. Should only the key personnel and graduate trainees of the other party to the RTA be taken into account, or does it apply to both domestic and all foreign key personnel and graduate trainees? In other words, does Article 124 EU-C&P contain an MFN obligation, a national treatment obligation, or both? Article 124 EU-C&P is titled 'key personnel and graduate trainees' and the definitions of these terms in Article 123 EU-C&P are limited to service suppliers of a party. However, the text of the obligation in Article 124.2 EU-C&P does not imply that the discrimination should solely be assessed vis-à-vis these service suppliers of the other parties. The limitations should not be measures concerning the entry into the EU territory of EU nationals. However, 'stay' could be interpreted more widely to cover measures regulating issues such as: (i) professional qualification or diploma requirements applicable to supplying the service (not those required for entry); (ii) remuneration requirements;[315] (iii) professional title requirements; or (iv) other practical requirements which discriminate between EU and Colombian or Peruvian key personnel and graduate trainees.[316] There

---

314 Article 122 EU-C&P.

315 Article 126.4 (d) EU-C&P refers to such a condition for contractual service suppliers.

316 Note that preambular paragraph 4 to Annex IX of the EU-C&P RTA appears to prevent 'social dumping' on the receiving party's labour market. Also see below, on the delineation between market access, national treatment and domestic regulation.

does not appear to be a textual basis for excluding the national treatment aspect of the obligation. Therefore, it is argued that, in the absence of qualifying language to the contrary, no discriminatory limitation may be upheld for key personnel or graduate trainees in comparison to *any* other key personnel or graduate trainees. This does not give an excessive scope to the obligation considering the strict definitions of these groups of natural persons, and the temporal limitation in Article 124.1 EU-C&P.

Finally, as noted above with regard to the additional non-discrimination obligation for establishment in the EU-Georgia DCFTA, discrimination is not determined by whether less favourable treatment is being accorded to like key personnel or graduate trainees. Any discrimination, whether it accords less favourable treatment or not, is sufficient to breach the non-discrimination obligation. This gives a broad reach to the obligation. Any formal difference in treatment is sufficient. For a *de facto* discrimination, it may suffice that the diagonal vector test leads to a finding of discrimination, although *in casu* the broad reach of this test is limited by the narrow scope of its beneficiaries, i.e. key personnel and graduate trainees. Nonetheless, it only prohibits discriminatory *limitations*. The term 'limitation' is used in the context of GATS to describe restrictions on the market access and national treatment obligations that are scheduled by a Member.[317] The 1993 Scheduling Guidelines use the term 'limitations' to refer to 'the 'terms', 'conditions', 'limitations' and 'qualifications' used in Articles XVI and XVII of the GATS'.[318] As with Article XVII GATS,[319] Article 124.2 EU-C&P does not contain an exhaustive list of what constitutes a 'limitation'. Therefore, 'discriminatory limitation' should be interpreted as any measure that is discriminatory and therefore limits the entry and temporary stay of key personnel and graduate trainees. Moreover, the key personnel or graduate trainees should not be like, although in practice the definitions of these categories of natural persons may be sufficiently narrow that the absence of the likeness criterion does not result in overly wide groups for comparison.

Article 8.14.2 EU-Singapore is almost identical to Article 124.2 EU-C&P.[320] However, its scope is wider, as the sectors liberalised pursuant to both establishment and cross-border trade in services define

---

[317] General Agreement on Tariffs and Trade, MTN.GNS/W/164, Scheduling of Initial Commitments in Trade in Services: Explanatory Note (3 September) para. 3.

[318] Ibid para. 3, footnote 2.

[319] Ibid para. 7.

[320] Article 8.14.1 EU-Singapore contains an obligation to allow the entry and temporary stay of key personnel and graduate trainees, subject to temporal

the commitments for the temporary presence of key personnel and graduate trainees. Annex 8-A-3 contains a list of all liberalised sectors and the limitations applicable to key personnel and graduate trainees.[321] The foregoing analysis of Article 124.2 EU-C&P applies *mutatis mutandis* to this Annex. The same analysis applies to Article 89.2 EU-Georgia, which again contains a quasi-identical obligation to that in Articles 124.2 EU-C&P and 8.14.2 EU-Singapore.[322] The scope is limited to commitments made for establishment. The EU scheduled specific limitations for key personnel and graduate trainees in Annex XIV-C.[323]

2.4 Constraints on Regulatory Autonomy

The constraints on regulatory autonomy resulting from the non-discrimination obligations in the selected EU RTAs operate at two levels. First, as concerns the likeness and less favourable treatment requirements, the constraints on regulatory autonomy are the same as under Article XVII GATS. Second, the non-discrimination obligations in the selected EU RTAs place greater constraints on regulatory autonomy than GATS in a number of ways.

With regard to establishment, the main constraints on regulatory autonomy are as follows:

a. The wider scope of the term 'establishment', i.e. including any type of economic activity constrains regulatory autonomy vis-à-vis the non-discrimination obligations in the selected EU RTAs due to the broadened application of the provisions.

---

limitations and the limitations in the Schedule. Article 8.15 EU-Singapore applies to business services sellers and is of a similar nature.

321 Preambular paragraph 4 to Annex IX of the EU-C&P RTA is duplicated in preambular paragraph 4 to Annex 8-A-3 of the EU-Singapore RTA. Paragraph 5 of the latter strengthens the protection of workers within the EU and therefore adds to the goal of preventing social dumping through temporary presence of natural persons for business purposes.

322 Article 89.1 EU-Georgia also contains an obligation to allow the entry of key personnel and graduate trainees in the territory of the parties, subject to temporal limitations and the limitations in the Schedule. Business sellers are the subject of Article 90 EU-Georgia, which is similar to Article 89.1. For contractual service suppliers and independent professionals, the same principle applies but additional conditions are set forth in Articles 91 and 92 respectively.

323 Preambular paragraphs 4 and 5 to Annex 8-A-3 of the EU-Singapore RTA are reiterated in preambular paragraphs 4 and 5 of Annex XIV-C EU-Georgia.

b. It is likely that the EU has undertaken more commitments for (or listed less limitations on) establishment in comparison to the GATS Schedule on Mode 3. This undoubtedly applies to the extension of the establishment Schedules to non-services sectors. The same is likely to be true for the negative listing approach taken in the relevant Schedule in the EU-Georgia DCFTA. This would place additional constraints on regulatory autonomy for these committed sectors.
c. In the EU-Georgia DCFTA, the addition of an MFN obligation may have substantial effects from the perspective of non-discrimination, but the constraints on regulatory autonomy appear limited. The multiplying effect of the MFN obligation merely extends the scope of the treatment already granted and therefore cannot be said to constrain regulatory autonomy beyond the main proposition of an MFN obligation, i.e. it is no longer possible to discriminate between foreign establishments and investors. Of course, the wider scope of 'establishment' and the sectoral commitments do extend the constraints resulting from the MFN obligation.
d. The additional non-discrimination obligations in the EU-Singapore and EU-Georgia RTAs may have far-reaching implications for the introduction of new measures. If my interpretation is correct, no discrimination whatsoever is allowed. Hence, treatment must be formally identical and a diagonal vector type test may mean that there is no margin whatsoever to discriminate between Singaporean and EU entrepreneurs and establishments, or between Georgian and EU juridical persons as concerns their establishment and operations. For the EU-Georgia DCFTA, this is in line with the objective of integrating the Georgian economy in the EU internal market. Therefore, the constraints resulting from this obligation could be characterised as an extension of EU law obligations. Clearly, this argument does not hold true for the EU-Singapore RTA: the broader scope of Article 8.12.2 EU-Singapore aggravates concerns regarding the obligation's constraints on regulatory autonomy.

For cross-border supply of services, there are no extra constraints on regulatory autonomy vis-à-vis the interpretation of Article XVII GATS, except for constraints that follow from any additional commitments in the relevant Schedule. The sole exception is the wide non-discrimination obligation in the EU-Singapore RTA, which constrains regulatory autonomy in the same way as with regard to establishment.

Finally, non-discrimination as concerns the temporary presence of natural persons for business purposes is limited to key personnel and graduate trainees. Again, it may be expected that there are more commitments in the relevant Schedules.[324] For these groups of service suppliers, the wider scope of commitments under establishment applies, albeit with specific limitations. It is argued that the prohibition of discrimination here encompasses both an MFN and national treatment type obligation. A Member may not adopt or maintain any measure that is discriminatory in limiting the entry and temporary stay of key personnel and graduate trainees. As noted, this language has a broad reach and discrimination can easily be found to exist. However, the constraints on regulatory autonomy resulting from this non-discrimination obligation are mitigated by the limited class of beneficiaries under this obligation. Nonetheless, within the scope of the obligation, very little room for regulatory manoeuvring remains.

3. OVERVIEW: NON-DISCRIMINATION OBLIGATIONS

Table 4.1 provides an overview of non-discrimination obligations in GATS and the selected EU RTAs. Naturally, the differences in scope between the Modes of supply in GATS and the selected EU RTAs should be taken into account for the interpretation of this table.

[324] This also applies to market access schedules. See Erik van der Marel and Sébastien Miroudot, 'The Economics and Political Economy of Going Beyond the GATS' (2014) 9 The Review of International Organizations 205, 205. Here, it is argued that the 'commitment gap' between GATS and RTA Schedules may be explained on the basis of 'asymmetries between negotiating partners and market size, together with endowments in mid-skilled labor and institutional governance'.

Table 4.1 Non-discrimination obligations

		GATS	EU-C&P RTA	EU-Singapore RTA	EU-Georgia DCFTA
Establishment	MFN	*unconditional; MFN exemptions*			*conditional; limitations; negative list; no likeness*
	National treatment	*conditional; limitations*	*conditional; limitations*	*conditional; limitations*	*conditional; limitations; negative list; no likeness*
	Standstill non-discrimination without likeness condition and less favourable treatment condition			*'in relation to' specific commitments; limitations*	*conditional; limitations*
	Specific exception for legal and technical differences				X
Cross-border trade in services	MFN	*unconditional; MFN exemptions*			
	National treatment	*conditional; limitations*	*conditional; limitations*	*conditional; limitations*	*conditional; limitations*
	Standstill non-discrimination, no likeness condition or less favourable treatment condition			*conditional; 'in relation to' specific commitments; limitations*	
Temporary presence of natural persons for business purposes	MFN	*unconditional; MFN exemptions*			
	National treatment	*conditional; limitations*			
	Discriminatory limitations on temporary entry and stay, no likeness conditions or less favourable treatment condition		*key personnel; graduate trainees; in establish-ment Schedule*	*key personnel; graduate trainees; in establish-ment and cross-border trade in services Schedules*	*key personnel; graduate trainees; in establish-ment Schedule*

5. Market access

1. THE MARKET ACCESS OBLIGATION IN GATS

1.1 Paragraph 1 of the Market Access Obligation

The market access obligation of Article XVI GATS states, in paragraph 1, that each Member shall accord services and service suppliers of any other Member treatment no less favourable than that provided for under the terms, limitations and conditions contained in the market access column of the Member's Schedule of specific commitments. Thus, the obligation is a conditional one: it applies only to committed sectors, and is subject to any scheduled limitations. The scope of Article XVI GATS is extended by footnote 8 to Article XVI:1 GATS, which explains that the movement of capital must be allowed for commitments in two situations. First, movement of capital must be allowed for Mode 1 commitments if the cross-border movement of capital is an essential part of the service itself. 'Cross-border movement of capital' covers both inward and outward movements of capital.[1] The obligation only extends to situations in which the movement of capital is an essential part of the service, thereby excluding movements that are merely related to the service.[2] Second, as concerns its Mode 3 commitments, a Member must allow the transfer of capital into its territory where such a transfer is related to the service. Thus, in such a situation, a Member must grant market access in the sense of Article XVI GATS. The scope of the obligation is dependent upon the meaning of 'granting market access', which is elaborated upon in paragraph 2 of the market access obligation and discussed in greater detail below.

However, before doing so, it should be noted that the market access commitments in the Schedules, which contain 'the terms, limitations and

[1] Panagiotis Delimatsis and Martín Molinuevo, 'Article XVI GATS' in Rüdiger Wolfrum, Peter-Tobias Stoll and Clemens Feinäugle (eds), *Max Planck Commentaries on World Trade Law: WTO – Trade in Services*, vol 6 (Martinus Nijhoff 2008) 373.

[2] Ibid.

conditions' of the commitments, are to be seen as minimum requirements.[3] They are to be applied on a non-discriminatory basis vis-à-vis all Members.[4] Therefore, the first paragraph of Article XVI GATS 'simply links a Member's market access obligations in respect of scheduled services to "the terms, limitations and conditions agreed and specified in its Schedule"'.[5] According to the Panel in *US – Gambling*, Article XVI:1 GATS does not prevent a Member from granting more favourable treatment to services and service suppliers of *all* Members.[6] In principle, this seems correct: the obligation does not prohibit granting better treatment. However, it is unclear why a Member could not grant more favourable market access treatment to one Member without violating Article XVI:1 GATS. The provision merely sets out a baseline standard, based on the commitments in a Member's Schedule, which should be applied to all Members on a non-discriminatory basis. It does not contain an obligation to extend more favourable treatment to all Members. Of course, such treatment could also constitute a violation of the MFN obligation of Article II GATS.

1.2 Paragraph 2 of the Market Access Obligation: Six Types of Prohibited Measures

1.2.1 Measures that should be scheduled

The market access obligation is limited in scope as it only provides for a number of specific market access restrictions. Article XVI:2 GATS lists six types of measures which a Member shall not maintain or adopt in sectors where specific commitments are scheduled, unless the relevant schedule contains a relevant limitation. This list is exhaustive.[7] Consequently, 'full market access' in the sense of Article XVI GATS is not

---

[3] *United States – Measures Affecting the Cross-Border Supply of Gambling and Betting Services* WT/DS285/R, Panel report adopted 20 April 2005 para. 6.263; *China – Measures Affecting Trading Rights and Distribution Services for Certain Publications and Audiovisual Products* WT/DS363/R, Panel report adopted 19 January 2010 para. 7.1353.

[4] *US – Gambling (Panel)* para. 6.265.

[5] *United States – Measures Affecting the Cross-Border Supply of Gambling and Betting Services* WT/DS285/AB/R, AB report adopted 20 April 2005 para. 235.

[6] *US – Gambling (Panel)* para. 6.264.

[7] Ibid para. 6298; *China – Publications and Audiovisual Products (Panel)* para. 7.1353. The AB declined to address the issue considering the scope of Antigua's appeal in *US – Gambling (AB)* para. 256, although it may be said to share the Panel's view in para. 215. There, the AB notes that the scope of the

equivalent to 'an undertaking's ability to execute its activities'.[8] The six types of measures, as listed in Article XVI:2 GATS, are the following:

(a) Limitations on the number of service suppliers whether in the form of numerical quotas, monopolies, exclusive service suppliers or the requirements of an economic needs test.
(b) Limitations on the total value of service transactions or assets in the form of numerical quotas or the requirement of an economic needs test.
(c) Limitations on the total number of service operations or on the total quantity of service output expressed in terms of designated numerical units in the form of quotas or the requirement of an economic needs test.[*]
(d) Limitations on the total number of natural persons that may be employed in a particular service sector or that a service supplier may employ and who are necessary for, and directly related to, the supply of a specific service in the form of numerical quotas or the requirement of an economic needs test.
(e) Measures which restrict or require specific types of legal entity or joint venture through which a service supplier may supply a service.
(f) Limitations on the participation of foreign capital in terms of maximum percentage limit on foreign shareholding or the total value of individual or aggregate foreign investment.

[*] Subparagraph 2(c) does not cover measures of a Member which limit inputs for the supply of services.

US' commitment meant that it would not maintain or adopt any of the six measures listed in Article XVI:2 GATS. See Markus Krajewski, 'Playing by the Rules of the Game? Specific Commitments after *US – Gambling and Betting* and the Current GATS Negotiations' (2005) 32 Legal Issues of Economic Integration 417, 431; and Eric Leroux, 'Eleven Years of GATS Case Law: What Have We Learned?' (2007) 10 Journal of International Economic Law 749, 769. Also see General Agreement on Tariffs and Trade, *MTN.GNS/W/164, Scheduling of Initial Commitments in Trade in Services: Explanatory Note (3 September)* para. 4.

[8] Delimatsis and Molinuevo, 'Article XVI GATS' 377. As the AB summarised in *US – Gambling (AB)* para. 215 (also see para. 233): 'In other words, the United States has undertaken to provide full market access, within the meaning of Article XVI, in respect of the services included within the scope of its [...] commitment. In so doing, it has committed not to maintain any of the types of measures listed in the six sub-paragraphs of Article XVI:2.' Compare this to the definition of 'market access' in the *Dictionary of Trade Policy Terms*, as reiterated by the Panel in *US – Gambling (Panel)* para. 6.274: 'the extent to which a good or a service can compete with locally-made products in another market. In the WTO framework it as a legalistic terms [sic] outlining the government-imposed conditions under which a product may enter a country under non-discrimination conditions'.

These types of measures, which limit market access, can be divided into three categories.[9] First, measures mentioned in subparagraphs (a)–(d) are limitations in the form of quantitative restrictions. Second, subparagraph (e) contains limitations on the form of establishment. Third, subparagraph (f) disciplines limitations on the participation of foreign capital.

Before analysing these limitations in more detail, it is helpful to address the scope of the list of prohibited measures in Article XVI:2 GATS. Four issues stand out. First, Article XVI GATS is applicable to discriminatory and non-discriminatory measures. This applicability was explicitly addressed in the 1993 Scheduling Guidelines, which have been followed by the panels and AB.[10] This applicability is 'the conventional wisdom' regarding Article XVI GATS.[11] A strong textual argument for this finding is that, while Article XVI:2 (a) GATS refers to *all* service suppliers (not just foreign service suppliers), Article XVI:2 (f) GATS

---

[9] *US – Gambling (AB)* para. 214.

[10] General Agreement on Tariffs and Trade, *MTN.GNS/W/164, Scheduling of Initial Commitments in Trade in Services: Explanatory Note (3 September)* para. 4; S/L/92 2001 Scheduling Guidelines para. 8. Panagiotis Delimatsis, 'Don't Gamble with GATS: The Interaction between Articles VI, XVI, XVII and XVIII GATS in the Light of the *US – Gambling* Case' (2006) 40 Journal of World Trade 1059, 1063 at footnote 22 stresses that the 2001 Scheduling Guidelines have been adopted by all Members in the CTS.

For an analysis of why this approach is not so different from the GATT 1994 distinction between Articles III:4 (national treatment) and XI (quantitative restrictions) despite the Ad Note to Article III:4 GATT 1994, Douglas A Irwin and Joseph Weiler, '*Measures Affecting the Cross-Border Supply of Gambling and Betting Services* (DS 285)' (2008) 7 World Trade Review 71, 100–101. More generally, on this distinction, see Joost Pauwelyn, 'Rien ne Va Plus? Distinguishing Domestic Regulation from Market Access in GATT and GATS' (2005) 4 World Trade Review 131, 142–148; Erich Vranes, 'The WTO and Regulatory Freedom: WTO Disciplines on Market Access, Non-Discrimination and Domestic Regulation Relating to Trade in Goods and Services' (2009) 12 Journal of International Economic Law 953. (It is, however, notable that an overlap between these provisions in not necessarily excluded: *India – Measures Affecting the Automotive Sector* WT/DS146/R, WT/DS175/R, Panel report adopted 5 April 2002 paras 7.224 and 7.306; P Van den Bossche and W Zdouc, *The Law and Policy of the World Trade Organization* (3rd edn, Cambridge University Press 2013) 354–355.)

[11] Donald H Regan, 'A Gambling Paradox: Why an Origin-Neutral "Zero-Quota" is Not a Quota Under GATS Article XVI' (2007) 41 Journal of World Trade 1297, 1299 and footnote 6.

refers only to *foreign* capital.[12] The rationale behind Article XVI GATS applying to both discriminatory and non-discriminatory measures may be that even non-discriminatory quotas are likely to be protectionist, as many systems allocating the places under the quota are more favourable for domestic service suppliers:

> Even if the selection is *de novo* and evenhanded, local suppliers are likely to have the best current knowledge of the market, and thus to be the most likely to apply and to succeed. Any system that cuts off free entry over time seems likely to favor locals, as compared to a system which allows free entry and exit.[13]

This wide approach risks further blurring the line between non-discriminatory and discriminatory measures. But it is true that even non-discriminatory quotas are unnecessarily trade-restrictive vis-à-vis their purported goal.[14] Nonetheless, the addition of non-discriminatory measures to the scope of Article XVI GATS has been criticised as a 'misconceived attempt' to subject such measures to the market access obligation.[15] In the current case law, this 'attempt' nonetheless appears to have been successful.

---

[12] Delimatsis, 'Don't Gamble with GATS: The Interaction between Articles VI, XVI, XVII and XVIII GATS in the Light of the *US – Gambling* Case' 1063 at footnote 22.

[13] Regan, 'A Gambling Paradox: Why an Origin-Neutral "Zero-Quota" is Not a Quota Under GATS Article XVI' 1308.

[14] Federico Ortino, 'Treaty Interpretation and the WTO Appellate Body Report in *US – Gambling*: A Critique' (2006) 9 Journal of International Economic Law 117, 142–143; Regan, 'A Gambling Paradox: Why an Origin-Neutral "Zero-Quota" is Not a Quota Under GATS Article XVI' 1309.

[15] James Flett, 'National Treatment under the General Agreement on Trade in Services (GATS)' in Anselm Kamperman Sanders (ed), *The Principle of National Treatment in International Economic Law: Trade, Investment and Intellectual Property* (Edward Elgar Publishing 2014) 78–80. Flett argues that the Scheduling Guidelines wrongly *require* a Member to schedule a non-discriminatory market access limitation. He notes that a Member wanting to grant non-discriminatory market access to a certain level, but also retain the right to discriminate beyond that level, must schedule their commitments accordingly. For example, a measure may limit the number of service suppliers to ten, of which five are non-discriminatorily divided between foreign and domestic service suppliers, but the Member retains the right to discriminate for the other five. A similar argument had been advanced as the central thesis in Petros C Mavroidis, 'Highway XVI Re-visited: The Road from Non-discrimination to Market Access in GATS' (2007) 6 World Trade Review 1, especially at 10–15.

Second, Article XVI GATS does not constrain a Member from restricting exports of domestically-owned or domestically-controlled service suppliers and services, even if the Member has made a full market access commitment.[16] However, this does not extend to exports of services by service suppliers established under Mode 3, even if the actual exports of these services occur through Modes 1 and 2.[17] The importance of this understanding for the scope of GATS should not be underestimated. A study reviewing whether GATS Schedules include specific limitations for exports concluded that 'nobody apparently anticipated the need for targeted limitations'.[18]

Third, in *US – Gambling*, the Panel found that a full market access commitment requires that the scheduling Member does not 'prohibit the use of one, several or all means of delivery of that service'.[19] Notably, the US appealed this finding but abandoned the argument in the oral hearings.[20] The AB subsequently upheld the Panel's findings.[21] Two of the challenged (federal) US measures 'specifically prohibit[ed] the use of communication or other facilities for gambling across state or international borders', and the combination of the challenged measures 'arguably prohibit[ed] the supply of cross-border gambling and betting services to consumers in the US'.[22] Hence, the measures prohibited the supply of online gambling services through Mode 1. However, if the

---

[16] *Mexico – Measures Affecting Telecommunications Services* WT/DS204/R, Panel report adopted 2 April 2004 para. 7.375; *China – Measures Affecting Electronic Payment Services* WT/DS413/R, Panel report adopted 31 August 2012 para. 7.618; Rudolf Adlung, 'Export Policies and the General Agreement on Trade in Services' 18 Journal of International Economic Law 495 and 498.

[17] As Adlung explains: 'While the trade flows flatly fall within the definitional scope of modes 1 and 2, [...] the right to generate such flows is contingent on the existence of commitments under mode 3'. Adlung, 'Export Policies and the General Agreement on Trade in Services' 498.

[18] Ibid. In Mode 4, the author notes, the problem is in practice much less poignant.

[19] *US – Gambling (Panel)* paras 6.287 and 6.290.

[20] *US – Gambling (AB)* para. 220.

[21] Ibid.

[22] Lode Van Den Hende, 'GATS Article XVI and National Regulatory Sovereignty: What Lessons to Draw from *US – Gambling*?' (2007) 20 Cambridge Review of International Affairs 93, 94–95; Leroux, 'Eleven Years of GATS Case Law: What Have We Learned?' 773. Trachtman disagrees, noting that only *part* of the mode of supply was banned. Joel P Trachtman, 'United States: Measures Affecting the Cross-Border Supply of Betting and Gambling Services, WT/DS285/AB/R' (2005) 99 American Journal of International Law 861, 866.

gambling services sector is considered as a whole there would have been no zero-quota,[23] as 'the measures, whilst certainly affecting certain possible modes of gambling, do not amount to a zero quota of the committed service in its totality'.[24] Note that the statement of the Panel is wide enough to lead to the same conclusion regardless of the approach: whether one uses the broader sector of 'gambling services' (in comparison to the more narrow category of 'online gambling services'), the measures at issue still restrict a complete *means* of supply, i.e. cross-border supply of gambling services. If a more narrow interpretation had been taken, for example 'online gambling services', the anti-protectionist rationale disappears as *both* domestic and foreign online gambling services suppliers would be prohibited from supplying their services.[25] Considering that the market access obligation does not require the demonstration of protectionist intent, this broader approach is perhaps also preferable from a policy, rather than a legal, perspective.

Nonetheless, the abovementioned statement of the Panel clearly raises questions as to the delineation of the relevant means of supply in combination with the relevant services sector. It does not leave a regulator with the autonomy to regulate a specific form of service supply without violating a market access commitment *after* the commitment was made. In order to justify such a violation, recourse would have to be had to the exceptions clauses. From a scheduling Member's perspective, two solutions exist to circumvent interpretative problems such as the one faced by the US:

a. A Member could limit the means of supply for a specific service in its Schedule. Prior to *US – Gambling*, it was suggested that the limitations that may be scheduled by a Member under Article XVI:2 GATS are only those mentioned in that provision and, consequently, limitations on a specific *means* of supply cannot be

---

[23] In *US – Gambling*, the sector of 'other recreational services', the residual category under which the Panel found that the US had committed to allowing gambling services, is overly broad to consider as the service in its totality. The Panel made use of the complainants' argumentation that the relevant services were 'gambling and betting services'. *US – Gambling (Panel)* para. 6.2.

[24] Irwin and Weiler, '*Measures Affecting the Cross-Border Supply of Gambling and Betting Services* (DS 285)' 88.

[25] Regan, 'A Gambling Paradox: Why an Origin-Neutral "Zero-Quota" is Not a Quota Under GATS Article XVI' 1308.

scheduled or prohibited by the market access obligation.[26] This suggestion cannot stand following the Panel ruling in *US – Gambling*, which noted that a commitment 'implies the right for other Members' suppliers to supply a service through all means of delivery, whether by mail, telephone, Internet etc., unless otherwise specified in a Member's Schedule'.[27] This safeguards, from a systemic point of view, the Members' autonomy to restrict certain means of supply of a service at the moment of scheduling.

b. A more detailed classification of services sectors could also mitigate the problem. For example, the EU explicitly differentiates between privately and publicly funded educational services in its Schedule, only making commitments for the latter category of services.

Although consistent with the technological neutrality of commitments in the Schedules,[28] the obvious problem with both solutions is that they require a Member to foresee *how* a service may be supplied in the future at the time of scheduling.[29]

Fourth, the Panel in *US – Gambling* differentiates between measures directed at services or service suppliers, and measures directed at consumers.[30] Concerning the latter, the Panel found that Article XVI GATS was not applicable, considering that the wording of Article XVI GATS is directed at service suppliers. This may 'reveal an interesting inconsistency or desired effect' of the market access obligation under

---

[26] Patrick Low and Aaditya Mattoo, 'Is There a Better Way? Alternative Approaches to Liberalization Under the GATS' in Pierre Sauvé and Robert M Stern (eds), *GATS 2000: New Directions in Services Trade Liberalization* (Brookings Institution 2000) 454.

[27] *US – Gambling (Panel)* para. 6.285; Nellie Munin, *Legal Guide to GATS* (Wolters Kluwer 2010) 191.

[28] See, explicitly, *US – Gambling (Panel)* para. 6.285; Sacha Wunsch-Vincent, 'The Internet, Cross-Border Trade in Services, and the GATS: Lessons from *US – Gambling*' (2006) 5 World Trade Review 319 329–334; Tania Voon, 'China and Cultural Products at the WTO' (2010) 37 Legal Issues of Economic Integration 254; Joost Pauwelyn, 'Squaring Free Trade in Culture with Chinese Censorship: The WTO Appellate Body Report on *China – Audiovisuals*' (2010) 11 Melbourne Journal of International Law 119, 131–132.

[29] Of course, this is especially tricky considering the rise of electronically supplied services since 1995.

[30] *US – Gambling (Panel)* paras 6.382–6.383, 6.397–6.398, 6.401–6.402 and 6.405–6.406. Note that the AB stated that the Panel was not entitled to rule on the four US state laws relevant here because Antigua failed to make a prima facie case. *US – Gambling (AB)* para. 254, referring to paras 149–155.

GATS: governments may be able to circumvent the application of the market access obligation by regulating the consumption of a service and not the supply of the service.[31] As explained below, this distinction may not hold up in light of the AB's findings regarding the scope of Article XVI GATS: if the measure has a quantitative thrust, it should not matter whether it is directed at consumers or service suppliers. Nonetheless, whether a measure is directed at consumers may influence the analysis of a measure's quantitative thrust.

1.2.2 Limitations in the form of quantitative restrictions

1.2.2.1 The targets of the prohibition of limitations in the form of quantitative restrictions Article XVI:2 (a)–(d) GATS prohibits certain types of measures in the form of quantitative restrictions. This is the subject of the next section. To understand the scope of the prohibitions in these subparagraphs, one must first determine, in the words of the AB,[32] their 'targets'. Article XVI:2 (a) GATS targets measures that constitute limitations on the number of service suppliers. Subparagraph (b) prohibits limitations on the total value of service transactions or assets. As for Article XVI:2 (c) GATS, the AB has noted that this subparagraph targets, first, the number of service operations, and, second, the quantity of the service output.[33] 'Service operations' are 'activities comprised in the production of a service'; service output is 'the result of the production of the service'.[34] For example, a measure limiting the broadcasting time for foreign films would fall within the scope of this subparagraph.[35] Finally, subparagraph (d) prohibits limitations on the total number of natural persons that may be employed in a particular service sector, or, the total number of natural persons that a service supplier may employ and who are necessary for, and directly related to, the supply of a specific service. According to the 1993 Scheduling Guidelines, this would also cover

---

[31] Wunsch-Vincent, 'The Internet, Cross-Border Trade in Services, and the GATS: Lessons from *US – Gambling*' 337–338; this observation was first made by Krajewski, 'Playing by the Rules of the Game? Specific Commitments after *US – Gambling and Betting* and the Current GATS Negotiations' 436.

[32] *US – Gambling (AB)* para. 246.

[33] *US – Gambling (AB)* para. 246.

[34] *US – Gambling (Panel)* para. 6.349.

[35] General Agreement on Tariffs and Trade, *MTN.GNS/W/164, Scheduling of Initial Commitments in Trade in Services: Explanatory Note (3 September)* para. 6.

limitations that restrict foreign labour, or restrict the wages paid in respect of such labour, to a certain percentage of total labour or wages.[36]

1.2.2.2 In the form of numerical quotas, monopolies, exclusive service suppliers or the requirements of an economic needs test

1.2.2.2.1 ARTICLE XVI:2 (A) GATS AND *US – GAMBLING* The seminal GATS market access case, *US – Gambling*, focused on the interpretation of Article XVI:2 (a) GATS. As noted, this provision disciplines limitations on the number of service suppliers, whether in the form of: (i) numerical quotas; (ii) monopolies; (iii) exclusive service suppliers; or (iv) the requirements of an economic needs test. According to the AB, the term 'form' is to be interpreted broadly, as the meaning of 'in the form of' is informed by all four types of quantitative restrictions mentioned in the provision.[37] As concerns numerical quotas, the AB stated, based on dictionary definitions of 'numerical' and 'quota' that the term encompasses 'limitations which, even if not in themselves a number, have the characteristics of a number'.[38] Thereafter, the AB (in)famously held: 'Because zero is quantitative in nature, it can, in our view, be deemed to have the "characteristics of" a number – that is, to be "numerical"'.[39] Therefore, a ban, which limits the number of service suppliers to zero, is a numerical quota in the sense of Article XVI:2 (a) GATS.[40] The Panel helpfully stated that:

> It is true that the wording of Article XVI:2(a) covers numerical quotas other than zero. […] Paragraph (a) does not foresee a 'zero quota' because paragraph (a) was not drafted to cover situations where a Member wants to maintain full limitations. If a Member wants to maintain a full prohibition, it is assumed that such a Member would not have scheduled such a sector or sub-sector and, therefore, would not need to schedule any limitation or measures pursuant to Article XVI:2.[41]

With regards to monopolies and exclusive service suppliers, the AB referred to the definition of 'monopoly supplier of a service' in Article XXVIII (h) and of 'exclusive service supplier' in Article VIII:5 GATS.

---

36 Ibid.

37 *US – Gambling (AB)* paras 226–227. In other words, the list in Article XVI:2 (a) GATS is exhaustive. See *US – Gambling (Panel)* paras 6.323–6.325.

38 *US – Gambling (AB)* para. 227.

39 Ibid.

40 Ibid para. 238.

41 *US – Gambling (Panel)* para. 6.331.

That provision states that the establishment of a service supplier as, in effect, the sole service supplier, constitutes a monopoly. On the other hand, the establishment of just a few service suppliers would constitute exclusive service suppliers.[42] Finally, the terminology 'the requirements of an economic needs test' does not prescribe a specific form.[43] Moreover, the AB supports its reasoning with an example of a limitation in the sense of Article XVI:2 (a) GATS given in the 1993 Scheduling Guidelines, i.e. 'nationality requirements for suppliers of services (equivalent to zero quota)'.[44] Similarly, scheduling practice highlights many limitations on market access commitments which are not explicitly 'in the form of' the relevant numerical limitations.[45]

This interpretation appears to be very broad: if the quantitative *effect* of a measure is sufficient for it to be a measure *in the form of* a quantitative limitation, the scope of Article XVI GATS could be stretched considerably. However, in the words of the AB, the foregoing does not mean 'that the words "in the form of" should be ignored or replaced by the words "that have the effect of"'.[46] It is nonetheless clear to the AB 'that the thrust of sub-paragraph (a) is not on the form of limitations, but on their *numerical*, or *quantitative*, nature'.[47] In the words of the Panel in *China – Electronic Payment Services*:

> even a measure that is not, for instance, called a 'quota' can fall within the scope of Article XVI:2(a), if it is quantitative in its thrust and therefore, limits the supply of a service as a quota would do.[48]

Similarly, for the other forms of limitations covered by Article XVI:2 (a) GATS, aside from a 'quota', it should be assessed whether a measure, with a quantitative thrust, has the effect of limiting the number of service suppliers to one ('in the form of a monopoly') or to a few ('in the form

---

[42] *US – Gambling (AB)* paras 228–230. This was reiterated in *China – Electronic Payment Services (Panel)* para. 7.586.

[43] *US – Gambling (AB)* para. 231.

[44] General Agreement on Tariffs and Trade, *MTN.GNS/W/164, Scheduling of Initial Commitments in Trade in Services: Explanatory Note (3 September)* para. 6.

[45] Van Den Hende, 'GATS Article XVI and National Regulatory Sovereignty: What Lessons to Draw from *US – Gambling*?' 107–108.

[46] *US – Gambling (AB)* para. 232.

[47] Ibid (emphasis original).

[48] *China – Electronic Payment Services (Panel)* para. 7.592. The Panel finds, at paras 7.623–7.624, that this is the case where a Chinese service supplier is the sole authorised supplier of the handling of bank card transactions.

of exclusive service suppliers').[49] It should be noted that, where the measure is a limitation in the form of the requirements of an economic needs test,[50] the relevant entry in the Member's Schedule should indicate the main criteria on which the test is based.[51] Therefore, in addition to an analysis of the quantitative limitation that is the result of the application of the economic needs test, it may be questioned by a complainant whether the limitation in the responding Member's Schedule actually covers the economic needs test in the measure.

1.2.2.2.2 DEMARCATING QUANTITATIVE AND QUALITATIVE THRUST The dividing line between measures with a quantitative and a qualitative thrust is not yet clear. As explained in Figure 5.1, the distinction made by the AB between 'in the form of' and 'the effect of' could be interpreted as follows: a measure could be in the form of and have the effect of a quantitative restriction (situation (1)); or a measure could be in the form of a quantitative restriction but without the effect of such a restriction (situation (2)). Situation (2) is not likely to be common, but, nonetheless, may exist. Where a measure has the effect of a quantitative restriction, but is not in the form of such a restriction, there are two options available. First, the measure may have a 'quantitative thrust' (situation (3)). Second, it may have a 'qualitative thrust' (situation (4)). Only in the fourth situation is the measure not disciplined by Article XVI:2 (a) GATS. Therefore, based on this reasoning, it is submitted that the AB did not 'read "form" and "numerical" out of Article XVI' GATS.[52]

Thus, the question becomes: how can one distinguish between type (3) and type (4) measures? In other words: how can a quantitative thrust be established? The analytical focus lies in determining whether the measure constitutes 'a limitation that is numerical and quantitative in nature'.[53] The Panel in *China – Electronic Payment Services* stated that a measure should impose an *express* limitation on the number of service suppliers

---

[49] Ibid para. 7.593.

[50] An economic needs test is a test by which the need for a service (supplier) is determined on an economic basis, normally taking into account supply and demand. Markus Krajewski, *National Regulation and Trade Liberalization in Services* (Kluwer Law International 2003) 89.

[51] S/L/93, Guidelines and Procedures for the Negotiations on Trade in Services (Adopted by the Council for Trade in Services 28 March 2001) para. 9 gives the example that 'if the authority to establish a facility is based on a population criterion, the criterion should be described concisely'.

[52] I thus disagree with Pauwelyn, 'Rien ne Va Plus? Distinguishing Domestic Regulation from Market Access in GATT and GATS' 160.

[53] *China – Electronic Payment Services (Panel)* para. 7.593.

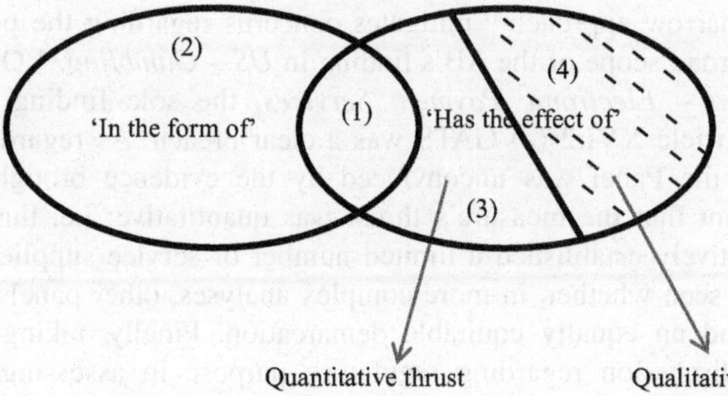

Figure 5.1 The universe of measures covered by Article XVI:2 (a)–(d) GATS

that is numerical or quantitative in nature.[54] In its attempt to delineate between measures with a quantitative or qualitative thrust, the Panel appeared to focus on a directly attributable effect. The *de facto* entrenchment of a limited number of service suppliers could breach Article XVI:2 (a) GATS.[55] Similarly, if the economic effect of the measure, or of a combination of the measures,[56] is that other service suppliers will not enter the market because doing so is not economically viable, that measure may breach Article XVI:2 (a) GATS.[57] The fact that the measure places a service supplier in a 'unique position' or grants it certain advantages vis-à-vis other service suppliers, however, does not suffice for such a violation.[58] In summary, a complainant must demonstrate, by providing evidence, that the measure under scrutiny produces economic effects so significant that they limit the number of service suppliers.[59]

---

[54] Ibid para. 7.600.

[55] Ibid para. 7.603.

[56] The Panel implies that a combination of a measure in violation of Article XVI:2(a) GATS with another measure could 'have the effect of converting' the latter measure 'into the type of measure referred to in Article XVI:2(a)'. Ibid para. 7.627.

[57] Ibid para. 7.604.

[58] Ibid para. 7.602.

[59] Ibid para. 7.504. The Panel explained, in the context of a claim that one domestic service supplier has a monopoly because of the measure at issue, that the Panel needs: 'evidence, e.g. economic analyses of profitability, price–cost margins, or demand elasticity, including in comparison with other markets, that would allow us to assess whether indeed the instruments at issue make it economically unviable for other [service] suppliers to establish themselves and operate [in the respondent's market]'.

This Panel's narrow approach[60] mitigates concerns regarding the potentially overly broad scope of the AB's finding in *US – Gambling*.[61] On the facts of *China – Electronic Payment Services*, the sole finding of a violation of Article XVI:2 (a) GATS was a clear breach. As regards the other claims, the Panel was unconvinced by the evidence brought by the complainant that the measure's thrust was quantitative; i.e. that the measure effectively established a limited number of service suppliers. It remains to be seen whether, in more complex analyses, other panels will be able to find an equally equitable demarcation. Finally, taking into account the discussion regarding regulatory purpose in assessing less favourable treatment under national treatment, it is submitted that no such purpose plays a role in the assessment of whether a measure is covered by Article XVI GATS.[62]

A notable line of reasoning, which assists in delineating between a quantitative and a qualitative thrust, may be explained as follows. As the 'nature of numericals is their quantifiable precision', a zero-quota, or a requirement of 'a majority' (an example given by the AB), would be covered by Article XVI:2 (a) GATS. Conversely, a measure with a quantitative impact without any precision, for example a measure that has a solely incidental impact on the quantity of service suppliers, would not be covered.[63] For instance, a driving test for taxi drivers would not limit the number of drivers to a specific, known number of taxi drivers passing

---

[60] Bernard M Hoekman and Niall Meagher, '*China – Electronic Payment Services*: Discrimination, Economic Development and the GATS' (2014) 13 World Trade Review 409, 431 and 436–437.

[61] This case can be seen as an example of Irwin and Weiler's analysis of the AB's findings in *US – Gambling*, with which I concur. Irwin and Weiler, '*Measures Affecting the Cross-Border Supply of Gambling and Betting Services* (DS 285)' 95.

[62] I therefore disagree with Ortino, 'Treaty Interpretation and the WTO Appellate Body Report in *US – Gambling*: A Critique' 135–146 and Leroux, 'Eleven Years of GATS Case Law: What Have We Learned?' 774–776; and agree with the conclusion of Delimatsis, 'Don't Gamble with GATS: The Interaction between Articles VI, XVI, XVII and XVIII GATS in the Light of the *US-Gambling* Case' 1072.

[63] Irwin and Weiler, '*Measures Affecting the Cross-Border Supply of Gambling and Betting Services* (DS 285)' 105, give the example that 'if a provider of cinematographic entertainment, or television transmission, is told that he may not allow children into certain types of movies or that certain types of transmissions may only take place at certain late hours of the night, he may not complain, absent discrimination, that this amounts to a restriction on his ability to provide services'.

such a test.[64] While helpful for understanding the scope of Article XVI GATS, this approach is more restrictive than necessary. The AB did not find that a zero-quota always comes within the scope of Article XVI:2 (a) GATS. The AB merely noted that such a quota could do so, if its thrust were quantitative. For example, a measure with the effect of a zero-quota but absent a quantitative thrust may well exist, perhaps *inter alia* because it is aimed at consumers, and, therefore, is *not* prohibited by Article XVI:2 GATS.[65] A crucial element is the distinction between a ban on a single method of supply and a ban on the whole of a committed sector (which serves a similar purpose to the definition of the market under the non-discrimination obligations): the quantifiable precision of a measure may disappear in the broader, sectoral context.

1.2.2.2.3 APPLICABILITY TO ARTICLE XVI:2 (B)–(D) GATS For the following reasons, the dividing line between a measure's quantitative and qualitative thrust under Article XVI:2 (a) GATS also applies to subparagraphs (b), (c) and (d). First, Article XVI:2 (c) GATS is grammatically ambiguous as it may be interpreted as containing two or three 'forms' of limitations. According to the AB, the provision may be interpreted to prohibit: (i) limitations expressed in terms of designated numerical units in the form of quotas; and (ii) limitations expressed in terms of the requirement of an economic needs test.[66] However, in an alternative reading, the provision may prohibit: (i) limitations expressed in terms of designated numerical units; (ii) limitations expressed in the form of quotas; and (iii) limitations expressed in terms of the requirement of an economic needs test.[67] Regardless of this uncertainty, the AB has found that the absence of express reference to numbered units in a

---

[64] Regan, 'A Gambling Paradox: Why an Origin-Neutral "Zero-Quota" is Not a Quota Under GATS Article XVI' 1302; Pauwelyn, 'Rien ne Va Plus? Distinguishing Domestic Regulation from Market Access in GATT and GATS' 170 gives this example, but goes on to say that the same applies to the requirement that gambling occurs face-to-face, as in *US – Gambling*. However, as Pauwelyn notes, a key difference is that in *US – Gambling*, the ban coincided with a complete method of supply.

[65] This reading may explain the 'apparent contradiction' between this differentiation, which exemplifies a strict reading of Article XVI GATS with deference to regulatory autonomy, and the application thereof to the facts in *US – Gambling* noted by Krajewski, 'Playing by the Rules of the Game? Specific Commitments after *US – Gambling and Betting* and the Current GATS Negotiations' 436.

[66] *US – Gambling (AB)* para. 245, at footnote 283.

[67] Ibid para. 245, at footnote 284.

measure does not preclude the applicability of subparagraph (c).[68] As with subparagraph (a), Article XVI:2 (c) GATS could cover measures equivalent to zero-quota.[69] Without reiterating its reasoning regarding the qualitative versus quantitative thrust of a measure, the AB indicated that differentiating between quantitative and qualitative measures is also key to the demarcation of Article XVI:2 (c) GATS.[70] Therefore, the diagram in Figure 5.1 may be applied to subparagraph (c).

Second and third, subparagraphs (b) and (d) prohibit: (i) measures in the form of numerical quotas or the requirement of an economic needs test; and (ii) measures in the form of numerical quotas or the requirement of an economic needs test respectively. Considering the overlap with the broader types of measures prohibited by Article XVI:2 (a) and (c) GATS, it is submitted that the AB's reasoning can be extended to these subparagraphs. Note that subparagraphs (b)–(d) refer to '*total* value', as compared to 'value' in subparagraph (a). The Panel in *US – Gambling* did not consider the addition of 'total' to be of particular relevance.[71] One author explains that the difference may stem from the exclusion of 'firm-related size limitations which might be maintained, for instance under competition or zoning laws' from the scope of Article XVI:2(a)–(d), in so far as these limitations do not affect the total amount of services that could be supplied.[72] In such an interpretation, the addition of 'total' to subparagraph (a) would have been meaningless.[73]

The above does not mean that Article XVI:2(a) GATS 'absorbs' subparagraphs (b)–(d) and renders them meaningless. The Panel in *Argentina – Financial Services* held that, precisely to give effect to subparagraphs (b)–(d), a measure that has the 'indirect effect' of limiting the number or value of service suppliers would not be covered by Article XVI:2(a) GATS. Only measures 'intended specifically' to do so are subject to that provision's disciplines.[74] The Panel appears to indicate that the complainant should have presented an argument under subparagraphs (b) or (c), rather than (a).[75]

---

68 Ibid para. 250.
69 Ibid para. 247.
70 Ibid paras 248–250.
71 *US – Gambling (Panel)* para 6.345.
72 Adlung, 'Export Policies and the General Agreement on Trade in Services' 496.
73 Ibid at footnote 21.
74 *Argentina – Measures Relating to Trade in Goods and Services*, WT/DS453, Panel Report not yet adopted paras 7.420–7.421.
75 Ibid para. 7.428.

1.2.3 Limitations on the form of establishment

In subparagraph (e), Article XVI:2 GATS contains a prohibition of 'measures which restrict or require specific types of legal entity or joint venture through which a service supplier may supply a service'. Note that there is no quantitative aspect in the text of this provision. Further, in contrast to the five other types of measures, there is no reference to 'limitations'. Some of these limitations are most likely non-discriminatory vis-à-vis foreign service suppliers and would apply to domestic service suppliers as well.[76] Others, however, apply solely to foreign service suppliers in a Mode 3 context.[77] An example of a limitation that would be covered by subparagraph (e) is a requirement, in a given services sector, that commercial presence must take the form of a partnership.[78] A further limitation in the sense of Article XVI:2 (e) GATS would be the requirement for foreign service suppliers to use contractual joint ventures in order to be able to supply services.[79]

1.2.4 Limitations on the participation of foreign capital

As noted, Article XVI:2 (f) GATS targets measures which place limitations on the capital participation of foreign investors. The provision prohibits such limitations in the form of (i) 'a maximum percentage of capital that can be held by foreign investors', or (ii) 'a total value of foreign investment, either by an individual investor or foreign investors as a whole'.[80] These limitations are inherently discriminatory.[81] For example, measures requiring that the domestic joint venture partner must hold the majority of equity in a contractual joint venture engaging in the distribution of audio-visual products were, in the absence of relevant limitations in the Member's Schedule, found in violation of Article

---

[76] Delimatsis and Molinuevo, 'Article XVI GATS' 387; Vranes, 'The WTO and Regulatory Freedom: WTO Disciplines on Market Access, Non-Discrimination and Domestic Regulation Relating to Trade in Goods and Services' 969–970.

[77] Delimatsis and Molinuevo, 'Article XVI GATS' 387.

[78] General Agreement on Tariffs and Trade, *MTN.GNS/W/164, Scheduling of Initial Commitments in Trade in Services: Explanatory Note (3 September)* para. 6.

[79] *China – Publications and Audiovisual Products (Panel)* para. 7.1356.

[80] Ibid para. 7.1360. The findings of the Panel regarding Article XVI:2 (f) GATS were not appealed.

[81] Delimatsis, 'Don't Gamble with GATS: The Interaction between Articles VI, XVI, XVII and XVIII GATS in the Light of the *US-Gambling* Case' 1072.

XVI:2 (f) GATS.[82] Subparagraph (f) is the sole GATS provision which refers explicitly to investment rather than commercial presence. That measures limiting investment are thus covered by Article XVI:2 (f) GATS, combined with the relatively broad scope of Mode 3, means that GATS can be considered 'an important international investment agreement'.[83] In that context, Article XVI:2 (f) GATS can be interpreted either narrowly or widely. In the narrow approach, subparagraph (f) only covers restrictions that affect the taking control of a service supplying enterprise. In the wide approach, all restrictions on investment may be covered in so far as they are linked to the supply of services and so long as ownership or control is acquired.[84] An even wider interpretation, which requires no link to the supply of services and no acquisition of ownership or control, has also been suggested. However, such an approach seems to contradict the language of GATS and would mean that any foreign equity limitation should be scheduled in GATS, regardless of a link to trade in services.[85] In such a case, no trade in services is at stake.[86]

1.3 Constraints on Regulatory Autonomy

Many regulatory measures have a restrictive impact on market access.[87] This explains the controversy surrounding the AB's finding in *US – Gambling* that measures which have a merely quantitative effect can be

---

[82] *China – Publications and Audiovisual Products (Panel)* paras 7.1376 and 7.1388.

[83] Bart De Meester and Dominic Coppens, 'Mode 3 of the GATS: A Model for Disciplining Measures Affecting Investment Flows?' in Zdenek Drabek and Petros C Mavroidis (eds), *Regulation of Foreign Investment: Challenges to International Harmonization* (World Scientific 2013) 105.

[84] Ibid.

[85] Munin, *Legal Guide to GATS* 200.

[86] De Meester and Coppens, 'Mode 3 of the GATS: A Model for Disciplining Measures Affecting Investment Flows?' 105.

[87] Irwin and Weiler, '*Measures Affecting the Cross-Border Supply of Gambling and Betting Services* (DS 285)' 96 give the following example: 'Imagine, say, a commitment in the Advertising Sector enabling the providers of foreign advertising services to enter the domestic market. Imagine then that the State that took such a commitment passed an origin-neutral law that forbade Billboard advertising in the interest of preserving the natural beauty of the environment as is now common in many countries. Imagine an agency whose specialty is that particular mode of providing advertising. It (and its domestic counterpart) would be faced with a measure having an effect equivalent to a zero quota'. Also see Emily Reid, 'Regulatory Autonomy in the EU and WTO: Defining and Defending Its Limits' (2010) 44 Journal of World Trade 877, 897.

covered by Article XVI:2 (a)–(d) GATS. The reasoning could have constituted a shift away from regulatory autonomy, and, in combination with the AB's finding that a zero-quota may be a measure with a quantitative effect in the sense of the market access obligation, could have had a chilling effect on regulators who want to ban the provision of certain services.[88] However, despite the many concerns raised in doctrine,[89] it is submitted that regulatory autonomy is not overly constrained. Indeed, in *US – Gambling*, the AB's 'attempt to decide on the measures at issue in the less intrusive manner possible is more than apparent'.[90] The Panel had foreseen the potential of criticism of its original findings. It stated, in a manner reminiscent of the famous AB finding in *US – Shrimp*:[91]

> We also wish to emphasize what we have *not* decided in this case. We have not decided that WTO Members do not have a right to regulate, including a right to prohibit, gambling and betting activities. In this case, we came to the conclusion that the US measures at issue prohibit the cross-border supply of gambling and betting services in the United States in a manner inconsistent with the GATS. We so decided, not because the GATS denies Members such a right but, rather, because we found, *inter alia*, that, in the particular circumstances of this case, the measures at issue were inconsistent with the United States' scheduled commitments and the relevant provisions of the GATS.[92]

As always with WTO dispute settlement, the factual constellation in *US – Gambling* should be given sufficient weight. As elucidated by Article 3.7 DSU, the primary aim of the dispute settlement system is to settle the

---

[88] Irwin and Weiler, '*Measures Affecting the Cross-Border Supply of Gambling and Betting Services* (DS 285)' 98.

[89] See e.g. Pauwelyn, 'Rien ne Va Plus? Distinguishing Domestic Regulation from Market Access in GATT and GATS' 161–168; Ortino, 'Treaty Interpretation and the WTO Appellate Body Report in *US – Gambling*: A Critique'; Mavroidis, 'Highway XVI Re-visited: The Road from Non-discrimination to Market Access in GATS'; Regan, 'A Gambling Paradox: Why an Origin-Neutral "Zero-Quota" is Not a Quota Under GATS Article XVI'.

[90] Delimatsis, 'Don't Gamble with GATS: The Interaction between Articles VI, XVI, XVII and XVIII GATS in the Light of the *US-Gambling* Case' 1068; similarly, see Wunsch-Vincent, 'The Internet, Cross-Border Trade in Services, and the GATS: Lessons from *US – Gambling*' 341–342.

[91] *United States – Import Prohibition of Certain Shrimp and Shrimp Products* WT/DS58/AB/R, AB report adopted 6 November 1998 para. 185.

[92] *US – Gambling (Panel)* para. 7.4 (emphasis original).

dispute at hand.[93] *US – Gambling* addressed a rare situation in which a Member made a full market access commitment for a sector in a mode of supply, but then denied all access to its market in that sector in that particular mode of supply.[94] In the context of the available information, the Panel and AB's interpretation of Article XVI GATS is convincing.[95] While the structure and the scope of the provision may be criticised, these are the responsibility of the Members, not of the panels or the AB.[96]

From a practical perspective, and as noted, it is overly broad to conclude from the case law that *any* ban would be sanctioned by Article XVI GATS. First, it should be recalled that the market access obligation is conditional in nature: a Member is only committed to providing market access in so far as it has scheduled commitments. Second, for a measure to be disciplined by the AB's interpretation of Article XVI (a)–(d) GATS, it must have a quantitative thrust. As evident from the Panel's reasoning in *China – Electronic Payment Services*, the distinction between measures with a quantitative and qualitative thrust should be made cautiously and on a case-by-case basis, without overstepping the boundaries of Article XVI GATS and with deference to regulatory autonomy. Indeed, many qualitative measures should not come within the ambit of Article XVI:2 (a)–(d) GATS. As stated by Irwin and Weiler, such qualitative measures are part of 'the market they have gained access to. The Member has promised access, but has not promised that Membership of the WTO will force it to change the social and cultural norms that are also reflected in its marketplace'.[97] Contrary to what some authors have argued, in my view, the AB's reasoning in *US – Gambling* does not stand in the way of

---

93 *United States – Measure Affecting Imports of Woven Wool Shirts and Blouses from India* WT/DS33/AB/R, AB report adopted 23 May 1997 19, where the AB noted that 'the basic aim of dispute settlement in the WTO is to settle disputes'.

94 Leroux, 'Eleven Years of GATS Case Law: What Have We Learned?' 772–773; however, note the above distinction between mode and method of supply in *US – Gambling*.

95 Therefore, I do not agree with Reid that the AB's finding is at odds with the preamble of GATS and the text of Article XVI GATS. Reid, 'Regulatory Autonomy in the EU and WTO: Defining and Defending Its Limits' 897.

96 Wunsch-Vincent, 'The Internet, Cross-Border Trade in Services, and the GATS: Lessons from *US – Gambling*' 346.

97 Irwin and Weiler, '*Measures Affecting the Cross-Border Supply of Gambling and Betting Services* (DS 285)' 103.

such an approach.[98] Undoubtedly, the fact that Article XVI GATS disciplines non-discriminatory measures has to be taken into account when interpreting the provision, as the application to such origin-neutral measures heightens the risk of constraining regulatory autonomy beyond what is acceptable.[99] The altered approach of the world trading system, in so far as it also applies to non-discriminatory measures grants regulators less leeway than a non-discrimination obligation does.[100] However, this is exactly why Article XVI:2 GATS has a limited scope, and is why the extension of the scope of subparagraphs (a)–(d) to measures with a quantitative thrust is defensible. Deciding otherwise would have made the obligation easy to circumvent. The provision has the purpose of balancing regulatory autonomy to adopt qualitative measures on the one hand and respect for freely given and negotiated quantitative market access commitments on the other.[101] Similarly, the inclusion of a zero-quota is not problematic if the quantitative thrust of the measure is established. It is for the complainant to provide proof of that quantitative thrust, and the bar for such proof has been set sufficiently high by the Panel in *China – Electronic Payment Services*.

1.4 The Relationship between Market Access and National Treatment

The demarcation between market access and national treatment is of crucial importance. This demarcation 'reflect[s] both economic and political preferences of certain types of policies over others' and the application of one obligation rather than the other 'lead[s] to drastically different disciplines and restrictions on the regulatory autonomy of WTO Members'.[102] Article XX:2 GATS grants some insight into the delineation between Articles XVI and XVII GATS. The provision states that

---

[98] Krajewski, 'Playing by the Rules of the Game? Specific Commitments after *US – Gambling and Betting* and the Current GATS Negotiations' 432, although Krajewski argues that the application of this principle by the AB in *US – Gambling* did not follow the 'cautious and balanced approach'.

[99] Reid, 'Regulatory Autonomy in the EU and WTO: Defining and Defending Its Limits' 900.

[100] Vranes, 'The WTO and Regulatory Freedom: WTO Disciplines on Market Access, Non-Discrimination and Domestic Regulation Relating to Trade in Goods and Services' 980–985.

[101] Irwin and Weiler, '*Measures Affecting the Cross-Border Supply of Gambling and Betting Services* (DS 285)' 92.

[102] Pauwelyn, 'Rien ne Va Plus? Distinguishing Domestic Regulation from Market Access in GATT and GATS' 133. At page 169, Pauwelyn notes that 'to preserve the regulatory autonomy of WTO Members under GATS it is, however,

measures which are inconsistent with both provisions are to be inscribed in the Schedule in the market access column, where they will also be considered as providing a qualification or condition to national treatment.[103] As such, Article XX:2 GATS safeguards certain measures from violating Article XVII GATS through limitations in the market access column of the Schedule.[104] On the basis of this provision, in combination with the broad scope of the national treatment obligation, it can be concluded that the scope of Articles XVI and XVII GATS is not mutually exclusive.[105] On the contrary, the wider *scope* of Article XVII GATS covers the scope of Article XVI GATS completely, although a measure that actually *violates* the market access obligation does not necessarily violate the national treatment obligation.[106]

The interpretation rejecting mutual exclusivity appears to be in accordance with the text of GATS and with the interpretation in case law. However, this interpretation does not immediately explain why the inherently discriminatory limitations of the types mentioned in Article XVI:2 (e)–(f) were added to the market access obligation. The answer lies in the following reasoning of the Panel in *China – Electronic Payment Services* on the meaning of Article XX:2 GATS. If a Member inscribes 'Unbound' in the market access column of its Schedule and a corresponding inscription of 'None' in the corresponding national treatment column, then Article XX:2 GATS means that the Member remains free to maintain the full range of limitations expressed in the six categories of Article XVI:2 GATS. This is the case irrespective of whether these limitations are discriminatory in the sense of Article XVII GATS.[107] Such an interpretation indeed also gives meaning to subparagraphs (e) and (f).

---

crucially important to narrowly define prohibited market access restrictions. If not, regulatory freedom under Article VI risks being emptied through per se prohibitions under Article XVI'.

[103] *China – Electronic Payment Services (Panel)* paras 7.657 and 7.661 affirmed that this specific scheduling rule applies when a measure is inconsistent with both Articles XVI and XVII GATS.

[104] Delimatsis, 'Don't Gamble with GATS: The Interaction between Articles VI, XVI, XVII and XVIII GATS in the Light of the *US-Gambling* Case' 1073.

[105] *China – Electronic Payment Services (Panel)* para. 7.658.

[106] Pauwelyn, 'Rien ne Va Plus? Distinguishing Domestic Regulation from Market Access in GATT and GATS' 149 and Figure 2 at 150. This does not mean that all measures that violate Article XVI GATS also violate Article XVII GATS, but merely that this is always a possibility.

[107] *China – Electronic Payment Services (Panel)* paras 7.654 and 7.661–7.664.

It should be noted that the opposite situation cannot be sustained. If a Member makes a full market access commitment, i.e. inscribes 'None', and a corresponding 'Unbound' commitment in the national treatment column, the Member is bound to respect Article XVI:2 GATS. Therefore, it cannot be true that the Member may take discriminatory measures of the types prohibited by Article XVI:2 (e)–(f) despite the full market access commitment, just because the national treatment obligation does not apply.[108] There is no market access limitation in the Schedule, so the obligations following from subparagraphs (e) and (f) must be respected. This finding is not altered by the fact that national treatment does not apply.[109]

The overlap between Articles XVI and XVII GATS, and the scheduling rule in Article XX:2 GATS may, in practice, seem very complex: the limitations scheduled under the market access obligation do not need to indicate whether the measures are discriminatory or not.[110] However, if one applies the scheduling convention of Article XX:2 GATS correctly, as clarified by the Panel in *China – Electronic Payment Services*, there may not be a problem of legal certainty. Instead, the problem may be regarding the value of market access commitments in so far as they are complemented by limitations.[111] Indeed, the interpretation of the overlap may prove relatively straightforward.[112] Consider the following example,

---

[108] This view has, in my view wrongly, been presented as the other side of the same coin to the conclusion reached by the Panel in *China – Electronic Payment Services* on Article XX:2 GATS by Wei Wang, 'On the Relationship Between Market Access and National Treatment Under the GATS' (2012) 46 The International Lawyer 1045, 1058–1059.

[109] Van Den Hende, 'GATS Article XVI and National Regulatory Sovereignty: What Lessons to Draw from *US – Gambling*?' 103 and footnote 11; Vranes, 'The WTO and Regulatory Freedom: WTO Disciplines on Market Access, Non-Discrimination and Domestic Regulation Relating to Trade in Goods and Services' 985.

[110] Aaditya Mattoo, 'National Treatment in the GATS: Corner-Stone or Pandora's Box?' (1997) 31 Journal of World Trade 107, 113.

[111] Mavroidis, 'Highway XVI Re-visited: The Road from Non-discrimination to Market Access in GATS' 9, considers that precisely this is the fault in the AB's understanding of Article XVI GATS: 'In the AB's view, a non-discriminatory statute can be found to be in violation of Art. XVI GATS. For this to be the case, however, a *necessary* condition is that the AB must have (at least implicitly) accepted that Art. XVI GATS covers market access for domestic services and services suppliers as well. This is what I find fault with' (footnotes omitted, emphasis original).

[112] Vranes, 'The WTO and Regulatory Freedom: WTO Disciplines on Market Access, Non-Discrimination and Domestic Regulation Relating to Trade

applicable to several EU Member States: for hospital services, a Mode 3 market access limitation reads 'The number of beds authorized is limited by a health services plan established on the basis of needs'.[113] (As noted, for Mode 3 supply of services, the market access and national treatment obligations apply, in principle, to both the pre- and post-establishment phase.) The market access limitation *juncto* Article XX:2 GATS means that a Member would be free to grant the number of beds *wholly* to foreign service suppliers. In such a case, the value of the market access commitment would be great. However, a Member would also be free to grant *all* of those beds to domestic service suppliers, as the measure is equally considered to be inscribed in the national treatment column. Consequently, the limitation would be of great value. This makes sense. Indeed, the Member scheduled the measure *as a limitation to its commitments*. The value of a full, corresponding national treatment obligation is therefore limited to *other* aspects of the treatment of foreign service suppliers, which are not covered by, *in casu* paragraph 2 (a) of, Article XVI GATS.[114]

This approach raises an important issue for regulatory autonomy: a Member's commitments under the market access obligation limit the Member's regulatory autonomy, *in so far as* these commitments apply to *domestic* service suppliers as well.[115] The following example illustrates the problem:

> Assume that by introducing the number 5 into its commitments on financial services (banks), Argentina has been limiting the number of bankers, domestic and foreign alike. As a result, Argentines will be in a position to access their domestic banking market under the conditions mentioned in GATS and not, for example, in a domestic statute. That is, Argentina, by signing the GATS, accepted a change at the level of regulation for its domestic citizens as well: it cannot unilaterally decide the number of Argentine bankers, their total value of transactions, their number of operations, the total number of natural persons they may employ, the legal entity under which they will operate; it

---

in Goods and Services' 982–985, concludes that 'In sum, the prima facie quite intricate relationship between Articles XVI and XVII can be analyzed in a relatively straightforward manner.'

113 EU 2006 consolidated Schedule 227–228. Such limitations apply, with slightly different wordings, to Austria, Belgium, France, Italy, Luxemburg and the Netherlands.

114 Flett, 'National Treatment under the General Agreement on Trade in Services (GATS)' 71–72.

115 Mavroidis, 'Highway XVI Re-visited: The Road from Non-discrimination to Market Access in GATS' 11.

cannot unilaterally decide any of the measures listed in Art. XVI GATS as far as Argentine suppliers are concerned.[116]

For some Members, this may be an unexpected effect of the scheduling of market access commitments. The effect is the result of the finding that the market access obligation also applies to non-discriminatory measures. The problematic nature of the effect is mitigated by the fact that the Scheduling Guidelines foresaw, whether correctly or not, the applicability of Article XVI GATS to non-discriminatory measures. Moreover, it should be assessed whether market access limitations in existing Schedules contain many such potentially problematic entries.

2. MARKET ACCESS OBLIGATIONS IN THE SELECTED EU RTAs

2.1 Market Access for Establishment

As with the non-discrimination provisions, the selected EU RTAs contain specific market access obligations for the different modes of supply. In the EU-C&P RTA, the market access disciplines for establishment are contained in Article 112. In the EU-Singapore RTA, this obligation is enshrined in Article 8.10. The structure of both provisions is similar to Article XVI GATS: the first paragraph contains a general principle, while the second lists specific types of measures that cannot be maintained for scheduled sectors, unless a limitation had been inscribed in the Schedule. Article 112.1 EU-C&P differs from Article XVI:1 GATS in two ways. First, 'establishments and investors' of another party are referred to as the beneficiaries of the obligation. This reflects the broad scope of the establishment chapter, which includes all economic activities through establishment – regardless of a connection to trade in services. Second, Article 112.1 EU-C&P merely reiterates that the treatment provided for *in the specific commitments* shall be granted to foreign actors, and does not, in contrast to Article XVI:1 GATS, refer to the terms, limitations and conditions in the Schedule. However, considering the structure of the Schedule, in which the commitments are inscribed in a column entitled 'Description of reservations', this omission does not seem to have undue implications. It may be noted that Article 8.10.1 EU-Singapore also refers to 'establishments and entrepreneurs', but, here, the provision includes a reference to the 'terms, limitations and conditions' of the Schedule.

116 Ibid.

In the respective paragraphs 2 of both Article 112 EU-C&P and Article 8.10 EU-Singapore, one can find a list of prohibited types of market access measures. Comparing these provisions to Article XVI:2 GATS highlights the following facts:

a. The introductory sentence of the paragraph is substantially copied from Article XVI:2 GATS.
b. Subparagraph (a) is also substantially copied from Article XVI:2 GATS. However, this provision refers, aside from numerical quotas and monopolies, to 'exclusive rights or other establishment requirements such as economic needs test'. The difference in wording found in subparagraph (a) is merely reflective of the wider scope of establishment in comparison to Mode 3 under GATS, which brings non-services sectors within the scope of this provision. Subparagraphs (b) and (c) are identical to their GATS counterparts. Footnotes 24 and 12 add that these first three subparagraphs do not cover measures taken in order to limit the production of an agricultural product. These footnotes can be contrasted with footnote 9 to Article XVI:2 (c) GATS, which exempts measures that limit inputs for the supply of services *only* from that subparagraph. The exemption under the EU-C&P RTA and the EU-Singapore RTA is thus, on the one hand, narrower than the GATS exemption in that it only applies to agricultural products (which are covered because establishment is defined more widely), and, on the other hand, wider than the GATS exemption in that it applies to subparagraphs (a), (b) and (c).
c. Article 112.2 (d) EU-C&P is identical to Article XVI:2 (d) GATS. Article 8.10.2 (f) EU-Singapore is also identical to Article XVI:2 (d) GATS, save for the exception that the limitation in Article 8.10.2 (f) does not apply to limitations on key personnel and graduate trainees as defined in Article 8.14. Instead, measures or limitations relating to key personnel and graduate trainees are subject to Article 8.14, which specifically applies to these categories of natural persons and is analysed below.[117] Market access restrictions on key personnel and graduate trainees do not fall under the market access obligation for establishment in the EU-Singapore

---

[117] In the version of the EU-Singapore RTA available at the time of writing, footnote 13 to Article 8.10.2 (f) refers to 'Article 8.15 (Key Personnel and Graduate Trainees)'. This is a mistake, which will likely be addressed in the scrubbing phase, as Article 8.14 is the correct article number.

RTA. Instead, they are subject to a separate market access obligation, which is discussed below. In comparison, the EU-C&P RTA would seem to grant greater market access to key personnel and graduate trainees. First, as in the case of the EU-Singapore RTA, such natural persons are subject to a specific market access obligation. Second, the market access obligation for establishment also applies to key personnel and graduate trainees covered by the EU-C&P RTA, as it does to all other natural persons.

d. Articles 112.2 (e) EU-C&P and 8.10.2 (d) EU-Singapore are identical to Article XVI:2 (f) GATS.

e. Finally, Article 122.2 (f) EU-C&P, which corresponds to Article XVI:2 (e) GATS, offers slightly more detail than its GATS counterpart:

> (f) measures which restrict or require specific types of establishment (subsidiary, branch, representative office) or joint ventures through which an investor of another Party may perform an economic activity.[†]
>
> [†] Each Party may require that in the case of constitution of juridical person under its own law, investors must adopt a specific legal form. To the extent that such requirement is applied in a non-discriminatory manner, it does not need to be specified in Annex VII (List of commitments on establishment) in order to be maintained or adopted by the Parties.

Annex VII Section B, which details the relevant commitments and limitations, explains this obligation further. Preambular paragraph 5 to this Annex states that non-discriminatory requirements as regards the types of legal form of an establishment are not included in the Schedule.[118]

This provision contains three notable elements. First, the specification of the types of establishment, in comparison to the broader 'types of legal entity' found in GATS, reflect the specific nature of the market access obligation for *establishment*. Nonetheless, it follows from the definition of 'establishment' in Article 110 EU-C&P that the scope of subparagraph (f) may be more limited than Article XVI:2 (e) GATS. For example, the 2001 Scheduling Guidelines note that the requirement for foreign service suppliers to create partnerships would fall under Article XVI:2 (e) GATS.[119]

---

[118] This provision, which is discussed below, has an impact on the relationship between the market access and national treatment obligations.

[119] S/L/92 2001 Scheduling Guidelines para. 12; Delimatsis and Molinuevo, 'Article XVI GATS' 387.

This requirement would not be covered by Article 122.2 (f) EU-C&P, unless it could be qualified as a joint venture.

Second, the scope of this subparagraph is further limited by the preambular paragraph, which limits the field of application of this provision to discriminatory limitations. Foreign investors cannot benefit from this obligation if the restriction on market access is non-discriminatory. While it may seem that the main market access restrictions for 'establishment' would be discriminatory, there could be non-discriminatory limitations on specific types of legal entity or joint venture. Such non-discriminatory limitations would fall within the scope of this provision's GATS counterpart. For example, the non-discriminatory requirement to use non-liability structures to supply specific services would need to be inscribed under GATS,[120] whereas such a requirement is not prohibited under Article 122.2 (f) EU-C&P. Indeed, this situation is specified in footnote [†]. Therefore, such non-discriminatory limitations are not covered by the national treatment obligation, as they are not discriminatory, and, by virtue of these provisions, neither are they covered by the market access obligation.

Third, the subparagraph refers to 'economic activity' rather than 'supply of a service' in order to be applicable to the entire scope of the establishment chapter.

In the EU-Singapore RTA, market access limitations on the type of legal entity are addressed in subparagraph (e), which is identical to Article XVI:2 (e) GATS, save that it applies to entrepreneurs performing any economic activity. However, preambular consideration 5 to Annex 8-A-2, in which the establishment commitments are listed, notes that non-discriminatory limitations on the type of legal establishment do not need to be scheduled in order to be maintained or adopted. This addition has the same meaning as in the EU-C&P RTA.

As noted, the EU-Georgia DCFTA contains no market access obligation for establishment. However, in contrast to the other RTAs under scrutiny here, the EU-Georgia DCFTA does include *inter alia* an MFN obligation. (Recall that the establishment Schedule for the EU-Georgia DCFTA is based on a negative list.) Therefore, if regulators do not discriminate between different foreign, or between foreign and domestic, establishments and investors, they remain free to erect market access barriers.

---

120 Delimatsis and Molinuevo, 'Article XVI GATS' 386.

This is reiterated by preambular consideration 4 to Annex XIV-A, which contains the reservations for establishment and notes that 'non-discriminatory requirements […] are not listed in this Annex as they are not prejudiced by the Agreement'.

2.2 Market Access for Cross-border Supply of Services

As concerns cross-border supply of services, the market access obligation in the EU-C&P and EU-Singapore RTAs are enshrined in Articles 119 and 8.5 respectively. Paragraph 1 and the introduction to paragraph 2 of each provision is substantively the same as their corresponding market access provisions for establishment. However, the subparagraphs are more limited than is the case for establishment, with each provision containing only subparagraphs (a)–(c). Each of the three subparagraphs are identical to their GATS counterparts in Article XVI:2 (a)–(c), including the footnote regarding inputs for the supply of services. In addition to GATS, however, an additional footnote 5 to Article 8.5 EU-Singapore clarifies that the scope of subparagraph (a) includes measures that require a service supplier to have an establishment within the meaning of the chapter on establishment, or to be resident in a party's territory as a condition for the cross-border supply of a service. This specification mirrors the EU's scheduling practice in its GATS Schedule, which includes several such limitations. For example, there is a limitation for Mode 1 which states that 'Establishment in Belgium is required for the provision of investment advisory services'.[121] The GATS Schedule does not specify whether this type of limitation falls under Article XVI:2 (a) GATS. Indeed, it could be argued that this type of limitation would fall under Article XVI:2 (e) GATS.[122] In the context of the EU-Singapore RTA, footnote 5 clearly indicates that such a measure would fall under subparagraph (a).

The consequences of this expansion of the scope of subparagraph (a) are unclear: if a service supplier is required to have an establishment as a condition for supplying a cross-border service, the services supplied through the establishment are delivered through 'Mode 3'. If a limitation requiring such establishment for Mode 1 means that the service cannot be supplied through Mode 1, the commitment is equal to 'unbound', and

---

[121] EU 2006 consolidated Schedule 456.

[122] As noted above, for the market access obligation for establishment in the EU-C&P and EU-Singapore RTAs, the relevant Annexes provide that non-discriminatory requirements as to the types of legal form of an establishment should not be scheduled.

thus meaningless. Such a limitation would need to be scheduled like the Italian Mode 1 limitation 'Unbound for "promotori di servizi finanziari" (financial salesmen)'.[123] The type of measure which is envisaged thus seems to concern a situation where the establishment is required, but the service itself is not supplied by the establishment – it is supplied by the foreign mother company. For example, a foreign bank may need to open a subsidiary in the receiving state for it to supply its services on the receiving state's market, even if the subsidiary itself does not supply the full range of services that the mother company offers. Considering that the footnote cannot be found in the EU-C&P and EU-Georgia RTAs, it could be that the negotiators had a country-specific situation in mind.

Neither RTA contains a prohibition of market access limitations of the types in Article XVI:2 (d)–(f) GATS concerning cross-border trade in services. At first sight, this omission does not seem to limit the scope of the market access obligation, as the main concern of subparagraphs (d)–(f) appears to be the supply of a service through establishment. Indeed, subparagraph (d) is predominantly concerned with Modes 3 and 4,[124] while the prohibition of joint venture requirements in subparagraphs (e) and (f) only applies to Mode 3.[125] Nonetheless, the EU GATS Schedule contains a limitation for France that concerns privately funded primary, secondary and higher education services delivered through Mode 1. The limitation states: 'Condition of nationality. However, third country nationals may obtain authorization from competent authorities to establish and direct an education institution and to teach'.[126] This limitation could be considered as falling under Article XVI:2 (d) GATS. Moreover, subparagraph (e) prohibits non-discriminatory limitations on the forms of establishment that are relevant for Modes 1, 2 and 3.[127]

The practical importance of this omission may nonetheless be limited. The EU GATS Schedule offers only a few examples of which measures could be covered by Article XVI:2 (e) GATS but would not be prohibited by Articles 119 EU-C&P and 8.5 EU-Singapore. For example, service suppliers in Lithuania supplying auditing services need to prepare the auditor's report in conjunction with an auditor accredited to practice in Lithuania.[128] Most limitations that could be considered as falling under XVI:2 (e) GATS are limitations for Mode 1 that require the establishment

---

123 EU 2006 consolidated Schedule 457.
124 Delimatsis and Molinuevo, 'Article XVI GATS' 382.
125 Ibid 388.
126 EU 2006 consolidated Schedule 430, 432 and 434.
127 Delimatsis and Molinuevo, 'Article XVI GATS' 386.
128 EU 2006 consolidated Schedule 341.

of foreign service suppliers to supply cross-border trade in services. For example, there is an establishment requirement for service suppliers to supply security services in Finland.[129] A further example concerns Austria, where a limitation is inscribed in the Schedule which prohibits promotional activity and intermediation on behalf of foreign subsidiaries or branches which are not established in the EU.[130] Similarly, Poland requires a commercial presence for the supply of travel agencies and tour operator services through Modes 1 and 2.[131] In the EU-Singapore RTA, these limitations are included by way of footnote 5 to Article 8.5 EU-Singapore.

In contrast to the situation for establishment, where the lack of a market access obligation is compensated for by broader non-discrimination provisions as compared to the other two RTAs, the EU-Georgia DCFTA does contain a market access obligation (but no MFN obligation) for cross-border trade in services. Article 84 EU-Georgia demonstrates the classical structure for a market access obligation for services. Paragraph 1 and the introductory sentence to paragraph 2 are identical to those found in the EU-C&P RTA for cross-border supply of services. As with the previous two RTAs, only subparagraphs (a)–(c) are included, and their wording is the same as above. There are no explanatory footnotes. First, as concerns the footnote regarding inputs for the supply of services, one must ask whether the ordinary meaning of subparagraph (c) includes measures limiting inputs for the supply of services. Considering the explicit inclusion in both GATS and the EU-C&P and EU-Singapore RTAs, and the contrasting exclusion there, it seems as if these measures would be included. Therefore, the scope of Article 84.2 (c) EU-Georgia would be wider than in GATS, the EU-C&P RTA and the EU-Singapore RTA. Second, the omission of a footnote which brings measures that require a service supplier to have an establishment (within the meaning of the chapter on establishment) within the scope of subparagraph (a), has the same consequences as for the EU-C&P RTA. Namely, the Mode 1 limitations that require establishment to supply a service are not covered by subparagraph (a).

---

129 Ibid.
130 Ibid 446.
131 Ibid 498.

2.3 Market Access for Temporary Presence of Natural Persons for Business Purposes

In addition to the market access obligations for establishment and cross-border supply of services, and as noted regarding the non-discrimination disciplines, the selected EU RTAs contain limited market access provisions for the temporary presence of natural persons for business purposes. The obligation is limited to key personnel and graduate trainees, and does not extend to the other types of natural persons covered by the chapter. In terms of sectoral coverage, the obligation applies to sectors in which specific commitments have been made under the establishment chapters. Consequently, similarly to the non-discrimination obligation for key personnel and graduate trainees, the scope of the market access obligation for the temporary presence of natural persons for business purposes also extends to non-services sectors. Although the limitations in the establishment schedule do not apply, specific limitations are scheduled in Annexes IX EU-C&P, 8-A-3 EU-Singapore and XIV-C EU-Georgia.

Article 124.2 EU-C&P RTA contains a non-discrimination provision for key personnel and graduate trainees. Further, this provision prohibits a party from adopting or maintaining limitations on the total number of natural persons that an investor may employ as key personnel and graduate trainees in a specific sector in the form of numerical quotas or a requirement of an economic needs test. Articles 8.14.2 EU-Singapore and 89.2 EU-Georgia contain very similar obligations. Clearly, these prohibitions are derived from Article XVI:2 (d) GATS. However, they differ from GATS and each other in several ways:

a. In contrast to GATS, the RTA obligations do not extend to limitations on the total number of natural persons that may be employed in a particular service sector. In this sense, the RTA obligations are narrower than GATS.
b. Also in contrast to GATS, the RTA obligations are not limited by the requirement that the covered natural persons are necessary for and directly related to the supply of a specific service. In this sense, the RTA obligations are wider than GATS.
c. Under the RTA obligations, the natural persons which fall within the beneficiary categories are limited to key personnel and graduate trainees. These natural persons must be, *inter alia*, employed by a juridical person of another party. The obligations cover their temporary transfer to an establishment (or for setting up such an establishment) of the juridical person that employs them. Although

the obligations apply solely to *investors* (in the EU-C&P RTA) or *entrepreneurs* (in the other two RTAs; as noted, the definitions of both terms overlap), and thus seem to be limited by the exclusion of *domestic* service suppliers wishing to attract foreign key personnel or graduate trainees, such a limitation actually follows from the scope of the beneficiary categories of natural persons. In conclusion, whilst Article XVI:2 (d) GATS may be said to also apply to measures limiting the number of *foreign* natural persons a *domestic* service supplier may employ, this is not the case for the market access obligations for temporary presence of natural persons for business purposes in the RTAs.

d. The term 'may employ', used in Article XVI:2 (d) GATS, is replicated in the EU-C&P and EU-Georgia RTAs. In the EU-Singapore RTA, this has been changed to 'may transfer'. This alteration may reflect the fact that some key personnel or graduate trainees do not need to be *employed* by the establishment of the foreign investor. The definitional requirements to qualify as a graduate trainee or intra-corporate transferee entail employment by the establishment. As such, this alteration is relevant only for 'business visitors for establishment purposes'. These form the second category of 'key personnel'. One can imagine that these natural persons are not employed by the establishment they seek to set up.
e. Finally, while not the case for market access under GATS or market access for cross-border trade in services or establishment in the RTAs, the criteria upon which an economic needs test for the temporary presence of key personnel and graduate trainees must be based are described in preambular paragraph 7 of Annex IX EU-C&P and paragraphs 8 of Annexes 8-A-3 EU-Singapore and 8 of XIV-C EU-Georgia. The main criteria for such a test will be (i) the assessment of the relevant market situation in the EU Member State, including with respect to the number of existing services suppliers, and (ii) the impact on these suppliers.

The relationship between the market access obligation for temporary presence of natural persons for business purposes, the market access obligation for cross-border supply of services and the market access obligation for establishment differs among the RTAs. First, as concerns cross-border supply of services, there is no overlap considering the omission of subparagraph (d)-type limitations from the relevant obligations and the definitional requirements for key personnel and graduate trainees. Second, as concerns establishment, it may be recalled that the

EU-Georgia RTA does not contain a market access obligation for establishment. Article 8.10.2 (f) EU-Singapore, which contains the market access limitation for the total number of natural persons for the establishment chapter, explicitly excludes key personnel and graduate trainees. Therefore, for these categories of natural persons, Article 8.14.2 contains the sole market access obligation. Such is not the case in the EU-C&P RTA. For example, absent any explicit exclusion, Article 112.2 (d) EU-C&P on market access for establishment, can be considered as covering measures that limit the total number of key personnel and graduate trainees. Under this RTA, key personnel and graduate trainees who are both necessary for and directly related to the performance of an economic activity can benefit from the wider scope of Article 11.2 (d) EU-C&P. More specifically, they may benefit from the prohibition of limitations on the total number of natural persons that may be employed in a particular economic activity.

2.4 Constraints on Regulatory Autonomy

The market access obligations in the selected EU RTAs largely coincide with Article XVI GATS. The provisions are very similar to their GATS counterparts, with the exception of market access for temporary presence of natural persons for business purposes. There are no indications in the text or context of the RTAs that the interpretations put forward above for GATS – on both the distinction between the quantitative and qualitative thrust of measures and on the relationship between the triad domestic regulation, market access and national treatment – do not apply to the EU-C&P, EU-Singapore and EU-Georgia RTAs. Therefore, the remarks on constraints on regulatory autonomy from Article XVI GATS apply equally in the RTA context.

Nonetheless, there are several notable differences between market access at the preferential level and market access at the multilateral level. First, market access in the RTAs is GATS– in four ways. First, there is no market access obligation for establishment in the EU-Georgia DCFTA. This is mitigated by the EU internal market-type non-discrimination obligation. Second, in the EU-C&P and EU-Singapore market access obligation for establishment, the equivalent to Article XVI:2 (e) GATS is limited to discriminatory measures. Third, for cross-border supply of services, there is no prohibition of limitations of the type covered by Article XVI:2 (d) and (e) GATS, even though such measures may impact cross-border trade in services. For measures of the type covered by subparagraph (e), this is partially alleviated by the mentioned footnote 5 in the EU-Singapore RTA. Fourth, market access for temporary presence of natural persons for business purposes is structurally limited to key personnel and graduate trainees.

Second, market access in the selected RTAs goes beyond Article XVI GATS, or is GATS+, in three ways. First, the scope of market access is extended to non-services sectors for establishment and the temporary presence of natural persons for business purposes. Second, in the EU-Singapore RTA, subparagraph (a) of the market access obligation for cross-border trade in services includes measures that require a service supplier to have an establishment or be resident in a party's territory as a condition for the cross-border supply of a service. Third, the market access obligation for graduate trainees and key personnel in all three RTAs is not limited by the requirement that the covered natural persons are necessary for and directly related to the supply of a specific service.

2.5 The Relationship between Market Access and National Treatment

Whereas GATS Schedules contain three columns (market access, national treatment and additional commitments), the Schedules in the selected EU RTAs contain only one column (limitations on market access and national treatment). As such, an Article XX:2 GATS counterpart in the RTAs is not necessary. However, this is not a reason for a different assessment of the relationship between market access and national treatment under the EU RTAs. Indeed, it is submitted that the interpretation set forth in the context of GATS applies fully in the RTA context.

6. Domestic regulation

1. DOMESTIC REGULATION OBLIGATIONS IN GATS

Article VI GATS on domestic regulation addresses the relationship between national regulators and individual service suppliers in six paragraphs. Paragraphs 1, 2, 3 and 6 contain transparency obligations. Paragraphs 4 and 5, however, encompass substantive obligations that are very much linked. Paragraph 4 contains the obligation to develop disciplines for measures relating to qualification requirements and procedures, technical standards and licensing requirements, while paragraph 5 contains disciplines which apply pending the entry into force of these new disciplines under Paragraph 4. Article VI:5 GATS clarifies that its obligations only apply to sectors in which specific commitments have been scheduled.

It must be stressed that the term 'domestic regulation' in the context of Article VI:5 GATS refers solely to measures relating to licensing and qualification requirements and technical standards.[1] It may be noted that, in *US – Gambling*, the Panel stated that Article VI:5 GATS covers measures that impose qualification requirements and procedures, technical standards and licensing requirements.[2] The Panel thus extended the scope of Article VI:5 GATS to cover qualification procedures. However, there does not appear to be any textual basis for this. Therefore, in my view, these measures are covered by Article VI:4 GATS only. In any case, the covered types of regulatory measures are commonly used to attain a wide variety of policy goals in many services sectors.[3]

---

[1] As noted below, licensing procedures are partially covered. I do not agree with Delimatsis that qualification procedures are submitted to the disciplines of Article VI:5 GATS. Panagiotis Delimatsis, *International Trade in Services and Domestic Regulations: Necessity, Transparency and Regulatory Diversity* (Oxford University Press 2008) 118.

[2] *United States – Measures Affecting the Cross-Border Supply of Gambling and Betting Services* WT/DS285/R, Panel report adopted 20 April 2005 para. 6.303.

[3] World Trade Organization, *Disciplines on Domestic Regulation Pursuant to GATS Article VI.4: Background and Current State of Play* (2011) 3.

This is particularly true for professional and financial services, as domestic regulation combats information asymmetries.[4] However, the exact scope of the types of regulatory measures which are covered is obfuscated; their exact meaning is the subject of the first subsection below. Second, the substantive obligations of Article VI:5 GATS are analysed. Third, the constraints on regulatory autonomy resulting from these provisions are addressed.

1.1 Licensing and Qualification Requirements and Technical Standards

The terms licensing requirements, qualification requirements and technical standards have not yet been interpreted in case law. However, they have been used in reports from panels and the AB, although this use has merely provided examples of measures within the scope of 'licensing requirements' and 'qualification requirements'. The term 'technical standards' has been used in case law but no guidance regarding its meaning can be derived from that use.[5] 'Licensing requirements' have been explained in *EC – Bananas III* as encompassing the requirements an exporter needs to fulfil in order to be granted an import licence for bananas.[6] The 1993 Scheduling Guidelines elucidate that licensing requirements are minimum requirements, such as minimum capital requirements for the establishment of a firm.[7]

In *Korea – Government Procurement*, the US argued that the conditions an enterprise needs to fulfil in order to bid for procurement contracts are 'qualification requirements'.[8] (In this case, the qualification requirements included having obtained licences, which highlights the

---

[4] Aaditya Mattoo and Pierre Sauvé, *The Preferential Liberalization of Services Trade* (NCCR Working Paper N°2010/13, 2010) 11.

[5] *Brazil – Measures Affecting Imports of Retreaded Tyres* WT/DS332/R, Panel report adopted 17 December 2007 paras 20 and 35 of Annex 1; *China – Measures Affecting Electronic Payment Services* WT/DS413/R, Panel report adopted 31 August 2012 paras 7.269 and 7.286.

[6] *European Communities – Regime for the Importation, Sale and Distribution of Bananas* WT/DS27/R, Panel report adopted 25 September 1997 paras 3.16–3.28. The complainants *inter alia* argued that these requirements were discriminatory. Ibid paras 4.53, 4.289, 4.293 and 4.371.

[7] General Agreement on Tariffs and Trade, *MTN.GNS/W/164, Scheduling of Initial Commitments in Trade in Services: Explanatory Note (3 September)* para. 5.

[8] *Korea – Measures Affecting Government Procurement* WT/DS163/R, Panel report adopted 19 June 2000 para. 4.448.

interconnectedness of these types of regulatory measures.) Qualification requirements may also consist of state rules that require personnel of publication import entities to be 'qualified'.[9] Moreover, in the 2001 Scheduling Guidelines, it is noted that 'approval procedures or licensing and qualification requirements, such as financial soundness or membership in a professional organization, are frequently stipulated as conditions to obtain a licence'.[10] In the same document, the following examples of 'licensing and qualification requirements' are given, as if these measures constitute one category rather than two discernible ones: (i) in order to work as a mountain guide or ski instructor, passing an examination is required; access to such exams for foreigners may be restricted; (ii) barristers and commercial lawyers in national law are required to be graduates of national universities; (iii) licences may be conditional upon one year of previous residency; (iv) three years of prior professional practice in the country are required to supply a service; and (v) non-residents must be registered and licensed in order to purchase unprocessed fish from primary producers and/or process fish.[11]

In a Note on the relevance of the TBT Agreement and the Import Licensing Agreement to Article VI:4 GATS, the Secretariat provided the following definitions of the terms under Article VI:5 GATS:

a. Licensing requirements 'are substantive requirements, other than qualification requirements, with which a service supplier is required to comply in order to obtain formal permission to supply a service. They include measures such as residency requirements, fees, establishment requirements, registration requirements, etc'.[12]
b. Qualification requirements 'comprise substantive requirements which a professional service supplier is required to fulfil in order to obtain certification or a licence. They normally relate to matters such as education, examination requirements, practical training, experience or language requirements'.[13]

---

[9] *China – Measures Affecting Trading Rights and Distribution Services for Certain Publications and Audiovisual Products* WT/DS363/AB/R, AB report adopted 19 January 2010 para. 147.

[10] S/L/92 2001 Scheduling Guidelines para. 10.

[11] Ibid 17.

[12] S/WPPS/W/9, The Relevance of the Disciplines of the Agreements on Technical Barriers to Trade (TBT) and on Import Licensing Procedures to Article VI:4 of the General Agreement on Trade in Services (Note by the Secretariat, 11 September 1996) para. 4.

[13] Ibid.

c. Technical standards 'are requirements which may apply both to the characteristics or definition of the service itself and to the manner in which it is performed. For example, a standard may stipulate the content of an audit, which is akin to definition of the service; another standard may lay down rules of ethics or conduct to be observed by the auditor'.[14] This definition was followed in a communication from Switzerland, which contained draft disciplines for technical standards under Article VI:4 GATS and explicitly added that both voluntary and mandatory standards would be covered by this category.[15] This differs from the concepts 'technical regulation' and 'standard' in the TBT Agreement. In Annex 1 to that agreement, a technical regulation is defined as laying down product characteristics or related processes and production methods with which compliance is mandatory. A standard is defined, in the same Annex, as a document containing rules, guidelines or characteristics for products or related processes and production methods, with which compliance is not mandatory.

These definitions seem to be coherent with the limited guidance from both case law and the Scheduling Guidelines and can therefore be upheld for the purposes of this section.[16]

1.2 Substantive Obligations of Paragraph 5 (and 4) GATS

The negotiations on domestic regulation disciplines based on paragraph 4 are part of the Doha Round and, so far, have not led to an agreement.[17] The outcome of these negotiations will directly constrain regulatory autonomy. However, addressing the many legal uncertainties and political sensitivities surrounding these negotiations goes beyond the scope of this

---

14 Ibid.

15 S/WPDR/W/32, Communication from Switzerland: Proposal for Disciplines on Technical Standards in Services (1 February 2005) para. 13.

16 These definitions have also been used by Panagiotis Delimatsis, 'Determining the Necessity of Domestic Regulations in Services: The Best is Yet to Come' (2008) 19 European Journal of International Law 365, 369.

17 An agreement would, on the basis of an 'unspoken working assumption' be integrated into the GATS as an Annex. Aik Hoe Lim and Bart De Meester, 'Addressing the Domestic Regulation and Services Trade Interface: Reflections on the Way Ahead' in Aik Hoe Lim and Bart De Meester (eds), *WTO Domestic Regulation and Services Trade* (Cambridge University Press 2014) 349.

book, especially as it is unclear whether the negotiations will be concluded at all.[18]

Pending an agreement on paragraph 4, Article VI:5 (a) GATS obliges Members to refrain from applying licensing and qualification requirements and technical standards that:[19]

a. '[A]re not based on objective and transparent criteria, such as competence and the ability to supply the service'.

   The term 'objective criteria' is reminiscent of the term 'neutral and objective criteria' in Article 8.2 (b) (ii) SCM Agreement. On the basis of Footnote 32 to that provision, this term means that such criteria may not favour certain regions beyond what is appropriate for the objective of the measure, *in casu* the elimination of regional disparities within the framework of regional development policy.

b. '[A]re more burdensome than necessary to ensure the quality of the service'.

   In the context of regulatory autonomy, it is important to note that, in the words of the Secretariat, necessity tests are, in general:

   > a means of reflecting the balance in WTO Agreements between the freedom of Members to set and achieve their own regulatory objectives through measures of their own choosing, and the goal of discouraging Members from adopting measures that unduly restrict trade.[20]

   The interpretation of 'necessary' has been the subject of much litigation in the context of the general exceptions in Articles XIV GATS and XX GATT 1994. However, its meaning here does not necessarily coincide with that under the general exceptions: their purposes differ. In Articles XIV GATS and XX GATT 1994, the necessity requirement is part of an exception, whilst in the context of, for example, Articles VI:5 GATS, 2.2 TBT Agreement and 2.2

---

[18] The latest annual report from the WTO's Working Party on Domestic Regulation highlights that Members are not discussing the development of actual disciplines. See S/WPDR/16, Annual Report of the Working Party on Domestic Regulation to the Council for Trade in Services (29 October 2013).

[19] Criteria a., b. and c. are the criteria set out in Article VI:4 GATS, to which Article VI:5 (a) refers back.

[20] S/WPDR/W/27/Add.1, 'Necessity Tests' in the WTO (Note by the Secretariat, Addendum, 18 January 2011) para. 4.

SPS Agreement,[21] it is part of an obligation.[22] Considering the difference in purpose,[23] it is argued that case law concerning the latter type of necessity test is most relevant for the interpretation of the necessity requirement in Article VI:5 GATS.

The Panel in *Mexico – Telecoms* summarised the AB's finding in *Korea – Beef*. The Panel noted that, in a GATS context:

> [T]he term 'necessary' can refer to a range of degrees of necessity, depending on the context, and the object and purpose of the provision in which it is used. At one end of this continuum, 'necessary' can be understood to mean 'indispensable' to achieving a policy goal; at the other end, 'necessary' can be taken to mean simply 'making a contribution to' a policy goal.[24]

By analogy to Article 2.2 TBT Agreement,[25] the necessity condition of Article VI:5 GATS requires a measure to not be more

---

[21] The necessity test in paragraph 5 (e) of the GATS Annex on Telecommunications is also part of an obligation.

[22] The Secretariat makes a general distinction between each type of necessity test. In the case of exception provisions, the necessity tests usually contain a closed list of policy objectives. By way of contrast, the obligation provisions usually contain an illustrative list. Moreover, for necessity in an exception provision, the burden of proof is on the respondent whilst, in an obligation provision, it is for the complainant to show that the measure is not necessary. S/WPDR/W/27/Add.1, 'Necessity Tests' in the WTO (Note by the Secretariat, Addendum, 18 January 2011) para. 6. This may influence the interpretation of such a necessity test: panels and the AB have not yet found a violation of Article 2.2 TBT Agreement, which contains a similar necessity test.

[23] This is in line with the AB's statement that the 'Panel would have been on safer ground had it compared the MFN obligation in Article II of the GATS with the MFN and MFN-type obligations in the GATT 1994', rather than with the national treatment obligation of Article XVII GATS. *European Communities – Regime for the Importation, Sale and Distribution of Bananas* WT/DS27/AB/R, AB report adopted 25 September 1997 para. 231.

[24] *Mexico – Measures Affecting Telecommunications Services* WT/DS204/R, Panel report adopted 2 April 2004 para. 7.338, referring to *Korea – Measures Affecting Imports of Fresh, Chilled and Frozen Beef* WT/DS161/AB/R, AB report adopted 10 January 2001 para. 161.

[25] *United States – Measures Concerning the Importation, Marketing and Sale of Tuna and Tuna Products* WT/DS381/R, Panel report adopted 13 June 2012 para. 7.456. The analysis under Article 2.2 TBT Agreement first entails assessing whether the technical regulation pursues or fulfils a legitimate objective.

burdensome than necessary for the achievement of its objective.[26] It should be stressed that it is a prerogative of a Member to determine the level of attainment or protection it deems appropriate in achieving a policy objective.[27] If a less burdensome and reasonably available alternative measure exists which achieves the same objective, the measure would not be necessary.[28] This alternative, less burdensome measure must reach the same level of attainment or protection. The burden of proof is on the complainant to establish that the measure is more burdensome than necessary and to identify an alternative measure.[29]

It is notable that the necessity test for domestic regulation requires the measure to be 'not more burdensome' than necessary, rather than the more common 'not more trade restrictive than necessary'.[30] In the context of negotiations on Article VI:4 GATS disciplines, the EU considers these concepts to be essentially the same.[31] In the context of Article VI:5 GATS, I do not agree with this equation, as it does not stem from the text of paragraph 4.[32] It is the first sentence of paragraph 4, and not the conditions in subparagraph (b) in which the necessity condition is contained, that refers to 'unnecessary trade barriers'. Paragraph 5 only refers to measures not more burdensome than necessary. Therefore, an interpretation of necessity under Article VI:4 (b) GATS by reference to paragraph VI:5 should rely on the meaning of the term 'not

---

26 Therefore, the test is not whether the policy objective itself is necessary. S/WPDR/W/27/Add.1, 'Necessity Tests' in the WTO (Note by the Secretariat, Addendum, 18 January 2011) para. 84.

27 See e.g. *United States – Continued Suspension of Obligations in the EC – Hormones Dispute* WT/DS320/AB/R, AB report adopted 14 November 2008 para. 523.

28 *US – Tuna II (Mexico) (Panel)* para. 7.460.

29 Ibid para. 7.468 on Article 2.2 TBT Agreement.

30 See however paragraph 3 of the Reference Paper on Basic Telecommunications, which also contains the phrase 'not more burdensome than necessary' in the context of universal service obligations.

31 S/WPDR/W/14, Communication from the European Communities and their Member States: Domestic Regulation: Necessity and Transparency (1 May 2001) para. 17. This view has been said to be shared by the other Members in Delimatsis, 'Determining the Necessity of Domestic Regulations in Services: The Best is Yet to Come' 390, although the sources referred to there do not confirm this statement.

32 Delimatsis, 'Determining the Necessity of Domestic Regulations in Services: The Best is Yet to Come' 390.

more burdensome', rather than the meaning of 'not more trade-restrictive'. It has been suggested that 'burdensome' is wider than 'trade-restrictive'.[33] Indeed, the two terms are largely overlapping, but not necessarily so. The ordinary meaning of 'burdensome' is 'onerous, cumbersome, oppressive, troublesome, wearisome'.[34] Obviously, unnecessary burdens may restrict trade. However, there may be situations in which unnecessary burdens do not restrict trade: covered domestic regulations may be more burdensome than necessary to ensure the quality of the service without deterring service suppliers from actually conforming to them, for example because the same burdensome procedure applies in both the host and the receiving state,[35] or because the expected gains are sufficient. Therefore, the Panel's finding in *US – Gambling* that Article VI:5 GATS allows Members to maintain (non-discriminatory) measures 'so long as they do not constitute "unnecessary barriers to trade in services", pursuant to the criteria contained in Article VI:5',[36] cannot be sustained. Similarly, trade restrictive measures may simply not be more burdensome than necessary.

Finally, the measure must be necessary to *ensure the quality of the service*. It has been argued that 'quality' should be interpreted widely and may also include 'externalities and public-regarding goals'.[37]

For a more comprehensive analysis of necessity, albeit in the context of the general exceptions provision of Article XIV GATS and with the caveats that come with transposing that interpretation to the context of Article VI:5 GATS, see below. It is also notable that many RTAs include necessity conditions based on Article VI:4 GATS in their disciplines on domestic regulation. Although these

---

[33] Jan Neumann and Elisabeth Türk, 'Necessity Revisited: Proportionality in World Trade Organization Law After *Korea – Beef*, *EC – Asbestos* and *EC – Sardines*' (2003) 37 Journal of World Trade 199, 223; Markus Krajewski, *National Regulation and Trade Liberalization in Services* (Kluwer Law International 2003) 142.

[34] Stevenson, *Oxford Dictionary of English (Online Version)*.

[35] Markus Krajewski, 'Article VII GATS' in Rüdiger Wolfrum, Peter-Tobias Stoll and Clemens Feinäugle (eds), *Max Planck Commentaries on World Trade Law: WTO – Trade in Services*, vol 6 (Martinus Nijhoff 2008) 188.

[36] *US – Gambling (Panel)* para. 6.303.

[37] David W Leebron, 'Regulatory Discrimination in Domestic United States Law: A Model for the GATS' in Aaditya Mattoo and Pierre Sauvé (eds), *Domestic Regulation & Service Trade Liberalization* (World Bank & Oxford University Press 2003) 52.

may influence the negotiations in the context of GATS,[38] they are unlikely to inform the interpretation of Article VI:5 GATS in the absence of concluded negotiations on paragraph 4.

c. '[A]re, in the case of licensing procedures, in itself a restriction on the supply of the service'.

This condition suggests that licensing procedures[39] are covered by Articles VI:4 and 5 GATS, even though licensing procedures are not listed in the types of measures covered by either provision. In order for the reference to subparagraph (c) of Article VI:4 in paragraph 5 to be meaningful, it is submitted that licensing procedures under Article VI:5 need only fulfil this condition.

d. '[C]ould not have been expected of that Member at the time the specific commitments in those sectors were made'.

This final condition limits the scope of Article VI:5 GATS to regulations introduced after scheduling,[40] although some measures which were introduced after the specific commitments were made could have been reasonably expected. Therefore, Article VI:5 is to be interpreted as a standstill clause.[41] Consequently, its scope is highly dependent on existing internal legislation at the entry into

---

[38] See Delimatsis, 'Determining the Necessity of Domestic Regulations in Services: The Best is Yet to Come' 381–384 and 401–408 for an analysis. Examples of such RTAs are MERCOSUR, the Trans-Pacific Strategic Economic Partnership between Brunei, Chile, New Zealand and Singapore; US – Australia, US – Chile and US – Singapore.

[39] Licensing procedures are defined as 'administrative procedures relating to the submission and processing of an application for a licence, covering such matters as time frames for the processing of a licence, and the number of documents and the amount of information required in the application for a licence'. S/WPPS/W/9, The Relevance of the Disciplines of the Agreements on Technical Barriers to Trade (TBT) and on Import Licensing Procedures to Article VI:4 of the General Agreement on Trade in Services (Note by the Secretariat, 11 September 1996) para. 4.

[40] Krajewski, *National Regulation and Trade Liberalization in Services* 153; J Anthony VanDuzer, 'A Critical Look at the Prospects for Robust Rules for Services in Preferential Trading Agreements' (2012) 39 Legal Issues of Economic Integration 29, 33.

[41] Joel P Trachtman, 'Addressing Regulatory Divergence through International Standards: Financial Services' in Aaditya Mattoo and Pierre Sauvé (eds), *Domestic Regulation & Service Trade Liberalization* (World Bank & Oxford University Press 2003) 31; Jan Wouters and Dominic Coppens, 'GATS and Domestic Regulation: Balancing the Right to Regulate and Trade Liberalization' in Kern Alexander and Mads Andenas (eds), *The World Trade Organization and Trade in Services* (Martinus Nijhoff 2008) 52.

force of GATS for a Member.[42] This condition would apply to licensing procedures, considering its position in Article VI:5 (a) (ii) GATS.

e. In the case where the licensing and qualification requirements and technical standards do not meet the four foregoing conditions, they are prohibited only in so far as they *nullify or impair the specific commitments of a Member*.[43] The scope of the provision is substantially limited by this nullification or impairment test. The burden of proof lies on the complaining Member to demonstrate that the responding Member's specific commitment is nullified or impaired by the measure.[44]

Paragraph (b) to Article VI:5 GATS adds that international standards of relevant international organisations applied by the Member shall be taken into account to assess the conformity with the four conditions set out above. Interpretative footnote 3 explains that only international bodies whose membership is open to the relevant bodies of at least all Members of the WTO are covered. The importance of this provision could be substantial if understood as a presumption in favour of such international standards, indicating that when a Member applies an international standard, domestic regulation that deviates from that standard is an unnecessary restriction to trade.[45] Of course, a Member could contend that it considered but rejected the international standard for an acceptable reason.[46] Considering that the discipline is rather soft (e.g. 'taking into account') and that it applies only to standards being applied by the Member, its constraints on regulatory autonomy are limited.

1.3 Constraints on Regulatory Autonomy

As a standstill provision, Article VI:5 GATS has been said to be of limited practical importance.[47] Moreover, the scope of the disciplines are considerably limited as:

---

[42] David Luff, 'Regulation of Health Services and International Trade Law' in Aaditya Mattoo and Pierre Sauvé (eds), *Domestic Regulation & Service Trade Liberalization* (World Bank & Oxford University Press 2003) 206 and 210.

[43] Peter Van den Bossche and Werner Zdouc, *The Law and Policy of the World Trade Organization* (3rd edn, Cambridge University Press 2013) 534.

[44] Krajewski, *National Regulation and Trade Liberalization in Services* 153.

[45] Ibid 152–153. Also see interpretative footnote 3 at Article VI:5 (b) GATS.

[46] Nellie Munin, *Legal Guide to GATS* (Wolters Kluwer 2010) 294.

[47] Joel P Trachtman, 'Lessons for the GATS from Existing WTO Rules on Domestic Regulation' in Aaditya Mattoo and Pierre Sauvé (eds), *Domestic*

a. The disciplines only cover certain types of domestic regulation.
b. The disciplines only apply to scheduled sectors (albeit without taking into account any limitations).
c. The domestic regulation could not have been reasonably expected at the time of submission of the schedule.
d. The application of the covered domestic regulation must nullify or impair specific commitments.
e. The covered domestic regulation is only prohibited if it is: (i) not based on objective and transparent criteria; (ii) more burdensome than necessary to ensure the quality of the service; or (iii) in the case of licensing procedures, in itself a restriction on the supply of the service.

Taking these limitations into account, it seems clear that future disciplines resulting from negotiations under Article VI:4 GATS have greater potential to constrain regulatory autonomy than disciplines under Article VI:5 GATS. Nonetheless, even the present disciplines are not toothless. The most relevant aspect of the Article VI:5 GATS analysis is the necessity requirement. It has been argued that necessity as a positive obligation leads to further constraints on regulatory autonomy, in comparison to necessity in an exception, because in the former situation, a measure needs to be necessary even before an inconsistency with a GATS obligation has been established.[48] A mitigating factor is that the 'burdensome' element of the necessity requirement in Article VI:5 GATS appears to focus on procedural rather than substantive elements.[49] Naturally, it may be alleged, for example, that professional qualification requirements, such as a doctor's education, are 'more burdensome then necessary' to ensure the quality of the service. However, unless these requirements are clearly disproportionate, such claims seem hard to justify considering a Member's right to set its own level of protection. If procedural elements

---

Regulation & Service Trade Liberalization (World Bank & Oxford University Press 2003) 77; Krajewski, 'Article VI GATS' 194.

[48] Maxine Kennet, Jan Neumann and Elisabeth Türk, *Second Guessing National Level Policy Choices: Necessity, Proportionality and Balance in the WTO Services Negotiations* (Center for International Environmental Law Discussion Paper, 2003) 4.

[49] See Krajewski, 'Article VI GATS' 188, where it is explained that in the context of negotiations on Article VI:4 GATS disciplines, the distinction between 'burdensome' and 'trade-restrictive' is made for procedural and substantive obligations respectively.

are considered too burdensome, a requirement to amend them appears to have relatively limited constraints on regulatory autonomy.

It has been remarked that, together, the transparency requirements and the necessity test allow the appropriateness of domestic regulation to be challenged, helping to ensure that measures 'serve legitimate objectives rather than mask protectionist interests, and hence create benefits for domestic consumers and users of services'.[50] However, in my view, this does not significantly constrain regulatory autonomy.

1.4 The Relationship between the 'Triad' of Market Access, National Treatment and Domestic Regulation[51]

The complexity of the interplay between Articles XVI and XVII GATS discussed above appears to be heightened if one adds Article VI:4–5 GATS to the equation. Although Members have 'made a greater effort' to differentiate between the domestic regulation disciplines on the one hand, and the market access and national treatment obligations on the other, 'the line is blurred and the scope of current and potential rules is uncertain'.[52] The main concern is the differentiation between domestic regulation and market access. If the market access obligation applies to too wide a category of measures that could have been expected to fall solely under the domestic regulation disciplines, 'regulatory freedom under Article VI risks being emptied through *per se* prohibitions under Article XVI'.[53] In contrast to the market access obligation, Article VI:4–5 GATS addresses measures that 'relate to the quality of the service supplied, or to the ability of the supplier to supply the service'.[54] In the words of one author:

> Article XVI restrictions impose 'maximum limitations' that cannot be overcome by any action of the supplier (e.g., under a measure limiting new banks to ten, a bank cannot establish itself once the quota of 10 is filled, whatever

---

[50] Mattoo and Sauvé, *The Preferential Liberalization of Services Trade* 16–17.

[51] Aaditya Mattoo, 'Services in a Development Round: Three Goals and Three Proposals' (2005) 39 Journal of World Trade 1223, 1231.

[52] Ibid.

[53] Joost Pauwelyn, 'Rien ne Va Plus? Distinguishing Domestic Regulation from Market Access in GATT and GATS' (2005) 4 World Trade Review 131, 169.

[54] General Agreement on Tariffs and Trade, *MTN.GNS/W/164, Scheduling of Initial Commitments in Trade in Services: Explanatory Note (3 September)* para. 4; S/L/92 2001 Scheduling Guidelines para. 8.

> the bank does). In contrast to such 'maximum limitation', Article VI:4/5 measures impose 'minimum requirements'; that is, they condition entry on specific requirements whose fulfilment is, in theory, in the hands of the service supplier (e.g., a minimum capitalization requirement to obtain a banking license can, in theory, be met by any bank as long as it has the money).[55]

The fact that both provisions apply to non-discriminatory measures is the main subject of the delineation problem. For example, domestic regulation disciplines could apply to non-discriminatory qualitative obligations imposing minimum requirements, and the market access obligation could apply to non-discriminatory quantitative measures that apply maximum limitations.[56] The largest potential for overlap is presented where the qualitative measure has a quantitative thrust. However, according to the Panel in *US – Gambling*, Articles VI:4–5 and XVI GATS are mutually exclusive.[57] The Panel referred to the 1993 and 2001 Scheduling Guidelines. However, on a different interpretation, these documents appear to indicate that there is no mutual exclusivity between both provisions.[58] It has been suggested that the latter view is supported by the discussions in the CTS and the Working Party on Domestic Regulation, as well as by the GATS negotiating history.[59] Nonetheless, considering that the AB refused to settle the issue (noting that it was unnecessary to

---

[55] Pauwelyn, 'Rien ne Va Plus? Distinguishing Domestic Regulation from Market Access in GATT and GATS' 153.

[56] Panagiotis Delimatsis, 'Don't Gamble with GATS: The Interaction between Articles VI, XVI, XVII and XVIII GATS in the Light of the *US – Gambling* Case' (2006) 40 Journal of World Trade 1059, 1070 and footnote 62.

[57] *US – Gambling (Panel)* para. 6.305.

[58] General Agreement on Tariffs and Trade, *MTN.GNS/W/164, Scheduling of Initial Commitments in Trade in Services: Explanatory Note (3 September)* para. 4; S/L/92 2001 Scheduling Guidelines para. 11; Pauwelyn, 'Rien ne Va Plus? Distinguishing Domestic Regulation from Market Access in GATT and GATS' 156. Also see S/WPPS/W/21, Draft Disciplines on Domestic Regulation in the Accountancy Sector (Adopted 30 November 1998) para. 1. These Accountancy Disciplines, the only disciplines that have so far emerged from the negotiating mandate in Article VI:4 GATS, commence with the explicit statement that they do not apply to measures subject to scheduling under Article XVI GATS.

[59] Delimatsis, 'Don't Gamble with GATS: The Interaction between Articles VI, XVI, XVII and XVIII GATS in the Light of the *US – Gambling* Case' 1069–1070, with many references in footnotes 57–59. Also see Erich Vranes, 'The WTO and Regulatory Freedom: WTO Disciplines on Market Access, Non-Discrimination and Domestic Regulation Relating to Trade in Goods and Services' (2009) 12 Journal of International Economic Law 953, 973–980.

go into the dividing line *in abstracto*),[60] it must be understood that, under current case law, Articles VI:4–5 and XVI GATS are mutually exclusive.

As to the delineation between Articles VI:4–5 and XVII GATS, the 2001 Scheduling Guidelines seem to suggest that, if a discriminatory measure violates Article XVII GATS, it may also be subject to Article VI:4–5 GATS.[61] However, the Panel in *US – Gambling* applied the same reasoning to the relationship between Articles VI:4–5 and XVII GATS.[62] Therefore, although not explicitly stated by the Panel, one may deduce that this Panel considered Articles VI:4–5 GATS and XVII GATS to be mutually exclusive. As one author explains, *discriminatory* licensing and qualification procedures and requirements and technical standards thus fall *exclusively* within the scope of Article XVII GATS (and could have been scheduled as a limitation); conversely, such measures that are *non-discriminatory* are disciplined by Article VI:5 GATS.[63]

The logical consequence of this position appears to be that a measure that is correctly scheduled as a limitation under Articles XVI and/or XVII GATS cannot violate Article VI:5 GATS. This *de facto* extends limitations that are correctly scheduled under Articles XVI and XVII GATS to the domestic regulation disciplines. This is not contradictory to the text of Article VI:5 GATS, which states that the obligation applies '[i]n sectors in which a Member has undertaken specific commitments'. First, Article VI:5 GATS applies if a measure is incorrectly scheduled as a limitation to Articles XVI or XVII GATS. Second, the scope of Article VI:5 GATS appears to be broader than simply covering a Member's specific commitment; it appears to encompass the *entire* sector even where the commitment is only partial.

In conclusion, the interplay between the 'triad' of market access, national treatment and domestic regulation in GATS is 'the thorniest

---

[60] *United States – Measures Affecting the Cross-Border Supply of Gambling and Betting Services* WT/DS285/AB/R, AB report adopted 20 April 2005 para. 250; the US had appealed this finding of the Panel.

[61] S/L/92 2001 Scheduling Guidelines para. 10; Pauwelyn, 'Rien ne Va Plus? Distinguishing Domestic Regulation from Market Access in GATT and GATS' 156.

[62] *US – Gambling (Panel)* paras 6.308–6.313. Also see S/WPPS/W/21, Draft Disciplines on Domestic Regulation in the Accountancy Sector (Adopted 30 November 1998) para. 1. As noted vis-à-vis Article XVI GATS, the Accountancy Disciplines do not apply to measures subject to scheduling under Article XVII GATS.

[63] Vranes, 'The WTO and Regulatory Freedom: WTO Disciplines on Market Access, Non-Discrimination and Domestic Regulation Relating to Trade in Goods and Services' 971–972.

systemic issue in GATS today'.[64] The previous two sections are summarised in Figure 6.1. According to the current case law, a measure may fall within:

a. Situation (1), a non-discriminatory measure in the form of one of the four quantitative limitations on market access expressly mentioned in Article XVI:2 (a)–(d) GATS.
b. Situation (2), a non-discriminatory measure that has the effect of limiting market access in the sense of Article XVI (a)–(d) GATS, in so far as the measure has a quantitative thrust.
c. Situation (3), a discriminatory measure, also subject to Article XVII GATS, in the form of one of the four quantitative limitations on market access expressly mentioned in Article XVI:2 (a)–(d) GATS. Situation (3) also covers the discriminatory limitations covered by Article XVI:2 (e) and (f) GATS.
d. Situation (4), a discriminatory measure, also subject to Article XVII GATS, that has the effect of limiting market access in the sense of Article XVI (a)–(d) GATS, in so far as the measure has a quantitative thrust.
e. Situation (5), a discriminatory measure that does not, in form or in effect (in so far as its thrust is quantitative), limit market access in the sense of Article XVI (a)–(f) GATS.
f. Situation (6), a measure that has a qualitative thrust and is not discriminatory, it can be covered by Article VI:5 GATS if it falls within that provision's scope.

(Note that this categorisation concerns *violations* of these provisions, not their initial *scope*.[65])

---

[64] Delimatsis, 'Don't Gamble with GATS: The Interaction between Articles VI, XVI, XVII and XVIII GATS in the Light of the *US – Gambling* Case' 1061.

[65] As noted, the scope of the national treatment obligation, for example, is very wide as it applies to any measure affecting trade in services. The differentiation is not always made clearly, e.g. Lode Van Den Hende, 'GATS Article XVI and National Regulatory Sovereignty: What Lessons to Draw from *US – Gambling*?' (2007) 20 Cambridge Review of International Affairs 93, 100, directly contrasts the national treatment obligation, on the one hand, with those measures that may violate the obligation, on the other.

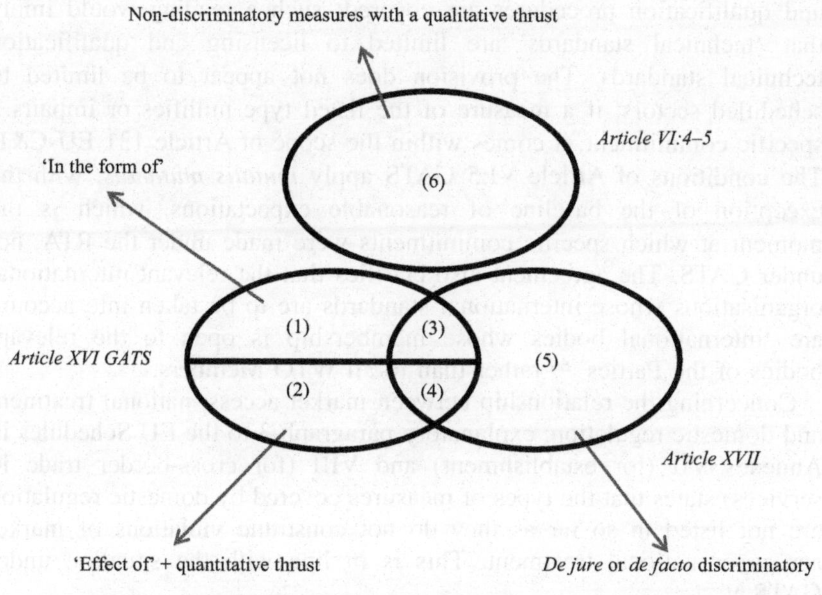

Figure 6.1 The relationship between market access, national treatment and domestic regulation

2. DOMESTIC REGULATION OBLIGATIONS IN THE SELECTED EU RTAs

2.1 The Article VI:5 GATS-like Approach in the EU-C&P RTA

In the EU-C&P RTA, Article 131.4 stipulates that the results of negotiations under Article VI:4 GATS or any similar negotiation undertaken in other multilateral fora shall be integrated into the agreement. The requirement that the negotiations are *undertaken* in a multilateral forum would include plurilateral agreements concluded in the context of the WTO, but not standalone plurilateral agreements – such as, for now, the Trade in Services Agreement (TiSA).

Pending an outcome of Article VI:4 GATS negotiations, Article 131.5–6 EU-C&P *de facto* integrate Article VI:5 GATS into the RTA. However, the scope of this domestic regulation obligation is wider than Article VI:5 GATS as it covers 'licensing and qualification requirements, procedures and technical standards'. It is unclear whether *only* licensing and qualification procedures are covered; such a reading would imply that 'technical standards' are limited to licensing and qualification technical standards. The provision does not appear to be limited to scheduled sectors: if a measure of the listed type nullifies or impairs a specific commitment, it comes within the scope of Article 131 EU-C&P. The conditions of Article VI:5 GATS apply *mutatis mutandis*, with the exception of the baseline of reasonable expectations, which is the moment at which specific commitments were made under the RTA, not under GATS. The agreement also clarifies that the relevant international organisations whose international standards are to be taken into account are 'international bodies whose membership is open to the relevant bodies of the Parties',[66] rather than to all WTO Members.

Concerning the relationship between market access, national treatment and domestic regulation, explanatory paragraph 3 to the EU Schedules in Annexes VII (for establishment) and VIII (for cross-border trade in services) states that the types of measures covered by domestic regulation are not listed in so far as they do not constitute violations of market access or national treatment. This is in line with the situation under GATS.[67]

2.2 More Elaborate Domestic Regulation Disciplines in the EU-Singapore and EU-Georgia RTAs

In the EU-Singapore RTA and the EU-Georgia DCFTA, the disciplines on domestic regulation are contained in Articles 8.18–8.20 and 93–95 respectively. Articles 8.18 and 93 set out the scope of the subsections on domestic regulation, which cover licensing requirements and procedures and qualification requirements and procedures. This enumeration is clearer than the one under Article 131 EU-C&P. Moreover, the types of measures covered are defined in paragraph 4 of Articles 8.18 and 93:

a. Licensing requirements are 'substantive requirements, other than qualification requirements, with which a natural or a juridical person is required to comply in order to obtain, amend or renew authorisation' to supply services or set up an establishment.[68] This definition is very similar to the one proposed by the WTO

---

66 Footnote 40 to Article 131.6 EU-C&P.

67 It is explicitly added that the measures covered by the domestic regulation disciplines apply to the investors and service suppliers of the signatory Andean countries.

68 Article 93.4 EU-Georgia and 8.18.4 EU-Singapore.

Secretariat;[69] indeed, it would seem that the negotiators based themselves on this proposal. The definition in the EU-Georgia DCFTA is the slightly broader of the two, in the sense that it covers amendments and renewals of authorisation. It also covers establishment in the sense of the EU-Georgia DCFTA, which, as noted, is wider than GATS Mode 3.

b. Licensing procedures are 'administrative or procedural rules' that a natural or juridical person seeking authorisation to supply services or set up an establishment, 'must adhere to in order to demonstrate compliance with licencing requirements'.[70] This includes the amendment or renewal of a licence. The influence of the Secretariat definition is less evident here. However, as with the latter, the link between licensing procedures and requirements is made clear.

c. Qualification requirements are 'substantive requirements relating to the competence of a natural person to supply a service, and which are required to be demonstrated for the purpose of obtaining authorisation to supply a service'.[71] This definition is almost identical to the one proposed by the Secretariat, although the definition in the EU-Georgia DCFTA may be more limited in that its scope is expressly limited to requirements related to the competence of the service supplier. Although, at first sight, there seems to be little practical difference, the Secretariat definition is unlike the EU-Georgia DCFTA definition, in that it is limited to professional service suppliers.

d. Qualification procedures are 'administrative or procedural rules that a natural person must adhere to in order to demonstrate compliance with qualification requirements, for the purpose of obtaining authorisation to supply a service'.[72] This is a more limited definition than the one proposed by the Secretariat, which expressly classifies these procedures as part of a wider category of administrative or procedural rules relating to the administration of qualification requirements.

---

69 S/WPPS/W/9, The Relevance of the Disciplines of the Agreements on Technical Barriers to Trade (TBT) and on Import Licensing Procedures to Article VI:4 of the General Agreement on Trade in Services (Note by the Secretariat, 11 September 1996) para. 4.

70 Article 93.4 EU-Georgia and 8.18.4 EU-Singapore.

71 Ibid.

72 Ibid.

On the one hand, the scope of both domestic regulation provisions is broadened because the application of these measures need not nullify or impair specific commitments: it suffices that they affect cross-border supply of services, establishment in their territory or temporary stay in their territory as covered by the agreement.[73] On the other hand, scheduled limitations and reservations apply.[74]

Substantively, Articles 8.19 EU-Singapore and 94 EU-Georgia contain obligations for licensing requirements and procedures and qualification requirements and procedures. In the case of the EU-Singapore RTA, Article 8.18.1 contains an obligation reminiscent of Article VI:4 (a) GATS, which requires that measures related to such requirements and procedures are both clear, objective and transparent, and pre-established and accessible to the public and interested persons. The addition of the latter condition reflects the link between domestic regulation and transparency obligations that is also evident from Article VI GATS. Similarly, paragraph 3 of the provision reiterates the obligation to maintain or institute judicial, arbitral or administrative tribunals or procedures for the review of administrative decisions. Finally, paragraph 2 requires the parties to grant an authorisation or license, subject to availability, as soon as it is established, in light of an appropriate examination that the conditions for granting the authorisation or licence have been met.

Article 94 EU-Georgia is more elaborate. Its first and second paragraphs are similar to Article VI:4 (a) GATS. They state that measures relating to licensing and qualification requirements and procedures are based on criteria, 'which preclude the competent authorities from exercising their power of assessment in an arbitrary manner'. These criteria are: (i) proportionate to a public policy objective; (ii) clear and unambiguous; (iii) objective; (iv) pre-established; (v) made public in advance; and (vi) transparent and accessible. Subsequently, the provision also contains paragraphs 2 and 3 of Article 8.18 EU-Singapore in Articles 94.3 and 94.4 EU-Georgia respectively. Finally, paragraphs 5 and 6 contain obligations for situations where the number of licences available for a specific activity is limited due to the scarcity of available natural resources or technical capacity. In such cases, a party must apply a selection procedure that provides full guarantees of impartiality and transparency. This especially includes transparency, i.e. adequate publicity about the launch, conduct and completion of the procedure. The rules

---

[73] Articles 8.18.1 EU-Singapore and 93.1 EU-Georgia.

[74] Articles 8.18.2–3 EU-Singapore and 93.2–3 EU-Georgia. Recall that establishment in the EU-Georgia DCFTA makes use of negative listing.

for these selection procedures may be established by taking into account public policy objectives, such as health, safety, the protection of the environment or the preservation of cultural heritage, subject to the other disciplines in Article 94 EU-Georgia. Once again, these obligations are related to transparency rather than substance.

Furthermore, Articles 8.20 EU-Singapore and 95 EU-Georgia proscribe an additional obligation for licensing and qualification procedures 'and formalities'. The first paragraph of Article 8.20 EU-Singapore and second paragraph of Article 95 EU-Georgia state that licensing and qualification procedures and formalities must be as simple as possible and shall not unduly complicate or delay the supply of the service. Any licensing fees[75] which the applicants may incur from their application should be reasonable. In the EU-Singapore RTA, it is held that the licensing fees should not in themselves restrict the supply of the service. In the EU-Georgia DCFTA, the licensing fees should be proportionate to the cost of the authorisation procedures in question. Additionally, Article 95.1 EU-Georgia requires licensing and qualification procedures and formalities to be clear and publicly available in advance. They should also provide the applicants with a guarantee that their application will be dealt with objectively and impartially. These requirements can be considered largely procedural, although some aspects do touch upon substance.

Paragraphs 2–8 of Article 8.20 EU-Singapore and 3–9 of Article 95 EU-Georgia contain the following procedural requirements: (i) impartiality of the procedures used by the competent authorities in the licensing or authorisation process, and of their decisions; (ii) independence of the competent authorities; (iii) a reasonable period of time for the submission of an application; (iv) processing of the application without undue delay, within a reasonable timeframe; (v) an opportunity to correct deficiencies or supplement incomplete applications;[76] (vi) the rejection of the application in writing and without undue delay; (vii) a granted licence or authorisation must enter into effect without undue delay and in accordance with the terms and conditions of the licence or authorisation.

---

[75] According to footnote 18 to Article 8.20.1 EU-Singapore and footnote 1 to Article 95 EU-Georgia, this does 'not include payments for auction, tendering or other non-discriminatory means of awarding concessions, or mandated contributions to universal service provision'.

[76] These conditions are said to reflect progress on domestic regulation in GATS in the Doha Round. Mattoo and Sauvé, *The Preferential Liberalization of Services Trade* 32.

2.3 Constraints on Regulatory Autonomy

The constraints on regulatory autonomy resulting from the domestic regulation provisions in the EU-C&P, EU-Singapore and EU-Georgia RTAs differ substantially. Nonetheless, in each of these agreements, it holds true that domestic regulation in RTAs is regulated:

> in a manner analogous to that found in Article VI of the GATS, i.e. with a focus on procedural transparency and ensuring that regulatory activity does not lead to unduly burdensome or disguised restrictions to trade or investment in services.[77]

The scope and reach of the disciplines in the EU-C&P agreement are most comparable to Article VI:5 GATS, although the disciplines apply to all sectors. This is not the case for the quasi-identical domestic regulation provisions in the EU-Singapore and EU-Georgia RTAs. On the one hand, these disciplines constrain regulatory autonomy beyond GATS because measures which merely (but in a sufficiently direct way) affect trade can be prohibited (in contrast to the nullification or impairment test), regardless of whether these measures could have been reasonably expected. Hence, these disciplines are not standstill obligations. On the other hand, technical standards are not covered and, more importantly, the only substantive obligation on domestic regulation is one similar to Article VI:4 (a) GATS. Therefore, the contentious necessity test is not part of these disciplines. The relatively extensive extra disciplines are largely procedural and are related to transparency. This may increase the possibilities for challenging protectionist domestic regulatory measures, but, once again, this does not seem to constrain regulatory autonomy. Indeed, the domestic regulation provisions in these three RTAs are not 'rule-making laboratories'.[78]

2.4 The Relationship between the 'Triad' of Market Access, National Treatment and Domestic Regulation

In contrast to the distinction between market access and national treatment, for which the RTAs contain no explicit guidance, some guidance may be found for distinguishing between domestic regulation on the one hand and market access and national treatment on the other. In all three RTAs, the preambles to the respective Schedules of specific commitments

---

77 Ibid 31.
78 Ibid.

for establishment, cross-border trade in services and temporary presence of natural persons for business purposes each contain a relevant paragraph on this relationship. Preambular paragraph 3 of Annexes VII EU-C&P and 8-A-2 EU-Singapore concerning establishment; paragraph 3 of Annexes VIII EU-C&P, 8-A-1 EU-Singapore and XIV-B EU-Georgia on cross-border trade in services; and preambular paragraph 4 of Annexes IX EU-C&P, 8-A-3 EU-Singapore and XIV-C EU-Georgia with regard to the temporary presence of natural persons for business purposes, are very similar. They each note that the Schedules do not 'include measures relating to qualification requirements and procedures, technical standards and licensing requirements and procedures when they do not constitute a market access or a national treatment limitation' within the meaning of the relevant provisions on market access and national treatment. The provisions continue by stating that such measures, even if not listed, apply in any case to the service suppliers, establishments or investors of the other party. The following examples of such measures are given:

a. For all three modes of supply: (i) the need to obtain a licence; (ii) the need to obtain recognition of qualifications in regulated sectors; and (iii) the need to pass specific examinations, including language examinations.
b. With respect to establishment and cross-border trade in services: (iv) universal service obligations.
c. Solely for establishment: (v) a non-discriminatory requirement that certain activities may not be carried out in environmental protected zones or areas of particular historic and artistic interest.
d. Solely for the temporary presence of natural persons: (vi) the need to have a legal domicile in the territory where the economic activity is performed.
e. Solely for the temporary presence of natural persons in the EU-C&P RTA: (vii) the need to comply with national regulations and practices concerning minimum wages and with collective wage agreements in the host country.

Two additions to the above should be pointed out. First, in the EU-C&P RTA, the Schedule for temporary presence of natural persons also states that measures regarding employment, work and social security conditions are not listed if they do not constitute such limitations on market access or national treatment. This exclusion appears largely unnecessary, as similar exclusions can be found in Articles 107.6 EU-C&P, 8.1.4 EU-Singapore and 76.5 EU-Georgia, which are applicable to all trade in services and establishment, *juncto* the specific exceptions for *inter alia* social security in Articles 167.2 EU-C&P and 134.3 EU-Georgia.[79] Second, in the EU-Singapore RTA a similar provision to those found in the preambular paragraphs to the Schedules is contained in Article 8.18 on domestic regulation, which applies to all modes of supply. Paragraph 3 of Article 8.18 states that 'These disciplines do not apply to measures to the extent that the measures constitute limitations as scheduled in Article 8.10 (Market Access) and/or Article 8.11 (National Treatment)'. A very similar provision can be found in Article 93.3 EU-Georgia. This confirms the interpretation under GATS that domestic regulation on the one hand, and market access and national treatment on the other, are mutually exclusive. Considering the above, there is no need for the addition in Article 131 EU-C&P which integrates Article VI GATS into the RTA.

3. OVERVIEW: CURRENT DOMESTIC REGULATION DISCIPLINES

Table 6.1 provides an overview of the domestic regulation disciplines that are currently in place in GATS and the EU-C&P, EU-Singapore and EU-Georgia RTAs.

[79] See below. The EU-Singapore RTA does not contain a similar exception.

Table 6.1 Domestic regulation disciplines

		Article VI:5 GATS	EU-C&P RTA	EU-Singapore RTA	EU-Georgia DCFTA
Disciplines applicable to		*scheduled sectors, limitations do not apply*	*all sectors*	*scheduled sectors, limitations apply*	*scheduled sectors, limitations apply*
To be covered, measure must		*nullify or impair specific commitments*	*nullify or impair specific commitments*	*affect trade in any of the four modes of supply*	*affect trade in any of the four modes of supply*
Exclusion for		*reasonably expected measures*	*reasonably expected measures*		
Types of measures covered	Licensing requirements	X	X	X	X
	Qualification requirements	X	X	X	X
	Licensing procedures	only in so far as it is itself a restriction on the supply of the service		X	X
	Qualification procedures	(VI:4 only)		X	X
	'Procedures'		X		
	Technical standards	X	X		
Applicable disciplines		Article VI:4 (a), (b) and (c) GATS	Article VI:4 (a), (b) and (c) GATS	≈ Article VI:4 (a) GATS; plus transparency and procedural	≈ Article VI:4 (a) GATS; plus transparency and procedural

7. Transparency

1. THE PRINCIPLE OF TRANSPARENCY IN GATS AND THE SELECTED EU RTAs

The principle of transparency can be considered as a cornerstone of WTO law[1] and is also central to the selected EU RTAs and their services chapters.[2] Transparency in the internal legal regimes of Members is key to facilitating trade as it reduces transaction and information costs and improves efficiency. Transparency has even been called the 'real jewel in the crown' of the WTO (as opposed to dispute settlement).[3] But, as explained below, transparency obligations rarely constrain regulatory autonomy. They are therefore mostly dealt with briefly in this book.

According to a WTO Secretariat definition, in the WTO agreements, the principle of transparency is three-pronged. The prongs encompass the following requirements: (i) to make information on trade-related laws, regulations and policies publicly available; (ii) to notify (changes to) laws

---

[1] M Krajewski, *National Regulation and Trade Liberalization in Services* (Kluwer Law International 2003) 124; Panagiotis Delimatsis, 'Article III GATS' in Rüdiger Wolfrum, Peter-Tobias Stoll and Clemens Feinäugle (eds), *Max Planck Commentaries on World Trade Law: WTO – Trade in Services*, vol 6 (Martinus Nijhoff 2008), 94.

[2] In the preamble of the EU-Singapore RTA, the parties recognise 'the importance of transparency in international trade to the benefit of all stakeholders'. Additionally, Chapter 14 of this RTA solely addresses transparency. Title X of the EU-C&P RTA contains provisions relating to transparency and administrative proceedings. Moreover, Article 287 EU-C&P contains a general obligation to cooperate in relevant bilateral and multilateral fora in order to increase transparency in trade-related matters. In the EU-Georgia DCFTA, Chapter 12 is wholly dedicated to transparency.

[3] Petros C Mavroidis and Robert Wolfe, *From Sunshine to a Common Agent: The Evolving Understanding of Transparency in the WTO* (European University Institute – Robert Schuman Centre for Advanced Studies, Global Governance Programme RSCAS Policy Paper 2015/01, 2015) 1.

and regulations; and (iii) to ensure that laws and regulations are administered in a uniform, impartial and reasonable manner.[4] The third prong is a form of due process[5] that is considered part of the principle of transparency here.

2. TRANSPARENCY OBLIGATIONS IN GATS AND THE SELECTED EU RTAs

GATS, the EU-C&P RTA, the EU-Georgia DCFTA and the EU-Singapore RTA contain many transparency requirements, of each of the three prongs of the principle of transparency. As noted, the obligations in the following overview may be considered burdensome, but – with one exception – cannot be said to constrain regulatory autonomy:[6]

a. Articles III:1–2 GATS, 288.1, 3 EU-C&P and 14.3.1 EU-Singapore contain the unconditional obligation to publish or make publicly available all relevant measures.
b. Article III:3 GATS contains the conditional obligation to inform of the introduction of certain measures.
c. Article III:4 GATS, 130.1 (a) EU-C&P, 97.1 EU-Georgia and 8.17 EU-Singapore contain unconditional obligations to respond to information requests and establish contact and enquiry points.
d. Articles V:7 (a) and (b), and V bis (b) GATS contain the unconditional obligation to notify integration agreements.
e. Articles VI:2 GATS, 292 EU-C&P, 14.6 EU-Singapore and 224 and 411 EU-Georgia contain the unconditional obligation to make available legal remedies.
f. Article VI:3 GATS and 131.2 EU-C&P contain conditional (for GATS) or unconditional (for the EU-C&P RTA) information obligations related to authorisation for the supply of services.
g. Article VI:6 contains obligations relating to adequate procedures to verify professional service suppliers' competence.

---

[4] WT/WGTI/W/109, Transparency: Note by the Secretariat (Adopted 27 March 2002) para. 5.

[5] As concerns Articles VI:1 and VI:3, this was confirmed in *United States – Measures Affecting the Cross-Border Supply of Gambling and Betting Services* WT/DS285/R, Panel report adopted 20 April 2005 para. 6.432.

[6] Krajewski, *National Regulation and Trade Liberalization in Services* 126.

h. Articles VII:4 GATS, 129.5 EU-C&P and 96.5 EU-Georgia contain unconditional transparency obligations related to recognition. The EU-Singapore RTA does not contain a similar provision.
i. Articles IX:2 GATS, 265 EU-C&P and 12.13 EU-Singapore contain the unconditional obligation to enter into consultations regarding business (for GATS) or competition practices.
j. Article XV GATS, 293.5 EU-C&P, 206 EU-Georgia and 12.9 EU-Singapore contain unconditional transparency requirements related to subsidies.
k. Articles 14.3 EU-Singapore and 221 EU-Georgia require that Members provide an explanation of the objective and rationale for measures of general application.
l. Articles 288.2 EU-C&P, 221.2 (b)–(c) EU-Georgia and 14.3.2 (b)–(c) EU-Singapore require each party, to the extent that is possible, to provide opportunities for interested persons to comment on any proposed measure relating to any matter covered by the agreement, and also to examine such comments, provided that they are relevant.

The one exception to the rule that transparency obligations do not constrain regulatory autonomy concerns a transparency obligation of the third prong. The conditional Article VI:1 GATS obliges Members to ensure that all measures of general application affecting trade in services are administered in a reasonable, objective, and impartial manner. Measures affecting (i) 'an unidentified number of economic operators', (ii) 'a range of situations or cases, rather than being limited in their scope of application',[7] or individual decisions establishing or abandoning a principle of general application all fall within the scope of this provision.[8]

It is said that the objective of Article VI:1 GATS is to ensure that foreign service suppliers are 'not impeded in their work by the arbitrary or biased administration of domestic regulations' affecting trade in

[7] Panagiotis Delimatsis, 'Due Process and "Good" Regulation Embedded in the GATS – Disciplining Regulatory Behaviour in Services through Article VI of the GATS' (2006) 10 Journal of International Economic Law 13, 20, with reference to case law on Article X GATT 1994, especially *United States – Restrictions on Imports of Cotton and Man-Made Fibre Underwear* WT/DS24/AB/R, AB report adopted 25 February 1997 21; and *European Communities – Selected Customs Matters* WT/DS315/R, Panel report adopted 11 December 2006 para. 7.116.

[8] Markus Krajewski, 'Article VI GATS' in Rüdiger Wolfrum, Peter-Tobias Stoll and Clemens Feinäugle (eds), *Max Planck Commentaries on World Trade Law: WTO – Trade in Services*, vol 6 (Martinus Nijhoff 2008), 170.

scheduled services sectors.[9] Such impediments need to be sufficiently serious: their importance 'in the commercial world' needs to be shown.[10] Hence, the provision does not discipline the content of the measure but the way in which it is administered.[11] This may apply to a whole system of administration, i.e. without a specific application of such administration.[12] The consequence is that the measures covered by Article VI:1 GATS need not be reasonable, objective or impartial *as such*.[13] Indeed, a violation of this provision would not require the withdrawal of the measure, but instead the correction of procedural practices linked to its application.[14] On the basis of GATT case law, it may be expected that the administration of a measure in a *single* case will not trigger the application of Article VI:1 GATS.[15] However, doubts have been raised as to whether this is a correct interpretation of Article VI:1 GATS; a safer interpretation may be that only a measure with individual reach and no general application is excluded from the scope of Article VI:1 GATS.[16]

In light of the above, it seems that only the administration of measures is covered. Nonetheless, in the context of Article X GATT 1994 (which is very similar to Article VI:1 GATS), the Panel in *Argentina – Hides and*

---

[9] Delimatsis, 'Due Process and "Good" Regulation Embedded in the GATS – Disciplining Regulatory Behaviour in Services through Article VI of the GATS' 28.

[10] Bart De Meester, *Liberalization of Trade in Banking Services: An International and European Perspective* (Cambridge University Press 2014) 239–240, on the basis of *Argentina – Measures Affecting the Export of Bovine Hides and the Import of Finished Leather* WT/DS155/R, Panel report adopted 16 February 2001 para. 11.77 and *United States – Anti-Dumping Measures on Certain Hot-Rolled Steel Products from Japan* WT/DS184/R, Panel report adopted 23 August 2001 para. 7.268.

[11] *US – Gambling (Panel)* para. 6.432. *In casu*, the Panel determined that Antigua had not made a *prima facie* case of violation of Article VI:1 GATS.

[12] Padideh Ala'i and Matthew D'Orsi, 'Transparency in International Economic Relations and the Role of the WTO' in Padideh Ala'i and Robert G Vaughn (eds), *Research Handbook on Transparency* (Edward Elgar Publishing 2014) 381, referring to *European Communities – Selected Customs Matters* WT/DS315/AB/R, AB report adopted 11 December 2006 para. 166.

[13] Delimatsis, 'Due Process and "Good" Regulation Embedded in the GATS – Disciplining Regulatory Behaviour in Services through Article VI of the GATS' 19.

[14] De Meester, *Liberalization of Trade in Banking Services: An International and European Perspective* 238.

[15] *US – Hot-Rolled Steel (Panel)* para. 7.268.

[16] De Meester, *Liberalization of Trade in Banking Services: An International and European Perspective* 239–240.

Leather expressed the view that cases exist in which the substantive content of a measure must be addressed.[17] This is the case when the substance of a measure is administrative in nature, i.e. when 'it provides for a certain *manner of applying* substantive rules'.[18] The AB subsequently narrowed the scope of such substantive review: the substance of a measure can only be challenged under Article X:3 GATT 1994 if it is alleged that such a measure leads to a lack of uniform, impartial, or reasonable administration of a legal instrument.[19] In this interpretation, Article VI:1 GATS could, *mutatis mutandis*, be construed as assessing the reasonableness, objectivity and impartiality 'of the very substance of numerous domestic regulatory measures that regulate the application or implementation of measures'.[20]

For those measures falling within its scope, Article VI:1 GATS sets out three obligations: (i) reasonableness; (ii) objectivity; and (iii) impartiality. Each obligation can be invoked independently.[21] First, reasonableness 'refers to notions such as "in accordance with reason", "not irrational or absurd", "proportionate", "having sound judgement", "sensible", "not asking for too much", "within the limits of reason, not greatly less or more than might be thought likely or appropriate", "articulate"'.[22] The objective, cause and rationale behind the administration of a measure are all relevant in determining reasonableness.[23] The obligation thus requires a rational *reason* for the behaviour that is said to be unreasonable.[24]

---

17 *Argentina – Hides and Leather (Panel)* paras 11.70–11.71.

18 Delimatsis, 'Due Process and "Good" Regulation Embedded in the GATS – Disciplining Regulatory Behaviour in Services through Article VI of the GATS' 21 (emphasis original).

19 *EC – Selected Customs Matters* (AB) paras 200–201.

20 Delimatsis, 'Due Process and "Good" Regulation Embedded in the GATS – Disciplining Regulatory Behaviour in Services through Article VI of the GATS' 24 (emphasis original), where this argument is made in the context of Article X GATT 1994.

21 Ibid 26–27, with reference to Article X GATT 1994 case law, in which only one of the three elements was claimed to be violated by the complainants.

22 *Argentina – Hides and Leather (Panel)* para. 11.94; *Dominican Republic – Measures Affecting the Importation and Internal Sale of Cigarettes* WT/DS302/R, Panel report adopted 19 May 2005 para. 7.385, referring to the ordinary meaning of the word. In the specific cases at hand, both Panels found that the respondents did not act reasonably.

23 *United States – Certain Country of Origin Labelling (COOL) Requirements* WT/DS384/R, WT/DS386/R, Panel report adopted 23 July 2012 para. 7.851.

24 Krajewski, 'Article VI GATS' 171. See, *a contrario*, *US – COOL (Panel)* para. 7.859, where a rational reason was deemed to be missing.

Second, in this context, objectivity implies the use of a rational *process*, without emotional or personal intentions.[25] Third, impartial means 'not partial; not favouring one party or side more than another; unprejudiced, unbiased, fair'.[26] Hence, no special consideration or privileged treatment can be granted to one party without being granted to the other,[27] unless, again, there is a good reason for such distinction.[28] The test is marginal: only where blatant impartiality is evident should a panel find that this standard has been violated.[29] The Panel in *Argentina – Hides and Leather* has offered some guidance regarding the interpretation of these conditions. The Panel explained that the real effect or potential impact of the administration of the measure on foreign economic actors must be assessed.[30]

The three obligations included in Article VI:1 GATS can be seen as manifestations of the principles of consistency and predictability.[31] On a more stringent interpretation, it has also been suggested that the obligations prohibit the discriminatory or arbitrary administration of decisions.[32] I do not agree with the argument that discriminatory administration is prohibited. Indeed, it may be that a rational reason for discrimination exists (for example, the difference in administration may be based on a legitimate regulatory distinction) and that therefore Article VI:1 GATS may not be violated. However, I do agree that arbitrary administration would violate Article VI:1 GATS; arbitrary discrimination is not reasonable and is unlikely to be objective.

---

[25] Krajewski, 'Article VI GATS' 171. See *Argentina – Hides and Leather (Panel)* para. 11.100 for an example of an application of this.

[26] *China – Measures Related to the Exportation of Various Raw Materials* WT/DS394/R / WT/DS395/R / WT/DS398/R, Panel report adopted 22 February 2012 para. 7.694.

[27] Krajewski, 'Article VI GATS' 171.

[28] Bart De Meester, 'The Interaction Between European and International Liberalisation of International Trade in Banking Services' (PhD Thesis, KU Leuven 2010) 325. The link between 'reasonable' and 'impartial' was also made in *Argentina – Hides and Leather (Panel)* para. 11.89.

[29] De Meester, 'The Interaction Between European and International Liberalisation of International Trade in Banking Services' 325.

[30] *Argentina – Hides and Leather (Panel)* para. 11.77; *China – Raw Materials (Panel)* para. 7.708.

[31] Delimatsis, 'Due Process and "Good" Regulation Embedded in the GATS – Disciplining Regulatory Behaviour in Services through Article VI of the GATS' 28; Delimatsis, 'Article III GATS' 104.

[32] Krajewski, *National Regulation and Trade Liberalization in Services* 128.

From the perspective of regulatory autonomy, Article VI:1 GATS raises several questions. The regulatory burden caused by this provision may be substantial.[33] Domestic legislation could cover at least some of the obligations arising from Article VI:1 GATS. Therefore, according to one author, its impact on domestic regulatory autonomy is likely to be limited.[34] Others have noted that the requirement is 'a potentially powerful mechanism for ensuring equitable treatment for traded services and service suppliers beyond the substantive disciplines of WTO law', noting that regulatory autonomy may be constrained, especially if the reasonableness of Members' administration of measures is assessed.[35] This concern may explain the AB's explicit statement that allegations of another Member's unreasonable or biased conduct are serious and should not be brought lightly or without solid evidence.[36] This applies *mutatis mutandis* to Article VI:1 GATS. In our view, the AB's statement serves to remind other Members that they should not bring frivolous complaints. Its statement therefore limits the potential chilling effect of a wide interpretation of Article VI:1 GATS. However, the Panel in *China – Raw Materials* reiterated that, as noted in Article 3.10 DSU, the use of dispute settlement procedures should not be considered a contentious act and that, consequently, a Member is free to bring a claim on the basis of Article X:3 GATT 1994.[37]

Nonetheless, it is true that Article VI:1 GATS could be a very powerful mechanism under some understandings of its scope and mandate. For example, regulatory autonomy could be constrained considerably if the provision was to be interpreted as allowing a WTO panel to test the consistency of domestic decisions or rulings with domestic laws or regulations. In *US – Stainless Steel*, the Panel noted that this was *not* the purpose of Article X:3 GATT 1994; this function is reserved for domestic courts.[38] A panel ruling on such a claim does not need to test such

---

[33] Ibid; Nellie Munin, *Legal Guide to GATS* (Wolters Kluwer 2010) 282.

[34] Krajewski, *National Regulation and Trade Liberalization in Services* 128.

[35] Andrew Mitchell and Tania Voon, 'Reasonableness, Impartiality and Objectivity' in Aik Hoe Lim and Bart De Meester (eds), *WTO Domestic Regulation and Services Trade* (Cambridge University Press 2014) 65.

[36] *United States – Sunset Reviews of Anti-Dumping Measures on Oil Country Tubular Goods from Argentina* WT/DS268/AB/R, AB report adopted 17 December 2004 para. 217.

[37] *China – Raw Materials (Panel)* para. 7.739.

[38] *United States – Anti-Dumping Measures on Stainless Steel Plate in Coils and Stainless Steel Sheet and Strip from Korea* WT/DS179/R, Panel report adopted 1 February 2001 para. 6.50.

consistency with domestic laws.[39] Another potential constraint on regulatory autonomy would be a far-reaching interpretation of the three distinct obligations, in combination with a broad interpretation of the scope of Article VI:1 GATS vis-à-vis substantive domestic measures. However, in light of the existing interpretations of the corresponding GATT 1994 case law, the potential has (as of yet) not been fulfilled. The balance struck under Article X:3 GATT 1994 could be transposed to Article VI:1 GATS. This would not overly restrict regulatory autonomy in the context of the object and purpose of the latter provision.

All three RTAs contain an unconditional obligation similar to the conditional GATS obligation to Article VI:1 GATS. First, Article 131.1 EU-C&P is identical in wording to Article VI:1 GATS. However, it applies to all measures of general application covered by the title on trade in services, establishment and e-commerce, i.e. it is unconditional.

Second, Article 223.1 EU-Georgia is substantively identical to its GATS counterpart but its scope of application covers the integral Title IV on trade. Moreover, in Article 223.2 EU-Georgia, the specific requirements of the obligation are detailed. The parties are required, when applying measures of general application to particular services or service suppliers, to:

a. Ensure that the procedures a party applies are based on and carried out in accordance with that party's law. This requirement gives foreign service suppliers the same guarantees as domestic service suppliers that domestic laws are applied, although enforcement may be much simpler for domestic service suppliers (for example due to standing, or from a purely practical perspective).
b. Endeavour, in the case of the initiation of administrative proceedings, to provide directly affected interested persons with reasonable notice, a description of the nature of the proceedings, a statement of the legal authority under which the proceedings have been initiated and a general description of any issues in controversy.
c. Afford such directly affected interested persons a reasonable opportunity to present facts and arguments before a final administrative action is undertaken in so far as time, the nature of the proceedings and, notably, public interest will allow.

---

[39] Andrew Mitchell, *Legal Principles in WTO Disputes* (Cambridge University Press 2008) 173, and see the case law on Article X:3 GATT 1994, most recently *United States – Countervailing and Anti-dumping Measures on Certain Products from China* WT/DS449/R, Panel report adopted 22 July 2014.

The relationship between these specific emanations and the general principles of reasonableness, objectivity and impartiality is not entirely clear. The general principles are not to be understood as being *exclusively* furthered by these specific emanations, as these are preceded by the words 'to this end'. As such, the specific emanations are merely explicit examples of what this obligation covers.

Third, although Article 14.5 EU-Singapore strongly resembles Article 223 EU-Georgia from a substantive point of view, its structure is fundamentally different. The three specific emanations are, in identical wording, also present in this provision. However, Article 14.5 EU-Singapore does not have a general first paragraph that sets out the obligation to administer all measures of general application in an objective, impartial and reasonable manner. Instead, it merely states that with a view to administering in a consistent, impartial and reasonable manner, the three specified conditions must be fulfilled. Hence, here, the furtherance of the general principles of objectivity, impartiality and reasonableness are themselves the objective of the specific emanations. This is unlike the situation under the EU-Georgia DCFTA, whereby the emanations contain certain additional obligations. Consequently, the obligation is, perhaps surprisingly, more limited than under the EU-C&P RTA and the EU-Georgia DCFTA. It could even be said to be GATS–.

Nonetheless, the provisions in all three RTAs do not constrain regulatory autonomy beyond those potential constraints which were identified with regards to Article VI:1 GATS. The interpretation of the three principles set forth in the analysis of Article VI:1 GATS applies to all three provisions *mutatis mutandis*.

8. Exceptions

1. EXCEPTIONS IN GATS

GATS contains several exception clauses which mitigate the reach of its obligations. Measures which violate GATS obligations may be justified using one of these provisions. Exceptions, by their very nature, create room for regulators. The carved-out regulatory autonomy was always part of the compromise: it is unlikely that a Member would have signed a GATS containing no exceptions. The most important issue for the present purposes is the interpretation of the exception clauses. In addition to some specific exceptions that have already been addressed, such as the exceptions to the MFN obligation, this chapter addresses the exceptions that are, for the most part, applicable to all obligations in GATS.

Article III bis GATS states that the agreement shall not require any Member to provide confidential information if the disclosure of such information would: (i) impede law enforcement; (ii) otherwise be contrary to the public interest; or (iii) prejudice legitimate commercial interests of particular enterprises, public or private. The provision appears to have been inserted following Article III because it is most applicable to transparency obligations.[1] However, it is applicable to all obligations arising from GATS, not only the unconditional general obligations related to transparency. Indeed, the provision contains a general exception for the protection of confidential information.[2] In practice, this provision seems most relevant as a defence vis-à-vis a breach of GATS transparency obligations.[3]

Since the 1970s, the world economy has, primarily, been based on flexible exchange rates. It has been noted that, in such an economy, there is less need, except in exceptional circumstances, to resort to trade

---

[1] Panagiotis Delimatsis, 'Article III bis GATS' in Rüdiger Wolfrum, Peter-Tobias Stoll and Clemens Feinäugle (eds), *Max Planck Commentaries on World Trade Law: WTO – Trade in Services*, vol 6, 108.

[2] WT/WGTI/W/109, Transparency: Note by the Secretariat (Adopted 27 March 2002) para. 43.

[3] Delimatsis, 'Article III bis GATS' 112.

measures to counterbalance payment issues.[4] Indeed, in a flexible exchange rate system, changes in the exchange rate seem 'the dominant method of balance-of-payments adjustment for at least the major industrialized countries'.[5] Moreover, 'capital markets have been liberalized and increasingly integrated', which will adjust a country's balance of payments.[6] Therefore, trade measures to combat balance of payment difficulties, for example import controls and export subsidies, are 'demonstrably ineffective tools' and 'should be relegated to the sidelines'.[7] The lack of dispute settlement on Articles XII GATS and GATT 1994 perhaps reflects the reluctance of Members to apply this exception.[8] The strict conditions of non-discrimination and necessity, combined with the decreased importance of trade measures vis-à-vis balance of payments difficulties in developed countries in the modern world economy, indicate that Article XII GATS is of limited importance.

Article XIV bis GATS and its goods-counterpart Article XXI GATT 1994 each contain a security exception and have been invoked only sparingly in the WTO context.[9] The case law in the context of GATT 1947 is equally sparse, being limited to two reports addressing the American embargo vis-à-vis Nicaragua.[10] This lack of practice may be

---

[4] Frieder Roessler, 'The GATT Declaration on Trade Measures Taken for Balance-of-Payments Purposes: A Commentary' (1980) 12 Case Western Reserve Journal of International Law 383, 383.

[5] C Fred Bergsten, 'Reforming the GATT: The Use of Trade Measures for Balance-of-Payments Purposes' (1977) 7 Journal of International Economics 1, 4.

[6] Karen McCusker, 'Are Trade Restrictions to Protect the Balance of Payments Becoming Obsolete?' (2000) 35 Intereconomics 89, 91.

[7] Bergsten, 'Reforming the GATT: The Use of Trade Measures for Balance-of-Payments Purposes' 5.

[8] The sole case concerning balance of payments addresses a developing country and focuses on Article XVIII:B GATT 1994 rather than Article XII GATT 1994: see the Panel and AB reports in *India – Quantitative Restrictions on Imports of Agricultural, Textile and Industrial Products*, WT/DS90. Also see *India – Measures Affecting the Automotive Sector* WT/DS146/R, WT/DS175/R, Panel report adopted 5 April 2002 paras 7.288–7.294, where India asserted, unsuccessfully, a balance of payments defence.

[9] The only interpretation can be found in *European Communities – Conditions for the Granting of Tariff Preferences to Developing Countries* WT/DS246/R, Panel report adopted 20 April 2004 para. 7.37. Here, the Panel explains that the security exceptions do not establish a positive obligation.

[10] *United States – Imports of Sugar from Nicaragua* L/5607, GATT Panel report, adopted 13 March 1984, BISD 31S/67; *United States – Trade Measures Affecting Nicaragua* L/6053, GATT Panel report, 13 October 1986, unadopted.

explained by a clear risk of abuse of the security exceptions,[11] as their ratio is the protection of essential security interests of a Member. Considering the sensitive nature of such interests, it is likely that a panel would grant extensive regulatory autonomy to the invoking Member and would only reject manifest misuse of the exceptions.[12] In turn, this risks eroding commitments.[13] Indeed, the exceptions have even been used in response to requests for consultations as a deterrent for the complaining Member to actually bring the dispute.[14] It has been argued that Article XIV bis GATS is a 'virtually unlimited escape clause',[15] the language of which 'substantially risks undermining WTO obligations'.[16] Admittedly, the language of the provision is quite broad. However, the limited practice under Articles XIV bis GATS and XXI GATT 1994 indicates that Members understand the systemic implications of using these security exceptions without restraint.[17] Nonetheless, from the perspective

---

Note, however, that the issue has generated substantial academic debate ever since. See e.g. Richard Sutherland Whitt, 'The Politics of Procedure: An Examination of the GATT Dispute Settlement Panel and the Article XXI Defense in the Context of the U.S. Embargo of Nicaragua' (1987) 19 Law and Policy in International Business 603; and more recently Andrew Emmerson, 'Conceptualizing Security Exceptions: Legal Doctrine or Political Excuse?' (2008) 11 Journal of International Economic Law 135.

[11] Thomas Cottier and Panagiotis Delimatsis, 'Article XIV bis GATS' in Rüdiger Wolfrum, Peter-Tobias Stoll and Clemens Feinäugle (eds), *Max Planck Commentaries on World Trade Law: WTO – Trade in Services*, vol 6 (Martinus Nijhoff 2008) 331.

[12] Cottier and Delimatsis (ibid) 343 make this remark only for subparagraph (b). However, it is submitted here that this applies equally to the other security exceptions. See, more extensively, Peter Lindsay, 'The Ambiguity of Gatt Article XXI: Subtle Success or Rampant Failure?' (2003) 52 Duke Law Journal 1277, especially 1281–1296.

[13] Cottier and Delimatsis, 'Article XIV bis GATS' 332.

[14] See *European Communities – The Cuban Liberty and Democratic Solidarity Act*, WT/DS38/2; *India – Import Restrictions*, WT/DS149; *Nicaragua – Measures Affecting Imports from Honduras and Columbia*, WT/DS188.

[15] Michael J Hahn, 'Vital Interests and the Law of GATT: An Analysis of GATT's Security Exceptions' (1991) 12 Michigan Journal of International Law 558, 558–559.

[16] Cottier and Delimatsis, 'Article XIV bis GATS' 331.

[17] Dapo Akande and Sope Williams, 'International Adjudication on National Security Issues: What Role for the WTO?' (2003) 43 Virginia Journal of International Law 365, 404. However, there has also been criticism of the US' past use of trade sanctions, which link trade to security interests. See Raj Bhala, 'National Security and International Trade Law: What the GATT Says, and What

of regulatory autonomy, it seems clear that actual security interests are safeguarded through Article XIV bis GATS.

1.1 General Exceptions[18]

The most important exceptions, both from a practical perspective and a regulatory autonomy perspective, are contained in the general exceptions clause of Article XIV GATS. The provision mirrors Article XX GATT 1994, which is a centrepiece of WTO law: the provision consists of a chapeau and a list of policy grounds. Article XIV GATS reads:

> Subject to the requirement that such measures are not applied in a manner which would constitute a means of arbitrary or unjustifiable discrimination between countries where like conditions prevail, or a disguised restriction on trade in services, nothing in this Agreement shall be construed to prevent the adoption or enforcement by any Member of measures:
>
> (a) necessary to protect public morals or to maintain public order;(**5**)
> (b) necessary to protect human, animal or plant life or health;
> (c) necessary to secure compliance with laws or regulations which are not inconsistent with the provisions of this Agreement including those relating to:
> (i) the prevention of deceptive and fraudulent practices or to deal with the effects of a default on services contracts;
> (ii) the protection of the privacy of individuals in relation to the processing and dissemination of personal data and the protection of confidentiality of individual records and accounts;
> (iii) safety;
> (d) inconsistent with Article XVII, provided that the difference in treatment is aimed at ensuring the equitable or effective (**6**) imposition or collection of direct taxes in respect of services or service suppliers of other Members;
> (e) inconsistent with Article II, provided that the difference in treatment is the result of an agreement on the avoidance of double taxation or

the United States Does' (1998) 12 University of Pennsylvania Journal of International Economic Law 263, 317.

[18] Although the exceptions in Articles XIV (d) and (e) GATS are exceptions specific to one obligation, i.e. national treatment and the MFN obligation respectively, they are addressed here and not, as with other MFN exceptions, in the discussion of the obligations. The key reason for doing this is the applicability of the chapeau to all subparagraphs. Further, the two-tiered structure of the general exceptions provision can be better explained and understood when taking Article XIV GATS as a whole.

> provisions on the avoidance of double taxation in any other international agreement or arrangement by which the Member is bound.

(footnote original) 5 The public order exception may be invoked only where a genuine and sufficiently serious threat is posed to one of the fundamental interests of society.

(footnote original) 6 [omitted].

In light of the textual overlaps between Articles XX GATT 1994 and XIV GATS, and the identical function of both provisions, the AB has clarified that case law on either provision is relevant to the other: 'like the Panel, we find previous decisions under Article XX of the GATT 1994 relevant for our analysis under Article XIV of the GATS'.[19] Thus, as with Article XX GATT 1994, if a measure is found to be inconsistent with an obligation under GATS, the measure – rather than the inconsistency[20] – may be justified through the general exceptions clause.[21] First, it will be assessed whether the measure can be preliminarily justified under one of the Article XIV subparagraphs. If this hurdle is satisfied, the measure's conformity with the requirements of the chapeau will be examined.[22]

---

19 See, on the interpretation of Article XIV GATS, *United States – Measures Affecting the Cross-Border Supply of Gambling and Betting Services* WT/DS285/AB/R, AB report adopted 20 April 2005 para. 291; *United States – Measures Affecting the Cross-Border Supply of Gambling and Betting Services* WT/DS285/R, Panel report adopted 20 April 2005 para. 6.448. See, interpreting Article XX GATT 1994 with reference to *US – Gambling* case law on Article XIV GATS (all referring to *US – Gambling (AB)* para. 306, for example, *Dominican Republic – Measures Affecting the Importation and Internal Sale of Cigarettes* WT/DS302/AB/R, AB report adopted 19 May 2005 para. 69; *Brazil – Measures Affecting Imports of Retreaded Tyres* WT/DS332/AB/R, AB report adopted 17 December 2007 paras 143, 146 and 182; *China – Measures Affecting Trading Rights and Distribution Services for Certain Publications and Audiovisual Products* WT/DS363/AB/R, AB report adopted 19 January 2010 paras 240 and 242; *Thailand – Customs and Fiscal Measures on Cigarettes from the Philippines* WT/DS371/AB/R, AB report adopted 15 July 2011 para. 179; *European Communities – Measures Prohibiting the Importation and Marketing of Seal Products* WT/DS400/AB/R, AB report adopted 18 June 2014 paras 5.169 and 5.215.

20 *United States – Standards for Reformulated and Conventional Gasoline* WT/DS2/AB/R, AB report adopted 20 May 1996 13–14; *Thailand – Cigarettes (Philippines) (AB)* para. 177; *EC – Seal Products (AB)* para. 5.185.

21 *US – Gasoline (AB)* 24.

22 *US – Gambling (AB)* para. 292 for GATS, reaffirming *US – Gasoline (AB)* 19.

1.1.1 First tier of the analysis: the list of policy grounds

The first tier of the Article XIV GATS analysis involves an assessment of whether the measure falls within the scope of a particular subparagraph. The AB has explained that this analysis constitutes two cumulative steps. First, the challenged measure must 'address the particular interest specified in that paragraph'. Second, there must be 'a sufficient nexus between the measure and the interest protected'.[23] The latter requirement is evident from the language of the subparagraphs,[24] i.e. the use of the terms 'necessary' (for subparagraphs (a)–(c)) and 'aimed at' (for subparagraphs (d)–(e)). The former requirement entails that the measure must be designed to attain the specific interest, for example to protect public morals or maintain public order.[25] In other words, the measure's object and purpose must be to attain the interest.[26] Note that the measure is not necessarily required to reflect the interest *directly*: it suffices that the concerns raised by the measure fall within the scope of the policy grounds listed in the subparagraph.[27] For example, a measure may be aimed at combating organised crime, and therefore fall within the scope of the public morals exception. Whether this condition is satisfied must be assessed for each subparagraph individually.

The analysis of a measure under Article XIV GATS requires that the objective of the measure is determined.[28] This determination impacts upon both the applicability of a subparagraph and on the necessity test, discussed below. In several cases, the AB has found that the panel erred in determining the objective of a measure.[29] For example, in *EC – Asbestos*, the Panel found that the objective of the measure was the protection of the health of workers, in other words, that the measure had a general objective of human health.[30] The AB, however, argued that the objective of the EU's measure was the elimination and reduction of

---

[23] *US – Gambling (AB)* para. 292.

[24] Ibid.

[25] *US – Gambling (Panel)* para. 6.455.

[26] Ibid para. 6.474.

[27] Ibid para. 6.487.

[28] See e.g. *EC – Seal Products (AB)* paras 5.133–5.167.

[29] Benn McGrady, 'Necessity Exceptions in WTO Law: *Retreaded Tyres*, Regulatory Purpose and Cumulative Regulatory Measures' (2009) 12 Journal of International Economic Law 153, 158–160; Chad P Bown and Joel P Trachtman, '*Brazil – Measures Affecting Imports of Retreaded Tyres*: A Balancing Act' (2009) 8 World Trade Review 85, 124–125.

[30] *European Communities – Measures Affecting Asbestos and Asbestos-Containing Products* WT/DS135/R, Panel report adopted 5 April 2001 paras 8.173–8.174.

health risks from asbestos fibres.[31] In *EC – Seal Products*, the Panel concluded that the 'objective of the EU Seal Regime is "to address the moral concerns of the EU public with regard to the welfare of seals"'.[32] The AB did not overturn the Panel's analysis, which had also included indigenous communities and other interests as part of the objectives of the measure, but concluded more clearly that 'the principal objective of the EU Seal Regime is to address EU public moral concerns regarding seal welfare, while accommodating IC [indigenous communities] and other interests so as to mitigate the impact of the measure on those interests'.[33] Clearly, a measure can have several different objectives. If this is the case, it seems the AB is of the opinion that a panel should determine, on the basis of the evidence before it, which is the principal objective.[34] If the measure consists of several elements, for example a general rule and exceptions to that rule, all aspects of the measure need to be taken *together as a whole* for the justification analysis.[35]

Related to the question of a measure's multiple objectives, the link between a measure and the exceptions to that measure has been addressed in the case law. In *Brazil – Tyres*, the Panel considered the measure, and the exemption from the measure, for MERCOSUR imports separately in its analysis of both a substantive obligation and the provisional justification of the measure under subparagraph (b) of Article XX GATT 1994. In its analysis under the chapeau, the Panel only examined the measure.[36] The AB clarified that 'the Panel might have opted for a more holistic approach', examining both the measure and the

---

[31] *European Communities – Measures Affecting Asbestos and Asbestos-Containing Products* WT/DS135/AB/R, AB report adopted 5 April 2001 para. 172.

[32] *European Communities – Measures Prohibiting the Importation and Marketing of Seal Products* WT/DS400/R, Panel report adopted 18 June 2014 para. 7.410.

[33] *EC – Seal Products (AB)* para. 5.167.

[34] Ibid paras 5.133–5.167. The extensive analysis of the objective of the measure by the Panel and the AB indicates that the criticism put forward by McGrady, that there is too little analysis, may not always hold true. See McGrady, 'Necessity Exceptions in WTO Law: *Retreaded Tyres*, Regulatory Purpose and Cumulative Regulatory Measures' 158–160.

[35] *US – Gasoline (AB)* 19; *EC – Seal Products (AB)* paras 5.193.

[36] *Brazil – Measures Affecting Imports of Retreaded Tyres* WT/DS332/R, Panel report adopted 17 December 2007 paras 7.106–7.107.

exemption together.[37] In *EC – Seal Products*, the AB continued in this direction, noting that the measure, i.e. an import ban, and the exceptions to this ban needed to be 'taken together', both for the assessment under substantive obligations and in the analysis of the general exceptions.[38] Thus, in line with the approach taken for a measure which has multiple objectives, the AB's preferred approach here appears to be an examination of the measure as a whole.

Before addressing the subparagraphs in greater detail, it is useful to point out that the list of policy grounds is exhaustive.[39] Consequentially, the scope of the general exceptions provision is limited to measures which address one of the listed public policies. In the context of Article XX GATT 1994, it has been remarked that the list of ten policy objectives is limited to the 'most compelling sort of regulatory interests'.[40] For GATS, the scope of the general exceptions provision is even narrower. Only five grounds are upheld, three of which feature under Article XX GATT 1994. Unlike GATT 1994, there are no exceptions for measures:

a. Relating to the importations or exportations of gold or silver.
b. Relating to the products of prison labour.
c. Imposed for the protection of national treasures of artistic, historic or archaeological value.
d. Relating to the conservation of exhaustible natural resources.
e. Undertaken in pursuance of obligations under any inter-governmental commodity agreement.

---

37 *Brazil – Retreaded Tyres (AB)* para. 126. Also see Tania Voon, 'Exploring the Meaning of Trade-Restrictiveness in the WTO' 14 World Trade Review 451, 472–474.

38 *EC – Seal Products (AB)* paras 5.188–5.189 and 5.193.

39 S/L/74, Work Programme on Electronic Commerce Progress (Report by the Council for Trade in Services 19 July 1999) para. 14; Petros C Mavroidis, *The General Agreement on Tariffs and Trade: A Commentary* (Oxford University Press 2005) 184; Thomas Cottier, Panagiotis Delimatsis and Nicolas Diebold, 'Article XIV GATS' in Rüdiger Wolfrum, Peter-Tobias Stoll and Clemens Feinäugle (eds), *Max Planck Commentaries on World Trade Law: WTO – Trade in Services*, vol 6, 297.

40 Robert E Hudec, 'GATT/WTO Constraints on National Regulation: Requiem for an "Aim and Effects" Test' (1998) 32 The International Lawyer 619, 622. Also see Aaditya Mattoo and Arvind Subramanian, 'Regulatory Autonomy and Multilateral Disciplines: The Dilemma and a Possible Resolution' (1998) 1 Journal of International Economic Law 303, 314.

f. Involving restrictions on exports of domestic materials necessary to ensure essential quantities of such materials to a domestic processing industry.
g. Essential to the acquisition or distribution of products in general or local short supply.

These exceptions have not been invoked often in the context of GATT 1994, bar the exception for measures relating to the conservation of exhaustible natural resources. This latter exception could seem more relevant in the context of goods than in the context of services. However, one could expect environmental services, for example, to play a role in the conservation of exhaustible natural resources too.[41] In the context of GATS, such measures would need to be justified through the exception for the protection of human, animal or plant life and health. On the other hand, in comparison to Article XX GATT 1994, an exception for the maintenance of public order has been included in Article XIV (a) GATS. Subparagraphs (d) and (e) are also unique to GATS.

1.1.1.1 Whether the measures address the particular interest

1.1.1.1.1 PUBLIC MORALS AND PUBLIC ORDER Article XIV (a) GATS covers measures necessary to protect public morals and maintain public order. As the Panel in *US – Gambling* stated, 'there may be sensitivities associated with the interpretation of the terms 'public morals' and 'public order' in the context of Article XIV'.[42] Therefore, the same Panel found that 'the content of these concepts for Members can vary in time and space, depending upon a range of factors, including prevailing social, cultural, ethical and religious values'.[43] Such an approach is consistent with the dynamic interpretation of Article XX (g) GATT 1994.[44] Moreover, it is for the Member to determine the level of protection, for the particular interest, which it deems appropriate.[45] In other words:

---

[41] Cottier, Delimatsis and Diebold, 'Article XIV GATS' 297.
[42] *US – Gambling (Panel)* para. 6.461.
[43] Ibid.
[44] Mark Wu, 'Free Trade and the Protection of Public Morals: An Analysis of the Newly Emerging Public Morals Clause Doctrine' (2008) 33 Yale Journal of International Law 215, 231.
[45] *US – Gambling (Panel)* para. 6.461 for Article XIV (a) GATS specifically, referring to *Korea – Measures Affecting Imports of Fresh, Chilled and Frozen Beef* WT/DS161/AB/R, AB report adopted 10 January 2001 para. 176 and EC – Asbestos (AB) para. 168.

> Members should be given some scope to define and apply for themselves the concepts of 'public morals' and 'public order' in their respective territories, according to their own systems and scales of values.[46]

This indicates that, with regard to 'similar interests of moral concerns', Members may set different levels of protection of public morals, i.e. a Member is not obliged by subparagraph (a) to address similar moral concerns in a similar way.[47] Therefore, there does not appear to be a requirement of consistency. This finding also seems applicable in the public order context.[48] It has been argued that this is an incorrect extrapolation of the 'appropriate level of protection' concept, which is discussed below as it is part of the necessity test.[49] However, it is clear, also from the AB's later finding in *EC – Seal Products*, that public morals (and, likely, public order) differ from the other policy grounds in the general exceptions provision. For example, a Member can define its *own* public morals, whereas it may have less leeway to do so for the content and scope of the other policy grounds.[50] Nonetheless, the broad public morals and public order interests that result from this interpretation remain limited by the 'public' character of both interests. This wording entails that, in order to be justifiable under Article XIV (a) GATS, a measure must be aimed at protecting either *the whole* of the people within a community, or, *the whole* of the people within a nation.[51] This issue is examined below.

Although there may be overlaps between the public morals and public order concepts, they are nonetheless distinct.[52] First, the protection of

---

[46] *US – Gambling (Panel)* para. 6.461.

[47] *EC – Seal Products (AB)* para. 5.200.

[48] *A fortiori*, as it is also applicable to Article XX (b) GATT 1994. See *EC – Asbestos (Panel)* paras 8.170–8.171.

[49] Nicolas Diebold, 'The Morals and Order Exceptions in WTO Law: Balancing the Toothless Tiger and the Undermining Mole' (2008) 11 Journal of International Economic Law 43, 52–53.

[50] According to Diebold (ibid 53), the AB explained that a Member may not define 'exhaustible natural resources' for itself in *United States – Import Prohibition of Certain Shrimp and Shrimp Products* WT/DS58/AB/R, AB report adopted 6 November 1998 para. 128. In my view, in the cited paragraph, the AB merely rejected the (strict) interpretation set forth by the complainant.

[51] *US – Gambling (Panel)* para. 6.463.

[52] Ibid para. 6.468. According to Cottier, Delimatsis and Diebold, 'Article XIV GATS' 299–300 and Diebold, 'The Morals and Order Exceptions in WTO Law: Balancing the Toothless Tiger and the Undermining Mole' 71–74, the concept of public morals falls completely within the concept of public order. This may well be the case, although there appears to be no reason to exclude the

public morals has been identified as one of the most important values or interests pursued by Members in their public policies.[53] The Panel in *US – Gambling* stated, in a finding upheld by the AB,[54] that the term 'public morals' 'denotes standards of right and wrong conduct maintained by or on behalf of a community or nation'.[55] For example, the protection of public moral concerns regarding the welfare of animals is an important value or interest.[56] From the perspective of regulatory autonomy, it should be emphasised that the relevant public morals for an Article XIV (a) GATS defence are those in the responding Member's society, community or nation.[57] However, it has been remarked, correctly, that it may be becoming progressively difficult, *inter alia* due to the digitised society, to determine common moral concerns among increasingly fragmented co-existing micro-communities – starting at the household level.[58] The consequences of this observation for the applicability of the public morals exception are unclear. How narrowly can 'community' be defined in the context of Article XIV (a) GATS? As elaborated upon in the next paragraph, the evidence required for the establishment of the existence of a public moral does not accommodate an overly fragmented approach. Of course, first and foremost, there must be a *measure* that aims at protecting public morals. A legislator is perhaps unlikely to regulate a concern not supported by a sufficiently large proportion of its constituency. Subsequently, as noted, the concern must be a *public* one, shared by the whole people within a community.[59] However, while the public

---

possibility of public morals concerns that do not fall within the scope of the term 'public order'. The authors argue that the key differentiation is footnote 5: if a threat to public order is insufficiently grave to meet the threshold set forth there, it could still be a concern that may nonetheless be justified through the public morals exception.

53 *China – Measures Affecting Trading Rights and Distribution Services for Certain Publications and Audiovisual Products* WT/DS363/R, Panel report adopted 19 January 2010 para. 7.817.

54 *US – Gambling (AB)* para. 299.

55 *US – Gambling (Panel)* para. 6.465.

56 *EC – Seal Products (Panel)* para. 7.632.

57 Panagiotis Delimatsis, 'Protecting Public Morals in a Digital Age: Revisiting the WTO Rulings on *US – Gambling* and *China – Publications and Audiovisual Products*' (2011) 14 Journal of International Economic Law 257, 275, notes that this approach equally is a 'convenient, wise and at the same time effective solution'.

58 Ibid 275–276 gives the example of two neighbours. The first runs a strict religious website; the second a pornographic one. Also see ibid 287–291.

59 *US – Gambling (Panel)* para. 6.463.

character of the exception must be taken into account, there is no inherent textual reason to require, for example, that a majority of the Member's population must endorse the public moral concerned.[60]

Whether a measure aims to protect public morals requires a two-step analysis:

> [F]irst, whether the concern in question indeed exists in that society; and, second, whether such concern falls within the scope of 'public morals' as 'defined and applied' by a regulating Member 'in its territory, according to its own systems and scales of values'.[61]

In practice, this means that it must be established (i) whether the evidence shows that there is a specific *public* concern and (ii) whether that public concern is a public moral – i.e. a standard of right or wrong – as defined and applied by the Member.[62] As concerns the first step, it is true that public morals can often not be identified or assessed through risk-assessment methods, such as scientific evidence.[63] Therefore, an assessment of the existence of a public concern can be based on the text or design of the measure,[64] and its legislative history.[65] However, a panel is not bound by the objectives of a measure as put forth by the Member taking the measure, and could find guidance in contrary evidence proffered by the complaining Member.[66] The second step can be rephrased as follows: are the public concerns identified in the first step 'anchored in the morality' of the responding Member's society?[67] This question may be answered by looking at the legislative history of the

---

[60] I therefore disagree with the statement in Diebold, 'The Morals and Order Exceptions in WTO Law: Balancing the Toothless Tiger and the Undermining Mole' 61.

[61] *EC – Seal Products (Panel)* para. 7.383; with implicit reference to *US – Gambling (Panel)* para. 6.461. Although this section of the *Seal Products* report deals with Article 2.2 TBT Agreement, the Panel explains in para. 7.382 that the public morals exception of Article XX (a) GATT 1994 is of relevance as the TBT Agreement and GATT 1994 should be interpreted in a coherent and consistent manner.

[62] *EC – Seal Products (Panel)* paras 7.384 and 7.403.

[63] *EC – Seal Products (AB)* para. 5.198.

[64] *EC – Seal Products (Panel)* paras 7.386–7.389.

[65] Ibid paras 7.390–7.398.

[66] *US – Gambling (AB)* para. 304.

[67] *EC – Seal Products (Panel)* para. 7.404.

measure,[68] other domestic laws and regulations of the responding Member,[69] or international legal instruments.[70]

In *US – Gambling*, the US put forth instrumental reasons (e.g. underage gambling risks and the relationship between gambling and organised crime) to justify the measure under Article XIV (a) GATS.[71] This differs from an approach in which non-instrumental reasons are presented for such a justification, i.e. through an expression of 'moral opprobrium'.[72] In *EC – Seal Products*, the EU put forth both instrumental and non-instrumental reasons.[73] The evidentiary burden set out by the Panel in *EC – Seal Products* for establishing the existence of public morals, thus allows non-instrumental reasons for the protection of public morals. This is very relevant to the scope of the public morals exception, which has matured into a fully-fledged exception that is likely to be crucial to the further development of justifications under Articles XIV GATS and XX GATT 1994.

Second, in *US – Gambling*, public order, read in conjunction with footnote 5 to Article XIV GATS was defined by the Panel as referring 'to the preservation of the fundamental interests of a society, as reflected in public policy and law. These fundamental interests can relate, *inter alia*, to standards of law, security and morality'.[74] This finding was upheld by the AB.[75] For example, such interests could be related to standards of safety, combating organised crime, or access to essential facilities.[76] The 'public' character of public order differs from that seen in the concept of

---

[68] Ibid paras 7.396 and 7.405.

[69] Ibid paras 7.405–7.407.

[70] Ibid paras 7.405 and 7.408; Markus Krajewski, 'Playing by the Rules of the Game? Specific Commitments after *US – Gambling and Betting* and the Current GATS Negotiations' (2005) 32 Legal Issues of Economic Integration 417, 440–441.

[71] *US – Gambling (AB)* para. 74; Robert Howse and Joanna Langille, 'Permitting Pluralism: The Seal Products Dispute and Why the WTO Should Accept Trade Restrictions Justified by Noninstrumental Moral Values' (2012) 37 Yale Journal of International Law 367, 412.

[72] Howse and Langille, 'Permitting Pluralism: The Seal Products Dispute and Why the WTO Should Accept Trade Restrictions Justified by Noninstrumental Moral Values' 412.

[73] See e.g. *EC – Seal Products (Panel)* para. 7.420, where the Panel refers to the EU's attempt to demonstrate that animal welfare is a 'global social norm' and a 'universal value'.

[74] *US – Gambling (Panel)* para. 6.467.

[75] *US – Gambling (AB)* para. 299.

[76] Cottier, Delimatsis and Diebold, 'Article XIV GATS' 300.

public morals. Indeed, 'public' should be interpreted more widely in the case of public order.[77] However, contrary to the case for public morals, footnote 5 limits the applicability to public order interests that are (i) fundamental interests, and (ii) challenged by a genuine and sufficiently serious threat.[78] Finally, public order must be differentiated from national security interests,[79] for which an exception is enshrined in Article XIV bis GATS.

It has been argued that the public order exception is broad and inclusive, providing for more regulatory autonomy under GATS than under GATT 1994, and that it should be interpreted to accommodate for the restricted, short list of policy objectives in Article XIV GATS.[80] Nonetheless, it is possible that few measures would qualify for justification under such an exception.[81] Footnote 5 limits the potential scope of the public order exception to a relatively narrow type of interest. By way of contrast, the relatively broad interpretation of public morals could be expected to overlap substantially with this public order exception.

1.1.1.1.2 HUMAN, ANIMAL OR PLANT LIFE OR HEALTH Whereas Article XX (b) GATT 1994 is very similar to Article XIV (b) GATS, the former is complimented by Article XX (g), which concerns measures related to the protection of exhaustible natural resources.[82] As noted above, no such policy ground can be found in GATS. This fact may be relevant in the interpretation of Article XIV (b) GATS.[83] The WTO's Committee on Trade and Environment noted that, at the end of GATS negotiations, most – but not all – Members agreed that subparagraph (b) included measures necessary for the protection of the environment, provided that such

---

[77] Diebold, 'The Morals and Order Exceptions in WTO Law: Balancing the Toothless Tiger and the Undermining Mole' 61–62.

[78] Cottier, Delimatsis and Diebold, 'Article XIV GATS' 301; Diebold, 'The Morals and Order Exceptions in WTO Law: Balancing the Toothless Tiger and the Undermining Mole' 62.

[79] M Krajewski, *National Regulation and Trade Liberalization in Services* (Kluwer Law International 2003) 158.

[80] Cottier, Delimatsis and Diebold, 'Article XIV GATS' 292 and 298; Rolf H Weber, 'Regulatory Autonomy and Privacy Standards under the GATS' (2012) 7 Asian Journal of WTO & International Health Law and Policy 25, 38.

[81] Krajewski, *National Regulation and Trade Liberalization in Services* 158.

[82] Concerning the overlap between Articles XX (b) and (g) GATT 1994, see Bradly J Condon, 'GATT Article XX and Proximity of Interest: Determining the Subject Matter of Paragraphs b and g' (2004) 9 UCLA Journal of International Law and Foreign Affairs 137.

[83] Cottier, Delimatsis and Diebold, 'Article XIV GATS' 302.

measures are made effective in conjunction with equivalent measures imposed domestically.[84] This may indicate that, in the context of GATS, subparagraph (b) should be interpreted widely. However, this does not mitigate the concerns raised by the exclusion of justification grounds like in Article XX (g) GATT 1994 for two reasons. First, the measure must still be necessary under Article XIV (b) GATS, as opposed to merely 'related to' under the aforementioned GATT 1994 provision. As discussed below, 'related to' is a much lower legal hurdle. Second, the term 'exhaustible natural resources' in Article XX (g) GATT 1994 includes not only living (i.e. animals and plants) but also non-living (e.g. air, water, soil) natural resources.[85] Certainly, 'living' natural resources can overlap with Article XX (b) GATT 1994. However, non-living exhaustible natural resources cannot be included in Article XIV (b) GATS unless a link with the protection of health or life can be established.

Aside from the necessity requirement, there should be an *identifiable* risk to life or health before a measure can be justifiable under subparagraph (b).[86] The responding Member must make a *prima facie* case that the risk exists and the complaining Member may seek to rebut this claim.[87] This risk may overlap with concerns related to public morals or public order. However, considering that the same necessity test would apply, this distinction is of no practical consequence here.[88] From a regulatory autonomy perspective, it is important to note that a Member is not required to treat all similar health risks in the same way.[89] Moreover, Members are free to determine, within the limits of the meaning of the terms, what constitutes a risk for life or health.[90] For example, a Member may base its policies on scientific sources that diverge from the majority opinion, such as maverick science.[91]

---

[84] WT/CTE/W/9, Committee on Trade and Environment, Environment and Services, 8 June 1995 para. 8.

[85] *US – Shrimp (AB)* para. 131.

[86] *EC – Asbestos (AB)* paras 157–163; *EC – Asbestos (Panel)* para. 8.170; *EC – Seal Products (AB)* para. 5.197.

[87] *US – Gambling (Panel)* para. 6.514.

[88] Cottier, Delimatsis and Diebold, 'Article XIV GATS' 303.

[89] *EC – Asbestos (Panel)* paras 8.170–8.171; an approach endorsed in *EC – Seal Products (AB)* para. 5.200.

[90] Cottier, Delimatsis and Diebold, 'Article XIV GATS' 306.

[91] *EC – Asbestos (AB)* paras 168 and 178.

1.1.1.1.3 EXTRATERRITORIALITY AND ARTICLES XIV (A) AND (B) GATS

The complex issue of extraterritoriality is outside the scope of this book, and is therefore only touched upon briefly. However, it must be noted that one crucial unanswered question remains regarding the scope of justifying measures with extraterritorial reach under the general exceptions. In GATS, these concerns are particularly relevant for subparagraphs (a) and (b). As noted by the AB:

> [c]onditioning access to a Member's domestic market on whether exporting Members comply with, or adopt, a policy or policies unilaterally prescribed by the importing Member may, to some degree, be a common aspect of measures falling within the scope of one or another of the exceptions (a) to (j) of Article XX.[92]

Extraterritorial concerns are most relevant for Modes 1 and 2, and are less – or not at all – relevant for Modes 3 and 4.[93] Taking the example of public morals, three types of extraterritorial measures can be envisaged:[94]

a. Measures protecting public morals of inhabitants in the Member's territory directly. For example, in *US – Gambling* the ban on internet gambling protected *inter alia* against organised crime in the US.
b. Measures protecting persons involved in the economic activity in the exporting Member. For example, an import ban on products produced through child labour.

---

[92] *US – Shrimp (AB)* para. 121. In *United States – Import Prohibition of Certain Shrimp and Shrimp Products (Recourse to Article 21.5 of the DSU by Malaysia)* WT/DS58/AB/RW, AB report adopted 21 November 2001, the AB made clear that para. 121 is 'a fundamental basis of the original holding' of the original *US – Shrimp* report. Robert Howse, 'The Appellate Body Rulings in the *Shrimp/Turtle* Case: A New Legal Baseline for the Trade and Environment Debate' (2002) 27 Columbia Journal of Environmental Law 491, 501.

[93] Diebold, 'The Morals and Order Exceptions in WTO Law: Balancing the Toothless Tiger and the Undermining Mole' 70 explains that: 'Regulations on consumption of services abroad (mode 2) are very likely to have extraterritorial effects, as for example the prosecution of a tourist in his country of origin for soliciting child prostitution in a foreign country. Similarly, regulations restricting the service crossing into a Member's own territory (mode 1) may have extraterritorial effects, for instance if they are designed to protect values in the country from which the service originates'.

[94] The typology and examples were set forth by Wu, 'Free Trade and the Protection of Public Morals: An Analysis of the Newly Emerging Public Morals Clause Doctrine' 235–236.

c. Measures targeted at an exporting Member because the importing Member finds the practices of or in the exporting Member against its own public morals. For example, a ban on imports from or exports to a dictatorial regime.

However, measures, such as the measures at issue in *EC – Seal Products*, will often cater for type a concerns (animal cruelty considered insupportable by the European public) and also type b concerns (animal welfare concerns abroad).[95] Similarly, an import prohibition for child pornography could clearly fall within types a and b. It remains to be seen whether a measure protecting public morals only in the sense of type b would be considered to fall within the scope of the public morals exception. The same applies for a type c measure.[96] In both cases, this could be seen as the imposition of moral values which may not be shared by the exporting Member.[97] A regulator may thus be well informed to clarify the purpose of public morals related measures in the broader sense, i.e. in so far as they address both domestic and foreign concerns. A contextual basis confirming this interpretation is the GATS preamble's mention of *national* policy objectives.[98] However, generally, it will not be overly difficult to find a domestic aspect to a legitimate public morals claim, as *EC – Seal Products* demonstrates.

---

[95] Steve Charnovitz, 'The Moral Exception in Trade Policy' (1998) 38 Virginia Journal of International Law 689, 695–696 gives several examples; Howse and Langille, 'Permitting Pluralism: The Seal Products Dispute and Why the WTO Should Accept Trade Restrictions Justified by Noninstrumental Moral Values' 414.

[96] Type c measures are potentially the most contentious from a systemic perspective as they bring us into the realm of the human rights and trade interplay, which is outside the scope of this book. For examples of this approach, see Robert Howse, 'The World Trade Organization and the Protection of Workers' Rights' (1999) 3 Journal of Small and Emerging Business Law 131; Michael J Trebilcock and Robert Howse, 'Trade Policy & Labor Standards' (2005) 14 Minnesota Journal of Global Trade 261; Gareth Davies, 'Morality Clauses and Decision Making in Situations of Scientific Uncertainty: The Case of GMOs' (2007) 6 World Trade Review 249.

[97] Diebold, 'The Morals and Order Exceptions in WTO Law: Balancing the Toothless Tiger and the Undermining Mole' 69. Diebold notes that the measure must be primarily aimed at type a protection of public morals.

[98] Ibid.

1.1.1.1.4 SECURING COMPLIANCE WITH LAWS OR REGULATIONS The Panels in *US – Gambling* and *Argentina – Financial Services* explained that a successful defence on the basis of Article XIV (c) GATS – a provision which is very similar to Article XX (d) GATT 1994 – requires that, aside from satisfying the necessity test, two cumulative conditions are met:[99]

a. The measure for which justification is claimed must secure compliance with other laws or regulations. 'Laws or regulations' comprises all 'rules that form part of the domestic legal system of a WTO Member' and therefore includes international rules if such rules are incorporated or have direct effect in the domestic legal system.[100] 'Securing compliance' has been interpreted to mean 'enforcing obligations under' such laws and regulations, rather than ensuring the attainment of the objectives of such laws and regulations.[101] The use of coercion is not necessary.[102] A measure does not need to be designed exclusively to secure such compliance.[103] In other words, the design of the measure must contribute to securing compliance.[104] As with the previous policy grounds, and linked to the necessity test, a Member is free to determine the level of enforcement it deems appropriate.[105]
b. These other laws or regulations must not be inconsistent with GATS. This requirement is crucial and was not fulfilled in several disputes concerning Article XX (d) GATT 1994.[106] The three types

---

[99] *US – Gambling (Panel)* para. 6.536; *Argentina – Measures Relating to Trade in Goods and Services*, WT/DS453, Panel Report not yet adopted para. 7.592.

[100] *Mexico – Tax Measures on Soft Drinks and Other Beverages* WT/DS308/AB/R, AB report adopted 24 March 2006 para. 69. They do not include international obligations resting on *another* Member.

[101] *European Economic Community – Regulation on Imports of Parts and Components* L/6657, GATT Panel report, adopted 16 May 1990, BISD 37S/132 paras 5.14–5.18; *US – Gambling (Panel)* para. 6.538.

[102] *Mexico – Taxes on Soft Drinks (AB)* paras 75 and 77.

[103] *Korea – Measures Affecting Imports of Fresh, Chilled and Frozen Beef* WT/DS161/R, Panel report adopted 10 January 2001 para. 658; *US – Gambling (Panel)* paras 6.539 and 6.554–6.556.

[104] *Mexico – Taxes on Soft Drinks (AB)* paras 75 and 77.

[105] *Korea – Various Measures on Beef (AB)* paras 176 and 181; *Dominican Republic – Import and Sale of Cigarettes (AB)* para. 23.

[106] *Brazil – Retreaded Tyres (Panel)* paras 7.387–7.388; *China – Measures Affecting Imports of Automobile Parts* WT/DS339/R, WT/DS340/R,

> of 'other laws or regulations' mentioned in Article XIV (c) GATS are merely illustrative.[107] Although Member's laws are presumed to be WTO consistent,[108] it is for the invoking Member to establish that the other laws and regulations are consistent with GATS if the complaining Member asserts that this is not the case.[109] The invoking Member must name the other law or regulation, explain it and provide the text of it.[110]

It may be noted that these two requirements have been considered together by the AB in the context of Article XX (d) GATT 1994,[111] which is textually very similar to Article XIV (c) GATS.[112]

1.1.1.1.5 EQUITABLE OR EFFECTIVE IMPOSITION OR COLLECTION OF DIRECT TAXES Measures inconsistent with Article XVII GATS can be justified under subparagraph (d) of Article XIV GATS if they are aimed at ensuring the equitable or effective imposition or collection of direct taxes.[113] In other words, if a measure is aimed at the objectives of equitable or effective imposition or collection of direct taxes, a Member may deviate from Article XVII GATS as long as the requirements of the chapeau are met.[114] Footnote 6 to the subparagraph lists, in a non-exhaustive way,[115] six types of equitable or effective measures. These

---

WT/DS342/R, Panel report adopted 12 January 2009 paras 7.293–7.296; *Thailand – Customs and Fiscal Measures on Cigarettes from the Philippines* WT/DS371/R, Panel report adopted 15 July 2011 para. 7.758.

[107] *US – Gambling (Panel)* para. 6.538.

[108] *United States – Countervailing Duties on Certain Corrosion-Resistant Carbon Steel Flat Products from Germany* WT/DS213/AB/R, AB report adopted 19 December 2002 para. 115; *US – Gambling (Panel)* para. 6.549.

[109] *US – Gambling (Panel)* para. 6.547. The Panel refers to WTO consistency, but the text of Article XIV (c) GATS clearly indicates that the other laws and regulations must be consistent with '*this* Agreement', i.e. with GATS.

[110] Ibid para. 6.550.

[111] *Korea – Various Measures on Beef (AB)* para. 157.

[112] *US – Gambling (Panel)* para. 6.537.

[113] Consequentially, Article XIV (d) GATS confirms that a direct income tax measure could fall within the scope of Article XVII GATS. See *United States – Tax Treatment for 'Foreign Sales Corporations'*, WT/DS108/R, Panel Report adopted 20 March 2000, para. 8.143.

[114] Cottier, Delimatsis and Diebold, 'Article XIV GATS' 311.

[115] Peter Van den Bossche and Werner Zdouc, *The Law and Policy of the World Trade Organization* (3rd edn, Cambridge University Press 2013) 592. According to Cottier, Delimatsis and Diebold, 'Article XIV GATS' 311, the listing is exhaustive. They refer to the General Agreement on Tariffs and Trade,

provisions are particularly relevant to measures seeking to combat tax avoidance.[116] Moreover, the footnote explains that any tax terms or concepts in the subparagraph and the footnote are to be 'determined according to tax definitions and concepts, or equivalent or similar definitions and concepts, under the domestic law of the Member taking the measure'. Nonetheless, Article XXVIII (o) GATS states that the concept of 'direct taxes':

> [c]omprises all taxes on total income, on total capital or on elements of income or of capital, including taxes on gains from the alienation of property, taxes on estates, inheritances and gifts, and taxes on the total amounts of wages or salaries paid by enterprises, as well as taxes on capital appreciation.[117]

It has been argued that the number of tax measures that could fall within the scope of subparagraph (d) is limited because few measures aiming at the protection of the Member's tax base or offsetting the avoidance or evasion of taxes will violate the national treatment obligation. This is the case because the purpose of these measures is precisely to maintain *equal* conditions of competition.[118] Thus, there would be no modification of the conditions of competition. This provision has not yet been interpreted in the case law. From the perspective of regulatory autonomy, this exception allows Members to discriminate between foreign and domestic like services and service suppliers, if the differentiation is aimed at the equitable and effective imposition and collection of taxes.[119]

1.1.1.1.6 AVOIDANCE OF DOUBLE TAXATION Article XIV (e) GATS has never been invoked or referred to in WTO dispute settlement. It provides a justification for measures that violate the MFN obligation, if the difference in treatment between Members is the result of an agreement or

---

MTN.GNS/W/178, Taxation Issues Related to Article XIV(d), Note by the Secretariat, 15 November (1993) para. 3. Here, the Secretariat notes that the absence of a term such as 'including' indicates that the listing is exhaustive. However, this document discusses a *draft* of GATS. In the final version, the term 'including' was added.

116 Krajewski, *National Regulation and Trade Liberalization in Services* 160.

117 On the linkages between the WTO and direct taxation, see Michael Lang, Judith Herdin and Ines Hofbauer (eds), *The WTO and Direct Taxation* (Kluwer 2005) and Michael Daly, *The WTO and Direct Taxation* (WTO Discussion Paper 9, 2005).

118 Cottier, Delimatsis and Diebold, 'Article XIV GATS' 310.

119 Krajewski, *National Regulation and Trade Liberalization in Services* 159.

provisions on the avoidance of double taxation. Double taxation occurs in the situation where 'the same income, in the hands of the same taxpayer, is liable to tax in different States'.[120] Article 59 SCM Agreement contains a similar exception for prohibited export subsidies.[121] Similarly to subparagraph (d), relatively few tax measures aimed at avoiding double taxation would violate the MFN obligation by modifying the conditions of competition between two Members.[122] For example, the WTO Secretariat has noted that according less favourable treatment to affiliates in low-taxed jurisdictions does not violate the MFN obligation because it does not distinguish on the basis of the country of origin of the service supplier but rather on the location of its affiliates.[123] Of course, this would not apply if the service supplier itself was located in a low-taxed jurisdiction. Similarly, maintaining a list of countries that either qualify or do not qualify for the application of a particular measure (e.g. because they are low-taxed jurisdictions) does not violate the MFN obligation if the list is based on 'objective criteria designed to counter tax avoidance and not on the basis of nationality distinctions'.[124]

Further, Article XXII:3 GATS notes that a Member may not invoke the national treatment obligation with respect to a measure of another Member that falls within the scope of an international double taxation agreement between them. This applies to the consultation phase preceding dispute settlement, but also vis-à-vis recourse to the actual dispute settlement and enforcement phases. In other words, a Member may not bring a claim of a violation of Article XVII GATS before WTO dispute settlement if it concerns a measure falling within the scope of a double taxation agreement. Article XX:3 GATS explains that if the Members do not agree whether the measure falls within such a scope, the matter may be referred to the Council for Trade in Services (CTS), which may then refer the matter for binding arbitration.

---

[120] *United States – Tax Treatment for 'Foreign Sales Corporations'*, WT/DS108/AB/R, Appellate Body Report adopted 20 March 2000, para. 137.

[121] See ibid paras 132 and 137.

[122] Cottier, Delimatsis and Diebold, 'Article XIV GATS' 310.

[123] General Agreement on Tariffs and Trade, MTN.GNS/W/178, Taxation Issues Related to Article XIV(d), Note by the Secretariat, 15 November 2.

[124] Ibid.

1.1.1.2 The required nexus between the measure and the policy ground

1.1.1.2.1 ARTICLES XIV (A)–(C) GATS: 'NECESSARY' The necessity test in Articles XIV GATS and XX GATT 1994 has been the subject of much case law and academic debate,[125] as it is a key factor in the assessment of the justifiability of a measure under the general exceptions in the aforementioned agreements.[126] In the words of the WTO Secretariat, necessity tests reflect the balance between preserving regulatory autonomy and discouraging undue restrictions on trade.[127] According to the current case law,[128] the necessity requirement should be interpreted as requiring the responding Member to make a prima facie case that the measure is 'significantly closer to the pole of "indispensable" than to the opposite pole of simply "making a contribution to"' achieving 'objectives relating to' the policy grounds in the relevant subparagraph.[129]

According to established case law, the necessity analysis is carried out through 'a process of weighing and balancing a series of factors'.[130] In *US – Gambling*, the AB summarised that, in most cases, four elements are especially relevant for this analysis. These are:

---

[125] See e.g. Donald H Regan, 'The Meaning of "Necessary" in GATT Article XX and GATS Article XIV: The Myth of Cost–Benefit Balancing' (2007) 6 World Trade Review 347; McGrady, 'Necessity Exceptions in WTO Law: Retreaded Tyres, Regulatory Purpose and Cumulative Regulatory Measures'; Gisèle Kapterian, 'A Critique of the WTO Jurisprudence on Necessity' (2010) 59 International and Comparative Law Quarterly 89.

[126] Emily Reid, 'Regulatory Autonomy in the EU and WTO: Defining and Defending Its Limits' (2010) 44 Journal of World Trade 877, 892 and 894.

[127] Henning Grosse Ruse-Khan, A Comparative Analysis of Policy Space in WTO Law (Max Planck Institute for Intellectual Property, Competition & Tax Law Research Paper 08-02, 2008) 22.

[128] The more recent, and more flexible, interpretation of necessity addresses inadequacies in the narrower, earlier construct. See, regarding the latter construct, Deborah A Osiro, 'GATT/WTO Necessity Analysis: Evolutionary Interpretation and its Impact on the Authority of Domestic Regulation' (2002) 29 Legal Issues of Economic Integration 123.

[129] *US – Gambling (AB)* paras 309–310, with reference to *Korea – Various Measures on Beef (AB)* para. 161.

[130] *Korea – Various Measures on Beef (AB)* para. 164. The actual 'weighing and balancing' occurs in a holistic manner and has been criticised. For example, Joel P Trachtman, 'International Legal Control of Domestic Administrative Action' (2014) 17 Journal of International Economic Law 753, 767–768.

a. The relative importance of the interests or values furthered by the challenged measure.[131] In the case of subparagraph (c), the relevant interests or values are those intended to be protected by the laws or regulations to be enforced.[132] If an interest is considered important, the measure is more likely to be considered necessary.[133] Whether societal interests are important can be discerned from, for example, parliamentary statements.[134] For instance, the AB has recognised that the protection of human health and life against life-threatening health risks is 'vital and important in the highest degree'.[135] The Panel in *US – Gambling* decided that the same applies to the 'threat of money laundering, organized crime, fraud and risks to children (i.e underage gambling) and to health (i.e. pathological gambling)'.[136] The evaluation of a policy objective by panels or the AB has been criticised as being illegitimate, for example by second-guessing domestic regulatory choices or hierarchising them.[137] Although this only mitigates the raised concern to some extent, it should be noted that no interest has been considered unimportant by a panel,[138] or by the AB.[139] More importantly, contrary to what has been suggested in the aforementioned criticism,[140] this element of the necessity analysis does *not* consist of a balancing test and actually *enhances* regulatory autonomy *if* the interest is considered

---

131 *US – Gambling (AB)* para. 306, with reference to *Korea – Various Measures on Beef (AB)* para. 162, and *EC – Asbestos (AB)* para. 172.

132 *US – Gambling (Panel)* paras 6.542 and 6.557–6.558.

133 Ibid para. 6.477, with reference to *Korea – Various Measures on Beef (AB)* para. 162.

134 *US – Gambling (Panel)* para. 6.559.

135 *EC – Asbestos (AB)* para. 172.

136 *US – Gambling (Panel)* paras 6.489 and 6.558.

137 See e.g. Maxine Kennet, Jan Neumann and Elisabeth Türk, *Second Guessing National Level Policy Choices: Necessity, Proportionality and Balance in the WTO Services Negotiations* (Center for International Environmental Law Discussion Paper, 2003) 3; Geert Van Calster, 'Faites Vos Jeux: Regulatory Autonomy and the World Trade Organisation after *Brazil Tyres*' (2008) 20 Journal of Environmental Law 121, 134; McGrady, 'Necessity Exceptions in WTO Law: *Retreaded Tyres*, Regulatory Purpose and Cumulative Regulatory Measures' 162–163; Kapterian, 'A Critique of the WTO Jurisprudence on Necessity' 118–121.

138 McGrady, 'Necessity Exceptions in WTO Law: *Retreaded Tyres*, Regulatory Purpose and Cumulative Regulatory Measures' 162–163.

139 Regan, 'The Meaning of "Necessary" in GATT Article XX and GATS Article XIV: The Myth of Cost–Benefit Balancing' 362–363.

140 Kapterian, 'A Critique of the WTO Jurisprudence on Necessity' 121.

important,[141] which would be the case for many policy objectives in Article XIV GATS. As summarised by one author:

> Granting an extra margin of appreciation is a regulator-*friendly* move. Of course, giving a greater margin of appreciation when the purpose is important logically entails giving a relatively lesser margin of appreciation when the purpose is less important; but I have just pointed out that, even without any margin of appreciation at all, if it is clear there is no less-restrictive alternative, the respondent Member wins. So the margin of appreciation works in principle to the regulator's advantage.[142]

b. The contribution of the measure to the realisation of the ends pursued by the measure.[143] The relevant ends are the ends pursued *by the measure*.[144] As noted, these do not necessarily reflect the interest of the subparagraph *directly*: it suffices that the ends pursued by the measure fall within the scope of the policy grounds listed in the subparagraphs.[145] For example, the ends pursued by a measure could be 'to protect public morals by avoiding the dissemination of goods containing prohibited [audio-visual] content'.[146] Under subparagraph (c), one must assess the contribution of the measure to the securing of compliance with the other laws or regulations.[147] A greater contribution indicates that the measure is more likely to be necessary.[148]

A Member should seek to establish the contribution of its measure to the achievement of the ends pursued through past or present evidence or data.[149] Considering the difficulty of establishing such a contribution in the short term, especially in the context of comprehensive policies consisting of multiple measures, it may be sufficient – in the context of the weighing and balancing of the several relevant elements of the necessity test[150] – for a Member to

---

141 Regan, 'The Meaning of "Necessary" in GATT Article XX and GATS Article XIV: The Myth of Cost–Benefit Balancing' 353.

142 Ibid (emphasis original).

143 *US – Gambling (AB)* para. 306, with reference to *Korea – Various Measures on Beef (AB)* para. 164.

144 *US – Gambling (Panel)* para. 6.494.

145 Ibid para. 6.487.

146 *China – Publications and Audiovisual Products (AB)* para. 243.

147 *US – Gambling (Panel)* paras 6.542, 6.557 and 6.559.

148 Ibid para. 6.477, with reference to *Korea – Various Measures on Beef (AB)* para. 163.

149 *Brazil – Retreaded Tyres (AB)* para. 151.

150 *EC – Seal Products (AB)* paras 5.210–5.215.

demonstrate that the measure is apt to produce a material contribution to the achievement of ends pursued by the measure.[151] A Member may demonstrate this through, for example, quantitative projections or qualitative reasoning based on hypotheses that are tested and supported by evidence.[152] More generally, the AB clarified that selecting 'a methodology to assess a measure's contribution is a function of the nature of the risk, the objective pursued, and the level of protection sought', and 'also depends on the nature, quantity, and quality of evidence existing at the time the analysis is made'.[153] This approach has been criticised by Bown and Trachtman, who have argued that the ruling means 'we must assume in the future that any measure that contributes to health, no matter how minimally, will satisfy the necessity test under Article XX(b)' GATT 1994.[154] Such a criticism has since been alleviated by subsequent AB rulings. First, as noted, in *China – Publications and Audiovisual Products*, the AB made it clear that it would not accept that a measure makes a material contribution without sufficient evidence from the respondent in that regard.[155] Second, in *EC – Seal Products*, the AB placed a strong emphasis on the weighing and balancing of all relevant elements in the necessity test.[156]

c. The restrictive impact of the measure on international trade.[157] What is crucial here is an assessment of the extent to which 'the provisions restrict those wishing to engage in importing'.[158] In other words, the relevant question is whether importation is suppressed by the measure.[159] Hence, the focus is on relations between

---

151 *Brazil – Retreaded Tyres (AB)* para. 151. In *China – Publications and Audiovisual Products (AB)* para. 294, the AB found that the Panel had erred in accepting that a measure was apt to produce a material contribution, in light of the absence of sufficient evidence from China that this would be the case.

152 *Brazil – Retreaded Tyres (AB)* para. 151.

153 Ibid para. 145.

154 Bown and Trachtman, '*Brazil – Measures Affecting Imports of Retreaded Tyres*: A Balancing Act' 125–126.

155 *China – Publications and Audiovisual Products (AB)* para. 294.

156 *EC – Seal Products (AB)* paras 5.210–5.215.

157 *US – Gambling (AB)* para. 306, with reference to *Korea – Various Measures on Beef (AB)* para. 164.

158 *China – Publications and Audiovisual Products (AB)* para. 308.

159 *Colombia – Indicative Prices and Restrictions on Ports of Entry* WT/DS366/R, Panel report adopted 20 May 2009 para. 7.597.

the complainant and the respondent.[160] Surges in exports from the Member taking the measure may be relevant in answering this question.[161] Nonetheless, the assessment of the restrictive impact of the measure on international trade *could* extend beyond the mere trade restrictive effect on imports.[162] These findings, held in the context of a dispute concerning a violation of the national treatment obligation, highlight that the interpretation of the condition of restrictive impact is to be assessed on a factual basis vis-à-vis the specific obligation that was violated by the measure.[163] If the measure is less restrictive on trade, it is more likely to be considered necessary.[164]

d. Whether a genuine, reasonably available and less trade restrictive alternative is available, taking into account the importance of the interests or values at issue.[165] The responding Member's (light) burden of proof to establish a *prima facie* case of necessity appears to be met when the Member shows that the measure is *bona fide* and reasonable vis-à-vis the policy goal.[166] It is then for the complaining Member to advance an alternative, following which the responding Member will seek to demonstrate that the alternative is not reasonably available.[167] The alternative should be consistent, or less inconsistent, with the WTO agreements than the original measure.[168] An alternative is not a genuine, reasonably available alternative where:
   (i) The alternative contributes less to the objective than the measure.[169] In the absence of a clear contribution by the measure under scrutiny, determining whether an alternative contributes equally or more to the objective may be a complex

---

160 *EC – Seal Products (Panel)* paras 7.472–7.482.

161 *Colombia – Ports of Entry (Panel)* para. 7.597.

162 *China – Publications and Audiovisual Products (AB)* para. 306.

163 Andrew Mitchell and Caroline Henckels, 'Variations on a Theme: Comparing the Concept of "Necessity" in International Investment Law and WTO Law' (2013) 14 Chicago Journal of International Law 93, 32 (of SSRN working paper).

164 *US – Gambling (Panel)* para. 6.477, with reference to *Korea – Various Measures on Beef (AB)* para. 163.

165 *US – Gambling (AB)* paras 307 and 311.

166 Eric Leroux, 'Eleven Years of GATS Case Law: What Have We Learned?' (2007) 10 Journal of International Economic Law 749, 789.

167 *China – Publications and Audiovisual Products (AB)* paras 319 and 324.

168 Ibid para. 318.

169 *Korea – Various Measures on Beef (AB)* paras 163 and 166.

undertaking.[170] For example, entering into bilateral consultations is a process, with uncertain outcomes, which cannot be compared to an actual unilateral measure.[171] Another example is the case where a proposed alternative is a complementary measure to the actual measure, rather than an alternative.[172] A complementary measure can, in abstracto, be distinguished from an alternative by examining three cumulative characteristics. First, a complementary measure is either in place or in the process of implementation. Second, it is aimed at the same objective as the measure under scrutiny. Third, it has a different effect on that objective as compared to the measure under scrutiny.[173]

As noted, if a measure's regulatory goal is construed narrowly, there would be fewer alternatives which contribute to that measure's objective. In other words, if a measure is part of a multi-pronged set of measures which, in turn, is part of a broader, encompassing policy, the complaining Member has less leeway to come up with alternatives. A more broadly defined objective allows a wider range of alternatives to contribute to that objective.[174] In *Brazil – Tyres*, the Panel interpreted the objective of Brazil's measure narrowly, with the aforementioned effects on the EU's proposed alternative. This narrow approach was subsequently criticised by Bown and Trachtman, who conclude that:

> Both the Panel and the Appellate Body failed to recognize that non-generation of waste tyres alone [the objective of the measure as defined by the Panel and the AB] is an impermissible level of

[170] Bown and Trachtman, '*Brazil – Measures Affecting Imports of Retreaded Tyres*: A Balancing Act' 126–127.

[171] *US – Gambling (AB)* para. 317.

[172] *Brazil – Retreaded Tyres (AB)* para. 172.

[173] These conditions have been proposed by McGrady, 'Necessity Exceptions in WTO Law: *Retreaded Tyres*, Regulatory Purpose and Cumulative Regulatory Measures' 167–168. According to Bown and Trachtman, '*Brazil – Measures Affecting Imports of Retreaded Tyres*: A Balancing Act' 127, the distinction should be based solely on the first factor. Whereas the second factor of McGrady's proposition is quite self-evident, the third is not. In my view, it is a correct addition.

[174] McGrady, 'Necessity Exceptions in WTO Law: *Retreaded Tyres*, Regulatory Purpose and Cumulative Regulatory Measures' 157–158, 166 and 168.

protection under Article XX. They therefore erroneously discounted alternative means of protecting health.[175]

However, a measure may be indirectly directed at an objective. Regulatory autonomy would be severely restricted if panels were to establish the regulatory goal of a measure in overly wide terms, such as 'the protection of health'. Of course, too narrow an understanding of a policy goal creates a situation in which no alternative would be suitable. Certainly, a balance must be struck.

(ii) The alternative is not less trade restrictive than the measure.[176] This condition has also been labelled 'not less WTO inconsistent'.[177] Consequently, it is not relevant whether the alternative, for example, leads to 'a less democratic regime'.[178] The footnote to Article 5.6 SPS Agreement

---

175 Bown and Trachtman, '*Brazil – Measures Affecting Imports of Retreaded Tyres*: A Balancing Act' 128–129.

176 *China – Publications and Audiovisual Products (AB)* para. 324.

177 See e.g. *Korea – Various Measures on Beef (AB)* para. 166.

178 Delimatsis, 'Protecting Public Morals in a Digital Age: Revisiting the WTO Rulings on *US – Gambling* and *China – Publications and Audiovisual Products*' 286–287, where Delimatsis argues the AB should have taken into account that the proposed alternative would lead to a less democratic regime regarding foreign publications in China. In his conclusion, at 292, he notes: 'the WTO judiciary advanced the view that a *more* democracy-impairing measure would be a *less* trade-restrictive measure' (emphasis original). In my view, this is the correct outcome when applying the necessity test as it stands. For a view opposing Delimatsis, but with the same approach to what the AB should have done, see Julia Ya Qin, 'Pushing the Limits of Global Governance: Trading Rights, Censorship and WTO Jurisprudence – A Commentary on the *China – Publications* Case' (2011) 10 Chinese Journal of International Law 271, 320–321. Both Delimatsis, arguing that the AB *should* have steered Chinese domestic politics, and Qin, who claims the AB has but shouldn't have, are thus unhappy with the AB's ruling. I do not share either author's concern. The task of the AB is to apply international trade law rules. Indeed, in the view of Michael Ming Du, 'Has the WTO Appellate Body Pushed the Limits of Global Governance in the *China – Publications* Case? A Reply to Julia Ya Qin' (2012) 11 Chinese Journal of International Law 227, 232, the AB showed deference to regulatory autonomy, which 'is politically savvy and indeed helps the AB steer clear of potential political thunderstorms that will otherwise arise from adjudicating on such a politically sensitive dispute'. In my view, the AB indeed followed such an approach in this case. Both Qin and Du point out that the result of the ruling may well be that China will enact more trade-restrictive and more stringent censorship rules, which will nonetheless be more consistent with WTO law. Although this

contains an additional requirement that the alternative is *significantly* less trade restrictive than the measure. The omission of such an explicit requirement in GATS and GATT 1994 indicates that this is not the case for an alternative under Articles XIV GATS or XX GATT 1994.[179] The Panel in *China – Publications and Audiovisual Products* did however explicitly recognise that an alternative that is not just marginally less trade restrictive would weigh heavier against finding that a measure is necessary.[180]

(iii) The alternative is merely theoretical in nature (e.g. where the Member is not capable of taking it).[181]

(iv) The alternative imposes an undue burden on the Member, such as prohibitive costs or substantial technical difficulties.[182] *Some* costs or burdens do not render an alternative unavailable.[183] In this sense, there is a cost-benefit analysis, balancing the trade cost against the cost of enforcing or implementing the alternative.[184]

(v) The alternative does not preserve the Member's right to achieve its desired level of protection with respect to the objective pursued under the subparagraph.[185] The 'level of protection' should be understood as the degree to which the objective is to be fulfilled.[186] (The contribution of the measure is thus the contribution to the level of protection set with regard to the objective.) The AB has held, explicitly, that the right of a Member to set their own level of protection includes the right to opt for the maximum level of protection.[187]

---

may not be a morally or politically wanted outcome it is, in my view, the consequence of applying WTO law.

179 In the view of Delimatsis, 'Protecting Public Morals in a Digital Age: Revisiting the WTO Rulings on *US – Gambling* and *China – Publications and Audiovisual Products*' 287, the alternative accepted by the AB in *China – Publications and Audiovisual Products* is insufficiently less trade restrictive than the measure to consider the measure not necessary.

180 *China – Publications and Audiovisual Products (Panel)* para. 7.899.

181 *Brazil – Retreaded Tyres (AB)* para. 156; *US – Gambling (AB)* para. 308.

182 *US – Gambling (AB)* para. 308.

183 Ibid; *China – Publications and Audiovisual Products (AB)* para. 327.

184 Regan, 'The Meaning of "Necessary" in GATT Article XX and GATS Article XIV: The Myth of Cost–Benefit Balancing' 349.

185 *US – Gambling (AB)* para. 308.

186 *Brazil – Retreaded Tyres (AB)* para. 140.

187 Ibid para. 170.

However, the level of protection declared by a Member may be scrutinised by a panel or the AB. For example, in *Korea – Various Measures on Beef*, the AB noted that, although Korea had stated that it aimed to eliminate *all* fraud in the context of beef sales, such elimination could not be achieved through the measure.[188] Consequently, the AB determined that, based on the measures taken by the Korean government, the level of protection sought by Korea was not total but rather considerable elimination of fraud.[189] This finding has been criticised. The finding is analogous to that concerning the measure in *EC – Asbestos*, where the AB did not find that the purported level of protection was the actual level of protection.[190] However, the EU *did* ban asbestos. The AB stated Korea's measure should have reflected the purported level of protection in the actual level of protection.[191] Note that this question differs from the contribution analysis; it rather appears to ask whether the measure is capable of achieving the purported level of protection. In my view, this issue is comparable to the determination of an objective: the statement by the Member is but one relevant aspect of the assessment, and a panel or the AB should, in case of doubt, examine whether such a statement reflects reality.[192] If a measure cannot fulfil the said level of protection, or perhaps contribute in the context of multifaceted policies, it may be questioned whether the statement regarding the level of protection is strategic – i.e. with the purpose of limiting the available range of alternatives.

In conclusion, the AB's approach has, correctly, been called 'pragmatic in the sense that it both retains *de jure* regulatory autonomy,

---

[188] *Korea – Various Measures on Beef (AB)* para. 178.

[189] Ibid.

[190] Douglas A Irwin and Joseph Weiler, '*Measures Affecting the Cross-Border Supply of Gambling and Betting Services* (DS 285)' (2008) 7 World Trade Review 71, 107; Kapterian, 'A Critique of the WTO Jurisprudence on Necessity' 109.

[191] *Korea – Various Measures on Beef (AB)* paras 178–181.

[192] I thus agree with Mitchell and Henckels, 'Variations on a Theme: Comparing the Concept of "Necessity" in International Investment Law and WTO Law' 35 (of SSRN working paper).

but *de facto* allows balancing scrutiny to root out indefensible, haphazardly set risk levels'.[193]

It should be emphasised that, from a regulatory autonomy perspective, if an alternative is considered reasonably available, and the measure therefore is not necessary, this does not entail that the responding Member *must* employ the alternative.[194] Rather, it means that the measure cannot be provisionally justified under the relevant subparagraph, and that the Member must bring its measure into conformity with its obligations – which the Member may do in the way it prefers.[195]

To assess these four elements of the necessity test, i.e. to assess whether a measure is necessary for the attainment of the policy objective, a panel should look at: (i) a Member's characterisation of the measure's objectives; (ii) the effectiveness of the Member's regulatory approach; (iii) the structure and operation of the measure; and (iv) contrary evidence offered by the complaining Member.[196] The first and second criteria are to be assessed by looking at, for example, 'texts of statutes, legislative history, and pronouncements of government agencies or officials'.[197]

1.1.1.2.2 ARTICLES XIV (D)–(E) GATS: 'AIMED AT' AND 'IS THE RESULT OF'

In contrast to the requirement that a measure is necessary for the policy objective, required by subparagraphs (a)–(c), subparagraphs (d) and (e) contain a different nexus requirement between the measure and the policy objective. Under Article XX GATT 1994, several nexus requirements, aside from necessity, can be found: essential (paragraph (j)); relating to (paragraphs (c), (e) and (g)); for the protection of (paragraph (f)); in pursuance of (paragraph (h)); and involving (paragraph (i)). In Article XIV GATS, two further nexus requirements are inscribed: aimed at (paragraph (d)); and is the result of (paragraph (e)). As the AB has noted:

> It does not seem reasonable to suppose that the WTO Members intended to require, in respect of each and every category, the same kind or degree of

---

[193] Michael Ming Du, 'Autonomy in Setting Appropriate Level of Protection under the WTO Law: Rhetoric or Reality?' (2010) 13 Journal of International Economic Law 1077, 1101, with reference to Joseph Weiler, 'Comment, *Brazil – Measures Affecting Imports of Retreaded Tyres* (DS322)' (2009) 8 World Trade Review 137, 141.

[194] *China – Publications and Audiovisual Products (AB)* para. 335.

[195] Ibid.

[196] *US – Gambling (AB)* para. 304.

[197] Ibid.

> connection or relationship between the measure under appraisal and the state interest or policy sought to be promoted or realized.[198]

This statement referred to the 'relating to' nexus in Article XX (g) GATT 1994. This nexus has been considered a 'very light touch review' of regulatory autonomy.[199] The same may be said of the nexus requirement in subparagraph (d), but, arguably, not for that in subparagraph (e).

Recall that it is not the *measure* subject to justification under Article XIV (d) GATS that must be 'aimed at' the imposition of taxes, but rather the *difference in treatment* (i.e. the less favourable treatment resulting from a violation of Article XVII GATS). This limits the analysis of the nexus under the subparagraph: the text of the Article XIV (d) GATS implies that (contrary to AB case law for other policy grounds in the general exceptions provisions) not the whole measure, but merely the actual violation needs to be taken into account in the 'aimed at' analysis. However, the exhaustive list in footnote 6 to Article XIV (d) GATS states that *measures* 'aimed at' the objective are listed. This obfuscates the difference between the measure being aimed at the collection of taxes, and the violation being aimed at such collection. Nonetheless, the nexus required by this subparagraph would be relatively easy for the invoking Member to demonstrate.

Under Article XIV (e) GATS, the difference in treatment, i.e. less favourable treatment under Article II GATS, must be *the result of* an international tax agreement. Again, not the measure as a whole, but the actual violation, is the subject of the nexus analysis. Whereas, under subparagraph (d), the nexus allowed some room for manoeuvring as to the contribution of the measure (or the violation) to the objective, the nexus under subparagraph (e) requires a *causal* link: the difference in treatment must have been the 'result of' the international tax agreement. The AB clarified that the ordinary meaning of 'result' is 'an effect, issue, or outcome *from* some action, process or design'.[200] *A fortiori* to the AB's reasoning, the less favourable treatment must be 'an effect, issue or outcome' of an international tax agreement, or the international tax

---

198 *US – Gasoline (AB)* 17–18.

199 Reid, 'Regulatory Autonomy in the EU and WTO: Defining and Defending Its Limits' 892 and 894.

200 *United States – Definitive Safeguard Measures on Imports of Certain Steel Products* WT/DS248/AB/R, WT/DS249/AB/R, WT/DS251/AB/R, WT/DS252/AB/R, WT/DS253/AB/R, WT/DS254/AB/R, WT/DS258/AB/R, WT/DS259/AB/R, AB report adopted 10 December 2003 para. 315 (emphasis original).

agreement must 'result' in the less favourable treatment.[201] In the context of the nullification or impairment test of Article XXIII:1 (b) GATT 1994, the Panel in *Japan – Film* explained that the requirement that a Member's benefit under the agreement is nullified or impaired *as the result of* the application of a measure by another Member, which it labelled as 'causality', is 'one of the more factually complex areas' of the dispute.[202] Furthermore, the Panel stated that:

> Four issues related to causation merit general discussion. First, the question of the degree of causation that must be shown – 'but for' or less. Second, the relevance of the origin-neutral nature of a measure to causation of nullification or impairment. Third, the relevance of intent to causality. And fourth, the extent to which measures may be considered collectively in an analysis of causation.[203]

Considering the different context in which the Panel's statement was made, and the, perhaps limited, practical relevance of Article XIV (e) GATS, it is sufficient to note that the Panel's statement clarifies the complex nature of a causality analysis. The responding Member, invoking the exception, would need to provide sufficient evidence that there is a causal link between the international tax agreement and the less favourable treatment.[204] From the perspective of regulatory autonomy, this nexus is stricter than that required by Article XIV (d) GATS.

1.1.2 Second tier of the analysis: the chapeau[205]

The purpose and object of the chapeau is to prevent abuse of the subparagraphs in the general exceptions clause.[206] The chapeau provides

---

[201] Ibid.

[202] *Japan – Measures Affecting Consumer Photographic Film and Paper* WT/DS44/R, Panel report adopted 22 April 1998 paras 10.82–10.83.

[203] Ibid para. 10.83. In paras 10.84–10.88, the Panel considers each element in more detail.

[204] Note that in *Uruguayan Recourse to Article XXIII* L/1923, GATT Panel report, adopted 16 November 1962, BISD 11S/95 para. 15; *United States – Imports of Sugar from Nicaragua* L/5607, GATT Panel report, adopted 13 March 1984, BISD 31S/67 paras 5.20–5.23; and *Japan – Trade in Semi-Conductors* L/6309, GATT Panel report, adopted 4 May 1988, BISD 35S/116 para. 131, the lack of evidence regarding the causal link explained by the Panel in *Japan – Film* was crucial to the assessment of the nullification and impairment claim.

[205] The AB in *EC – Seal Products* rejected the Panel's approach of applying the same legal test to the chapeau and Article 2.1 TBT Agreement. *EC – Seal Products (AB)* paras 5.310–5.313.

[206] *US – Gasoline (AB)* 22.

a balancing mechanism between the right of a Member to invoke an exception and the duty of that Member to respect its obligations under the WTO agreements. In other words, the chapeau seeks to prevent a Member from abusing its rights.[207] In fact, the chapeau has been said to be an 'expression of the principle of good faith'.[208] Moreover, the AB has explained the importance of the chapeau under Article XIV GATS as follows:

> By requiring that the measure be *applied* in a manner that does not to constitute 'arbitrary' or 'unjustifiable' discrimination, or a 'disguised restriction on trade in services', the chapeau serves to ensure that Members' rights to avail themselves of exceptions are exercised reasonably, so as not to frustrate the rights accorded to other Members by the substantive rules of the GATS.[209]

The subparagraphs thus constitute a conditional exception to the substantive obligations, the condition being that compliance with the requirements of the chapeau can be demonstrated.[210] It should be stressed that the policy goal, under which the measure is provisionally justified, cannot provide the rationale or justification under the standards of the chapeau.[211]

A crucial element of the chapeau analysis is that it focuses 'not so much [on] the questioned measure or its specific contents as such, but rather [on] the manner in which that measure is applied'.[212] In order to be justifiable under the chapeau, a measure must not be applied in a manner that: (i) may constitute an arbitrary or unjustifiable discrimination between countries where like conditions prevail; and/or (ii) is a disguised restriction on trade.[213] These elements place both substantive and procedural requirements on the measure.[214] Moreover, the elements should be considered in the application of the measure resulting from the text of the

---

207 *US – Shrimp (AB)* para. 156.

208 Ibid para. 158.

209 *US – Gambling (AB)* para. 339 (emphasis original, footnote omitted).

210 *United States Section 337 of the Tariff Act of 1930* L/6439, GATT Panel report, adopted 7 November 1989, BISD 36S/345 para. 5.9; *US – Shrimp (AB)* para. 157.

211 *US – Shrimp (AB)* para. 149.

212 *US – Gasoline (AB)* 22 (footnote omitted).

213 See, for an application in the specific context of GATS, *US – Gambling (Panel)* para. 6.607.

214 *US – Shrimp (AB)* para. 160.

measure, from which the expected application may be derived,[215] and from the actual practice of applying the measure.[216] As concerns the text of the measure, it is relevant to examine the design, the architecture, and the revealing structure of a measure.[217] To illustrate this distinction, it may be noted that, in *US – Gambling*, the AB did not accept the 'inconclusive' evidence on the actual application of the measure in practice, which had been put forward by Antigua and accepted by the Panel. Rather, the AB said that, taking into account the limited evidence on the practical application of the measure, the Panel should have focused on the text of the provision to determine whether the application resulted in a violation of the chapeau requirements.[218]

Before addressing the three elements of the chapeau, it may be noted that it is unclear from the case law *how* precisely to distinguish between the three standards in the text of the chapeau. Namely, these standards are: (i) 'arbitrary discrimination'; (ii) 'unjustifiable discrimination'; and (iii) 'disguised restriction on trade'. The AB has noted that these three elements can be 'read side-by-side; they impart meaning to one another'.[219] Further, the AB has explained that the standards established in the chapeau are 'necessarily broad in scope and reach' and that '[w]hen applied in a particular case, the actual contours and contents of these standards will vary as the kind of measure under examination varies'.[220]

1.1.2.1 Arbitrary or unjustifiable discrimination between countries where like conditions prevail Although the requirement that a measure is not applied in a manner that constitutes arbitrary or unjustifiable discrimination between countries where like conditions prevail contains two different standards, these two conditions which are usually examined together in case law. The AB has clarified that three elements are relevant to an assessment of this condition:[221]

---

215 *EC – Seal Products (AB)* para. 5.302.
216 *US – Shrimp (AB)* para. 160.
217 *EC – Seal Products (AB)* para. 5.302.
218 *US – Gambling (AB)* paras 352–357.
219 *US – Gasoline (AB)* 25.
220 *US – Shrimp (AB)* para. 120. The AB explicitly states that, depending on the policy objective of the subparagraph under which the measure is provisionally justified, the standard of each element of the chapeau analysis may be different.
221 Ibid.

a. Whether the measure results in discrimination, of a different nature and quality to that under the substantive obligations. The circumstances leading to a finding of discrimination under a substantive obligation can be the same as those examined under the chapeau.[222] This element of discrimination encompasses both national treatment and MFN type discrimination.[223]

For example, in *US – Shrimp*, the discrimination analysis under the chapeau focused on the application of the measure, Section 609, through guidelines circulated by the US Department of State and through the practice of administrators responsible for certification requirements, as inscribed in Section 609.[224] Consequently, it was considered that the practical application of the measure resulted in discrimination. In *US – Gambling*, the Panel found instances of discrimination in the application of three federal statutes *in practice*, and *in the text* of a fourth measure, the Interstate Horseracing Act. The AB only upheld the finding of discrimination as concerns the discrimination 'at face' in the latter instance.[225] The former finding was rejected and the AB clarified that isolated examples of enforcement (in the context of Article XIV (c) GATS) are insufficient to determine whether the measure is 'enforced in a manner that discriminates between domestic and foreign service suppliers'. This was because the proper context of such a determination 'might include evidence on the overall number of suppliers, and on patterns of enforcement, and on the reasons for particular instances of non-enforcement', as well as on the wording of the measure.[226]

b. Whether that discrimination is arbitrary or unjustifiable in character. Consequentially, a certain degree of discrimination is allowed, as long as it is not arbitrary or unjustifiable.[227] In order to assess this

---

[222] *EC – Seal Products (AB)* para. 5.298. In para. 5.318, the AB concludes that 'in the present case, the causes of the "discrimination" found to exist under Article I:1 of the GATT 1994 are the same as those to be examined under the chapeau'.

[223] *Argentina – Measures Affecting the Export of Bovine Hides and the Import of Finished Leather* WT/DS155/R, Panel report adopted 16 February 2001 para. 11.314; *China – Measures Related to the Exportation of Rare Earths, Tungsten, and Molybdenum* WT/DS431/R, WT/DS432/R, WT/DS433/R, Panel report adopted 2 September 2014 para. 7.351.

[224] *US – Shrimp (AB)* para. 161.

[225] *US – Gambling (AB)* paras 368–369.

[226] Ibid paras 352–357.

[227] *China – Rare Earths (Panel)* para. 7.354.

element, one may focus on the *cause* or rationale of the discrimination, in light of the objective of the measure. In other words, there is arbitrary or unjustifiable discrimination when 'the reasons given for this discrimination bear no rational connection to the objective [of the measure[228]] falling within the purview of a paragraph of Article XX, or would go against that objective'.[229] Whether the discrimination is rationally related to the policy objective that has led to provisional justification is one more of the most important factors in the assessment of this element.[230] It should be noted that, although important, the rationale of the discrimination is not the only relevant element.[231] For example, the *effects* of the discrimination are another aspect which may be taken into account when assessing whether the discrimination is arbitrary or unjustifiable.[232]

Whether the application of a measure amounts to arbitrary or unjustifiable discrimination is a highly factual matter. The analysis is guided by the general principle that the purpose of the chapeau is to prevent abuse of the exceptions. For example, the Member should make comparable efforts vis-à-vis different categories of affected economic operators.[233] If basing treatment on statistics, the Member should treat countries with similar statistical characteristics in the same manner.[234] The Member's measure should take into account different circumstances in other Members, and the specific policies of those Members aimed at the same policy objective as the measure at issue.[235] The Member may not introduce price discrimination between domestic and foreign buyers by way of export quota for so-called conservational purposes where domestic consumption exceeds exports.[236]

In the context of measures with different objectives, the rational connection test may be considered overly stringent. The measure in *EC – Seal Products*, which effectively banned imports of seal

---

228 *Brazil – Retreaded Tyres (AB)* para. 232. Indeed, it is the objective of the measure under scrutiny which must bear a rational connection to the discrimination.

229 Ibid paras 229 and 246; *EC – Seal Products (AB)* paras 5.306 and 5.318.

230 *EC – Seal Products (AB)* para. 5.306.

231 *US – Shrimp (AB)* para. 176.

232 *Brazil – Retreaded Tyres (AB)* para. 230.

233 *US – Shrimp (Article 21.5 – Malaysia) (AB)* para. 122; *EC – Seal Products (AB)* para. 5.337.

234 *EC – Tariff Preferences (Panel)* paras 7.228–7.229 and 7.233–7.235.

235 *US – Shrimp (AB)* paras 163–164.

236 *China – Rare Earths (Panel)* paras 7.660–7.663, 7.835–7.836 and 7.962.

products, contained, *inter alia*, an exception for seal products resulting from hunting by indigenous communities (IC). According to the EU, the purpose of this exception was to mitigate the negative effects on those communities, which are protected through various international instruments, from the ban. Nonetheless, the AB argued that the EU had not explained:

> [W]hy the need to protect the economic and social interests of the Inuit and other indigenous peoples necessarily implies that the European Union cannot do anything further to ensure that the welfare of seals is addressed in the context of IC hunts, given that 'IC hunts can cause the very pain and suffering for seals that the EU public is concerned about'.[237]

This finding was exacerbated by the fact that the measure allowed, in its potential application, abuse of the IC exception. Ambiguities in the application of the exception meant that seal products from an IC hunt could enter the EU market even if they had been dubbed 'commercial'. By way of contrast, seal products from non-IC commercial hunts could not enter the EU market.[238] The application of the IC exception, which is designed without an anti-circumvention clause, leaves substantial discretion to the designated bodies who decide on the application of the exception.[239] Indeed, where the application of (part of) the measure is 'singularly informal and casual' and 'conducted in a manner such that these processes could result in the negation of rights of Members', there may be arbitrary or unjustifiable discrimination.[240] The AB considered these elements to be problematic, even though the protection of the economic interests of the IC was part of the rationale put forward by the EU for the inclusion of the IC exception.[241]

Therefore, it seems as if criticism that a measure cannot cater for multiple policy objectives and pass the rational connection test should take into account that the IC exception was faulted for allowing abuse. If that had not been the case, as with the other two exceptions to the measure, the lack of a rational connection may have been mitigated by a clearly circumscribed, explainable discrimination between commercial hunts and non-commercial IC

---

237 *EC – Seal Products (AB)* para. 5.320 (footnote omitted).

238 I.e. not, in reality, falling under the Seals Regulation's 'partial use' or 'subsistence' criteria.

239 *EC – Seal Products (AB)* paras 5.322–5.327.

240 *US – Shrimp (AB)* para. 181.

241 *EC – Seal Products (AB)* paras 5.322–5.330.

hunts. What is clear from the case law is that a Member must provide some degree of certainty that the application of the measure, or of parts of the measure, will be applied in a fair and just way by the designated domestic bodies.[242]

Finally, as noted, it is unclear how one should differentiate between arbitrary discrimination on the one hand and unjustifiable discrimination on the other.[243]

c. Whether the discrimination occurs between countries where like conditions prevail. Note that, under Article XX GATT 1994, the chapeau requires that the conditions between countries are *the same*, not just *like*. This difference in the text has not led to a different interpretation,[244] although it may be said that the language in GATS is more restrictive than under GATT 1994, in that it widens the group of countries regarding which discrimination may have occurred.

This third condition has been interpreted widely. For example, the importing Member and exporting Members may be countries where like conditions prevail.[245] However, only conditions relevant for the purpose of establishing whether there is discrimination, which is, moreover, arbitrary or unjustifiable 'in the light of the specific character of the measure at issue and the circumstances of a specific case' are to be taken into account.[246] Therefore, relevant conditions include those conditions relating to the particular policy objective under the applicable subparagraph, and those conditions relating to the finding of a violation of a substantive provision.[247]

In light of the intertwined nature of the three abovementioned elements, it is important to note that panels and the AB enjoy a large margin of

---

[242] *US – Shrimp (AB)* para. 181; *EC – Seal Products (AB)* para. 5.328.

[243] *US – Shrimp (AB)* para. 177, where the AB notes that the same findings that led to the conclusion that the discrimination in the application of the measure was 'unjustifiable' also constitute evidence that the discrimination is 'arbitrary'. In *Brazil – Retreaded Tyres (Panel)* para. 7.225, these two conditions are considered together because of the close relationship between them.

[244] See *US – Gambling (Panel)* paras 6.577–6.578, noting that the AB in *US – Shrimp* provided guidance on the interpretation of 'arbitrary or unjustifiable discrimination between countries where like conditions prevail', even though that case addressed Article XX GATT 1994, where the chapeau requires 'same conditions'.

[245] *US – Gasoline (AB)* 23–24.

[246] *EC – Seal Products (AB)* para. 5.299.

[247] Ibid para. 5.300.

discretion in the application of these elements, which should be interpreted 'as a whole' and 'in context'.[248]

1.1.2.2 Disguised restriction on trade The condition that a measure may not constitute a disguised restriction on trade overlaps with, but is not limited to, restrictions amounting to arbitrary or unjustifiable discrimination if the latter are disguised as a measure formally within the terms of a subparagraph.[249] Indeed, the term 'restriction' should not be interpreted narrowly, and includes discriminatory restrictions.[250] Moreover, a measure 'need not be formally "hidden" or "dissimulated"' to constitute a disguised restriction on trade.[251] As with the interpretation of the previous element, a finding that a measure is a disguised restriction on trade can be based on a range of relevant factors.[252] In practice, there has been considerably more attention on the previously discussed element, 'arbitrary or unjustifiable discrimination'.[253]

1.1.3 Implications for regulatory autonomy

Three elements in the analysis of the general exceptions discussed in this section have clear implications for regulatory autonomy: (i) the scope of the subparagraphs; (ii) the necessity test; and (iii) the chapeau analysis. First, the lack of an exception clause for the conservation of exhaustible natural resources in Article XIV GATS may become problematic when taking into account the way in which services have become integral to trade in goods.[254] However, aside from the more stringent necessity test, compared to the 'relating to' test in Article XX (g) GATT 1994, the exception for the protection of human, animal or plant life or health may, in many situations, suffice to justify measures which are aimed at protecting the environment. Moreover, recent case law on the public morals exception has clarified that the exceptions clause will be construed with deference to regulatory objectives that may not, at first sight, be covered by the exceptions. If a Member can establish that a measure protects a domestic public moral (for which, arguably, the threshold is not overly high) the measure may be justified under Article XIV (a)

---

248 Cottier, Delimatsis and Diebold, 'Article XIV GATS' 323–324.

249 *US – Gasoline (AB)* 25.

250 *EC – Asbestos (Panel)* para. 8.235.

251 *Brazil – Retreaded Tyres (Panel)* para. 7.319.

252 Ibid paras 7.321–7.322.

253 Cottier, Delimatsis and Diebold, 'Article XIV GATS' 325.

254 See e.g. National Board of Trade Sweden, *Everybody is in Services – The Impact of Servicification in Manufacturing on Trade and Trade Policy*.

GATS. This constitutes an important safety valve through which the list of policy grounds can reflect changing realities.

Second, as explained, the current interpretation of the necessity test in subparagraphs (a)–(c) allows ample room for regulators. It is true that, to some extent, the pragmatic approach may be criticised for falling short of 'a coherent legal doctrine on the degree of deference to be afforded to Members'.[255] However, the AB's analysis is already complex, often lengthy and contains many moving parts that allow adjudicators to weed out measures that should *not* be considered necessary. An overly formulistic and check-box-ticking approach should be avoided, and greater confidence should be placed in the AB and panels. Indeed, it appears that, while its legal reasoning may sometimes be criticised, the actual outcome of the AB's analysis is considered acceptable in the vast majority of cases. Therefore, in terms of balancing legal predictability with the dispute settlement mechanism's mandate to settle disputes, the current necessity test case law can be lauded.

Third, as concerns the interpretation of the chapeau, it remains true that, despite a substantial volume of case law, it is hard to draw general conclusions because the findings are so case-specific.[256] As the AB stated:

> The task of interpreting and applying the chapeau is, hence, essentially the delicate one of locating and marking out a line of equilibrium between the right of a Member to invoke an exception under Article XX and the rights of the other Members under varying substantive provisions […] The location of the line of equilibrium, as expressed in the chapeau, is not fixed and unchanging; the line moves as the kind and the shape of the measures at stake vary and as the facts making up specific cases differ.[257]

The requirement that the application of the measure does not constitute arbitrary or unjustifiable discrimination appears to be a strict test.

It has been argued that the impact of the chapeau on regulatory autonomy is less than that of the cumulative scope of the subparagraphs (and the omission of certain policy objectives therefrom).[258] The reason for this is that the chapeau mostly concerns the *application* of the measure. Consequentially, the chapeau should not review the Member's policy preferences. However, the line between the application of a

[255] Kapterian, 'A Critique of the WTO Jurisprudence on Necessity' 118.

[256] Krajewski, *National Regulation and Trade Liberalization in Services* 162; Cottier, Delimatsis and Diebold, 'Article XIV GATS' 322.

[257] *US – Shrimp (AB)* para. 159.

[258] Krajewski, *National Regulation and Trade Liberalization in Services* 163.

measure and the measure itself may be blurry.[259] As noted, for example, the design of the measure is reconsidered when examining the (potential) application of the measure (as it is considered in establishing whether the measure violates a non-discrimination obligation, and in the examination of the necessity test). However, my review of the case law does not confirm that the current interpretation of the chapeau is at odds with a Member's prerogative to adopt a particular level of protection.[260] On the contrary, it would seem that the chapeau safeguards regulatory autonomy, so long as it is exercised 'in good faith'.[261] That the analytical focus in WTO dispute settlement is on the chapeau rather than the domestic regulatory 'recipe' means that Members are left with 'sufficient breathing space' to regulate the subject matters which they deem important. Indeed, the focus is on the manner in which the recipe is applied.[262] Moreover, even if a violation of the chapeau is found, a Member maintains the possibility of bringing the measure into conformity without altering the level of protection; it must, however, eliminate discrimination in the application of the measure. Arguably, this can, in many cases, be achieved without repealing the measure, but by making minor alterations to its structure or application.

A notable observation in this regard – which also applies beyond the context of the general exceptions – is that when a Member must bring its measure into conformity with its WTO obligations, the modified measure may lead to *more* regulation or *more* trade restriction. Three examples may serve to explain this argument. First, in *US – Clove Cigarettes*, the panel and AB found that the US measure accorded less favourable treatment to (mainly imported) clove cigarettes compared to (mainly domestic) menthol cigarettes. As a consequence of this finding, it was asked 'whether the outcome has opened the domestic policy space so as to facilitate stronger health regulation'.[263] In order to bring its measure into conformity, the US could choose to ban menthol cigarettes as well – thereby advancing the objective of reducing health risks related to

---

[259] Reid, 'Regulatory Autonomy in the EU and WTO: Defining and Defending Its Limits' 894–895.

[260] Ibid.

[261] Sungjoon Cho, *Free Markets and Social Regulation: A Reform Agenda of the Global Trading System* (Kluwer Law International 2003) 4.

[262] Ibid 58–60.

[263] Benn McGrady, 'Menthol Cigarettes and *US – Clove Cigarettes*' (*O'Neill Institute for National and Global Health Law, Georgetown University*, 2013) <http://www.oneillinstitutetradeblog.org/menthol-cigarettes-and-us-clove-cigarettes/> accessed 10 January 2015, no longer available online.

smoking. (Perhaps the WTO ruling could even be used to counter domestic resistance against a ban on menthol cigarettes).[264] This observation casts doubt upon the view that WTO rulings generally have a deregulatory, pro-trade impact on non-trade policies.[265] Of course, equally, the US could choose to repeal the measure and allow clove cigarettes to be sold on its market once again. It is crucial to understand that WTO adjudicators do not require, or even prefer, one solution over the other. It may well be said that, in this regard, the WTO discourages policymakers from introducing a policy objective in gradual steps, *in casu* towards a total ban on smoking. (This does not apply to measures which do not discriminate.) Second, the same effect can be seen in *EC – Seal Products*. Here, the EU's measure was found to violate Article XX GATT 1994, mainly due to the IC exception. Consequently, in order to bring its measure into conformity, the EU has proposed abolishing an exception for marine resource management, and making the IC exception subject to more stringent conditions.[266] The consequence thereof would be less trade in seal products. These examples are reflected in *US – Shrimp*: the AB famously stated 'we wish to underscore what we have not decided in this appeal' and subsequently noted that the only problem with the measure at issue was that its application constituted arbitrary and unjustifiable discrimination between Members.[267]

In conclusion, I subscribe to the following statement:

> Health and environmental policies […] enjoy not only the protection of GATT Article XX but also the sympathy of the Appellate Body – unless, that is, they discriminate without a suitable reason. […] The Appellate Body's message to WTO Members, not for the first time, is (almost) straightforward: if your objectives are legitimate and your measures reasonable, don't worry too much about technicalities; the system is with you. But do worry about discrimination – we won't tolerate that, unless it is a logical part of your protective policy.[268]

---

[264] See above on the function of exogenous constraints on regulatory autonomy to induce domestic reforms.

[265] McGrady, 'Menthol Cigarettes and *US – Clove Cigarettes*'.

[266] European Commission, *COM(2015) 45 final, Proposal for a Regulation of the European Parliament and of the Council Amending Regulation (EC) No 1007/2009 on Trade in Seal Products* (2015) 2.

[267] *US – Shrimp (AB)* paras 185–186.

[268] Hannes Schloemann, '*Brazil Tyres*: Policy Space Confirmed under GATT Article XX' (2008) 12 Bridges.

Indeed, although the GATS general exceptions allow considerable regulatory autonomy—part of 'the deal' when subscribing to GATS in the first place – there is no flexibility in the analysis of the exceptions, and, especially, the chapeau, vis-à-vis arbitrary discrimination caused by the measure.[269] The interpretation of the 'regulatory autonomy gateway' of the general exceptions by the AB and panels has 'matured' into a focus on the overall design and application of the regulatory measure; in particular, the question is whether protectionism is present.[270] The focus on the design and application, rather than the substance, of the measure *appears* to be more deferent to regulatory autonomy as it focuses, solely, on preventing abuse: this approach to the chapeau has been called a 'due process' approach.[271] However, this *apparent* deference to regulatory autonomy resulting from the 'proceduralisation' of the chapeau analysis is not necessarily what happens in practice: covert substantive review may still occur.[272] However, it is evident that any focus on substantive review has been relaxed.[273] This is perhaps best exemplified by the divided analysis of the AB's finding concerning Chinese censorship rules in *China – Publications and Audiovisual Products*.[274] Therefore, it may be said that the case law supports the conclusion that the AB and panels display 'significant sensitivity to domestic regulatory concerns'.[275]

2. EXCEPTIONS IN THE SELECTED EU RTAs

As with GATS, the exceptions to the obligations in the EU-C&P, EU-Singapore and EU-Georgia RTAs form an integral part of the compromise between the parties. The balance between obligations on the one hand and exceptions on the other has been carefully struck. As this section highlights, GATS has, once again, proven to be a major source of

---

[269] Ibid.

[270] Van Calster, 'Faites Vos Jeux: Regulatory Autonomy and the World Trade Organisation after *Brazil Tyres*' 121 and 129.

[271] Ibid 130.

[272] Andrew Lang, *World Trade Law after Neoliberalism: Reimagining the Global Economic Order* (Oxford University Press 2011) 346–348.

[273] Ibid 329.

[274] See above, and, for example, Delimatsis, 'Protecting Public Morals in a Digital Age: Revisiting the WTO Rulings on *US – Gambling* and *China – Publications and Audiovisual Products*' 286–287.

[275] Sacha Wunsch-Vincent, 'The Internet, Cross-Border Trade in Services, and the GATS: Lessons from *US – Gambling*' (2006) 5 World Trade Review 319, 348.

inspiration for the exceptions clauses in the RTAs, even if the encompassing nature of RTAs has meant some exceptions have been moved around within the agreement. By and large, the four major exceptions in GATS are also present for the services chapters of the RTAs. Considering the wider scope of the latter, it is unsurprising that some of the RTA exceptions also extend beyond the scope of their GATS counterparts. Additionally, the RTAs contain exceptions related to taxation for which no alternative exists under GATS.

Article 130.2 EU-C&P, which concerns the protection of confidential information under the RTA's title IV on trade in services, establishment and electronic commerce, is identical to Article III bis GATS. Also identical to Article III bis GATS is Article 289 EU-C&P, which is applicable to the whole of the EU-C&P agreement. Furthermore, this generally applicable provision is also found in Articles 17.11 EU-Singapore and 97.2 EU-Georgia. Considering the identical wording of all four provisions to Article III bis GATS, it is submitted that the above analysis applies *mutatis mutandis*.

Articles 170.2-3 EU-C&P, part of the chapter on current payments and movement of capital, allow the EU, in exceptional circumstances, to adopt safeguard measures with regard to capital movements. In the EU-Georgia DCFTA, Article 139, also part of the chapter on current payments and movement of capital, contains a very similar exception. The EU-Singapore RTA does not contain a similar exception for difficulties in the operation of exchange rate policy or monetary policy.

In the EU-C&P RTA, in addition to the exception for difficulties for the operation of exchange rate policy or monetary policy, Article 297 contains a provision for balance of payments safeguards which is applicable to the entire agreement. This provision is very similar to Article XII GATS. Article 17.9 EU-Singapore contains a very similar provision to Article 297 EU-C&P. Equally, Article 17.9 EU-Singapore is applicable to the entire agreement. Here, the safeguard measure must be in accordance with Article XII GATS and the other WTO agreements and may only be imposed for six months.

In conclusion, the balance of payments exception in the EU-Singapore RTA bears the closest resemblance to Article XII GATS, and Article 139 EU-Georgia is the widest exception. However, even under this wide exception, the measure must be 'strictly necessary', a steep hurdle considering the interpretation of 'necessity' in the general exceptions. The EU-C&P RTA has different provisions for the two types of financial difficulties. The balance of payments safeguard follows the GATS approach, whereas measures tackling difficulties for the operation of exchange rate policy or monetary policy can be taken freely, so long as they are not protectionist. Thus, the EU-C&P RTA is most lenient in this regard.

2.1 General Exceptions

The general exceptions clauses of the selected EU RTAs' services chapters closely resemble Article XIV GATS. Indeed, their structure is identical: a closed list of policy grounds in the subparagraphs and a chapeau applicable once a measure has been provisionally justified under a subparagraph. Therefore, my analysis of the general exceptions in the EU-Colombia & Peru, EU-Singapore and EU-Georgia RTAs focuses on the difference between these provisions and Article XIV GATS.

2.1.1 First tier of the analysis: the list of policy grounds

2.1.1.1 Whether the measures address the particular interest

2.1.1.1.1 PUBLIC SECURITY, PUBLIC MORALS AND PUBLIC ORDER Paragraphs (a) of Articles 167.1 EU-C&P, 8.62 EU-Singapore and 134.2 EU-Georgia are the RTAs' counterpart to Article XIV (a) GATS. However, the provisions in the RTAs are wider, in that they cover measures 'necessary to protect public security or public morals or to maintain public order'. The concept of 'public security' has not been clarified in the context of WTO dispute settlement, but may be linked to the 'essential security interests' that are the subject of the security exceptions. The scope of the term 'public security' is likely to overlap with that of the security exceptions. However, whereas, the security exceptions are limited to certain interests that are 'essential' to a Member's security, the category of 'public security' interests is broader. This is mitigated by the more stringent nexus required between the measure and the policy ground: the measure must be necessary to protect public security. The scope of the term 'public security' is unclear, although the use of the concept in RTAs is neither new nor limited to the EU.[276] In one interpretation, public security refers to 'the protection of persons, their

---

[276] For example, the EU-Mexico RTA, signed in 1997, contains a similar exception. Also see Article 8 of the Free Trade Agreement between the Republic of Estonia, the Republic of Latvia and the Republic of Lithuania and Article 21 of the Free Trade Agreement between the Arab Republic of Egypt and the EFTA States.

goods and assets, the rule of law and democratic institutional development from threats posed by a variety of crimes, violence and corruption'.[277] In contrast, national security is defined as 'concerned with protection of the state, territorial integrity and sovereignty, and essential state functions and agencies from threats by other states or trans-state actors (e.g. terrorism, organised crime and the like)'.[278] Although the security exceptions could be interpreted without such definitions being taken into account, the texts of these exceptions do seem to confirm the idea that they protect 'national' security interests. The 'public' security exception in subparagraphs (a) of the aforementioned provisions could then logically be construed to fit the foregoing definition. As with public morals and public order, a Member would have some leeway to determine the scope of what it considers such interests to be. In order to fit with the interpretation of public morals and public order, as derived from WTO case law, a public security interest must have a sufficiently public character. Nonetheless, the relevance of the public security exception appears relatively limited, as a combination of the interpretation of the public morals and public order and security exceptions would, in many cases, be sufficient to justify a measure aimed at the protection of 'security' interests. Therefore, the addition of these interests may be considered more as an additional safeguard than as a substantial expansion of the scope of subparagraph (a).

It should be noted that, in the EU-C&P and EU-Singapore RTAs, the public order exception is limited, in the same way as under Article XIV (a) GATS, by substantively identical footnotes which state that the exception may only be invoked when a genuine and sufficiently serious threat is posed to a fundamental interest of society. Article 134.2 EU-Georgia does not contain such a footnote. Consequently, the EU-Georgia obligation must be interpreted in a broader manner than under the EU-C&P and EU-Singapore RTAs or under GATS. Indeed, the threshold for justifying measures under the public order exception is lower. For example, the exception could be invoked in situations that may not relate to a *fundamental* interest of society; or in cases where the threat is not *yet* genuine and sufficiently serious. Nonetheless, the

---

[277] Nelson Michaud, 'Security Policies in the NAFTA Environment' in Gordon Mace (ed), Regionalism and the State: NAFTA and Foreign Policy Convergence (Ashgate 2013).

[278] John Bailey, 'Public Security and Democratic Governability: Theorizing about Crime, Violence, Corruption, State and Regime' (Annual Meeting of the Midwest Political Science Association, Chicago, 14–17 April 2004) footnote 3.

definition of public order remains relatively narrow, even in the absence of the limiting footnote.

2.1.1.1.2 HUMAN, ANIMAL OR PLANT LIFE OR HEALTH As seen in Article XIV (b) GATS, subparagraphs (b) of Articles 167.1 EU-C&P, 8.62 EU-Singapore and 134.2 EU-Georgia contain an exception for measures necessary to protect human, animal or plant life or health. In light of their identical wording, it is submitted that the scope of these subparagraphs is identical to that of the GATS provision. However, one exception to this is Article 167.1 (b) EU-C&P, which extends the scope of the provision to 'those environmental measures necessary to this effect'. This extension is reminiscent of US practice. For example, the general exceptions clauses in NAFTA, the Korea-US RTA, the Australia-US RTA and the Korea-Australia RTA explicitly incorporate Article XX GATT 1994 and/or XIV GATS *mutatis mutandis*. Furthermore, these provisions add, inter alia, that subparagraph (b) is understood to 'include environmental measures necessary to protect human, animal, or plant life or health'. Notably, with respect to Article XX (g) GATT 1994, these provisions, incorporating the general exceptions in an RTA, also explain that 'exhaustible natural resources' comprise living and non-living natural resources. As noted, this is the interpretation given to Article XX (g) GATT 1994 in case law.[279] Could the addition of 'environmental measures' to the scope of subparagraph (b) be a similar codification? This seems to be the case for the abovementioned approach to subparagraph (b) advocated by many Members in the Committee on Trade and Environment.[280]

As noted, a wide interpretation of Article XX (g) GATT 1994 creates an overlap with subparagraph (b) for living exhaustible natural resources. Article 167.1 (b) EU-C&P confirms this conceptual overlap. However, more important than this expansion of the scope (or perhaps mere clarification of a wide scope), is the addition, in subparagraph (c) of the EU-C&P, EU-Singapore and EU-Georgia general exceptions clauses, of a full-blown subparagraph for the conservation of exhaustible natural resources.

---

[279] *United States – Restrictions on Imports of Tuna* DS21/R, GATT Panel report, 3 September 1991, unadopted, BISD 39S/155 para. 4.9; *Canada – Measures Affecting Exports of Unprocessed Herring and Salmon* L/6268, GATT Panel report, adopted 22 March 1988, BISD 35S/98 para. 4.4; and, most clearly, but after NAFTA was enacted, *US – Shrimp (AB)* paras 128–131.

[280] WT/CTE/W/9, Committee on Trade and Environment, Environment and Services, 8 June 1995 para. 8.

2.1.1.1.3 THE CONSERVATION OF EXHAUSTIBLE NATURAL RESOURCES

Addressing one of the main shortcomings of Article XIV GATS, Articles 167.1 EU-C&P, 8.62 EU-Singapore and 134.2 EU-Georgia contain, in subparagraphs (c) to their general exceptions clauses, an exception for measures relating to the conservation of natural resources. This exception applies if such measures are applied in conjunction with restrictions on domestic entrepreneurs or investors, or on the domestic supply or consumption of services. It may be noted that the conservation of exhaustible natural resources is a policy ground with a direct link to the preamble of the WTO Agreement, which states that the purposes and objectives of the WTO Agreement include the protection and preservation of the environment.[281] For a measure to be justifiable under Article XX (g) GATT 1994, it must '(i) "relate to" the "conservation" of an "exhaustible natural resource", and (ii) be "made effective" "in conjunction" with "restrictions" on "domestic production or consumption"'.[282] These conditions should be assessed holistically.[283] For a measure to be justified under subparagraph (c) of Article XIV GATS, Articles 167.1 EU-C&P, 8.62 EU-Singapore and 134.2 EU-Georgia, it must fulfil the above conditions, with two alterations. First, a notable difference in wording between Article XX (g) GATT 1994 and the corresponding RTA provisions is that, whereas the former provision requires that the measure is made effective in conjunction with domestic restrictions, the latter provisions require that the measure must be applied in conjunction with domestic restrictions. Second, the relevant domestic restrictions are specified as restrictions vis-à-vis domestic entrepreneurs or investors, or on the domestic supply or consumption of services. As GATS does not contain such an exception, the following analysis is based on the case law on Article XX (g) GATT 1994.

To summarise, in order to be justifiable under subparagraph (c), the measure must:

a. 'Relate to' the conservation of exhaustible natural resources. The 'relating to' nexus is addressed below.
b. Fall within the scope of the concept 'exhaustible natural resources'. Although not the case for the EU-Singapore and EU-Georgia RTAs, Article 167.1 (c) EU-C&P expressly confirms that the term

---

281 *EC – Tariff Preferences (Panel)* para. 7.52.

282 *China – Rare Earths (Panel)* para. 7.240; *China – Measures Related to the Exportation of Various Raw Materials* WT/DS394/R/WT/DS395/R/WT/DS398/R, Panel report adopted 22 February 2012 para. 7.361.

283 *China – Rare Earths (Panel)* para. 7.240.

exhaustible natural resources applies to both living and non-living 'resources'. (It is interesting to note that Article 167.1 (b) and (c) EU-C&P thus appear to have been inspired by US practice on clarifying GATT 1994 and GATS general exceptions in its RTAs. However, this is perhaps unsurprising considering that the 2006 US RTAs with Colombia and Peru, which predate the EU-C&P RTA, also contain such clarifications).[284] This is merely a codification of the case law. The AB and panels have interpreted exhaustible natural resources as including clean air,[285] petroleum,[286] mineral resources,[287] and even fish[288] and sea turtles.[289] As the AB noted:

> One lesson that modern biological sciences teach us is that living species, though in principle, capable of reproduction and, in that sense, 'renewable', are in certain circumstances indeed susceptible of depletion, exhaustion and extinction, frequently because of human activities. Living resources are just as 'finite' as petroleum, iron ore and other non-living resources.[290]

However, despite the above, qualifying the term 'resources' with the phrase 'exhaustible natural' does limit the scope of the policy ground: there comes a point where processed raw materials no longer constitute exhaustible natural resources.[291] Nonetheless, in order to fall within the scope of the subparagraph, it is not necessary for a measure to be imposed *directly* on such resources, rather, the measure may simply support or contribute to the conservation of exhaustible natural resources.[292]

c. Relate to the 'conservation' of exhaustible natural resources. The AB has clarified that the term conservation means 'the preservation

---

[284] See Articles 22.1 US-Colombia Trade Promotion Agreement and US-Peru Trade Promotion Agreement.

[285] *US – Gasoline (AB)* 14.

[286] *US – Shrimp (AB)* para. 128.

[287] Ibid; *China – Raw Materials (Panel)* para. 7.369; *China – Rare Earths (Panel)* paras 7.365, 7.689 and 7.854.

[288] *US – Tuna (Mexico) (GATT Panel)* para. 4.9; *Canada – Herring and Salmon (GATT Panel)* para. 4.4.

[289] *US – Shrimp (AB)* para. 131.

[290] Ibid para. 128.

[291] *China – Rare Earths (Panel)* paras 7.248–7.249.

[292] *US – Gasoline (AB)* 19, as interpreted by *China – Rare Earths (Panel)* para. 7.250.

of the environment, especially of natural resources'.[293] However, according to the Panel in *China – Rare Earths*, the meaning of conservation is not limited to preservation.[294] Moreover, Members have the right to use their natural resources for the promotion of their own development whilst also encouraging the regulation of exhaustible natural resources to ensure sustainable development.[295] This does not mean that a Member may regulate a resource market for *any* purpose:[296] 'WTO Members' right to adopt conservation programmes is not a right to control the international markets in which extracted products are bought and sold'.[297]

d. 'Be applied' in conjunction with restrictions on domestic entrepreneurs or investors, or on the domestic supply or consumption of services. As noted, in Article XX (g) GATT 1994, the term 'made effective' is used. However, in interpreting this term, the AB has referred to the Spanish and French (the official languages of the WTO other than English) versions of the term to confirm its interpretation.[298] These versions, using the terms 'se appliquen' and 'sont appliquées' respectively, clarify that 'be applied' and 'made effective' are to be interpreted identically, i.e. as 'measures brought into operation, adopted, or applied'.[299]

e. Be applied 'in conjunction with' restrictions on domestic entrepreneurs or investors, or on the domestic supply or consumption of services. In light of the difficulty of establishing causation, and the fact that the effects of a measure in the field of conserving exhaustible natural resources may only be seen years after the enactment of the measure, this requirement does not establish an 'empirical effects' test.[300] Rather, it is a requirement of even-handedness.[301] In other words, there must be domestic restrictions

---

293 *China – Measures Related to the Exportation of Various Raw Materials* WT/DS394/AB/R, WT/DS395/AB/R, WT/DS398/AB/R, AB report adopted 22 February 2012 para. 355.

294 *China – Rare Earths (Panel)* para. 7.266.

295 Ibid para. 7.265.

296 Ibid para. 7.268, referring to *United States – Final Countervailing Duty Determination with Respect to Certain Softwood Lumber from Canada* WT/DS257/AB/R, AB report adopted 17 February 2004 para. 67.

297 *China – Rare Earths (Panel)* para. 7.268.

298 *China – Raw Materials (AB)* para. 356.

299 Ibid.

300 *US – Gasoline (AB)* 18–19.

301 Ibid 18.

in place in order for the measure to be even-handed.[302] These domestic restrictions must operate jointly with the restrictions provided for by the measure.[303] This even-handedness requirement cannot be analysed in light of the even-handedness requirement in Article 2.1 TBT Agreement. The latter requirement draws directly from the chapeau of Article XX GATT 1994 and any transposition would bring elements of the chapeau analysis into the analysis of a subparagraph. This would constitute a 'legal error'.[304]

f. Finally, the measure must be applied in conjunction with 'restrictions' on domestic entrepreneurs or investors, or on the domestic supply or consumption of services. In the context of Article XX (g) GATT 1994, the AB has defined 'restriction' as '[a] thing which restricts someone or something, a limitation on action, a limiting condition or regulation'.[305] If no such restrictions are imposed on domestic actors, the measure cannot be said to be designed for implementing conservationist goals.[306] To be a restriction on domestic supply or consumption, there must be a *quantitative* restriction which is 'set at a level that is lower than the expected demand for the period of time over which the restriction is intended to apply'.[307] This restriction must be capable (in reality rather than merely 'in the books') of limiting the amount of supply or consumption in comparison to the situation prior to the restriction. Further, the restriction must be enforced.[308]

The broader scope of the establishment provisions in the services chapters of the EU RTAs is the likely reason for the inclusion of an exception for measures relating to the conservation of exhaustible natural resources. Indeed, the application of certain disciplines in these chapters to goods requires the addition of this policy ground in order to preserve regulatory autonomy to the same extent as it is preserved under GATS. However, even if informed by this broader scope, the inclusion impacts

---

302 *US – Shrimp (AB)* para. 143; *China – Raw Materials (Panel)* para. 7.462.

303 *China – Raw Materials (AB)* para. 356.

304 *China – Rare Earths (Panel)* para. 7.336.

305 *China – Measures Related to the Exportation of Rare Earths, Tungsten, and Molybdenum* WT/DS431/AB/R, WT/DS432/AB/R, WT/DS433/AB/R, AB report adopted 2 September 2014 para. 5.91.

306 *US – Gasoline (AB)* 18.

307 *China – Rare Earths (Panel)* paras 7.308–7.310.

308 Ibid paras 7.308–7.310. Note that this is not an analysis of discrimination between restrictions applicable to domestic and foreign actors. Such problems would be assessed under the chapeau: see para. 7.312.

upon measures affecting trade in services. Considering the breadth of trade in services, and the importance of services in today's economy, one can imagine situations in which measures relating to the conservation of exhaustible natural resources affect trade in services in a way that violates one of the obligations in the services chapters of the selected EU RTAs. Therefore, it is clear that this inclusion is important from the perspective of regulatory autonomy. Considering its slight overlap with subparagraphs (a) and (b), the most significant aspect of the inclusion of subparagraph (c) is likely to be the required nexus: 'relating to' rather than 'necessary'. Nonetheless, where this is not the case, the exception for measures related to the exhaustion of natural resources is a welcome addition for regulators.

2.1.1.1.4 EXTRATERRITORIALITY AND THESE POLICY GROUNDS For public security, public morals, public order, and human and animal life or health in the selected EU RTAs, the remarks on extraterritoriality made vis-à-vis Articles XIV (a)–(b) GATS are applicable. The addition of the conservation of exhaustible natural resources policy ground in the respective subparagraphs (c) of the general exceptions in the EU RTAs requires some further attention.[309] In the context of the equivalent Article XX (g) GATT 1994, the AB famously stated:

> We do not pass upon the question of whether there is an implied jurisdictional limitation in Article XX (g), and if so, the nature or extent of that limitation. We note only that in the specific circumstances of the case before us, there is a sufficient nexus between the migratory and endangered marine populations involved and the United States for purposes of Article XX(g).[310]

This finding has been criticised for not addressing the jurisdictional limits of Article XX GATT 1994 directly. However, by focusing on the 'sufficient nexus approach' (to be differentiated from the nexus between the measure and the policy ground, such as the necessity test), the AB 'did the next best thing'.[311] For our purposes, the analysis, made in the

[309] The topic of trade and environment has been explored in-depth elsewhere. See e.g. Geert Van Calster and Denise Prévost (eds), Research Handbook on Environment, Health and the WTO (Edward Elgar Publishing 2014); Erich Vranes, Trade and the Environment: Fundamental Issues in International Law, WTO Law, and Legal Theory (Oxford University Press 2009).

[310] *US – Shrimp (AB)* para. 133.

[311] Lorand Bartels, 'Article XX of GATT and the Problem of Extraterritorial Jurisdiction: The Case of Trade Measures for the Protection of Human Rights' (2002) 36 Journal of World Trade 353, 388.

context of subparagraphs (a) and (b) of Article XIV GATS holds true vis-à-vis the exception for the conservation of exhaustible natural resources. Indeed, the 'sufficient nexus approach' can be construed within the aforementioned analytical framework of three types of extra-territorial measures.[312] The lesson to take from the *US – Tuna (Mexico)*, *US – Tuna II (Mexico)* and *US – Shrimp* saga may well be that a measure should have, and also be framed to have, a direct 'territorial' link,[313] i.e. a measure should address both domestic and foreign concerns. According to one author, this link is present, inherently, in the conditions of the exception. This is because the measure must be applied in conjunction with domestic restrictions. Indeed, '[t]he purpose of a territorial nexus is to prevent a state that lacks legitimate concern from using a global environmental problem as a pretext for protectionist interventionism'.[314] Combined with the more relaxed 'relating to' nexus for this policy ground, the potential to justify measures for the protection of the environment under this subparagraph is greater than the potential under subparagraph (b). Nonetheless, the chapeau of the general exceptions provision allows for the 'policing' of unilateral measures, such as the extraterritorial measures at issue here.[315]

2.1.1.1.5 THE PROTECTION OF NATIONAL TREASURES Subparagraphs (d) of Articles 167.1 EU-C&P, 8.62 EU-Singapore and 134.2 EU-Georgia are identical and relate to the protection of national treasures of artistic, historic or archaeological value. This policy ground is reflected in Article XX (f) GATT 1994, but no corresponding provision can be found in Article XIV GATS. The only difference between the RTA clauses and Article XX (f) GATT 1994 is that the former provisions require the measure to be 'necessary' whereas the latter provision simply requires the

---

312 Wu, 'Free Trade and the Protection of Public Morals: An Analysis of the Newly Emerging Public Morals Clause Doctrine' 235–236.

313 Bartels, 'Article XX of GATT and the Problem of Extraterritorial Jurisdiction: The Case of Trade Measures for the Protection of Human Rights' 386–390.

314 Howse, 'The Appellate Body Rulings in the *Shrimp/Turtle* Case: A New Legal Baseline for the Trade and Environment Debate' 504.

315 Asif H Qureshi, 'Extraterritorial Shrimps, NGOs and the WTO Appellate Body' (1999) 48 International and Comparative Law Quarterly 199, 204–205; Bartels, 'Article XX of GATT and the Problem of Extraterritorial Jurisdiction: The Case of Trade Measures for the Protection of Human Rights' 389–390, noting that the AB condemns coercive unilateral measures; Howse, 'The Appellate Body Rulings in the *Shrimp/Turtle* Case: A New Legal Baseline for the Trade and Environment Debate' 504–511.

measure to be 'imposed for' such protection. Article XX (f) GATT 1994 has not been invoked in case law. The exception may be relevant for measures that promote cultural identity or diversity, if the concept of national treasures is interpreted broadly.[316] It has been argued that the term is narrower than the broader notion of cultural property.[317] However, it has also been said that the protection of cultural heritage is a 'universally recognized interest in international law', and that the term national treasures of artistic, historic or archaeological value should be interpreted as covering cultural property in its entirety.[318] Regardless of the correct interpretation, the relevance of the exception appears to be very limited in the context of trade in services. As with the exception for the conservation of exhaustible natural resources, it appears that the main reason for including the exception is the broader scope of establishment. However, whereas, for exhaustible natural resources, this has led to a substantially wider exception for services, the same does not appear to hold true for the protection of national treasures.

2.1.1.1.6 SECURING COMPLIANCE WITH LAWS OR REGULATIONS An exception for measures necessary to secure compliance with certain laws or regulations, like that in Article XIV (c) GATS, can be found in subparagraphs (e) of Articles 167.1 EU-C&P, 8.62 EU-Singapore and 134.2 EU-Georgia. Substantively, there is no difference between GATS and the selected EU RTAs for this exception. The RTAs' provisions follow the structure of their GATS counterpart: a general sentence, followed by an open list of three types of laws or regulations. The wording used for these three measures is identical to that in GATS. However, as concerns the first sentence of the subparagraph, GATS and the three RTAs have slightly different fields of application. For example, the EU-Singapore and EU-Georgia RTA provisions apply to the services, establishment and electronic commerce chapters. However, in the EU-C&P RTA, the provision applies to Title IV, on services, establishment and electronic commerce, and to Title V on current payments and movement of capital. Therefore, violations of the obligations in the EU-Singapore and EU-Georgia RTAs that correspond to Title V of the

316 Van den Bossche and Zdouc, The Law and Policy of the World Trade Organization 572.

317 Jia Min Cheng, 'The Problem of National Treasure in International Law' (2010) 12 Oregon Review of International Law 141, 152–153.

318 Nele Matz-Lück, 'Article XX lit. of GATT 1994' in Rüdiger Wolfrum and others (eds), Max Planck Commentaries on World Trade Law: WTO – Technical Barriers and SPS Measures, vol 3 (Martinus Nijhoff 2008) 138.

EU-C&P RTA cannot be justified on the basis of subparagraph (e) of their respective general exceptions clauses, whereas this would be possible under the EU-C&P RTA.[319] In the case of Peru, footnote 55 to Article 167.1 EU-C&P clarifies 'for greater certainty' that 'the execution of measures that prevent a monetary transfer through the equitable, non-discriminatory and good faith application of Peruvian Laws', relating to five listed policy objectives, shall not be considered inconsistent with the provisions of Titles IV and V of the RTA.[320] (The addition of the term 'for greater certainty' highlights that these measures should not automatically be considered violations of the obligations vis-à-vis trade in services or capital transactions.)

2.1.1.1.7 EQUITABLE OR EFFECTIVE IMPOSITION OF DIRECT TAXES The general exceptions provision of Articles 8.62 EU-Singapore and 134.2 EU-Georgia contain an exception for discriminatory measures where the difference in treatment is aimed at ensuring the equitable or effective imposition or collection of direct taxes in respect of economic activities, entrepreneurs or service suppliers of the other party. These provisions, found in subparagraphs (f) of the exceptions clauses are very similar to Article XIV (d) GATS, including the explanatory footnote. Nonetheless, despite having no substantial implications for their interpretation, there are four ways in which these exceptions differ slightly from their GATS counterpart:

a. Whereas, in the EU-Singapore and EU-Georgia RTAs, the exception applies to national treatment for cross-border trade in services and establishment,[321] the exception also applies to the MFN obligation for establishment in the EU-Georgia DCFTA. This exception allows derogation from the MFN obligation vis-à-vis the other party. As noted, this MFN obligation seeks to ensure that the

---

[319] The text of Article 167.1 (c) EU-C&P may seem to suggest that the only measures which can be justified under this provision are those falling within the ambit of Title IV. However, the chapeau of Article 167.1 clarifies that the general exceptions clause applies to Title V in full.

[320] If such measures relate to: (a) bankruptcy, insolvency, or the protection of the rights of creditors; (b) issuing, trading, or dealing in securities, futures, options, or derivatives; (c) criminal or penal offences; (d) financial reporting or record keeping of transfers when necessary to assist law enforcement or financial regulatory authorities; or (e) ensuring compliance with judicial or administrative orders or rulings in judicial or administrative proceedings.

[321] Recall that there is no national treatment obligation for temporary presence of natural persons for business purposes.

economic actors of either party will always be granted the most preferential treatment given to any country. Consequently, in order to safeguard regulatory autonomy for the effective imposition or collection of direct taxes, taking into account differences that may arise between Georgia and any third country, this MFN exception is a necessary addition to the exception.[322]

b. The language of subparagraph (f) in each RTA has been adapted to the wider scope of establishment, in comparison to GATS, through the words 'in respect of economic activities, entrepreneurs and service suppliers'.
c. The equivalent to explanatory footnote 6 to Article XIV (d) GATS is inserted at the end of the provision, instead of after the word 'effective'. This does not impact upon the meaning of the footnote. It also appears to make more sense, considering that the footnote should not be understood to refer only to 'effective', but rather lists types of measures that are aimed at ensuring the equitable or effective imposition or collection of direct taxes.
d. Whereas Article 8.2 (a) EU-Singapore copies the definition of 'direct taxes' from GATS, the EU-Georgia DCFTA contains no such definition. Therefore, in accordance with the interpretative footnote to Article 134.2 (f) EU-Georgia, the definition of 'direct taxes', for the purpose of this exception, is to be determined under the domestic law of the party taking the measure.

The EU-C&P RTA does not contain a policy ground exception in its general exceptions provision, but rather in Article 296.3 that addresses taxation specifically.

2.1.1.2 The required nexus between the measure and the policy ground

2.1.1.2.1 'NECESSARY' AND 'AIMED AT' In light of the (almost) identical wording of subparagraphs (a), (b), (d) and (e) Articles 167.1 EU-C&P, 8.62 EU-Singapore and 134.2 EU-Georgia, it is submitted that the nexus 'necessary' should be interpreted identically to the necessity test under Article XIV GATS. The same applies to subparagraph (f) in Articles 8.62 and 134.2 EU-Georgia for the 'aimed at' nexus.

---

[322] For a confirmation of this interpretation, see Article 135 EU-Georgia, discussed below.

2.1.1.2.2 'RELATING TO' The nexus under subparagraphs (c) of Articles 167.1 EU-C&P, 8.62 EU-Singapore and 134.2 EU-Georgia, which contain an exception for measures relating to the conservation of exhaustible natural resources, is an important addition to the nexuses discussed above. The case law on Article XX (g) 1994, which contains an identical exception, has evolved from a necessity-type analysis to a more relaxed legal standard,[323] since GATT 1947 case law.[324] In *US – Gasoline*, the AB rejected the Panel's approach, noting that 'the Panel Report appears to have applied the "necessary" test not only in examining the baseline establishment rules under Article XX(b), but also in the course of applying Article XX(g)'.[325] The AB continued by noting that the different nexuses must be interpreted differently.[326] Relying on the dictionary meaning of 'relating to', the AB explained that the term means 'having some connection with', or 'being connected to'.[327] This connection has been clarified as being a relationship between the measure and the policy ground that is 'close and real'.[328] This would not be the case where a measure is inadvertently or incidentally aimed at the conservation of exhaustible natural resources.[329] Moreover, the measure may not be disproportionately wide in its scope and reach vis-à-vis the policy ground, as it must reflect a reasonable means and ends relationship.[330] Finally, the text of the exception does not proscribe an empirical effects test.[331] This is especially so considering the difficulties of determining causation.[332] However, this does not mean that such effects may not be taken into account. Indeed, 'actual effects may be used to confirm the predictable effects of a challenged measure'.[333]

In order to assess whether a measure is related to the conservation of exhaustible natural resources, a panel may look at: (i), primarily, the

---

[323] *Korea – Various Measures on Beef (AB)* para. 104.

[324] *United States – Standards for Reformulated and Conventional Gasoline* WT/DS2/R, Panel report adopted 20 May 1996 para. 6.40.

[325] *US – Gasoline (AB)* 16.

[326] Ibid 17–18.

[327] *China – Raw Materials (AB)* para. 355; *China – Rare Earths (AB)* para. 5.105.

[328] *US – Shrimp (AB)* para. 141.

[329] *China – Rare Earths (AB)* para. 5.90.

[330] *US – Shrimp (AB)* para. 141.

[331] *US – Gasoline (AB)* 20.

[332] *China – Rare Earths (AB)* para. 5.112.

[333] Ibid para. 5.113.

design and structure of the measure;[334] (ii) the text of the measure;[335] (iii) in the policy and regulatory context of the challenged measures, 'and not only in isolation';[336] and (iv) on a case-by-case basis through 'careful scrutiny of the factual and legal context in a given dispute'.[337] Moreover, the analysis of the nexus should not be artificially separated from the analysis of the other conditions of the subparagraph: the overall assessment should be holistic.[338]

2.1.2 Second tier of the analysis: the chapeau

The general exceptions in all three selected EU RTAs follow the two-tiered structure of Article XIV GATS. Although very similar to the GATS chapeau, the chapeaux in these provisions do differ slightly from the GATS provision, and from each other, in the following ways:

a. As concerns the 'like conditions' element, Article 167.1 EU-C&P does not contain a requirement that the arbitrary or unjustifiable discrimination occurs between countries where like conditions prevail. The provision merely states 'between the parties'. This indicates that, for the purposes of the general exceptions provision, the conditions are deemed to be like. Considering the broad interpretation given to these terms in WTO case law, as described above, this omission does not appear to render the chapeau substantially more stringent. However, the possibility of applying WTO case law to determine that the conditions are unlike is of course precluded.

   Article 8.62 EU-Singapore does include the requirement that the arbitrary or unjustifiable discrimination occurs 'against the other Party where like conditions prevail'. This change reflects that, as noted, only conditions relevant for the purpose of establishing whether there is arbitrary or unjustifiable discrimination 'in the light of the specific character of the measure at issue and the circumstances of a specific case' are to be taken into account.[339] In other words, the conditions between countries may be like vis-à-vis one measure, but not the next. As such, the change simply adapts the text of the chapeau to address the situation in which there are

334 *US – Shrimp (AB)* paras 135–137; *China – Raw Materials (AB)* para. 355.
335 *China – Rare Earths (Panel)* para. 7.290.
336 Ibid para. 7.289.
337 Ibid para. 7.292.
338 Ibid paras 7.363 and 7.240.
339 *EC – Seal Products (AB)* para. 5.299.

only two parties (the EU and Singapore), thereby clarifying the meaning of the condition.

In contrast, Article 134.2 EU-Georgia copies the GATS formulation, stating that the application of the measure may not lead to 'arbitrary or unjustifiable discrimination between countries where like conditions prevail'. This decision by the negotiators was likely informed by the MFN obligation in the agreement, which brings measures vis-à-vis third countries under the ambit of the EU-Georgia DCFTA.

b. The 'disguised restriction' element, which, under GATS, refers solely to a disguised restriction on trade in services, has been clarified in all three RTAs to mean 'disguised restriction on establishment or cross-border trade in services'. On the one hand, this broadens the scope of the condition vis-à-vis Article XIV GATS in order to reflect the broader scope of the establishment chapter.

On the other hand, this wording may seem more restrictive than GATS, in that it makes no reference to the temporary presence of natural persons for business purposes. It may be recalled that the non-discrimination and market access obligations for temporary presence of natural persons are limited to key personnel (defined as business visitors and intra-corporate transferees), and graduate trainees.[340] The definitions of these categories of natural persons indicate that: (i) business visitors are senior personnel setting up an establishment in the other party; (ii) intra-corporate transferees are executives, managers or specialists, further defined in the RTAs, employed by an establishment in the other party; and (iii) graduate trainees are employed by an establishment in the other party for career development purposes or to obtain training in business techniques or methods.[341]

Consequently, the scope of the 'disguised restriction' element appears to cover both the pre-establishment activities of business visitors and the post-establishment activities of intra-corporate transferees and graduate trainees. In other words, the wording does not limit the scope of the 'disguised restriction' element compared to GATS, taking into account the limited scope of Mode 4 supply of services in the RTAs;

c. As noted above in the analysis of Article 167.1 (e) EU-C&P, the scope of this subparagraph in the EU-C&P RTA differs from that in

340 See Articles 124.2 EU-C&P, 8.14.2 EU-Singapore and 89.2 EU-Georgia.
341 Articles 123 EU-C&P, 8.13.2 EU-Singapore and 88.2 EU-Georgia.

the other RTAs. The chapeau of Article 167.1 EU-C&P makes it clear that this observation holds true for the entire general exceptions provision. The chapeau states that 'nothing in this Title *and Title V (Current Payments and Capital Movements)* shall be construed to prevent the adoption or enforcement by any Party of measures' (emphasis added). Consequently, violations of obligations in Title V of the EU-C&P RTA may be justified on the basis of the general exceptions. This is not the case for the corresponding obligations in the EU-Singapore and EU-Georgia RTAs.

d. Finally, Article 134.1 EU-Georgia, which precedes the 'classical' general exceptions provision in paragraph 2, notes that, without prejudice to the security exceptions, the provisions of the chapter on establishment, trade in services and electronic commerce, and all relevant annexes, are subject to the general exceptions provision in Article 134 EU-Georgia. Considering that Schedules are considered an integral part of GATS by virtue of Article XX:3 GATS, this final addition merely seems to reflect that this also applies to this chapter. Indeed, considering the explicit statement in the chapeau of Article 134.2 EU-Georgia that 'nothing in this Chapter shall be construed to prevent the adoption or enforcement by any Party of measures' which meet the requirements of a subparagraph, it is unclear why this paragraph was added to the general exceptions clause.

Aside from the application of the general exceptions in the EU-C&P RTA to obligations related to capital transactions, the above differences do not appear to be substantial. In any case, they do not affect the interpretation of the scope of the general exception provisions as compared to the analysis of the chapeau under Article XIV GATS.

2.1.3 Implications for regulatory autonomy

Considering the strong resemblance between the general exceptions under GATS and those in the selected EU RTAs, the implications for regulatory autonomy discussed in the context of Article XIV GATS remain relevant. The main exception to this statement relates to the addition of an exception for measures related to the conservation of exhaustible natural resources. This addition to the selected EU RTAs is a substantial improvement on Article XIV GATS. It is an economic reality that services are strongly linked to other economic activities and that many services are directly linked to environmental concerns. Undoubtedly, the inclusion of this policy ground was fuelled by the broader scope of establishment under the EU RTAs, as compared to Mode 3 under GATS. Nonetheless, its impact extends to services. As noted, the main improvement of this inclusion is that 'relating to' is a less stringent nexus than 'necessary'. Therefore, under the EU RTAs, regulatory autonomy has been broadened considerably for measures which relate to the conservation of living and non-living exhaustible natural resources.

2.2 Security Exceptions

Considering the sensitive nature of the security exceptions, it is unsurprising that the three selected EU RTAs also contain provisions safeguarding the parties' essential security interests. At the outset, it can be noted that these exceptions do not provide substantially more or less leeway for regulators in comparison to Article XIV bis GATS.

2.3 Exceptions Related to Taxation

Finally, Articles 296 EU-C&P, 17.6 EU-Singapore and 135 EU-Georgia contain several exceptions related to taxation that are relevant for trade in services.[342] In the former two RTAs, this exception applies to the entire agreement. In the latter RTA, the exception applies only to the chapter on establishment, trade in services and electronic commerce. Moreover, the exceptions vary substantially between the agreements.

The general exceptions provisions of the EU-Singapore and EU-Georgia RTAs contain an exception, in subparagraphs (f), for discriminatory measures where the difference in treatment is aimed at ensuring the equitable or effective imposition or collection of direct taxes in respect of economic activities, entrepreneurs or service suppliers of the other party. This exception is based on Article XIV (d) GATS. In the EU-C&P general exceptions provision, there is no such policy ground. However, the generally applicable provision containing taxation exceptions does contain an exception for this policy ground: Article 296.3 (a) EU-C&P states that nothing in the agreement shall be construed to prevent a party from adopting or enforcing any measure which aims at ensuring the effective and equitable imposition and collection of direct taxes. This exception is broader than its counterparts in Article XIV GATS and the general exceptions of the EU-Singapore and EU-Georgia RTAs. First, it applies to a violation of *any* obligation, not just national treatment (and, in the EU-Georgia DCFTA, the MFN obligation). Second, justification under the exception does not require a chapeau

[342] Article 296.3 (d) EU-C&P contains an exception related to tax measures for MFN obligations. Considering that the services and establishment chapter does not contain such an obligation, this exception is not further assessed.

analysis: it suffices that the measure is aimed at ensuring effective and equitable imposition and collection of direct taxes. It should also be noted that paragraph 4 of Article 296 EU-C&P reiterates footnote 6 to Article XIV (d) GATS, holding that tax terms not defined in the agreement are to be interpreted according to the domestic tax law of the enacting Member. However, Article 296.4 EU-C&P sets out a general interpretational principle, whereas footnote 6 solely applies to Article XIV (d) GATS.

Furthermore, Articles 296.2–3 EU-C&P and 17.6.2–4 EU-Singapore contain three, supplementary exceptions for taxation. First, nothing in either RTA shall be construed to prevent a party from adopting or enforcing any measure that differentiates, in certain circumstances, between tax payers. In the EU-C&P RTA, the envisaged differentiation is in the application of the relevant provision of domestic fiscal legislation. This includes those measures aimed at ensuring the imposition or collection of duties. However, the differentiation can only be made between tax payers who are not in the same situation, 'in particular with regard to their place of residence or with regard to the place where their capital is invested'. In other words, the exception only allows differentiation in the *application* of domestic fiscal law between tax payers who are not in the same situation. In the context of Article 5.5 SPS Agreement, the term 'different situations' was given a broad meaning.[343] The language of the RTA, i.e. 'not in the same situation', may indicate that an even broader meaning was envisaged. Indeed, *a contrario*, the term 'same situation' was given a rather strict meaning in the context of Article VI:5 GATT 1994.[344]

In the EU-Singapore RTA, paragraph 3 of Article 17.6 adapts this wording, resulting in a broader provision. Here, any differentiation (hence not only in the application of domestic fiscal law) is acceptable,

---

[343] *European Communities – Measures Concerning Meat and Meat Products (Hormones)* WT/DS26/R, WT/DS48/R, Panel report adopted 13 February 1998 paras 8.176 and 8.179, stating that 'both parties in dispute agree that the scope of "different situations" contained in Article 5.5 includes situations which deal with the same substance as well as situations which involve the same adverse health effect'.

[344] *United States – Definitive Anti-Dumping and Countervailing Duties on Certain Products from China* WT/DS379/AB/R, AB report adopted 25 March 2011 paras 567–568. Also see *United States – Definitive Anti-Dumping and Countervailing Duties on Certain Products from China* WT/DS379/R, Panel report adopted 25 March 2011 paras 14.116–14.117.

as long as it is based on rational criteria, such as taxpayers which are not in the same situation. An explanatory footnote 4 to this provision clarifies that:

> For greater certainty, the Parties share an understanding that nothing in this Agreement shall prevent any taxation measure aimed at social welfare, public health or other socio-community objectives, or at macroeconomic stability; or tax benefits linked to place of incorporation and not the nationality of the person owning the company. Taxation measures aimed at macroeconomic stability are measures in reaction to movements and trends in the national economy to address or to prevent systemic imbalances which seriously threaten the stability of the national economy.

This footnote sheds light on the type of situations for which the exception was construed. Considering that the footnote states that 'nothing in the agreement' shall be construed to prevent the adoption or maintenance of such a measure, the 'rational criteria' element of Article 17.6.3 EU-Singapore is to be considered fulfilled when the measure is aimed at social welfare, public health, other socio-community objectives, macroeconomic stability or tax benefits linked to the place of incorporation. In other circumstances, the ordinary meaning of the term 'rational criteria' is criteria that are '[b]ased on or derived from reason or reasoning, [especially] as opposed to emotion, intuition, instinct, etc.', or '[i]n accordance with reason; reasonable, sensible; not foolish, absurd, or extreme'.[345] Indeed, a measure is rational when it is based on a rationale.[346] The AB has used 'rational' and 'reasonable' interchangeably when assessing the relationship between a measure and the risk assessment in the context of Article 5.1 SPS Agreement.[347] Moreover, the Panel in *Japan – DRAMs (Korea)* noted that a decision by Japan's investigating authorities on countervailing duties was not irrational because the authorities had followed distinct analytical phases, taking into account objective

---

[345] Stevenson, *Oxford Dictionary of English (Online Version).*

[346] *Brazil – Retreaded Tyres (AB)* para. 232.

[347] *European Communities – Measures Concerning Meat and Meat Products (Hormones)* WT/DS26/AB/R, WT/DS48/AB/R, AB report adopted 13 February 1998 paras 193–194.

findings on the commercial reasonableness of investor actions.[348] These fragmented findings confirm the ordinary meaning of the term 'rational criteria'.

In comparison to the similar exception in the EU-C&P RTA, the exception in Article 7.16.3 EU-Singapore goes further – or, at least, makes it easier for regulators to craft rules that may fall under this exception. Under the EU-C&P RTA, the exception only applies to the *application* of domestic fiscal legislation. As noted, the application of a measure is a central element to the chapeau analysis under Article XIV GATS. The expected application of the measure can be derived from the text of the measure,[349] for which the design, the architecture, and the revealing structure of a measure can be assessed.[350] The actual practice of applying the measure should also be taken into account.[351] Such considerations are also likely to play a role under the EU-Singapore RTA. However, here, there is no room for discussion as to whether it is the measure itself or its application that distinguishes between tax payers.

Second, Articles 296.2 EU-C&P and 17.6.2 EU-Singapore confirm that the RTA shall not affect the rights and obligations under tax agreements[352] between an EU Member State and Colombia or Peru, or an EU Member State and Singapore. In case of inconsistency between such an agreement and the RTA, the former agreement prevails, to the extent of the inconsistency. This primacy of tax agreements carves out policy space to address tax issues between the parties at a later stage, or to let tax *lex specialis* prevail over the more general trade agreements.

Third, Articles 296.3 (c) EU-C&P and 17.6.4 EU-Singapore state that nothing in either agreement shall be construed to prevent a party from adopting or enforcing any measure which aims at preventing the avoidance or evasion of taxes pursuant to the tax provisions of double taxation agreements, other tax arrangements or domestic fiscal legislation. Although similar to Article XIV (e) GATS, these exceptions are wider than their GATS counterpart as they (i) apply to any obligation, not just the MFN obligation; and (ii) are not limited to international agreements

---

348 *Japan – Countervailing Duties on Dynamic Random Access Memories from Korea* WT/DS336/R, Panel report adopted 17 December 2007 paras 7.129–7.132.

349 *EC – Seal Products (AB)* para. 5.302.

350 Ibid.

351 *US – Shrimp (AB)* para. 160.

352 The EU-C&P RTA uses the term 'tax convention', which is defined in footnote 85 to that provision as 'a convention for the avoidance of double taxation or other international taxation agreement or arrangement'.

but also apply to domestic fiscal law aimed at preventing tax avoidance or evasion. Once again, the broad scope of these exceptions safeguards regulatory autonomy in the fight against tax avoidance and evasion.

In comparison to the EU-C&P and EU-Singapore RTAs, the taxation exception in EU-Georgia is very limited.[353] Article 135 EU-Georgia, which, as noted, applies solely to the services and establishment chapter, only contains an exemption for the application of the MFN obligation. That obligation shall not apply to the tax treatment provided on the basis of agreements *between the parties* that are designed to avoid double taxation.

3. OVERVIEW: EXCEPTIONS

Table 8.1 provides an overview of the applicable exceptions in GATS and the selected EU RTAs. At an aggregate level, and as explained for each exception, regulatory autonomy appears to be well safeguarded by the elaborate exceptions. Nonetheless, a crucial understanding in this regard is that the burden of proof rests upon the invoking party. For example, in the case of exceptions, the burden of proof rests upon the respondent. This is especially important where, for example, non-discrimination obligations are not conditional upon the likeness of foreign and domestic actors, or upon the demonstration that treatment of foreign actors is less favourable. For all exceptions besides the general exceptions, the effects of this *caveat* are strongly mitigated due to the lack of a nexus or chapeau requirement. Nonetheless, it remains true that trade agreements, by their very nature, are inherently biased towards trade. Indeed, it is only in the justification phase, i.e. under the exceptions clauses, that other societal considerations become crucial.[354]

353 It may be noted that Article 416 EU-Georgia, which is applicable to the entire EU-Georgia DCFTA, contains a non-discrimination obligation, vis-à-vis the EU, *between Georgian firms, companies and nationals*. In other words, the EU cannot discriminate between Georgian economic actors.

354 See above, and Cho, *Free Markets and Social Regulation: A Reform Agenda of the Global Trading System* 2–5.

Table 8.1 Exceptions

	GATS	EU-C&P RTA	EU-Singapore RTA	EU-Georgia DCFTA
Confidential information	X	X	X	X
Exchange rate policy; monetary policy; balance of payments	*only balance of payments*	*most lenient*	*only balance of payments*	*wider scope, but 'strictly necessary'*
General exceptions				
Chapeau	X	X	X	X
Public morals and public order	*necessary*	*necessary; + public security*	*necessary; + public security*	*necessary; + public security*
Human, animal and plant life or health	*necessary*	*necessary*	*necessary*	*necessary*
Conservation of exhaustible natural resources		*relating to*	*relating to*	*relating to*
Compliance with laws or regulations	*necessary*	*necessary*	*necessary*	*necessary*
Imposition of direct taxes	*aimed at*	*no nexus; no chapeau*	*aimed at*	*aimed at*
Double taxation	*is the result of*	*broad*	*broad*	*narrow*
National treasures		*imposed for*	*imposed for*	*imposed for*
Security exceptions	X	X	X	X
Other taxation				
Differentiation between tax payers in different situations		X	X	
Primacy of tax agreements		X	X	

Concluding remarks*

In 1998, Renato Ruggiero, at that point the Director-General of the WTO, addressed the 'Conference on Trade in Services' in Brussels. In his speech, he stated that:

> [T]he GATS provides guarantees over a much wider field of regulation and law than the GATT; the right of establishment and the obligation to treat foreign services suppliers fairly and objectively in all relevant areas of domestic regulation extend the reach of the Agreement into areas never before recognised as trade policy.
>
> I suspect that neither governments nor industries have yet appreciated the full scope of these guarantees or the full value of existing commitments.[1]

This observation still holds true in 2015. The economic importance of services, and the economic potential of trade in services, is unquestionable. Conversely, the regulation of trade in services is still an opaque and highly technical matter. At the multilateral level, one may argue that this characterisation is no longer fully accurate. However, few would make the same claim vis-à-vis the preferential level. The technical complexity of the many disciplines and commitments provided for by RTAs and GATS reduces the potential for governments and industries to realise the full value of these disciplines and commitments.

This book has attempted to shed some light on these issues. It did so from the perspective of trade in services as defined and disciplined in GATS. Naturally, such a perspective has skewed my view of the regulation of services in the EU RTAs, in so far as such regulation is

---

* I am indebted to Dylan Geraets for his very helpful suggestions on an earlier draft of these conclusions.

[1] World Trade Organization, 'Renato Ruggiero, "Towards GATS 2000 – a European Strategy", Address to the Conference on Trade in Services, organized by the European Commission, Brussels, 2 June 1998' (1998) <http://www.wto.org/english/news_e/sprr_e/bruss1_e.htm> accessed 17 January 2015. He continued that: 'But the suppliers of services are not the only beneficiaries, and not even the most important ones. Consumers – whether private individuals or businesses – will always be the most important beneficiaries of competition.'

influenced by or based on EU law. Further, this book focused on the practical potential of the disciplines to constrain regulatory autonomy. Nonetheless, this approach has also highlighted the opposite side of the coin: as presented by Ruggiero, a regulator's right to regulate is limited in the diverse field of regulatory measures covered by the guarantees in GATS and the services chapters of the EU RTAs. In order to make the book manageable in scope, it has taken a case study approach to allow an in-depth analysis of the constraints on regulatory autonomy resulting from the liberalisation of trade in services at the multilateral and the preferential level – the main objective of the book.

As with any binding international law, it cannot be denied that the international regulation of trade in services constrains regulatory autonomy. This is not necessarily problematic. Indeed, it is perhaps the primary purpose of international regulation. Needless to say, what matters is the balance between regulatory autonomy and the constraints resulting from any obligations. A research project exploring the challenges faced by Members participating in the multilateral trading system has demonstrated some of the practical effects of constraints on regulatory autonomy.[2] Through 45 case studies, the effects of participation in the WTO system were assessed against economic, political and social outcomes. The project found that regulatory outcomes depend on domestic governance. Very seldom are regulatory outcomes determined by regulatory autonomy constrains resulting from WTO rules. An analysis of these case studies suggests that, although the WTO agreements 'constrain government actions in the regulation of trade, [...] none of those constraints appears in any of these case studies as a hurdle for governments or for businesses'.[3] The editors of the case study volume note that, even where WTO rules do constrain a government's regulatory choices, the WTO rules *and* the constraints resulting therefrom, 'seem likely to lead to more opportunities for trade and growth'.[4]

However, this does not mean that the constraints are not limiting the right to regulate where regulators seek to achieve other objectives, or prefer other pathways to trade and growth. Indeed, the editors state that:

> The case studies tell us that the decisions that matter to members most of the time are not made in Geneva. They are decisions made by governments in

---

[2] Peter Gallagher, Patrick Low and Andrew L Stoler (eds), *Managing the Challenges of WTO Participation: 45 Case Studies* (Cambridge University Press 2005).

[3] Ibid 21–22.

[4] Ibid.

> direct contact with other members within the framework of the WTO system, or they are decisions made autonomously by governments about the allocation of resources within their own economies.[5]

Moreover, the effect of constraints on regulatory autonomy resulting from the liberalisation of trade in services may have origins other than the regulation of trade in services, such as endogenous political or economic constraints. Finally, the practical effects of the constraints may be restricted by the limited enforcement of the obligations. A *de facto* variant of the *de minimis* principle likely prevents governments from bringing claims from which insufficient economic gains can be made, or where insufficient domestic pressure in favour of bringing a claim exists.[6] For that reason, governments 'get away' with 'minor' violations, of which many are undoubtedly present in existing regulation. Of course, at some point, a sufficient economic or political interest could turn these into actual disputes. Nonetheless, government decisions *are* guided and constrained by WTO rules. Therefore, it is tempting to make a value judgement regarding the constraints on regulatory autonomy resulting from the multilateral and preferential liberalisation of trade in services.

However, making such a value judgement is not what this book seeks to do. Ultimately, the balance between constraints and regulatory autonomy reflects political choices. What this book does attempt to do, is to assess how the regulation of international trade in services constrains regulatory autonomy. Thus, it seeks to expose the intended, and potentially unintended, consequences of the aforementioned political choices. It is also clear that, especially when combining the multilateral and preferential levels, the regulation of trade in services is not what one would call 'clear' and 'predictable', even if it may, mostly, be considered 'consistent'. Many examples of ambiguity and uncertainty, and some of inconsistency, have been highlighted. Of course, the comparative nature of this book precisely aimed at uncovering such ambiguities, uncertainties and inconsistencies.

At the multilateral level, the complexity of GATS can be excused by the fact that the agreement was negotiated to deal with a topic that was novel at the time. GATS has not been changed since its negotiation,

---

5 Ibid.

6 From a practical perspective, there may be room for a breach of a Member or a party's obligations as the risk of a complaint being brought would be limited in these cases. In cases of *de minimis* breach, there is no incentive (economic, political or systemic) to litigate, which creates leeway for governments to violate their obligations.

despite tremendous changes in the landscape of international trade in services. Within those limits, and taking into account the limited guidance from case law specifically addressing GATS, the lack of clarity and predictability is perhaps no greater than what it can, minimally, be. Taking into account the case law, the constraints on regulatory autonomy resulting from an application of GATS do not seem to go beyond what could have been expected by the Members. The complexity of the agreement and the Schedules cannot be denied, but, as has been argued throughout this book, their interpretation by panels and the AB has, as of yet, not been overly constraining. Moreover, the interpretation of those provisions which have not yet been clarified in case law would likely also strike this balance.

At the preferential level, in many cases, only minor changes have been made to the GATS framework.[7] This indicates that the main reason for having services chapters in RTAs is to increase the number and depth of specific commitments.[8] Moreover, the minor differences are probably the result of the bilateral nature of the negotiations, in which the EU has always been the economically stronger partner. The EU's template for services chapters has been the starting point. Subsequently, this template has been adapted to accommodate for some specific requirements of the EU's counterparties. Therefore, in my view, the differences between the agreements should not be overemphasised. Nonetheless, two arguments

---

[7] As explained at the outset of this book, an important caveat to this conclusion is that specific sectoral obligations are not part of the analysis. It could well be that these obligations are the emanation of RTAs as 'rule-making laboratories'. Aaditya Mattoo and Pierre Sauvé, *The Preferential Liberalization of Services Trade* (NCCR Working Paper N°2010/13, 2010) 32. GATS-X obligations are also noteworthy here.

[8] Indeed, this is an important feature of services regulation in RTAs: Martin Roy, Juan A Marchetti and Aik Hoe Lim, 'The Race Towards Preferential Trade Agreements in Services: How Much Market Access Is Really Achieved?' in Marion Panizzon, Nicole Pohl and Pierre Sauvé (eds), *GATS and the Regulation of International Trade in Services* (Cambridge University Press 2008) 80–83, present a dataset that explains that Mode 1 and Mode 3 commitments have substantially larger (almost double compared to GATS) sectoral coverage. However, in the EU RTAs that are part of their sample, the EU has not undertaken substantially more commitments in the sectors that are specifically addressed (distribution services, education services, audio-visual services (excluded by the EU, as noted), professional services), except in those areas subject to sectoral disciplines (financial services, telecommunication services). The EU has likely been more successful in opening foreign markets, considering both the relatively liberal commitments in the EU's GATS Schedule and the importance of its market to its negotiating counterparts in the RTAs.

that criticise these outcomes should be considered. First, in the selected RTAs, the EU has not been able to enhance the clarity and predictability of the regulation of trade in services, even though these can be said to be lacking in the context of GATS. This is regrettable as, both from the perspective of the regulator and from the perspective of the users of these agreements, the complexity and incomprehensibility of the regulation of trade in services reduces their appeal. A regulator would be better served by fully comprehending the constraints on regulatory autonomy that result from the regulation of trade in services. Purposeful complexity cannot be considered beneficial to regulators, as the burden of proof will often lie with the regulator.[9] The users of the agreements will also be better served by more understandable rules: if not for the benefit of economic actors, why are the agreements negotiated? Therefore, the lack of clarity and predictability in the regulation of trade in services is problematic. The small alterations made to established GATS phrases and principles have not created clearer, more predictable rules. Often, they have had the opposite effect. Finally, while the reuse of the main GATS obligations in the selected EU RTAs indicates that these rules are considered to be suitable for unlocking the potential of trade in services, the complexity of the rules is a likely reason for their under-utilisation.

Aside from identifying the increased complexity of the regulatory landscape, this comparative analysis of constraints on regulatory autonomy at the multilateral and preferential levels did not indicate that the EU RTAs' services chapters constrain regulatory autonomy in a fundamentally different way to GATS. There are notable differences. However, whereas some key obligations in the selected EU RTAs are considerably wider than under GATS, more exemptions from the scope of the chapters and a wider range of exceptions arguably serve to mitigate any unwarranted constraints on regulatory autonomy resulting from these obligations. This applies to most obligations, with the exception of the additional wide non-discrimination obligations in the EU-Singapore and EU-Georgia RTAs. Aside from these elements, the broad scope of establishment is remarkable from a GATS perspective. However, the overall balance between regulatory autonomy constraints resulting from GATS and the EU RTAs appears to be well guarded. This is not to say that the situation is perfect: the negotiators for the services chapters of the EU RTAs did not seize the opportunity to solve many

---

[9] A violation of, for example, the non-discrimination obligations in many of the EU-Singapore and EU-Georgia RTAs, can be easily established, compared to GATS. Consequentially, recourse will need to be had to the exceptions, where the invoking party, i.e. the respondent, will face the burden of proof.

GATS issues (indicating that the balance found in GATS and its interpretation is acceptable to the EU), rather, it may be said that they contributed to the proliferation of overlapping and slightly varying rules governing trade in services. Nonetheless, the services obligations in these agreements are legally binding, even if, so far, there is no enforcement of EU RTA provisions through dispute settlement. Other ways of utilising trade preferences in these RTAs could be, for example, through diplomatic pressure or business lobbying. Therefore, one should tread lightly, ensuring that an overview and understanding of the obligations arising from the plethora of applicable rules is kept at both governmental and business levels. Finally, it may well be that the constraints on regulatory autonomy from these RTAs primarily lands on the EU's counterparties, because the EU at least partially extends its internal market approach.

The recent surge in developments related to trade in services illustrates that this topic is a 'moving target'. The 'servicification' of the global economy,[10] especially in the wake of the rise of global value chains, should lead to more attention for the liberalisation, and regulation, of trade in services. The need for more manageable rules and an updated rulebook for trade in services is only set to increase. For the EU, negotiations concerning the Transatlantic Trade and Investment Partnership (TTIP) and the plurilateral Trade in Services Agreement (TiSA) are among the most high profile ways in which the foundations for a future regulatory framework for trade in services will be laid. These negotiations will address technical questions, such as whether to adopt a positive listing, negative listing or hybrid approach to scheduling commitments;[11] whether to create

[10] Servicification 'refers to manufacturing firms purchasing, producing and selling more and more services to their customers (both domestically and abroad) at all stages along the value chain'. Lucien Cernat and Zornitsa Kutlina-Dimitrova, 'Thinking in a Box: A "Mode 5" Approach to Service Trade' (2014) 48 Journal of World Trade 1109, 1116.

[11] The EU-Georgia DCFTA and CETA highlight that the EU's 'classical' approach, i.e. scheduling through positive listing, is changing. In the EU-Georgia DCFTA, the Schedule for establishment (to which no market access obligation applies) is based on the negative listing approach. In CETA, market access commitments are, for the first time, subject to the negative list approach. In TiSA, a draft EU Schedule was published with a document explaining that the market access column is 'like a GATS schedule', whereas the national treatment commitments are 'scheduled on the basis of a Horizontal National Treatment'. The latter should be understood as a negative listing approach. European Commission, *Initial EU TiSA Offer* (2013).

horizontal or sectoral disciplines;[12] and how to move forward in creating 'regulatory coherence' through, *inter alia*, mutual recognition.[13] They will also reflect political and tactical preferences, for example: continuing a mainly bilateral tactic of competition in a race for market access;[14] the relationship with China in TTIP and TiSA negotiations and in the Trans-Pacific Partnership;[15] making truly ambitious offers in a coalition-of-the-willing context;[16] or, allowing all negotiating parties to maintain blanket exemptions of specific categories of services.[17] However, most importantly, these negotiations have the potential to redesign the entire approach to the regulation of trade in services, setting a new standard even for parties not included in these negotiations. For example, a leaked document relating to talks on the 'new, enhanced disciplines' for services in TiSA

---

[12] ICTSD, 'TISA Negotiators Report Progress on New, Enhanced Disciplines Talks' (2014) 18 Bridges Weekly Trade News Digest, noting that discussions in TiSA are 'focused on texts regarding financial services; telecommunications; e-commerce; domestic regulation and transparency; and air, maritime, and road transport. Initial discussions were also held on competitive delivery services and energy services'. See also European Commission, *A Modular Approach to the Architecture of a Plurilateral Agreement on Services* (Non-Paper Circulated by the European Union at the Occasion of the Exploratory Talks for a Potential Plurilateral Services Agreement (known today as 'Trade in Services Agreement – TiSA'), 2012).

[13] Simon Lester and Inu Barbee, 'The Challenge of Cooperation: Regulatory Trade Barriers in the Transatlantic Trade and Investment Partnership' (2013) 16 Journal of International Economic Law 1.

[14] For an early assessment of the impact of TTIP on third countries, see Sinan Ülgen, *Locked In or Left Out? Transatlantic Trade Beyond Brussels and Washington* (Carnegie Endowment for International Peace Europe, 2014) and Philip I Levy, *Bargains among Behemoths: TPP and TTIP Implications for Developing Countries* (Paper written for the International Trade Department of the World Bank, 2013).

[15] There have been suggestions that China is interested in joining TiSA talks, but that the US and Japan are declining, for geopolitical reasons. Iana Dreyer and Jennifer Freedman, 'Take-Aways from Last Week's TiSA Talks' (*BorderLex*, 2014) <http://www.borderlex.eu/take-aways-last-weeks-tisa-talks/> accessed 14 February 2015.

[16] Kenneth Heydon, 'Plurilateral Agreements and Global Trade Governance: A Lesson from the OECD' (2014) 48 Journal of World Trade 1039.

[17] I am referring to the GATS negotiations, where Canada and the EU lobbied in favour of an exemption from the scope of GATS for audio-visual services. The systemic argument is that if all parties are allowed to carve out sectors from the *scope* of an agreement, this undermines the efficiency of the agreement. If a party wishes to limit its commitments, it may do so by using the flexibility of the agreement, for example by scheduling limitations.

that had been announced by the negotiators,[18] shows US proposals for local presence, local content and local technology disciplines, and horizontal provisions regulating the movement of information and open networks, network access and network use.[19] Nonetheless, TiSA is set to have the same scope as GATS, utilising its definitions and key obligations.[20]

The concluded Comprehensive Economic and Trade Agreement (CETA) negotiations, which have been set to provide the blueprint for the EU-US Transatlantic Trade and Investment Partnership,[21] may have taken a crucial turn in an opposite direction. GATS Modes 1 and 2 are still addressed, as in the three selected case studies in this book, as 'cross-border trade in services', and GATS Mode 4 remains applicable only to the 'temporary presence of natural persons for business purposes'. However, the integration of Mode 3 and investment, already witnessed through the broad scope of 'establishment' in the EU RTAs, has been completed without regulating 'Mode 3': the provisions on establishment have been integrated in the investment chapter. In other words, the basic structure of 'trade in services' through the four GATS modes of supply has been abandoned. This approach undoubtedly reduces the complexity of the existing regulatory regime: the overlap between services and investment is eliminated. Moreover, some exceptions provisions appear to have been revisited to (further) safeguard regulatory autonomy.[22] The solution in CETA appears to be to take the overlap out of the regulation of trade in services and to address such measures solely through the

---

[18] ICTSD, 'TISA Negotiators Report Progress on New, Enhanced Disciplines Talks'.

[19] Associated Whistleblowing Press, *Secret Trade in Services Agreement (TISA) New Provisions Applicable to All Services (April 25, 2014) Annex on Professional Services [as at 5 September 2014]* (TISA – US CONFIDENTIAL Information, 2014).

[20] ICTSD, 'TISA Talks Making Strong Progress, Officials Say' (2014) 18 Bridges Weekly Trade News Digest. Also see European Commission, *How to Read the TiSA Initial Offer of the European Union? (Schedule)* (2013); European Commission, *How to Read the TiSA Initial Offer of the European Union? (Text)* (2013).

[21] Jeremy Fleming, 'Commission ISDS Report: Fireworks for the New Year' (*EurActiv*, 2014) <http://www.euractiv.com/sections/ttip-and-arbitration-clause/commission-isds-report-new-years-firework-310764> accessed 15 February 2015.

[22] See Armand CM de Mestral, 'When Does the Exception Become the Rule? Conserving Regulatory Space under CETA' 18 Journal of International Economic Law 641.

provisions on investment.[23] Similarly, a recent proposal on 'Mode 5', comprising trade in services where 'services exports are domestic intermediate services inputs that are incorporated in one country's merchandise exports', highlights that the four modes are no longer sufficient to regulate trade in services.[24]

The future of the regulation of international trade in services looks exhilarating. If the eventual outcome of on-going negotiations is a less complex and more transparent regulatory framework, in which the current balance between regulatory autonomy and constraints thereon can be maintained, all involved actors will benefit. However, these pending changes also represent a major challenge for regulators and negotiators. In light of the social, political and economic importance of domestic regulation of services, great care must be taken to ensure that the balance between constraints and regulatory autonomy is maintained. Capacity must be built in order to, first, understand what the proposed changes imply, and, second, utilise any new rules to their full potential. I sincerely hope that this book can contribute to achieving these aims.

[23] An important remark, from the perspective of regulatory autonomy, is that inclusion in the investment chapter may have implications for the enforcement of the obligations. If, under the investment chapter, investor-state dispute settlement is available, a larger regulatory chill could be expected, in comparison to state-state dispute settlement under the services chapter.

[24] Cernat and Kutlina-Dimitrova, 'Thinking in a Box: A "Mode 5" Approach to Service Trade' 1116.

Selected bibliography

Adlung R, 'Public Services and the GATS' (2006) 9 Journal of International Economic Law 455
Adlung R, 'Export Policies and the General Agreement on Trade in Services' (2015) 18 Journal of International Economic Law 487
Adlung R and Carzaniga A, 'MFN Exemptions under the General Agreement on Trade in Services: Grandfathers Striving for Immortality?' (2009) 12 Journal of International Economic Law 357
Adlung R and Molinuevo M, 'Bilateralism in Services Trade: Is There Fire Behind the (BIT-)Smoke?' (2008) 11 Journal of International Economic Law 365
Adlung R and Morrison P, 'Less than the GATS: "Negative Preferences" in Regional Services Agreements' (2010) 13 Journal of International Economic Law 1103
Adlung R and Roy M, *Turning Hills into Mountains? Current Commitments under the GATS and Prospects for Change* (World Trade Organization Economic Research and Statistics Division Staff Working Paper ERSD-2005-01, 2005)
Barnard C, *The Substantive Law of the EU: The Four Freedoms* (3rd edn, Oxford University Press 2010)
Bartels L, 'Article XX of GATT and the Problem of Extraterritorial Jurisdiction: The Case of Trade Measures for the Protection of Human Rights' (2002) 36 Journal of World Trade 353
Bartels L and Ortino F (eds), *Regional Trade Agreements and the WTO Legal System* (Oxford University Press 2006)
Cernat L and Kutlina-Dimitrova Z, 'Thinking in a Box: A "Mode 5" Approach to Service Trade' (2014) 48 Journal of World Trade 1109
Cho S, *Free Markets and Social Regulation: A Reform Agenda of the Global Trading System* (Kluwer Law International 2003)
Cossy M, *Determining 'Likeness' under the GATS: Squaring the Circle?* (World Trade Organization Economic Research and Statistics Division Staff Working Paper ERSD-2006-08, 2006)
Davey WJ and Sapir A, 'The Soft Drinks Case: The WTO and Regional Agreements' (2009) 8 World Trade Review 5
De Meester B, 'Testing European Prudential Conditions for Banking Mergers in the Light of Most Favoured Nation in the GATS' (2008) 11 Journal of International Economic Law 609

De Meester B, *Liberalization of Trade in Banking Services: An International and European Perspective* (Cambridge University Press 2014)

De Meester B and Coppens D, 'Mode 3 of the GATS: A Model for Disciplining Measures Affecting Investment Flows?' in Z Drabek and PC Mavroidis (eds), *Regulation of Foreign Investment: Challenges to International Harmonization* (World Scientific 2013)

Delimatsis P, 'Don't Gamble with GATS: The Interaction between Articles VI, XVI, XVII and XVIII GATS in the Light of the *US–Gambling* Case' (2006) 40 Journal of World Trade 1059

Delimatsis P, 'Due Process and "Good" Regulation Embedded in the GATS – Disciplining Regulatory Behaviour in Services through Article VI of the GATS' (2006) 10 Journal of International Economic Law 13

Delimatsis P, 'Determining the Necessity of Domestic Regulations in Services: The Best is Yet to Come' (2008) 19 European Journal of International Law 365

Delimatsis P, *International Trade in Services and Domestic Regulations: Necessity, Transparency and Regulatory Diversity* (Oxford University Press 2008)

Diebold N, *Non-Discrimination in International Trade in Services: 'Likeness' in WTO/GATS* (Cambridge University Press 2010)

Diebold N, 'Standards of Nondiscrimination in International Economic Law' (2011) 60 International and Comparative Law Quarterly 831

Du MM, 'Domestic Regulatory Autonomy under the TBT Agreement: From Non-discrimination to Harmonization' (2007) 6 Chinese Journal of International Law 269

Du MM, 'Autonomy in Setting Appropriate Level of Protection under the WTO Law: Rhetoric or Reality?' (2010) 13 Journal of International Economic Law 1077

Ehring L, 'De Facto Discrimination in World Trade Law: National and Most-Favoured-Nation-Treatment or Equal Treatment?' (2002) 36 Journal of World Trade 921

Flett J, 'WTO Space for National Regulation: Requiem for a Diagonal Vector Test' (2013) 16 Journal of International Economic Law 37

Flett J, 'National Treatment under the General Agreement on Trade in Services (GATS)' in Sanders A Kamperman (ed), *The Principle of National Treatment in International Economic Law: Trade, Investment and Intellectual Property* (Edward Elgar Publishing 2014)

Gallagher P, Low P and Stoler AL (eds), *Managing the Challenges of WTO Participation: 45 Case Studies* (Cambridge University Press 2005)

Horn H, Mavroidis PC and Sapir A, 'Beyond the WTO? An Anatomy of EU and US Preferential Trade Agreements' (2010) The World Economy 1565

Howse R and Langille J, 'Permitting Pluralism: The Seal Products Dispute and Why the WTO Should Accept Trade Restrictions Justified by Noninstrumental Moral Values' (2012) 37 Yale Journal of International Law 367

Irwin DA and Weiler J, 'Measures Affecting the Cross-Border Supply of Gambling and Betting Services (DS 285)' (2008) 7 World Trade Review 71

Jackson JH, *Sovereignty, the WTO and Changing Fundamentals of International Law* (Cambridge University Press 2006)

Kolsky Lewis M and Frankel S (eds), *International Economic Law and National Autonomy* (Cambridge University Press 2010)

Krajewski M, *National Regulation and Trade Liberalization in Services* (Kluwer Law International 2003)

Krajewski M, 'Public Services and Trade Liberalization: Mapping the Legal Framework' (2003) 6 Journal of International Economic Law 341

Lang A, 'The GATS and Regulatory Autonomy: A Case Study of Social Regulation of the Water Industry' (2004) 7 Journal of International Economic Law 801

Lang A, *World Trade Law after Neoliberalism: Reimagining the Global Economic Order* (Oxford University Press 2011)

Leroux E, 'What is a "Service Supplied in the Exercise of Governmental Authority" Under Article I:3(b) and (c) of the General Agreement on Trade in Services?' (2006) 40 Journal of World Trade 345

Leroux E, 'Eleven Years of GATS Case Law: What Have We Learned?' (2007) 10 Journal of International Economic Law 749

Lester S and Mercurio B (eds), *Bilateral and Regional Trade Agreements: Commentary and Analysis* (Cambridge University Press 2009)

Lim AH and De Meester B (eds), *WTO Domestic Regulation and Services Trade* (Cambridge University Press 2014)

McGrady B, 'Necessity Exceptions in WTO Law: Retreaded Tyres, Regulatory Purpose and Cumulative Regulatory Measures' (2009) 12 Journal of International Economic Law 153

Marchetti JA and Mavroidis PC, 'The Genesis of the GATS (General Agreement on Trade in Services)' (2011) 22 European Journal of International Law 689

Marchetti JA and Roy M (eds), *Opening Markets for Trade in Services: Countries and Sectors in Bilateral and WTO Negotiations* (Cambridge University Press 2008)

Mathis J, 'WTO, Turkey – Restrictions on Imports of Textile and Clothing Products' (2000) 27 Legal Issues of Economic Integration 103

Mathis J, *Regional Trade Agreements in the GATT/WTO: Article XXIV and the Internal Trade Requirement* (TMC Asser Press 2002)

Mathis J and Laurenza E, 'Services and Investment in the EU–South Korea Free-Trade Area: Implications of a New Approach for GATS V Agreements and for Bilateral Investment Treaties' (2012) 13 The Journal of World Investment & Trade 157
Mattoo A, 'National Treatment in the GATS: Corner-Stone or Pandora's Box?' (1997) 31 Journal of World Trade 107
Mattoo A, 'Services in a Development Round: Three Goals and Three Proposals' (2005) 39 Journal of World Trade 1223
Mattoo A and Sauvé P (eds), *Domestic Regulation & Service Trade Liberalization* (World Bank & Oxford University Press 2003)
Mavroidis PC, 'Highway XVI Re-visited: The Road from Non-discrimination to Market Access in GATS' (2007) 6 World Trade Review 1
Mavroidis PC, 'WTO and PTAs: A Preference for Multilateralism? (or, the Dog That Tried to Stop the Bus)' (2010) 44 Journal of World Trade 1145
Mitchell A, *Legal Principles in WTO Disputes* (Cambridge University Press 2008)
Molinuevo M, *Protecting Investment in Services: Investor-State Arbitration Versus WTO Dispute Settlement* (Wolters Kluwer 2012)
Munin N, *Legal Guide to GATS* (Wolters Kluwer 2010)
Ortino F, 'The Principle of Non-Discrimination and its Exceptions in GATS: Selected Legal Issues' in K Alexander and M Andenas (eds), *The World Trade Organization and Trade in Services* (Martinus Nijhoff 2008)
Panizzon M, Pohl N and Sauvé P (eds), *GATS and the Regulation of International Trade in Services* (Cambridge University Press 2008)
Pauwelyn J, 'Rien ne Va Plus? Distinguishing Domestic Regulation from Market Access in GATT and GATS' (2005) 4 World Trade Review 131
Pauwelyn J, 'The Unbearable Lightness of Likeness' in M Panizzon, N Pohl and P Sauvé (eds), *GATS and the Regulation of International Trade in Services* (Cambridge University Press 2008)
Poretti P, *The Regulation of Subsidies Within the General Agreement on Trade in Services of the WTO: Problems and Prospects* (Kluwer 2009)
Porges A and Trachtman JP, 'Robert Hudec and Domestic Regulation: The Resurrection of Aim and Effects' (2003) 37 Journal of World Trade 783
Regan DH, 'A Gambling Paradox: Why an Origin-Neutral "Zero-Quota" is Not a Quota Under GATS Article XVI' (2007) 41 Journal of World Trade 1297
Roessler F, 'Increasing Market Access Under Regulatory Heterogeneity: The Strategies of the World Trade Organisation' in OECD (ed), *Regulatory Reform and International Market Openness* (OECD 1996)

Roy M, Marchetti JA and Lim H, 'Services Liberalization in the New Generation of Preferential Trade Agreements (PTAs): How Much Further than the GATS?' (2007) 6 World Trade Review 155

Sauvé P and Stern RM (eds), *GATS 2000: New Directions in Services Trade Liberalization* (Brookings Institution 2000)

Shan W, Simons P and Singh D (eds), *Redefining Sovereignty in International Economic Law* (Hart 2008)

Trachtman JP, 'Toward Open Recognition: Standardization and Regional Integration under Article XXIV of GATT' (2003) 6 Journal of International Economic Law 459

Van Damme I, 'The Interpretation of Schedules of Commitments' (2007) 4 Journal of World Trade 1

Van Damme I, *Treaty Interpretation by the WTO Appellate Body* (Oxford University Press 2009)

Van den Bossche P and Zdouc W, *The Law and Policy of the World Trade Organization* (3rd edn, Cambridge University Press 2013)

Van Den Hende L, 'GATS Article XVI and National Regulatory Sovereignty: What Lessons to Draw from *US–Gambling*?' (2007) 20 Cambridge Review of International Affairs 93

VanDuzer JA, 'Health, Education and Social Services in Canada: The Impact of the GATS' in JM Curtis and D Ciuriak (eds), *Trade Policy Research 2004* (Minister of Public Works and Government Studies Canada 2004)

Verhoosel G, *National Treatment and WTO Dispute Settlement: Adjudicating the Boundaries of Regulatory Autonomy* (Hart 2002)

Vranes E, 'The WTO and Regulatory Freedom: WTO Disciplines on Market Access, Non-Discrimination and Domestic Regulation Relating to Trade in Goods and Services' (2009) 12 Journal of International Economic Law 953

Wolfrum R, Stoll P-T and Feinäugle C (eds), *Max Planck Commentaries on World Trade Law: WTO – Trade in Services*, vol 6 (Martinus Nijhoff 2008)

Wu M, 'Free Trade and the Protection of Public Morals: An Analysis of the Newly Emerging Public Morals Clause Doctrine' (2008) 33 Yale Journal of International Law 215

Wunsch-Vincent S, 'The Internet, Cross-Border Trade in Services, and the GATS: Lessons from *US–Gambling*' (2006) 5 World Trade Review 319

Zdouc W, 'WTO Dispute Settlement Practice Relating to the GATS' (1999) 2 Journal of International Economic Law 295

Zdouc W, 'WTO Dispute Settlement Practice Relating to the General Agreement on Trade in Services' in F Ortino and E-U Petersmann (eds), *The WTO Dispute Settlement System 1995–2003* (Kluwer Law International 2004)

Index